THE EIGHTIES

From Eleanor 2019 birthday.

THE EIGHTIES

THE DECADE THAT TRANSFORMED AUSTRALIA

FRANK BONGIORNO

Published by Black Inc.,
an imprint of Schwartz Publishing Pty Ltd
37–39 Langridge Street
Collingwood VIC 3066 Australia
enquiries@blackincbooks.com
www.blackincbooks.com

Copyright © Frank Bongiorno 2015
Frank Bongiorno asserts his right to be known as the author of this work.

ALL RIGHTS RESERVED.
No part of this publication may be reproduced, stored in a retrieval system, or transmitted in any form by any means electronic, mechanical, photocopying, recording or otherwise without the prior consent of the publishers.

National Library of Australia Cataloguing-in-Publication entry:

> Bongiorno, Frank, 1969– author.
> The eighties : the decade that transformed Australia / Frank Bongiorno.
> 9781863957762 (hardback)
> 9781925203592 (ebook)
> Nineteen eighties.
> Australia—Social life and customs—History.
> Australia—Politics and government—History.
> Australia—History—1976–1990.
> 994.06

Cover design by Peter Long
Cover image: Paul Mathews, Fairfax
Endpapers: Fairfax (front) and Alan Pryke, Newspix (back)
Text design by Tristan Main

Printed in Australia by McPherson's Printing Group.

Contents

Introduction
Stories of the 1980s ix

Chapter 1
A Good Run 1

Chapter 2
Keeping Afloat 33

Chapter 3
'Vanishing Aussie'? 59

Chapter 4
Power and Passion 85

Chapter 5
The Deal-Makers 119

Chapter 6
Taking Credit 155

Chapter 7
New Pleasures, New Dangers 191

Chapter 8
The Identity Card 227

Chapter 9
The Crash 263

Afterword
What Did It All Mean? 303

Acknowledgments and Author's Note 307

Endnotes 313

Credits 357

Index 359

For Amy

Introduction
Stories of the 1980s

It was the biggest party Australia had ever seen – at least that's how its promoters touted it. In January 1988 – the same month Australia would celebrate its Bicentenary – Queensland's Gold Coast hosted the Ultimate Event. Paying visitors watched tennis and golf played by some of the world's greats, laughed at the comedy acts and enjoyed the glamour of the fashion parades. Young Whitney Houston belted out a few numbers, and so did that renowned grandson of a Tenterfield saddler, Peter Allen, on a summer visit to the land he still called home. But the ultimate event of the Ultimate Event was the appearance of Frank Sinatra: 40,000 turned out to see the 72-year-old perform some old favourites through a river of his sweat, as the world's most famous crooner battled the effects of his dinner jacket and bow tie, the stage lights and the subtropical humidity. Singing for an hour with the help of three teleprompters, Sinatra was said to have cleared $1.4 million for his efforts. It was a good night: even the rain which had been so unkind to the party previously, nearly wrecking the Whitney Houston concert, stopped for Ol' Blue Eyes.[1]

The occasion for the Ultimate Event was the opening of Sanctuary Cove, a residential, shopping, hotel and leisure development on the Gold Coast's Hope Island. It was a very 'eighties' kind of place: expensive homes, big marina, golf courses, luxury hotel, boutiques and even its own local brew, served in a German-style beer hall.[2] Sanctuary Cove was the vision of a bustling, overweight businessman named Mike Gore, who had arrived from Sydney in 1973 with just $400 in his pocket. As visitors contemplated the extraordinary if still incomplete development, there was no doubting his ability to make magical things happen. His friend the advertiser John Singleton thought that, 'In 200 years Australians will look around and this will be one of the biggest things a single man has completed.'[3] Gore was regarded as the leader of the white-shoe brigade, a group of 'can-do' Gold

Coast businessmen who wielded considerable influence over the conservative state government.

In one of the early advertisements for Sanctuary Cove – headed 'Are There 900 Civilised Human Beings in Queensland?' – Gore explained the concept behind his development. Surfers Paradise, with its 'ugly towers' and 'miles of glitzy neon and greasy takeaways', was 'Paradise Lost'. His 600 acres, however, were 'Paradise Regained':

> Shelly's Farm, Hope Island.
> 600 acres of salt marsh, leeches and scrub.
> She was battered, and she'd been raped, but I could see she was a lady.
> I fell in love instantly, and within hours, she was mine.
> Later I discovered her sad history. She'd been a fertile farm once. But 30 years ago, the sand miners had moved in, dumped thousands of tonnes of silt in her natural harbour, destroyed the drainage, and formed the swamp.
> I spent more than two million dollars on drainage.
> I swore to restore the harbour.
> I was hooked.

Gore thought of it as 'the place where we could make a new beginning, without the mistakes of the past', and claimed that development would 'complement the natural beauty of the place. Not compete with it or destroy it.'

The sexual imagery of Gore's promotional material was ripe, but his appeal to conservation was in tune with the times. Sanctuary Cove, however, also had a darker side, promoting itself as 'unashamedly elitist'.[4] It was, in effect, a gated residential community.

Gore would not stick around long to bathe in the glory of the Ultimate Event. He sold his share in Sanctuary Cove soon afterwards and later, in 1988, it was taken over by a Japanese company. He then experienced a series of business disasters and an expensive divorce, leaving for Canada with a new and much younger wife in 1992, owing his creditors a cool $25 million.[5] Like several other entrepreneurs of the 1980s, the chain-smoking, hard-living Gore did not live long after his fall, dying of a heart attack in 1994 at just fifty-three.

Mike Gore's is just one story of Australia's eighties, but his career captures a striking number of its familiar elements: the optimism, the energy, the elitism (frequently combined with a pretend egalitarianism), the excess and the crash. Yet today such complexities are overlooked by many of us, who too frequently see the decade only through rose-tinted glasses. On FM radio and in television mini-series, it is the era of big hair and shoulder pads, synthesised pop and 'greed is good'; of Michael Jackson, Madonna and Ronald Reagan; of British boy and girl bands, Live Aid for Ethiopia and Margaret Thatcher; of yuppies and 'masters of the universe' – as Tom Wolfe memorably called his New York stockbrokers in *The Bonfire of the Vanities*. It is the decade that began in the shadow of the bomb and ended in the joyful dismantling of the Berlin Wall. The world's most famous political prisoner, Nelson Mandela, began the 1980s in much the same way he had lived for twenty years – as a captive of a racist white regime in South Africa – and ended it a free man, in time to assume his country's presidency.

Australians participated in these happenings, sharing the excitements, challenges and surprises of the decade, and adding a few of their own. For us, it was the era of Hawke and Keating, of *Neighbours* and *Crocodile Dundee*, of let-it-rip capitalism and corporate excess, of assertive nationalism and cultural and sporting success. The decade has been treated as both an alpha and an omega. The journalist Paul Kelly famously claimed that the eighties saw the end of the Australian Settlement, the suite of ideas and policies that had underpinned the nation from the early twentieth century. White Australia, Industry Protection, Wage Arbitration, State Paternalism and Imperial Benevolence: all, said Kelly, were broken by the end of the 1980s – and, he suggests, a jolly good thing, too.[6] But another journalist, George Megalogenis, saw the eighties less as an end than as a beginning, a prelude to 'The Australian Moment', his name for the vindication of twenty-five years of policy reform that came with the economy's astonishing resilience during the global financial crisis of 2008.[7]

In these accounts, the Hawke government is the 'gold standard' for reformist governments of whatever stripe. Giants once strode the land: politicians who did not allow themselves to be diverted by last week's focus group, this week's opinion poll or today's 24-hour news cycle. Yet one of the leading participants in that government, Gareth Evans, recently commented that 'it did not always feel that way on the inside'.[8] Indeed, it is hard not to conclude that there is a certain forgetfulness operating when modern politicians, bureaucrats and journalists paint the 1980s as a political golden age. It is an aim of this book to provide an antidote to that amnesia.

The growing ascendancy of eighties youth in our own time might help to account for the decade's rosy hue. We have had just one Generation X prime minister, Julia Gillard (born 1961), but eighties teenagers and twenty-somethings are already prominent among the nation's political class. In April 2014, when Mike Baird (born 1968) became the premier of New South Wales, a friend located him very much as a child of the decade: 'He has shocking taste in music. It's embarrassingly dated. It's kind of stuck in a time warp of 1980s music that was bad then and is dreadful still. You know – power ballads, bad pop.'[9] At the time of writing, six out of eight Australian premiers or chief ministers were, like Baird, born between 1968 and 1973. All probably know quite a few power ballads. Eighties youth are also coming into their own in business, education and culture.

The growing prominence of this generation would perhaps be sufficient justification for an account of the Australia that made them. But to tell the story of Australia's eighties, it is not enough merely to evoke the experience of the young, the elite or the globally aware; there were other 1980s, too: those of the newly arrived migrant, the displaced manufacturing worker, the Aboriginal battler, the working mother, the nervous pensioner, the struggling – or wealthy – farmer, the disappointed radical, the disgruntled conservative. There was continuity as well as change, collectivism alongside individualism, the old and the durable hanging on alongside the new and disposable. A 1986 federal government inquiry into folklife concluded that white Australians were the heirs to 'living traditions' – games, rhymes, sayings, yarns, songs, dances, poems, customs, superstitions, recipes and skills – that ran 'deep, giving each of us our own sense of cultural identity, yet binding us together as Australians'.[10] This folk culture, with its powerful sense of continuity and roots in the European past, would reveal its enduring strength during the Bicentenary of 1988, despite the glitzy overlay of celebrity song and corporate branding.

When did the 1980s start and end? Graeme Turner has argued that the 1980s which circulate in popular memory began with Australia's victory in the America's Cup in September 1983 and ended with the Bicentenary of 1988. For Turner, it is 'a newly confident Australian nationalism' that defines the remembered eighties.[11] My own definition of the period is a little more capacious than his. The story begins with the optimism of Bob Hawke's long-anticipated ascension to the Labor leadership in early 1983, and runs through to its end, the bitter contest that culminated in Paul Keating's elevation as prime minister in December 1991. The period began and ended in national pessimism. Australia of the early 1980s was still an overwhelmingly white country of just 15 million people, with 'double-digit' unemployment, inflation and interest rates, a trifecta that in combination with the drought led some pundits to consider that the country was in the grip of a deep and possibly permanent malaise. Pessimists warned of the possibility of an Argentine fate for Australia, a future of 'economic stagnation ... social intolerance ... political decay, and ... nostalgic memories of a good life'.[12]

The 1980s ended, as they began, in economic recession, as well as in corporate collapse and political scandal. This was the rather depressing vantage point from which most Australians reflected on the decade they had just lived through. And many, unsurprisingly, did not much like what they saw, being more likely to repudiate the values of individualism and hedonism already synonymous with the decade than recall it with the warm glow of nostalgia that is so much in evidence today. They knew nothing of the era about to open up before them, with the arrival in the mid-1990s of both the World Wide Web and happier economic times. These surprises would divide the merely globalising world of the 1980s from the hyper-globalisation of our own times.

When I told people I was writing a book on this transformative decade, they often felt impelled to share something of their own 1980s with me, even if it was no more than a recollection of a favourite band, a fashion item, or a medal acquired at school to mark the Bicentenary. One told me that her first date with the boy who would later become her husband was on the shores of Sydney Harbour on Australia Day, 1988; another recalled the 1980s as a bit of a haze, a scramble to combine the roles of mother, businessman's wife and academic. It is experiences such as these that have been largely missing from accounts of the period, which have so far been preoccupied with grand transformations and great men – or at least with men who imagined they were great. The big changes and the great men will have their due in the pages that follow, but my aim has been, above all, to enlarge our sense of both the ordinary and the extraordinary things that happened to Australia and Australians during this liveliest of decades in our recent history.

1
A Good Run

The people were worried about their future, but stubborn in clinging to the notion of the lucky country.
                              PAUL KELLY, *THE HAWKE ASCENDANCY*

In the Christian calendar, Ash Wednesday is a time of fasting that signals the beginning of Lent, the six-week period before Easter. In 1983 it fell on 16 February, a day of fierce heat across south-eastern Australia. A devastating drought and deep economic recession gripped the country.

In Sydney, the new leader of the Opposition Australian Labor Party (ALP), Bob Hawke, gave his party's election campaign policy speech inside a packed and expectant Sydney Opera House. Hawke thought he was addressing the nation's most pressing emergency: that posed by the recession. But there was a far more urgent and elemental crisis unfolding in the country's south-east, as people feared not for their jobs but their lives, as bushfire choked or incinerated those in its path, as the advancing flames razed the tinder-dry landscape and visited destruction on homes and possessions – all in apparent mockery of the effort to subject the country to the templates of order, reason and progress.

But Hawke was a man who believed in order, reason and progress. At fifty-three, he had maintained a slim, even athletic physique. His luxuriant, well-tended head of dark wavy hair was already turning grey, as if to signal the growing distance between the boozy, aggressive and randy union leader of the 1970s, and the more mature, self-controlled, statesmanlike figure now bidding for the prime ministership. Journalists – most no doubt aware of Hawke's philandering ways – still played up his charisma and sex appeal, even as they paid tribute to his discipline in having given up his heavy drinking. The arched, almost triangular eyebrows remained, as did the bad temper and habit of intimidation. His minders, however, had ensured that there would be no repetition of his furious on-screen explosion on the night he became leader, when he was asked by interviewer Richard Carleton if he was embarrassed at the blood on his hands. Indeed, when he delivered his speech at the Opera House, he read it so slowly, and his style was so subdued, that he ran out of time and had to skip much of the text. Peter Bowers in the *Sydney Morning Herald* noted the emergence of 'the quiet persuader'.[1] Hawke had already been active in Australian public life for a quarter of a century. He had spent the turbulent 1970s as president of the Australian Council of Trade Unions (ACTU), and the early 1980s as a member of parliament and shadow minister. Under this charismatic new leader, Labor was expected to return to office for the first time since 1975.

The man Hawke had tipped out of the leadership just a couple of weeks before, Bill Hayden, sat in the second row of the Opera House auditorium that day. A former Queensland policeman, Hayden had served the party as leader with doggedness, and in the 1980 election managed a swing of 4 per cent. But doubts had grown about his ability to win a federal election. Although Hayden had withstood a challenge to his leadership from Hawke in July 1982, his days appeared numbered after the ALP achieved a swing of a miserly 3.5 per cent at a by-election in the Victorian Liberal-held seat of Flinders late in 1982. Support for his leadership ebbed, and critically, the powerful NSW Labor Right faction had for some time wanted to replace him with Hawke.

But it was John Button, a Victorian and Labor leader in the Senate, who delivered the coup de grâce. In recent months Button, a Hayden supporter, had come to think of the Labor leader as having squandered his political opportunities. His performance in the media was poor; Hayden remained 'an unrepentant bad communicator'.[2] Button travelled to Brisbane on 6 January 1983 in an effort to persuade Hayden to stand down as leader. Hayden, however, dug in; Hawke, he said, was 'a shallow man'. Button 'did not disagree with this view', and 'did not think that many people in the Party did either', but 'there were a number of important attributes in politics': 'integrity', 'decency' and 'desire for social change', on the one side; the ability to communicate and to command the confidence of voters on the other. Button's implication was that while Hawke had both, Hayden was deficient in the latter. But Hayden refused to accept his time was up. He was an 'existentialist' who, like Macbeth, went into battle and 'never asked for mercy ... if he lost the next election, he would not ask for mercy either'. Button was unimpressed; what about all of those thousands in the ALP who were not existentialists, and would find cold comfort in such an attitude if Labor lost the next election? 'I suppose that's right,' Hayden replied.[3]

Having failed in his mission, Button followed up with a decisive letter late in January 1983, reiterating his belief that Hayden could not win the next election. 'You said to me that you could not stand down for a "bastard" like Bob Hawke', Button wrote, but '[i]n my experience in the Labor Party the fact that someone is a bastard (of one kind or another) has never been a disqualification for leadership of the party'. The power of Button's missive lay not only in that it came from a friend and supporter, but also that its author seemed as alive to Hawke's weaknesses as he was to Hayden's:

> I am personally not one of those who believe that we can necessarily coast into office on the coat-tails of a media performer and winner of popularity polls. On the other hand I believe Hawke's leadership would give us a better chance of success . . . even some of Bob's closest supporters have doubts about his capacities to lead the party successfully, in that they do not share his own estimate of his ability.[4]

Among Labor politicians such as Button, who had witnessed at first hand the unravelling and then dismissal of the Whitlam government in 1975, there was now a hard pragmatism that rejected the party's sentimental attachment to failed leaders, as well as its too-easy acceptance of honourable defeat. Malcolm Fraser, meanwhile, was planning an early election when Button wrote his letter on 28 January. The authority of his Liberal–National Party coalition government was ebbing away in the face of a faltering economy, the embarrassing exposure of tax evasion by many wealthy Australians, and a bitter, occasionally violent struggle in Tasmania over a proposal by the state Liberal government to build a dam in the south-west wilderness.

On 3 February, finally bowing to unrelenting internal party pressure, Hayden resigned as ALP leader during a meeting of the shadow cabinet. At the same time as Labor was dealing with the leadership issue in Brisbane, Fraser was in Canberra seeking from the governor-general a double dissolution of parliament, so that an election could be held on 5 March. Dubious that Labor would be able to manage a smooth leadership transition, Fraser expected that he would be facing Hayden, but the ALP called his bluff by pragmatically switching leaders.[5] Hayden memorably told the media that he thought 'a drover's dog' could lead the Labor Party to victory at the next election 'the way the country is'.[6] But with Bob Hawke's ascent to the leadership, persistent doubts about the ALP's ability to defeat Fraser melted away. The electoral and the psychological advantage passed decisively to Labor.

Hawke's focus was on ending what he called 'the politics of division, the politics of confrontation'.[7] A Labor campaign slogan was 'Bringing Australia Together'; he stressed a politics of consensus. Not everyone among Labor's elite reacted favourably to Hawke's plan for an election campaign based on 'recovery, reconstruction and reconciliation'. The highly popular and successful premier of New South Wales, Neville Wran, thought he had stumbled on 'a meeting of the fucking Hare Krishnas ... Give them something to vote for. These greedy bastards want a quid in their pockets.'[8] Hawke would not forget Wran's 'greedy bastards'; his campaign speech promised both income tax cuts and an end to the wage freeze imposed by the Fraser government.

Hawke evoked a sense of crisis in his speech, and to the extent that he outlined an economic policy, it was a cautious but unmistakable Keynesianism which aimed to reduce unemployment and lift demand through 'controlled, responsible stimulation of the Australian economy'. A Hawke government would support centralised wage determination as part of its Prices and Incomes Accord with the union movement; this was a formal agreement signed before the election which committed the unions to wage restraint in return for government spending, such as on a new health insurance scheme to be called Medicare. Tariffs were to be maintained until the crisis in manufacturing had been overcome; government would offer industry 'a necessary breathing space until steady growth is restored'. Hawke ended by invoking the memory of his hero, John Curtin, and the Second World War, the 'time of Australia's gravest crisis, when our very existence as a nation was at stake', and the people had given Labor their support 'to take Australia through to final victory'. He enjoined his audience to see the recession and the drought as 'a very different kind of crisis', but one that posed the same challenge: 'to bring Australians together in a united effort until victory is won'.[9]

*

Even as thousands of enthusiastic Labor supporters left the Opera House on 16 February, a great tragedy was unfolding further south. Throughout the summer, there had been hundreds of bushfires in south-eastern Australia.[10] On 8 February, when the Melbourne temperature soared beyond forty-three degrees, squally winds gathered about 50,000 tonnes of topsoil into a vast cloud of red and brown that formed in the parched Wimmera Mallee region in the morning, hitting Melbourne just before three o'clock. Day turned into night as the cloud deposited a thousand tonnes of dust on the city, the ferocious winds uprooting trees and unroofing homes.[11]

The religious-minded had long been used to regarding such phenomena as a warning from God. It is a pity that the belief in such omens had declined, for it might have better prepared people for 16 February. The day before Ash Wednesday in southern Victoria had been cloudy, with light rain and temperatures in the mid-twenties to low thirties. Perhaps these mild conditions, in the midst of the hottest, driest summer in living memory, bred complacency. The following morning, the skies in southern Victoria began clearing at around eight o'clock. Temperatures climbed, humidity dropped, and a strong north wind blew. Melbourne's temperature again reached forty-three degrees. Combined with the fuel provided by a dry, brittle countryside, the conditions were ideally fitted for fires, and ninety-three were soon burning in Victoria alone.[12] In South Australia, the commuter suburbs in the Adelaide Hills were fast developing into a raging fire zone, and large blazes also broke out in the Clare wine-growing district and the south-east near the Victorian border. Adelaide was soon covered in dust and smoke; radio broadcasts in Britain contained the alarming but fortunately false intelligence that 400 people had died and half the city had been destroyed; Australia House in London was flooded with inquiries from concerned relatives.[13]

Meanwhile, in Victoria, several large fires erupted during the afternoon – near Warrnambool in the Western District; in the Otway Ranges, extending to coastal towns such as Lorne, Anglesea and Aireys Inlet; at Macedon, an area already devastated by a fire on 1 February; and several places in the Dandenong Ranges. Apart from the Warrnambool fire, all were on the fringe between Melbourne and its hinterland, and they were driven south during the afternoon by the prevailing winds. But in the early evening, a strong south-westerly that had been making its way from South Australia during the day finally hit the country near Melbourne, kickstarting the fires' most deadly phase. All but one death in Victoria occurred after the wind changed direction.[14] Towns that had seemed safe were now suddenly threatened by fast-moving walls of fire and the balls of flame they deposited like grenades.[15]

One town that found itself confronted by the danger was Cockatoo: a small community in the Dandenong Ranges about fifty kilometres from

Melbourne, a place of fibro and weatherboard homes, many previously holiday houses now owned by battling young families unable to afford a place closer to the city.[16] Residents were surprised by a fire that seemed to appear out of nowhere on the rise above the town. Cockatoo was soon alight, with residents assembling pets, photographs and treasured belongings, bundling them into their cars and seeking refuge on safer ground. The roads quickly became choked with traffic, the chaos heightened by a cacophony of car horns, exploding fireballs and gas bottles, powerful winds and thick smoke. Not all could leave; about 120 children with their mothers and pets spent a terrifying evening inside the local kindergarten, covered with wet towels – towels that repeatedly dried out as a result of the extreme heat – as parents tried to shield them from the frightening scenes outside. The children remained surprisingly calm. With great courage, two men spent the evening sitting on the roof, hosing down the modern circular building of brick, steel and glass as it was surrounded by fire.[17]

The power cut out just after nine o'clock, the telephone went dead, and the smoke in the building became thicker every moment. Torches were not needed: the glow of the nearby fire 'eerily lit the whole interior'.[18] The adults debated whether to move some of the children from the overcrowded kindergarten to a nearby building. A mother of two told a journalist the following day: 'I knew that any minute we would probably be incinerated and I just hoped that I would die first so I didn't have to listen to their dreadful screams of pain and fear.'[19] The fire passed without touching the building. But a couple engaged to be married in a few weeks who took refuge in a culvert were found dead the next day, their arms still around each another. At nearby Beaconsfield, twelve firefighters, including one woman, died after being trapped inside a ring of fire.

At Macedon a group of about 250 took refuge in a hotel. Like those in the Cockatoo kindergarten they survived, helped by firefighters who remained outside protecting the building with hoses. But at Kalangadoo in eastern South Australia, a 25-year-old man ran into trouble when his car became bogged during an effort to rescue his neighbours, a woman and her four young children. All perished. Another neighbourly effort at Greenhill in the Adelaide Hills was also in vain, when a burning man emerged from his home: '[T]here was nothing I could do. I touched him and his skin came off.' Thousands of properties were destroyed, from the humblest seaside and mountain cottages to the stately homes that adorned Summit Road in the Adelaide Hills. Kym and Julie Bonython lost their home, valuable art and the country's largest collection of jazz records.[20] The Adelaide radio journalist Murray Nicol remained on air to give an eyewitness account of his own property burning. He won a Walkley Award for journalism, but lost his home.[21] There were also stories of lucky escapes, such as the school bus full of children in the Adelaide Hills that was mistakenly directed into a fire zone. When some of the children became hysterical, a sixteen-year-old girl told them to 'sit down, shut up and stop panicking' so that the bus driver could concentrate on getting them out of the fire. The English-born driver calmly negotiated his way through the smoke and fire; 'a born-again Christian', he 'believed the Lord would bring us through to safety – and he did'.[22]

Since colonial times, Australians had grasped for a language and an imagery with which to convey their experience of fire. For one resident, the Ash Wednesday fire at Cockatoo 'sounded like a battle' but for another, the fire 'roared down the hill like a jumbo jet'.[23] The progress of the Belgrave fire up a hill recalled for witnesses an express train. At seaside Anglesea in Victoria, the movement of the fire was for two firefighters 'like a thousand horses coming down the gully'.[24] The SA Labor premier, John Bannon, thought that the forests he had seen looked 'as if a nuclear holocaust' had been through them.[25] Fraser compared the effects of the fires in coastal Victoria to an invasion of Panzer tanks, while a fire captain at Macedon also favoured a Second World War theme, the 'spotting' in that fire – the deposit of fiery material ahead of the main front – being like the film *The Dambusters*.[26] Others recalled more recent conflicts: the fire was like an attack with napalm.[27] Almost everyone seemed to agree they had experienced a holocaust.

Seventy-five people died in the Ash Wednesday bushfires – forty-seven in Victoria, twenty-eight in South Australia – and 2300 buildings were lost, as well as 350,000 livestock.[28] In the days that followed, bodies were extracted from burned-out houses and cars. Families who had lost contact on the night of the fires looked for one another, occasionally in vain. Thousands of homes were incinerated; whole towns had been largely wiped out; blackened chimneys remained where buildings had once stood. But there was, as usual in such fires, a capriciousness to which properties survived and which were left as piles of smouldering ashes and rubble. Scenes on 17 February recalled waves of wartime refugees: men, women and children with blank faces carried garbage bags containing their few remaining possessions to centres that had been set up to provide them with temporary shelter and meals.[29] Others rummaged through the remains of their homes for anything that had survived; a woman at Aireys Inlet searched desperately for her engagement ring.[30] The media celebrated the courage of firefighters and the community spirit of people who had stood up to the terrifying walls of flame. But petty jealousies soon emerged, resentment that children who had lost their homes received toys and holidays from donors while others who suffered missed out, and that 'undeserving' residents were presented with lovely new properties while those whose homes had survived still had just 'a normal house' – and perhaps a burned-out garden to go with it.[31]

The Ash Wednesday bushfires served to remind white Australians of their vulnerability in a land that, even after almost two centuries, they were only beginning to know. But there would be no revolution in how they managed the risk of fire. Bushfire science benefited from an immediate injection of resources and prestige, but things soon returned to normal. Many rebuilt their houses in much the same style on the same block as before. And it was all too easy, once the fires were out, the government inquiries had done their work and the lush regrowth had made its appearance, to return to fatalism. Australians' belief that they might defy nature, that luck might preserve them from future disaster, had survived the tragedy.[32]

*

The party leaders called a short truce in the federal election contest after the fire. Fraser, restored to the role of national leader rather than campaigning politician, toured devastated areas, consulted with the two state premiers, Bannon and John Cain (in Victoria), and promised government assistance. Hawke elected to remain in Melbourne; he did not wish to divert resources from the relief effort to hosting him and his entourage. No one, he said, could doubt his compassion for the victims.

Political commentators quickly went to work explaining how the fires were likely to affect the election campaign. Labor was ahead in the polls on 16 February, but with the Liberals seemingly reducing the gap between the parties. Most thought that Fraser would enjoy the advantage: a national crisis allowed a politician to become a statesman. Incumbency would yield its political rewards; the message of Hawke's policy speech had been lost in the smoke and dust of Ash Wednesday. But the bushfires had wiped out campaign time, recalling Fraser from the urgent task of fostering doubt about his opponent, and the national mood seemed to favour Hawke more than ever. Wasn't the central message of his campaign about cooperation in the face of adversity, Australians pulling together in a crisis?

In any case, the momentum remained with Hawke and the Labor Party.

On 19 February the WA branch of the Labor Party won 'a crushing victory' in the state election, delivering what the *Australian* described as 'a savage blow' to Liberal Party morale across the country.[33] The new premier, Brian Burke, turned thirty-six a few days after his victory. A former journalist who had greatly reduced his weight and drinking in the quest for office, Burke was the son of a federal Labor politician. He combined elements of the old Catholic machine politics with a newer style of Labor pragmatism that had helped leaders such as Neville Wran in New South Wales, John Cain in Victoria and John Bannon in South Australia into power. Wran, a former leading barrister with a rasping voice, a fiery temper and, in private conversation, a foul mouth, was the acknowledged master, having led the ALP in New South Wales to a narrow victory at the 1976 state election. When he followed up with massive victories at elections in 1978 and 1981 – dubbed 'Wranslides' – his electoral and policy success seemed to point a way forward for political leaders elsewhere in Australia. Wran gestured towards the social progressivism of the Whitlam era – the government championed the environment and the arts, and in 1984 Wran would himself move a successful private member's bill decriminalising homosexuality. But it was his reassuring persona, political nous and common touch, combined with a cautious approach to public finance and administration, that were the essential ingredients of his success.[34]

Labor leaders elsewhere emulated Wran's cautious pragmatism, although none could quite manage it so well as he did. Still, Cain had achieved a notable breakthrough in Victoria in April 1982; Labor had last won an election in that state thirty years before, when Cain's father led the party during its first ever term of majority government. Meanwhile, in November 1982 Bannon led Labor in South Australia back into office in contrasting circumstances; the ALP had only been in opposition there for a single term. Bannon had been a Labor staffer during the Whitlam years and had seen at first hand what happened when governments abandoned discipline and cohesion. Like Wran and Cain, he fostered an image of political moderation and, as premier and treasurer, a presidential profile, assisted by a personable style that appealed to Adelaide's small-town media.

All four of these Labor premiers, keen to distance themselves from the 'old' Labor Party's suspicion of capitalism, wanted close relations with business. But their background as lawyers, journalists or professional political operatives also meant that business was a world to which they had enjoyed only limited exposure. They could see how business might help Labor governments revitalise their respective states, but Cain and Bannon would eventually reveal themselves to be much less skilled in recognising the dangers of its wicked ways. For his part, Burke fancied himself a wheeler-and-dealer in a way that none of the other Labor premiers ever seriously contemplated. In this, his methods more closely resembled those of Queensland National Party premier Joh Bjelke-Petersen than his Labor counterparts. Burke consciously modelled himself on the infamous Louisiana governor Huey Long, cultivating a populist style based on the ruthless exploitation of government patronage in the interests of his mates and supporters. Burke's biographer also sees him as nursing a sense of grievance against Western Australia's 'old money', born of a Catholic working-class upbringing and the failure of his father's political career.[35] It led him to look for businessmen who might be willing to help him, and whom he would help in turn. A letter sent to a prospective political donor by a businessman close to Burke revealed the new premier's methods:

> There is absolutely no guarantee that a donation will result in any kind of preferential treatment for the donors should Brian Burke become the Premier, but what I can guarantee is that any point of view that a donor wishes to present to Mr Burke ... can be presented through his brother Terry ... and it will be given every consideration. If the matter is important enough Terry will arrange an appointment with Brian.[36]

Here was a glimpse of the old-fashioned Catholic machine politician in all his clannish glory.

One of those Burke persuaded to help him was Laurie Connell, a Liberal Party supporter and owner of the investment bank Rothwells. Connell agreed to donate $25,000 to Labor's 1983 campaign: small beer for a man whose wealth was growing rapidly through his merchant banking activities. Rothwells had been a venerable Brisbane menswear company with a history stretching back to the 1920s. In the early 1980s its board turned it into a 'cashbox' with the aim of converting the firm into a bank; that is, the company was stripped of pretty much everything except its cash. Rothwells qualified for trustee status, which meant it was able to get into the potentially lucrative business of managing trust funds. As such, the company was an attractive proposition to any raider confident they could persuade the Queensland government to offer a measure of patronage so that it could operate successfully as a financial institution. Two rising entrepreneurs who would give the 1980s much of its notoriety in the history of Australian business, Laurie Connell and a young Melbourne high-flyer named Christopher Skase, were in the running to take control, but Connell won. The Queensland National–Liberal Party government granted Rothwells 'the first money market dealer's licence issued by the Queensland Treasury in its more than 120 years of existence'. More importantly, Connell's supporters in the Queensland political establishment helped him give potential clients the impression that his was a sound enterprise, that it had government backing. The premier, Joh Bjelke-Petersen, launched the new merchant bank at a lavish party in Brisbane that was attended by members of the political, judicial and business establishment. Bjelke-Petersen's 'right hand man', Sir Edward Lyons, attended as chairman of Rothwells board. Happily, he was also chairman of the TAB (Totalisator Administration Board), which decided to channel the substantial cash flow gathered from the state's punters through Connell's little bank. Lyons's good friend the chief commissioner of police, Sir Terence Lewis, was also on hand to enjoy the hospitality; he had only recently intervened to try and make a drink-driving charge go away when Lyons, as 'full as a fowl', had been caught by police after a Christmas party.[37] Rothwells got its start in the world of Queensland conservative political cronyism, but it would acquire its fame in the no less spectacular Labor cronyism of the golden west, where it would also, eventually, suffer a sad demise.

*

In Canberra, on 4 March – the evening before the federal election – another Labor man anticipated that the turn of the political wheel was likely to bring him success, influence and riches. The 1980s should have been David Combe's time. During an arduous career as a political operative – most recently as ALP federal secretary – the stocky, woolly-haired Combe had shown exceptional organisational skill and financial acumen in helping bring the party organisation back from the brink. As he did so, he painstakingly built up his political and business networks with an eye on the party's future – as well as his own. In 1976 he had loyally taken the political hit – or at least much of its impact – following a gross miscalculation by Whitlam to consent to the pursuit of party funding from Iraq.[38] After resigning as ALP secretary in 1981, Combe set up as a 'government relations consultant' – or lobbyist – and his next goal was to use his old party contacts to make serious money.[39] Although in this respect a man completely in tune with the times, Combe was sadly hampered by one disabling legacy from the past: he could not let go of 1975.

He remained committed to the theory that the Central Intelligence Agency (CIA) had played a major role in the demise of the Whitlam government, and carried with him an open hostility to the United States on that score. It was an attitude common enough among the ALP left but increasingly played down by the new pragmatists who had taken control of the party. It was an attitude that would cost Combe his career and reputation.[40]

Combe was not yet forty when he fatefully accepted an invitation to dine with a young Russian diplomat named Valery Ivanov on election eve. One business on whose behalf Combe had been working was the Commercial Bureau, which had a unique status as the only Australian trading house accredited in the Soviet Union. The company was run by a mysterious businessman named Laurie Matheson; he seemed very rich, which impressed Combe, had a background in naval intelligence, and in due course it would become all too clear that he was also an informer for the Australian Security Intelligence Organisation (ASIO), if not something more sinister. Matheson's main business problem was that his former managing director had left to establish a rival organisation that was providing Commercial Bureau with unwelcome competition. In particular, he was having difficulty in New South Wales, and needed to gain a hearing with the Labor government there. Perhaps Combe might help him? Combe, as a member of the Australia–USSR Friendship Society, was about to travel with his wife to the Soviet Union. Combe undertook to work on Matheson's behalf while in Moscow.[41]

The First Secretary in Canberra's Soviet Embassy responsible for liaison with the Friendship Society was Ivanov, who was only thirty-three years old when he arrived in Australia in 1981. His youth was one factor that aroused ASIO's suspicion that he might be an intelligence officer; a Soviet diplomat of his seniority would normally be at least in their late thirties. The interest in him grew and, with it, interest in his connection to David Combe. It would later come to light that Ivanov had organised Combe's invitation to Moscow. By the time Combe arrived back in Canberra from Moscow late in 1982, ASIO was convinced that Ivanov was a member of the KGB.[42]

After his return, Combe provided Matheson with a report, based on his consultations with officials in Moscow, on how he could develop his company's trade with the Soviet Union. Combe pointed out that political tensions between Australia and the Soviet Union were a barrier to trade and recommended that Commercial Bureau might try to ease these tensions by participating in the Australia–USSR Friendship Society. He also suggested an upgrade of relations between the Communist Party of the Soviet Union and the Australian Labor Party, to be engineered by none other than David Combe, government relations consultant. Combe billed Matheson for $2500; ASIO soon had copies of both the report and the bill.[43]

As ASIO built its case against Ivanov, it considered approaching Combe to warn him of his predicament; perhaps he could be persuaded to report on his new friend, thereby helping ASIO make its case? That approach was never made, and to this extent, the self-serving claims later made by the ASIO director-general, Harvey Barnett, that he had saved 'Combe from himself', or from the clutches of the KGB, should not be taken too seriously.[44] In the context of the expulsion of KGB spies from other Western countries during this period, as well as local criticism from both right and left concerning ASIO's capacity, the organisation needed to catch a spy of its own.

On the evening of 4 March, Combe arrived at the home of Ivanov, his wife, Vera, and their seven-year-old daughter, Irina. Combe had already had plenty to drink; by his own account, he 'probably would not have run the gamut of a random breath testing unit' on the way to the house. By the time he left – after many hours of food, conversation, vodka, beer, red wine, white wine and liqueur – he was 'pretty well gone'. Whether Combe on that evening had revealed himself as a threat to national security would later be debated passionately. That he was a menace to traffic safety is beyond question.

The conversation during the evening was often rambling and, in Combe's case, increasingly slurred. He did most of the talking and had great hopes for the future – the country's and his own – under the Labor government that now seemed an inevitability. 'I was going to put in my list of requests on ... about Thursday or Friday,' he told Ivanov. 'I thought I'd ask to be Chairman of Qantas for first choice, and then Ambassador to Moscow, something like that you know.' 'Being Ambassador to Moscow, David, you'll keep your hand on the pulse,' replied the homesick diplomat wistfully. After a couple of years of money-making as a lobbyist, Combe explained, 'then I'll say, right, "I'm entitled to something, I want my job for the boys, Ambassadorship, Moscow will suit me very much."' Ivanov was confused; who were 'the boys'? Combe gave an impromptu lesson in Australian English, explaining that he meant patronage. Combe told Ivanov that he – Combe – was one of 'the boys', and payday had now arrived:

> I'm putting myself in a situation where, I'll level with you because you're a friend, Valeriy, I'm going to make the next two years, they're going to be the two most economically fruitful years of my life. I've

worked a long while for the Labor movement.... I've got nothing for it; in financial terms the next two years with a Federal Government and four State Governments, I'm in enormous demand, I mean I'm in a situation where I can say to Esso, you know, IBM, and all these companies, well, you know, I'll listen to your proposition and I'll make a decision in due course whether I'm going to work for you... in the next few weeks they're the decisions I have to make. Whom do I work for and on what basis, and I'm going to charge very big money... the buggers are going to be paying.

Combe went on to discuss with Ivanov the possibility of working for the Soviet Union to find opportunities for trade in Australia. But he was also representing a particular company with interests in the Soviet trade, Commercial Bureau, and he said that Ivanov would need to decide whether Combe could work for both.[45] Combe eventually thanked his hosts and wandered out into the night. The whole conversation had been recorded by ASIO, which had a listening device installed in the ceiling of the Ivanov home.

*

The day after Combe dined with Ivanov, 5 March 1983, Labor won a handsome 25-seat victory, in a house of 125. Hawke, accompanied by his wife Hazel, arrived in triumph that evening at the national tally room in Canberra. Combe was there to watch, having been hired as an expert commentator by a Sydney radio station. In Melbourne, where the Liberal Party had to share the Southern Cross Hotel with a Melbourne soccer team's big bash, Malcolm Fraser's 'granite face cracked' as he both conceded defeat and announced that he would resign the leadership of his party.[46] 'Mr Fraser's final surrender to a public display of emotion stunned observers,' reported Deborah Snow in the *Australian Financial Review*, and he 'dissolved into tears as he went into the embrace of his eldest son'. An angry crowd catcalled as he left the Southern Cross Hotel with his family, determined to take this final opportunity to hurl insults at him. The next day, he 'looked frail and shaken'.[47]

On the day following the election, Hawke, incoming treasurer Paul Keating – a 39-year-old Sydney politician of vaulting ambition – industry minister John Button and their advisers met with Treasury officials John Stone and Dick Rye in the saloon bar of Canberra's Lakeside Hotel. The federal election campaign had seen a flight of capital from the country: there were estimates that $2 billion had gone in the previous ten days alone, producing a liquidity crisis on the money markets and forcing up interest rates as local funds dried up. Labor blamed Fraser and the new Opposition for having told voters that under a Labor government the safest place for their money would be under the bed. Economists and business leaders were now calling for devaluation of the Australian dollar. Farmers and mining companies argued that it would boost exports. Manufacturers hoped a cut would stimulate local production by making imports dearer. The ACTU indicated that it would not use the devaluation as the basis for wage demands. So while there was a danger of unleashing inflation which made Stone nervous, that Sunday the politicians and bureaucrats agreed that devaluation was needed, but that the government should wait until Tuesday before making an announcement. They would watch the markets on Monday; when the capital flight continued, Hawke decided to devalue by 10 per cent, double the rate Stone advised.[48] As necessary as it was, such a drastic devaluation ensured that a bet on the value of the currency steadily rising afterwards was a sure one, thereby convincing some of the government's economic advisers that the existing system of setting exchange rates centrally had outlived its usefulness.

Many commentators expected the Labor government to sack John Stone, the Treasury Secretary, as soon as it came to office, because of his conservative politics, his differences with the new government over wages policy and his long-standing rivalry with Hawke, a fellow WA Rhodes scholar. But Stone also held the Fraser government in contempt for its poor economic performance and had voted Labor, for only the second time in his life, the previous Saturday. He gave Hawke and Keating budget figures at the Sunday meeting which they later examined more closely. The numbers did not come as a complete surprise; Hawke had received a tip late in the campaign that there was a much larger deficit being projected than the Fraser government was letting on. Treasury figures revealed that the forecast for 1983–84, at $9.6 billion, was considerably larger than the $6 billion that the Liberal treasurer, John Howard, had indicated during the campaign. If Labor's spending promises remained in place, the budget deficit would approach $12 billion, or about 6.5 per cent of gross domestic product (GDP), 'a record for the postwar period by a margin of nearly 4 percentage points'.[49] Hawke quickly recognised that he had inherited a fiscal mess but 'political gold'; the large budget deficit would, paradoxically, grant the government the freedom to cast aside many of its election promises. The expectations of Labor supporters could be hosed down, and the abandonment of Labor's spending promises laid conveniently at the feet of its political opponents. In these circumstances, it should not have surprised anyone that Keating, with Hawke's agreement, also decided to keep Stone on at Treasury; his retention would reassure the doubters that this was not another Whitlam government, that Keating could cope with a public servant known for his fiscal conservatism and forthright views. There would be no repetition of the guerrilla warfare between the Whitlam government and Treasury.[50]

In the meantime, the planning for a national economic summit – which Hawke treated as the centrepiece of Labor's transition to government – began. In his February policy speech, he had promised a meeting 'fully representative of Australian industry, the Australian work-force and the Australian people through their elected governments'. It was not, said Hawke, to be a substitute for government policy but an effort 'to create a climate for common understanding of the scale and scope of Australia's present crisis'.[51] In place of the normal gladiatorial combat of parliament, the chamber would become a place of reasoned debate among leading citizens grappling conscientiously and patriotically with the country's manifold economic problems. Hawke's opening address on 11 April concluded by appealing to 'innovation, initiative, independence, tolerance – and need I say, mateship – the qualities which we like to think are distinctively Australian'. And as in his February policy speech, he recalled the Second World War, drawing a parallel with the crisis of national survival the country faced in 1942.[52]

The summit embodied Hawke's election themes of cooperation and consensus, yet by inviting individual businessmen – many of them personal friends – along with the representatives of employer organisations, Hawke ensured there was little prospect that business could unite against government economic policy. Nor, so soon after the ringing endorsement of the Labor Party at the polls, was it in any position to challenge the Prices and Incomes Accord's basic assumptions and goals, such as an early return to centralised wage fixation.[53] If business was indeed under such an illusion, it had been well and truly shattered by the end of the first day.

On the opening afternoon of the summit, a 35-year-old union official with an unruly head of hair 'stole the limelight' and so announced his arrival as a leading member of the power elite. Bill Kelty, the young ACTU secretary, had already acquired a reputation as a tough union negotiator with a strong allegiance to the working class in which he had been raised, and out of which his economics degree, intellect and talent had taken him.[54] On the summit's first day, Kelty overshadowed the unassuming ACTU president Cliff Dolan to deliver a speech that stressed the commitment of the union movement to reasonable wage restraint and its willingness to accept higher taxes under the Accord.[55] His conciliatory tone heightened the expectation that business would respond in kind with a mildness of its own.[56] Kelty paved the way for further ACTU contributions on the second day which, like his own speech, mingled compromise and obduracy in a manner that offered employers little room for manoeuvre. The young junior vice-president, Simon Crean, was the son of the treasurer in the Whitlam government and an altogether shinier figure than Kelty; he had to work harder to prove his working-class credentials in a union movement which was still growing accustomed to accepting the leadership of the tertiary educated and the middle class. But on this occasion, Crean struck a perfect note, worrying employers with the barely concealed threat that the alternative to centralised wage fixation was that individual unions in 'key sectors' would push for increases based on 'sector productivity'.[57] Crean's was a deliberately provocative suggestion, for no one wanted anything like the kind of inflationary wages explosion that had helped destroy the Fraser government. Business leaders – some of whom had expressed their scepticism about centrally determined wage rises in line with inflation – now had to reassess their position, or they risked being seen as less flexible than the unions, and of dealing themselves out of any influence over government wages policy.[58]

The summit was a sea of blue, grey and black – someone joked of a 'suit-led recovery'. Paul Keating, not yet forty, looked like a gilded youth in such company; at the reception, his work was cut out for him 'fending off handshakes and jovial arms around his shoulder like an Academy Award winner on the way to receive his Oscar'. Yet he chewed his lip nervously, as if the man who had learned his politics at the feet of firebrand former NSW premier Jack Lang should not allow himself to get too matey with anyone, let alone a gaggle of corporate bosses.[59] The gregarious Hawke had no such qualms; he moved as easily among the captains of industry as among trade unionists, and he ensured that close friends such as Sir Peter Abeles, who headed the transport company TNT, were present to help things along. On the final day, Abeles suggested that the Accord should be turned 'into a trilateral agreement' that included business 'as an equal partner'; how would Hawke feel, he asked, if like the business representatives at the summit, he had 'been invited to play singles tennis against a champion doubles combination'?[60] In practice, however, the summit had already brought business within the scope of the Accord.[61] Geoff Kitney in the *National Times* concluded that the gathering had seen 'the coalition's traditional constituency desert it and embrace the policies of the Labor Party'.[62] 'Embrace' was perhaps too strong a word. But it was true that business had now committed itself to working with the government and unions towards an economic recovery. The occasion was a triumph for Hawke, and the share market was already showing signs of revival by the end of the summit.[63]

But what of the rest of society? Almost everyone present at the summit was white and male; the only interests fully recognised – apart from a single representative of the Australian Council of Social Service – were businesses, unions and the professions of law, medicine and accountancy. Other groups, such as the Australian Conservation Foundation and the Women's Electoral Lobby, had only observer status; like children, they were to be seen but not heard. Susan Ryan, a Labor senator who combined the role of minister of education and youth affairs with that of assisting the prime minister on the status of women, was the only woman with speaking rights. If the summit was any indication of women's status in Australian society, she had plenty of work to do: 'spotting a woman amongst the delegates was like finding a mango in a choko patch. They looked exotic simply because they weren't dressed in suits.' Nor were Aboriginal people, the churches, the young, the old, the sick or ethnic groups seen to warrant representation. Producers were conspicuous, but not consumers. A bulletin released by feminist critics of the conference defined 'consensus' as a 'collective noun covering businessmen, unionists and politicians', as in the phrase: 'A consensus got on the booze last night.'[64]

When the summiteers did have an opportunity to get on the booze, during a reception at the Lodge, good manners were on display. Many offered their congratulations to the Maoist leader of the Builders' Labourers' Federation (BLF), Norm Gallagher, on his release from a brief stint in prison for contempt of court. Gallagher was a burly industrial warrior of the old school, one who believed that while bosses were bastards in general, there were some good blokes among them – notably those who did as they were told or who generously shared their wealth with union officials. But Gallagher held his tongue when a captain of industry, standing within earshot at the economic summit, decided to deliver a smug lecturette on how talk of 'class society' was such a load of old nonsense.[65] Critics of the summit wondered whether Australia was developing its own brand of corporatism, one in which government, business and unions ran the country as a cosy partnership, the conflicts between them being frozen 'by a permanent truce'.[66] Others countered that Labor had long operated on the assumptions embodied by the summit: if you were in business or paid work, your interests would be represented; but if you were dependent on the earnings of someone else, or on the taxpayer through the welfare system, you were to be 'maintained by the state, but effectively excluded from its political processes'.[67] You were, in practice, something less than a complete citizen.

Others were also frozen out. Barry Jones, the science minister, found himself excluded from proceedings when it became clear to his colleagues that he intended delivering the message that government should give less support to declining manufacturing industry and more to sunrise industries deploying new and sophisticated technologies. That was a message which would not do in an audience that included both union leaders and manufacturers who depended on being propped up by government.[68] Keynesian economists involved in the early days and weeks of the Hawke government quickly also found themselves on the margins. John Langmore in Keating's office, who was heavily involved in preparing for the summit, resigned within months.[69] Another Keynesian, Peter Sheehan, had been arguing for a substantial fiscal stimulus; that one went down like a lead balloon with Treasury mandarins, whom Sheehan suspected of excessively cautious forecasts of economic growth for the coming financial year.[70] John Cain, his boss back in Melbourne and an admirer, later considered that federal Treasury regarded Sheehan 'as a pest'.[71] Cain was right. Sheehan was being touted by some as a successor to Stone, but according to Hawke, 'big-spending Keynesian economists were not the need of the day'. So far as he was concerned, 'the debate was already over'.[72]

On the industrial front, matters remained more complicated; builders' labourers were not to be brushed off as lightly as Keynesian economists. The union movement had been able to speak with a single voice at the summit but it was far from clear that the ACTU could now bind unruly unions to the agreements it had made. Indeed, even while the summit was being held in Canberra – with Norm Gallagher sitting among the delegates – 150 building sites in south-eastern Australia were being picketed by BLF members in an industrial campaign for a 36-hour week and a $40 per week pay rise.[73]

Unimpressed by the BLF's cheeky swagger under the Eureka flag, the Fraser government and employers had placed an application for its deregistration before the Arbitration Commission; in a scathing 1982 report, royal commissioner John Winneke had described the BLF as 'a lawless organization'.[74] Industrial tactics such as interrupting a concrete pour caused dismay among employers but underlined the tactical strength of the union. The BLF, said Winneke, 'penetrates into almost every corner of the building site', giving it a strength unlike any other union in the construction industry. Gallagher was himself a popular figure, inspiring, according to Winneke, 'a degree of awe' among BLF members.[75]

Gallagher wanted a good deal for his members, but did not neglect his own interests either: he had been accepting benefits from employers. With a bewildering absence of discretion, the BLF's Victorian and federal secretary had even been seen driving a truck owned by the Grollos, successful Italian migrants who ran their own construction company. Generosity towards Gallagher was for them a small price to pay for his union's goodwill; along with several other employers, the Grollos had provided him with free labour and building supplies for his and his son's beach houses.[76] In 1983 a few of the employers Winneke identified as having paid such benefits – Bruno Grollo, George Herscu and Maurice Alter – received fines and good behaviour bonds. But other builders – notably those associated with the Master Builders Association – were not prosecuted.[77] Gallagher would eventually have his own day in court, but his corruption was really of little moment to the Labor administrations in Melbourne, Sydney and Canberra as they contemplated how the mateyness between government, unions and business on display at the summit could be put to work for the national economy. In this context, it was the BLF's militancy, and its record of industrial success, that worried them. The BLF was a menace to the Accord, to 'consensus', and even – if matters were allowed to get out of hand – to the Hawke government itself. Matthew Butlin, a Treasury official, judged that strong action would need to be taken against the BLF to prevent it from pursuing sectional claims that would then flow on to other workers, reprising the kind of inflationary spiral that had bedevilled the two previous federal governments. Deregistration accompanied by the threat of other unions poaching BLF members, and disaffiliation from the ACTU, were possibilities that he suggested 'should be investigated as matters of urgency'.[78] Bob Carr, then a journalist, warned that a wages breakout led by the building unions 'would just about put the seal on the Hawke Government'. A showdown, he thought, was inevitable; any challenge to the Accord had to be 'crushed'.[79]

*

Rather like the businessmen at the national economic summit, Harvey Barnett, a career spy and now the director-general of ASIO, had every reason to wish to start off on a sound footing with Hawke and the new government. A Labor government had established ASIO in the late 1940s, but the ALP's relations with the security agencies had often been fraught in the years since. David Combe and Valery Ivanov presented Barnett with a useful opportunity, and he picked his mark exceedingly well when he sidestepped his own minister, Attorney-General Gareth Evans, and went straight to Hawke. Combe was obviously a hostile witness, but it is hard to disagree with his assessment that like the good spy he was, Barnett had 'studied his target, assessed his strengths and weaknesses, selected which strings to play upon and which drums to beat'.[80] Barnett would have known that Hawke, despite the support he had received from the left in his bid to become ACTU president in 1970, had strongly pro-American and equally vigorous anti-communist – and especially anti-Soviet – opinions. As a union leader, he had enjoyed friendly – critics on the left thought rather *too* friendly – relations with US officialdom in Australia.[81] And in 1979 the Soviet authorities had humiliated Hawke in connection with his fruitless effort to negotiate the passage of Jewish 'refuseniks' from the country. Hawke felt doublecrossed and claims to have contemplated suicide;[82] he was clearly someone who would be receptive to a strongly anti-Soviet message from the director-general of ASIO.

Barnett made an appointment to see Hawke late on the afternoon of 20 April and told him that ASIO had not only identified a KGB agent but had also uncovered an effort, by that same agent, to turn a former national secretary of the ALP into an agent of influence for the Soviet Union. Central to the case was that Ivanov had recently suggested in a conversation with Combe recorded by ASIO that the relationship between them should become clandestine. Barnett also told Hawke about Combe's 'jobs for the boys' boasting and his offer to work for the Soviet Union in commercial matters. Combe, Barnett reported, had expressed bitterly anti-American views, was convinced of the CIA's role in the dismissal of the Whitlam government and had shown sympathy with the goals of the Soviet Union.[83]

The director-general had been in no great hurry to let the government know what his spies had found – many weeks had passed since the fateful 4 March dinner. Yet on hearing Barnett's story, Hawke determined that the government needed to move quickly. He and Barnett discussed three possibilities: Combe could be called in for a talk – or, to put it in Hawke's own later words before the royal commission, 'I could call Mr Combe in and carpet him.' Hawke and Barnett saw several problems with this option: Combe, for instance, might talk to Ivanov; or once the news got out, the government might be seen to have compromised Australian security by giving special treatment to one of its own. A second possibility was that Ivanov could be quietly expelled, and that was quickly dismissed as well. So a public expulsion would occur, an option that Barnett plainly admitted would suit ASIO in view of the favourable publicity it would inevitably generate.[84] Hawke also saw benefits for his government beyond sending out the right message about its commitment to national security: he had just returned from the summit, an occasion intended to underline the government's willingness to deal openly and fairly with anyone committed to solving the nation's problems. The perception that a former senior party official was working hard behind the scenes, exploiting his connections on behalf of favoured clients, would have inconveniently undermined this central message. Hawke clearly recognised the danger of having Combe on the loose, selling access to the government, or even being seen as capable of doing so.[85]

The cabinet's National and International Security subcommittee (NISC) was quickly convened that evening, with all but two members present. Barnett briefed members, and he made the case against Combe in particular seem damning. Hawke gave his full support to Barnett's version of events; ministers were not permitted to see the transcript of the crucial 4 March dinner. Hayden, now foreign minister, told the royal commission that 'we left concluding that something very nasty and sinister and improper had been concluded or was about to be concluded between Combe and Ivanov'. As they left the room, Hayden said to another minister, Mick Young, that he would never have thought Combe capable of spying against his own country. 'I was quite distressed,' Hayden recalled, and he thought Young, who as a fellow South Australian was even closer to Combe, 'was equally upset'. But as Hayden later told the royal commission, once ASIO officials started reading selections from the transcripts to ministers the following day, 'the whole thing started to fall apart very quickly ... the very sinister connotations which had been put to us did not stand up'.[86] He could see nothing in the 4 March conversation other than a lobbyist doing his job or, at worst, a greedy man seeking to enrich himself through a commercial arrangement. Ministers did not like what they saw; but Combe's actions, so far as they could see, made him neither traitor nor potential traitor.

The NISC, however, decided that Ivanov should be expelled and Combe placed under surveillance. The former ALP national secretary's phones were tapped. On 22 April Hayden called in the Soviet ambassador and told him Ivanov had a week to leave the country; four days later, a cabinet meeting in Adelaide decided to cut off Combe's access to ministers in his capacity as a lobbyist. The government had destroyed Combe's livelihood; the prime minister even went to the trouble of calling two men with whom Combe was about to go into business to warn them off doing so.

With so many messages being sent here and there, Canberra was awash with rumours. On 8 May the *Sunday Telegraph* carried the journalist Laurie Oakes's claim that 'a member of the Prime Minister's own party' who knew Ivanov had, as a result of a recent government decision, been frozen out of contact with ministers.[87] Paul Kelly in the *Sydney Morning Herald* on 10 May revealed that ASIO had been watching the activities of a 'senior Labor man' who was 'one of the most important and influential figures in the party over the past two decades'. The security service had told the government he was 'a potential security risk'; the Labor man was 'determined to clear his name' and intended presenting Hawke with a document setting out his case.[88] It is a measure of the suspicion ASIO still aroused within the Labor Party that at the caucus meeting held that morning, Tom Uren, a left-wing government minister who had also been a member of the Whitlam government, asked Hawke whether he – Uren – was the figure being referred to in Kelly's story.[89]

The Opposition was also asking questions in parliament that afternoon: three in the space of a few minutes. It was the third question, posed by National Party heavyweight Ian Sinclair, which let the cat out of the bag; he asked whether members of the government had been instructed to dissociate themselves from David Combe, naming him for the first time.[90] That afternoon, in a sensational front-page story headed 'Russian Spy: Labor Official Named', Sydney's *Daily Mirror* claimed that a senior ALP official had 'been named a Soviet spy by Australia's security forces'.[91] No one could now fail to associate the gathering rumours with Combe. But when members of the government saw this article, they were unsure whether to laugh or cry. It was an outrageous libel and, at a time when Cold War conflict was still central to international affairs, a deeply damaging accusation. Combe was effectively being called a traitor. Yet the article ironically offered a way out for everyone, since if Combe decided to sue he would surely be the recipient of a massive windfall.[92] The following day, the government issued a ministerial statement declaring that 'Combe's relationship with Ivanov had developed to the point that it gave rise to serious security concern' to the extent that it was inappropriate for the government to deal with him in his capacity as lobbyist. Combe, Hawke reported, 'understands and accepts' this decision – there had been conversations with Combe going on behind the scenes as the government sought to contain the damage. Combe, Hawke hastened to add, had committed no criminal offence, nor was there any foundation for the allegation that he was 'in any sense a Soviet spy'.[93]

Combe could take little consolation from this statement, except that it potentially strengthened his case for a libel suit against the *Mirror*. But he was out of business, he and his family were besieged by the media, and he would soon be widely portrayed 'as some sort of buffoon'.[94] The story of the family's not inconsiderable suffering is related in an account by Combe's wife, Meena Blesing, who reported that her husband 'was psychologically destroyed and could not face the ruin of his life. The family disintegrated.'[95] Combe's sons suffered schoolyard taunts about their father the communist spy as the media laid siege to their Canberra home. The Combes felt shunned and even betrayed by old friends, while the government's decision to call a royal commission under Justice Robert Hope, who had inquired into the intelligence services on the initiative of the Whitlam government in the mid-1970s, only prolonged the family's agony. It was an exercise designed to vindicate the government's actions in the affair, which it did, ably assisted by a three-day appearance in the witness box by the prime minister himself. Combe, meanwhile, used his many contacts in the party and the media to arouse sympathy for his plight and a measure of support.

Eventually, there was a rehabilitation of sorts. The government feared the book that Combe was writing about his treatment. The Labor Left, increasingly angry over a range of government policies, was also threatening to make an issue of the affair – if necessary, on the floor of the national conference in 1984. Combe himself appeared regularly in the media and at public events to give his side of the story and attack the government. So the party effectively brought Combe back into the fold. Hawke even spoke on the floor of conference, reiterating that he had acted in defence of the national interest rather than out of any animus, and emphasising that there was now 'no blackball against David Combe'.[96] In 1985 Combe would be sent to western Canada as trade commissioner; another government overseas appointment followed in the early 1990s. Combe would eventually make a successful career in the private sector, as an executive in the wine industry.

Combe had behaved unwisely in many ways, but his desire to build a lucrative career for himself after many years of loyal party service was understandable. Combe's mistake was to boast about it in a manner that rubbed the noses of senior members of the government – indeed, even the nose of the prime minister himself[97] – in the money he was making or about to make on the back of his party connections. Yet in this respect Combe exemplified the spirit of the era that was opening up in the 1980s. There was money to be made, and he wanted in on the act. His weakness was that he also remained preoccupied with fighting the battles of the 1960s and 1970s – especially those of 1975 – and underestimated the continuing power of the Cold War to generate fear and loathing.[98]

Barnett and ASIO, for their part, held a fanciful and self-serving view of the influence Combe was likely to be able to wield under a Labor government. It is true that Combe was well connected and certainly well placed to work as a lobbyist, but Barnett's later suggestions concerning his likely clout were comically far-fetched. The case apparently showed the KGB's ability and taste for targeting 'the top echelon of Australian opinion-formers' and its desire for 'some degree of rapprochement' between the ALP and the Soviet Communist Party – all, according to Barnett, with the aim of 'neutering' social democratic parties so that, 'when any crunch came', they would be 'quiescent in the face of Soviet power'. Combe, claimed Barnett, 'was within a hair's breadth of entering the grand gallery of KGB spies, along with Philby, Burgess, Maclean, Fuchs, Blunt ... I like to think I saved him from such a fate'.[99] Kim Philby had been a senior MI6 officer while spying for Moscow; yet it is notable that not even the royal commission was able to identify what kind of material a lobbyist such as Combe, even if he had been inclined to do so, would have been able to pass on to the Russians.[100]

The reputation of the intelligence agencies suffered further damage when in late November 1983, ASIS – Australia's overseas intelligence service – conducted a training exercise that went embarrassingly wrong at the Sheraton Hotel in Melbourne. The operation involved a role-play in which a hostage being held in a room by foreign intelligence agents would be rescued by ASIS. Unfortunately, ASIS informed neither the police nor hotel staff beforehand. Not only were the premises damaged when officers used a sledgehammer to break down a door, but the masked rescuers threatened hotel staff with the weapons they carried. The only aspect of the operation that revealed a modicum of either common sense or judgment was that the trainees were not presented with live ammunition, although traumatised hotel staff were not to know that when automatic pistols and submachine guns were pointed at them. The busy royal commissioner, about to report on Combe and Ivanov, now had another incident to investigate.[101]

Those of progressive views who imagined that the new Labor government might be able to recapture the reforming spirit of the Whitlam era were sometimes inclined to see the shadowy activities of the intelligence community as a mere relic of a Cold War that had run its course. In this regard, they badly misread their times. The baby boomer generation coming into its own during the 1980s had rarely been required to pay the kind of price for its dissent that had been customary for earlier left-wing victims of the security service. It could perhaps afford to regard ASIO and ASIS as risible and contemptible in something like equal measure. But many of those who now occupied the commanding heights of government power – including within the Labor Party itself – had grown up between the 1930s and the early 1960s. Most were themselves products of the Cold War, and they well understood the passions it was capable of arousing in the Australian public. For the security services themselves and their defenders, the intensification of Cold War conflict during the early 1980s lent ample justification to their activities. Australia in the 1980s was still a Cold War battleground and not only – as it has increasingly been recalled in recent years – the setting for a bold adventure in economic reform.

*

Another major Australian challenge, the drought of 1982–83 – now recognised as one of the major El Niño events of the twentieth century – had created great hardship for many, but it would also prove a turning point in understandings of Australia's climate.[102] When the rain finally fell early in autumn, the Australian Wheat Board's bulletin was explaining the connections between El Niño – the periodic warming of the eastern Pacific – and dry conditions in eastern Australia, as well as reporting on the development of computer modelling that might 'in about 10 years' make drought forecasting a reality.[103] In fact, the Bureau of Meteorology began issuing seasonal climate outlooks regularly before the end of the decade. A mysterious land had become a little less so, as Australian farmers glimpsed how their lives were being shaped not only by the state of the international economy in which they traded, but also by the oceanic temperature off the Pacific coast of South America. Here was a form of globalism that few had contemplated.

By March 1983 much of eastern Australia had enjoyed at least some rain, bringing a little joy to long-suffering farmers. The Wimmera region of north-western Victoria, usually a rich wheat-growing area but during the drought a desiccated wasteland, witnessed 'soaking rain' in late March; it had 'been several years' since the farmers of Nhill and Kaniva enjoyed 'such a good early break'.[104] Queensland farmers were said to be 'jubilant' over the heavy falls in March; parts of southern Queensland reputedly had their best rain for seven years, and there seemed a real likelihood of a successful wheat planting, as well as winter fodder, after further falls over Easter.[105]

The story in New South Wales was much the same. The old copper-mining town of Cobar, along with its surrounding red-soil plains, was awash with 'the best soaking rains' many locals could recall. The town was soon isolated by floodwaters; over three days in March, it received more rain than in all of the previous year.[106] At Bourke there was rain over the Easter weekend in early April, and with grass shooting up on most properties, graziers were bringing their animals back from other districts. Experts warned them that hand-feeding should continue: the new grasses would be quickly eaten out if their stock were let loose on the fragile earth.[107] But the Easter rains meant that the winter cereal crops of barley and oats – used to feed stock – could be planted with a fair chance of success.[108] NSW irrigators were also relieved: before the rains, many had faced the possibility of receiving no water allocation at all for the coming year, and of being forced either to abandon their properties or to resort to dry-farming. Dams across the country, some of them nearly empty in March, captured the precious gift.[109] In the north-west of New South Wales, rain washed away the film of black earth which dust storms had deposited on dying trees; Moree, Narrabri and Tenterfield all enjoyed good falls in late April. There was a greater imposition on the patience of farmers in the central-west wheat belt, where the drought took longer to break, but it too saw rain towards the end of April.[110]

Few took for granted that a bumper wheat crop would follow, but when so many areas saw rain followed by dry weather, which was in turn followed by more rain, there was an outbreak of optimism. The rains lifted people's spirits and although it would be some time before a wheat cheque arrived, they also helped to open their wallets and purses. One grazier commented in early April: 'You can see the change in the locals already... They look different and, instead of frowning, are smiling. At last they can see some hope.'[111] Canberra shared in this joy, for the effects of drought flowed through the economy. The *Land* commented that the new prime minister 'must feel he is blessed with good fortune... A continuing autumn break will do more for the economic recovery of this country... than a dozen' economic summits.[112]

The drought, combined with the horrendous bushfire season, had brought rural Australia once again to the forefront of the national imagination. Yet there were suggestions in the rural press that city-dwellers' 'brief flirtation of identity with rural problems' would pass with the season; that the autumn rains would wash away not only the dust left by a long, hot summer but the bonds between town and country forged in drought and fire.[113] The unexpected appearance on the national scene of an old-timer who might have walked straight out of the fictions of Henry Lawson or Steele Rudd suggested that the mighty bush would not be so quickly forgotten.

The Otway Ranges, on the edge of Victoria's Western District, had been the setting for a devastating fire on Ash Wednesday. At Beech Forest on their northern edge, 61-year-old Cliff Young made a bare living growing potatoes on a 230-acre block of 'mostly unimproved land', which his more successful younger brother used to run stock. A bachelor and, by his own later account, a virgin, Young lived with his 89-year-old mother. Although he would later be described as a farmer in the media, Young was hardly one at all. The land which he purportedly farmed had mostly 'been left to nature';[114] he was really a poor rural labourer who, in time-honoured Australian tradition, had as a younger man gone on the road looking for work far from home, cutting cane in Queensland, picking grapes in Mildura, apples in Tasmania, tobacco in New Zealand. Cliffy disliked farming; he found the idea of slaughtering animals, along with a bad stew cooked by one of his sisters a few years before, so distasteful that he had become a vegetarian.[115]

Young took up running late in middle age, after failing at hang-gliding, and found that he was good at it; the longer the distance, the better he went. In April 1982 he had triumphed in a gruelling 100-mile race in Sydney, completing the course in bare feet after his running shoes caused him pain. With this success came a developing media interest in him.[116] But it was the Westfield Sydney-to-Melbourne Ultramarathon that would make Young famous. Westfield had large retail shopping complexes in both cities, at Parramatta and Doncaster; the idea was that competitors would make the journey between the two of them, a distance of some 875 kilometres. The prize was $10,000, put up by Westfield. Although media interest was strong, and Neville Wran was present to send the runners on their way, promoters did not even have official permits authorising the eleven competitors to use as a running track the country's busiest highway; the athletes and their support crews would be sharing it, day and night, with cars and trucks travelling at high speed. Rain made the business even more treacherous; it is a wonder that no one was killed.[117]

Young, with a support crew of family and friends, emerged as an early leader in the race despite a fall in which he injured a shoulder, getting by on just a few hours' sleep over five and a half days, often running through driving rain.[118] His shuffle became famous; it also turned out to be a highly effective way for him to conquer a long distance in good time without wearing himself out. He would be briefly passed only once, about two-thirds of the way to Melbourne, but as soon as he found out that Joe Record, his running mate, had caught up to him, the determined Young postponed sleep and went straight back on the road.

As he passed through each town along the highway, enthusiastic crowds – many wearing pyjamas and dressing gowns as they stood in the rain – lined the streets to cheer him on. When the lights of Melbourne came into blurry view, the crowds became larger and the traffic heavier, adding exhaust fumes as a new source of suffering. At Kalkallo just outside the city, drinkers rushed out of the hotel to cheer as he approached; Young rushed into the toilet in an unsuccessful effort to overcome the constipation that now afflicted him, in addition to his damaged shoulder and blisters. That would be his last stop before the finish line: Young, wearing a red waterproof jacket, ran through the night.

Race officials feared for the little man's life. He was in obvious distress despite his smile and all the waving at wellwishers – with his right hand only, because his left arm was now unusable. 'The pain in my entire body, not just the shoulder, became worse and worse,' Young recalled. 'Sometimes it got so bad I would scream in agony, but never when there were crowds around. I had my pride, you know.' He claimed to have forgotten about the prize money; 'all that counted was to finish and end the pain'.[119] Young could not be persuaded to rest even once he reached the city. Continuing straight to Westfield in Doncaster, he was greeted just after 1.30 am by fireworks, marching girls, a brass band playing the theme from the film *Rocky*, and an excited, chaotic crowd of several thousand – including his proud, bewildered mother.

Young achieved instant celebrity as the farmer who lived with his old mum, grew spuds and trained in gumboots while herding cows. The *Australian* praised his victory as 'a gut-wrenching demonstration of determination and toughness';[120] it was as if Young had shuffled out of the nation's dream-life, a folk hero possessing the virtues that Australians liked to think defined them as a people. 'I'm glad because of the type of bloke he is', explained one Colac civic leader, 'he doesn't skite about his success'.[121] Above all, Young was a man from the bush – or at least the forest – with 'a heart as big as the trees in the Otway rain forest where he trains'.[122]

Young's triumph was seen as a victory for improvisation over planning, of 'old-fashioned methods' over the new and fashionable, of old over young, country over city, small places over large. The *Colac Herald* explained to its readers that Cliff had been 'running for the first prize of $10,000 and to promote Colac and the Otways'. He was feted by politicians, journalists and television personalities, honoured at public receptions. The Colac council declared a 'Cliff Young Day', dressed him in the mayoral robes and regalia, and asked Australia Post to create a stamp in his honour. The Otway shire council did its best to live down the embarrassment that it had refused to provide him with official support. Following a civic reception in Melbourne's City Square, there was a homecoming parade in Colac followed by a ceremony at the Paradise Discount Store; a sign on the building declared 'Cliff, the hero of a nation'. The people of Beech Forest put on a dance to welcome him home.[123] Cliff enjoyed the dance, but bemoaned the lack of 'younger chicks ... Most were my age, not a breeder among them.'[124]

Bob Hawke lunched with him at the football in Geelong; John Cain in Victoria's Parliament House. Latter-day Homers, Virgils and Banjo Patersons churned out doggerel in his honour.[125] Businesses moved in for the kill: the representative of a sportswear company offered Young's support team $1000 if he would wear its running shoes and t-shirt across the finish line. And soon after his win, a canned-fruit company ran an advertisement which claimed that Young had consumed two cases of its pear halves during his run. Young would not become a wealthy man on the back of his celebrity, but admitted to having 'more money than I'd ever seen in the world before, the sort of money I thought only bank managers saw'. He would at least be able to clear his bank debt; and he had not given up hope of finding a 'breeder' – that is, a wife. She would soon present: in 1984 he wed Mary Howell, a woman in her mid-twenties.[126]

The mayor of Colac described Young's triumph in the ultramarathon as 'an inspiration to all at a time when we need it'.[127] Indeed, the rains that had made Young's journey along the Hume Highway so miserable augured well for a bumper harvest after the many disappointments of recent years. Farmers looked longingly at the fat green stalks that jostled for room in their moist paddocks.[128] And their hopes were not disappointed: in the summer, the country's silos were unable to cope with the harvest. Temporary bunkers were built to store the excess grain, while trucks lined up for hours at storage centres as farmers waited to offload their bounty. Railway carriages groaned under their enormous weight; galahs so filled their bellies that many were too loaded to avoid being run down by traffic on country roads. The harvest of almost 22 million tonnes was easily the largest ever.[129] Continuing rain did some damage to crops and hip pockets, but $3 billion was added to a national economy that desperately needed it.[130]

Drought, fire, rain and a rich harvest; a Cold War spy scandal; an economy that gave signs it could still deliver affluence; a Labor government led by a reformed larrikin committed to social cooperation and the fair go; a modest hero who emerged from farm and forest to remind the nation of its soul – it seemed that the cycles of Australian history, rather like the seasons themselves, were set on their familiar course. Guided by this illusion, few saw coming what would soon sweep over all: some of the most rapid, momentous and unsettling changes since the early years of the twentieth century.

2

Keeping Afloat

... yacht racing, and the America's Cup in particular, is usually as exciting to the average layman as a tennis match without a net.

Time, 3 October 1983

Few Australians of the early 1980s took a close interest in yachting, and yet it would soon come to play a central role in the national psyche. A sport enjoyed by the wealthy, yachting did not arouse anything like the passions, or level of interest, of the major football codes, cricket or even that other rich man's sport of horseracing, whose popularity derived in large part from its association with the genuinely popular national pastime of gambling. All the same, everyone knew about the America's Cup, at least from the time that Australian syndicates began their efforts in 1962 to unbolt the trophy from its cabinet in the New York Yacht Club (NYYC), which had held the cup since the first contest, in England, in 1851. No foreign challenge since had even come close. The Australian media magnate Frank Packer made a bid with his yacht *Gretel* in 1962, ultimately losing the series 4–1. Australians had won only two further races against the Americans in five subsequent challenges at Newport, Rhode Island. The 1974 series had seen an American clean sweep when *Courageous* defeated *Southern Cross* 4–0. On that occasion, the humiliated leader of the Australian syndicate was a stocky property developer from Perth named Alan Bond.[1]

Bond was an English migrant who, as a child in 1950, had come to Australia with his family. He performed poorly at school yet would later claim to have been an outstanding pupil, able to speak four languages. (An early employer, when asked about Bond's claims to such accomplishment, commented that 'he could hardly speak English'.) The young Bond exuded pushy arrogance. Bond began his working life as an apprentice sign-writer, but his success even in this modest trade was hampered by his poor spelling. A humble upbringing and lowly prospects did not prevent his marrying Eileen Hughes, the red-headed daughter of a well-to-do Perth Catholic family. Bride and groom were seventeen; Eileen was pregnant.[2]

To the relief of his employer, Bond's apprenticeship ended before he had finished its five-year term, and in partnership with his father he began a business called Nu-Signs. The sign-writing business – which extended into the retailing of electrical goods – did well, although Bond was far from the millionaire whiz-kid of legend. Constantly pursued by creditors, the company received complaints from clients about the poor quality of its paint jobs as well as from unions and workers about underpayment of wages. To the chagrin of the company's creditors, Bond began using the cash flow from his heavily indebted business to buy up real estate. A skilled salesman, he was also able to persuade local finance companies to hand over large sums for his ventures in a booming Perth property market. By the late 1960s Bond was rich enough to take up yachting, but too despised by the city's business establishment to gain membership of the Royal Perth Yacht Club.[3]

Bond's bid for the 1974 America's Cup was connected with his business aspirations in general, and his particular desire to create a city among the white sandhills of Yanchep, fifty-six kilometres north of Perth. The idea was that when he won the cup, he would bring it back to Yanchep Sun City where it would be defended. Bond would be able to build the resort he planned for the unpromising site and sell off land for residential development. In the meantime, he had gained the support of the WA government, built a marina and arranged for some of the site's desolate sandhills to be painted green to make them look better in the brochures. The project, however, foundered on the defeat of *Southern Cross* at Newport in 1974, which coincided with the near-collapse of Bond's business empire back in Australia. Propped up by banks worried about losing even more money if he went broke, Bond subsequently managed to rebuild his fortunes and bought the Swan brewery in Perth. At Newport in 1980, Bond's team even took a race from the Americans with their yacht *Australia*. He was determined to make a stronger bid in 1983. No expense would be spared in ensuring that he had the fastest boat, and a crew capable of making the most of its speed.[4]

Ben Lexcen was a self-taught man who had been designing boats for Bond since the late 1960s. He came up with two yachts that would compete in the 1983 America's Cup: the more conventional *Challenge 12* eventually raced in a syndicate led by the Melbourne businessman Richard Pratt; the other, a more radical departure, was *Australia II*. Its most significant innovation was an inverted winged keel, which modelling in a Dutch laboratory had found would reduce the yacht's drag and redistribute its mass.[5] Lexcen would be celebrated as the 'shaggy-haired genius' who came up with this idea;[6] the story was that the Dutch did no more than provide the facilities for testing. The concept's provenance mattered because race rules required that the yacht be designed by the challenging nation. NYYC officials, aware that Lexcen was no physicist, suspected the Dutch had been rather more involved than anyone was letting on, and they would eventually send a representative to the laboratory to get formal confirmation of what they strongly suspected.[7] Recent testimony from one of the scientists involved suggests that the Americans' suspicions were justified: the keel was designed by a highly qualified team of Dutch physicists. One of the leading scientists received $25,000 after the victory, courtesy of the syndicate's chief; it might be interpreted either as a reward for effort or hush money, depending on your view of Alan Bond.[8] In any case, American efforts to prove that the keel contravened the rules of twelve-metre yacht racing suggested bad sportsmanship at the same time as they repeated the legend of cheeky, heroic and improvising larrikins who battled both the odds and the Americans.

Australia II, under Olympic bronze medal–winning helmsman John Bertrand, defeated yachts from Australia, England, Canada, France and Italy to win the right to challenge the American yacht *Liberty* in a best-of-seven series in September 1983. Bertrand, a 37-year-old sail-maker from Melbourne who held a master's degree in marine engineering from the Massachusetts Institute of Technology, looked the very epitome of the moustachioed Australian sportsman of the era. His opponent was a Californian veteran, Dennis Conner, who had a bulky frame closer to Bond's than Bertrand's. Conner also had the inferior boat, but if anyone could overcome such a handicap, it was this fierce and wily sailor. The early races in the series seemed to bear this out: assisted by gear failures on *Australia II*, *Liberty* easily won the first two races in the series. *Australia II* enjoyed success in the third, but *Liberty* followed with a victory in the fourth; Conner had gambled successfully by using an unfamiliar sail which, worryingly for the Australians, had turned *Liberty* into the faster boat.

By this time, with the Americans leading 3–1, the Australian media was losing interest in a contest that looked like it would yield the usual result. Bond's reassurance that Australia would 'fight and win ... Just like we did at Gallipoli' was not reassuring to anyone who had paid more attention than he had in history lessons at school.[9] But the Australians won the next two contests in the series, to set up a seventh race that would decide the regatta. *Australia II* began well but Conner gained a narrow lead after about twenty minutes and then pulled further ahead. At the fourth mark, *Liberty* led by fifty-seven seconds, a margin usually regarded as fatal to a competitor at such a late stage in a race. But *Australia II* then began narrowing the gap and taking full advantage of wind changes, it effected a remarkable turnaround to lead *Liberty* by twenty-one seconds at the fifth and final mark before the finish line. In a desperate effort to close the gap between the boats, Conner then tacked forty-five times during the last leg, with Bertrand covering him painstakingly on each occasion. *Australia II* eventually crossed the finish line forty-one seconds ahead of its rival, amid a lot of manly hugging and crying on board, and to the joyous strains of 'Waltzing Matilda' across the spectator fleet.[10]

Thousands of Australians had travelled to Newport to see the series, and scenes of wild jubilation ensued. In an apparently spontaneous unveiling ceremony, Bond finally allowed the public to view the fabled winged keel; Donald Horne thought he did it like a man showing off the first wheel. Several Australian television networks screened the race, and millions sat glued to their television sets early in the morning, willing *Australia II* over the line. Horne, watching in Sydney, was reminded of the times when, as a boy, he had listened to the radio hoping that Charles Kingsford Smith would make it to Batavia, and that Don Bradman 'would survive the bodyline bowling of the perfidious English'. Australia's towns and cities erupted into a sea of green and gold, in celebrations that reminded those old enough to remember of the end of the Second World War. The song that had become a virtual anthem of the challenge, the Australian group Men at Work's 'Down Under', shot back up the music charts. The boxing kangaroo, an Australian symbol which had fallen into desuetude, had also been revived by the team as its own, and now vied for prominence with the national flag.[11]

For some, Australia's victory simply made them proud to be Australian – a common enough remark in the immediate aftermath – but editorial writers projected all kinds of fantasies onto the event, as if it had taken a twelve-metre yachting race to reveal the very core of a national identity after decades of futile navel-gazing. The Brisbane *Courier-Mail* was sure that it had witnessed not only a victory for yachting, but for Australia's 'good-hearted and generous' nationalism.[12] The *Australian*, one of the challenge's sponsors, had before the final race already deprecated the 'pseudo-socialist philosophy' behind the 'tediously trendy attitude' that the America's Cup was just an occasion for millionaires to play with their toys.[13] The victory, it said, showed that 'we can still do anything when we try'; the paper's proprietor, Rupert Murdoch, was conspicuous among the revellers in Newport.[14] But by the following day, the *Australian*'s editorialist was concerned that the euphoria might be wearing off. Australians, like the sailors on *Australia II*, 'should try to realise that we are all in the same boat'. Once they did, it hoped, those greedy unions might then abandon the concept of comparative wage justice.[15] The *Australian Financial Review* was convinced that the win had shown the superiority of individual initiative over government intervention. Sure, there were petty and mean-minded types who might say that yachting was a rich man's sport, but 'bold initiatives like those of Alan Bond' would do more for those struggling on the dole 'than any amount of wowserism'. Migrants of his kind had helped make of Australia 'a rough, egalitarian, success oriented society', which it needed to remain if it was 'not to decline into a lazy, isolated, self-indulgent society of parasites'.[16] The Melbourne *Age* appeared to agree with this interpretation when it asked rhetorically: 'Have we not seen in Mr Bond a triumph of the believer over the sceptic, the achiever over the knocker ... a demonstration ... that in a dynamic society talent will prevail over privilege? ... vigorous entrepreneurs can achieve much'.[17]

These editorialists might have been less inclined to such flights if they had been aware that Bond and Richard Pratt, just a few months earlier, had approached the federal government requesting millions of dollars of support for their efforts. The businessmen had proposed that the government allow them to rely on the same provision in the tax law, 10BA, which had been used since 1981 to encourage investment in the Australian film industry. They planned to pull off this stunt by maintaining that they were making a film about the America's Cup. Although any film's actual production costs would be, perhaps, half a million dollars, they wanted to claim $6 million which, under the generous 10BA, would have meant a concession in the order of $4 million. Unsurprisingly, at a time when it was suffering considerable damage over 'bottom-of-the-harbour' schemes of tax evasion (see chapter 4), the Fraser government had been unreceptive to this highly imaginative proposal.[18]

Many seemed convinced that the eyes of the world, and especially those of America, had turned to Australia. It is true that before the race, President Reagan had sent the *Liberty* crew a telegram telling them that 'Nancy and I will be rooting our hardest for you' – an undertaking that caused some mirth among Australians – while Reagan met Bond, Bertrand and other members of the winning team at a graceful reception in the White House Rose Garden.[19] But in the United States, the event had been tucked away on a cable channel where few saw it; as so often before, Australians performed for 'an imaginary grandstand'.[20] Yet the *West Australian*, from Bond's home town, was sure that the cup victory had produced 'a pride that will mark the national consciousness, and will help to alter for the better the way in which the world sees Australia and Australians see themselves'.[21] Some even expected '[t]he flow-on from the technological advances involved in the creation of our yacht will help Australia in the on-rush of the digital culture which is already upon us'.[22] The famous winged keel occupied a special place in this utopian 'high-tech' future, suggesting that a self-taught larrikin-genius like Lexcen – and who knew how many more were out there? – could take on and beat the rest of the world.

Australia II's victory was also an exercise in commercial nationalism.[23] The businesses that had sponsored the bid quickly manoeuvred themselves to make the most of the triumph. A banner flying from the Westpac bank's head office in Sydney declared: 'We unbolted it!!!' – the message accompanied by the image of a golden spanner supposedly to be used to take the cup from its cabinet at the NYYC.[24] In its post-race advertising, Comalco hinted none too subtly that there would not have been much of a bid without its aluminium.[25] Meanwhile, the syndicate's advertising agency, the Melbourne firm of Monahan Dayman Adams (MDA), felt compelled 'to send condolences to the nine advertising agencies in the top ten, whose yacht didn't win yesterday'.[26] The decidedly 'un-Australian' characteristic of skiting had suddenly become all the rage, a boastfulness unleashed by triumph over 'the blue-blazered [sic], straw-hatted and red-trousered gentlemen' of the NYYC.[27] The portrayal of the NYYC as snooty, effete and unsporting allowed the Americans to play the role of proxy English in the Australian imagination. English cricket captain Douglas Jardine's famous multi coloured harlequin cap from the 1932–33 Bodyline series was seemingly reincarnated in the 'pink pantalooned members of the New York Yacht Club'.[28]

With an unerring political instinct, Bob Hawke – as at the national summit a few months before – was able to place 'himself in the centre of an event ... expressing the prevailing mood and emotion'.[29] Conveniently, a cabinet meeting was scheduled to be held in Perth that day; Hawke stayed up watching the race and then headed to the Royal Perth Yacht Club to join in the fun. To this day, his exuberant performance for the cameras remains fixed in many people's memories as the defining moment of the America's

Cup victory of 1983, more significant even than *Australia II* crossing the finish line. Hawke, now well and truly off the booze, was nonetheless sprayed with champagne; he did not even seem to mind when someone affectionately ruffled his now sodden grey hair. There was the garish jacket he was handed, covered with the word 'Australia' along with little Australian maps emblazoned with the national flag, Hawke's colour blindness possibly lowering any inhibitions he might have felt about wearing it. There was his heartfelt declaration that the win was 'one of the greatest moments in Australian history'.[30] Then there was his remark that '[a]ny boss who sacks anyone for not turning up today is a bum'.[31] Hawke, said the journalist Greg Hywood, had now taken 'a lead on his opponents' that would need 'the political equivalent of a winged keel to close'.[32] Alan Ramsey merely considered that his performance in Perth 'was probably worth 5 per cent in the opinion polls'.[33] By early 1984 Hawke's personal approval rating was 73 per cent.[34]

Few doubted that Bond would use the win to sell more Swan Lager and inflate the price of his Perth property.[35] The America's Cup boosted the prestige of Bond and of 'larrikin capitalists' like him; men who set themselves apart from 'old money' in Australia, much as Bond and the *Australia II* bid had confronted the establishment they saw represented in the NYYC.[36] Politicians also looked forward to the benefits that might come from the Australian defence of the cup in 1987. The federal cabinet meeting in Perth held on the day of the victory, recognising its potential in attracting American tourists, invited John Brown, the enterprising tourism minister, to submit a proposal to a future cabinet meeting. He eventually asked for a special appropriation of $5 million and extra staff. He got only $2 million, but that was on top of an already enhanced allocation from the 1983–84 budget.[37]

The *Sydney Morning Herald* captured the moment perfectly when it looked forward to a 'spinnaker-led recovery'.[38] But except for those who made their money from selling flags and souvenirs, the economic benefits of the victory were hard to find. Perhaps it helped stimulate American tourism, which undeniably increased in the 1980s, but the immense popularity of the film *Crocodile Dundee* and the simultaneous collapse of the Australian dollar surely contributed more. The WA port city of Fremantle could eventually thank the America's Cup win for the millions spent on it in preparation for the 1987 defence. Yet the victory also imposed economic costs. The use Bond made of his new prestige to extract billions from the banks would, after he had lost it all and been sent to prison, lend his 1983 victory a grim irony. *Australia II*'s triumph nonetheless contributed to a sense of national optimism that matched perfectly the end of the drought and the shoots of economic recovery which, by the spring of 1983, already hinted at the better times ahead. And it contributed more than its fair share to the rising national pride of the early Hawke era, giving that moment a dreamlike quality in the more straitened times of the later 1980s and early 1990s.

*

At the time of *Australia II*'s victory, those entrusted with the nation's finances, Paul Keating and John Stone, were in the United States for a meeting of the International Monetary Fund in Washington. But the call of duty did not keep them away from Newport for the final race, where Keating and Stone – the latter decked out in 'navy blazer and commodore's cap' – found a relaxed Malcolm Fraser also enjoying the excitement.[39] In possibly the most unlikely intimate moment in the history of Australian politics, Fraser took Keating in what the historian Manning Clark might have called a manly embrace, after *Australia II* won the race.[40] But when Keating and Stone returned to Australia soon afterwards, they faced a problem that Fraser had allowed to fester during the final years of his government: Australia's creaking financial system. The rapid development of international money markets and the growth of the non-bank financial sector in Australia rendered outmoded a regulatory system whose essential character had emerged in the immediate aftermath of the Second World War. The Fraser government had appointed a committee headed by Sir Keith Campbell, a leading businessman, to inquire into the system. It reported in 1981 recommending comprehensive deregulation, but there was little political will to follow through.[41] By the time the new government settled in to office in the autumn of 1983, with the Accord as the formal centrepiece of its economic policy and ending the recession its overwhelming goal, much of whatever momentum there was for reform of the financial system seemed to have fizzled. Labor formally favoured a tighter regulation of the financial system, not the loosening of control. But as would so often prove to be the case with this government, outward appearances were deceptive: Hawke, Keating and their key economic advisers were interested in what a less regulated financial system could do for a sclerotic economy.

For over a decade Australian governments had been grappling with a global financial order in which the certitude of the golden age of capitalism following the war had disappeared. The challenge to US dominance posed by the rise of Japan and Germany, and the relative decline of Britain and

France, led to an unravelling of the Bretton Woods system of fixed exchange rates on which the stability of the international financial order had rested since the 1940s. In 1971 a US administration reeling from the combined costs of Lyndon Johnson's war on poverty at home, and on Vietnamese communists abroad, had ceased to guarantee that its currency could be exchanged for gold. This decision of the Nixon administration effectively ended the Bretton Woods system. The rise of computer technology, the divergent economic performances of the major capitalist nations and the growing integration of international capital markets in the 1970s and early 1980s placed even greater pressure on national financial authorities. Speculators were increasingly able to move capital rapidly around the globe and, where opportunities arose, to profit from fluctuations in exchange rates – which effectively became one-way bets on currency movements.

Countries responded to the challenges of the new environment in different ways. One response from some smaller countries was to peg the local currency to that of a major player. In the Australian case, the peg had become the US dollar in 1971, but from 1976 the rate was set by reference to what was called the trade weighted index, a figure derived from a basket of currencies reflecting Australia's trading patterns. The daily exchange rate was then expressed in relation to the US dollar. The rate itself was set at a morning meeting of three and later four wise men: senior officials from each of the Reserve Bank of Australia (RBA), Treasury, Finance and the Prime Minister's Department. In effect, only the RBA was permitted to deal in foreign exchange, since the trading banks had to settle their accounts at the end of each day.[42] But the currency crisis that greeted the new government in March 1983 and resulted in devaluation appears to have played a decisive role in convincing many – although as we shall see, not all – of the key players that the old system was finished.

What had emerged was a cat-and-mouse game in which, to the extent that exchange controls permitted, speculators sought to profit at the expense of the Reserve Bank, and therefore ultimately the Australian taxpayer, by anticipating the exchange rate decisions of the authorities. After devaluation in March, the Reserve Bank was on a hiding to nothing but this time from speculation about an appreciation of the currency. The devaluation had been driven largely by political factors – the Coalition's election scaremongering about what a Labor government would do with people's savings – so there was little prospect of the Australian dollar falling further, and every likelihood of a rapid recovery. Treasury in any case had long favoured an overvalued currency as a means of countering inflation, a preference widely known in the markets. Predictably, foreign exchange began flowing back into the country soon enough, and within a few months the dollar was reset at its pre-devaluation level. In the meantime, the government had been focused on the national economic summit, wages policy and the budget deficit. In order to set its spending priorities, it relied on an Expenditure Review Committee (ERC) comprising the prime minister and senior economic ministers. This became 'the engine-room of the Hawke Government', the place where all spending proposals except those in the forward estimates would be subjected to close scrutiny and, when found wanting, knocked firmly on the head.[43] In practice, at least in the early years of the government, 'ERC decisions were de facto cabinet decisions', as one of its hardest heads, Peter Walsh, would explain in his memoirs.[44]

The ERC epitomised the discipline of the new government, and its determination not to be seen as reprising the spendthrift ways of the Whitlam era. It reinforced the new trend towards fiscal caution. In May Keating had delivered an economic statement which foreshadowed a bond tender – effectively a government loan – of $1.5 billion, reductions in the exceedingly generous treatment of superannuation benefits, and a budget deficit of $8.5 billion. In August he unveiled the budget itself.[45] But financial matters had not, in the meantime, slipped off the agenda. Also in May, Keating had appointed a committee – under businessman Vic Martin – to review the proposals advanced in 1981 by the Campbell inquiry.[46] By commissioning its own report, the Labor government would be able 'to dress Campbell in Labor cloth'.[47]

Events, however, would overtake the Martin inquiry, at least insofar as the exchange rate was concerned. In the spring of 1983, a wave of cash flowed into the economy, prompting a decision for a partial float at the end of October. The Reserve Bank withdrew from any role in setting forward rates, and the trading banks took over. Meanwhile, the spot rate – that is, the rate determined each day by government officials – would still be set each morning, but the actual rate at which banks could convert their foreign exchange would be established at the end of the day, to allow traders greater freedom to buy and sell in response to movements on international markets. The RBA also no longer required the banks to convert the entirety of their foreign exchange accounts into Australian dollars each evening; it would set a limit for each bank.[48] These changes, taken together, were expected to give traders experience of taking on risk; a common attitude among the government's economic advisers was that a full float would ensue before long, possibly during a quiet period for the markets over the Australian summer.[49] More immediately, there were hopes that these changes would discourage further speculation on movements in the Australian dollar. But currency traders considered the Australian dollar undervalued, especially in view of the overwhelming evidence of economic recovery. Hundreds of millions of dollars entered the country in early December, the inflow of money threatening the government's ability to regulate the amount of cash in the economy, thereby undermining the prospect of economic recovery. The burden of the flow of capital would be carried by interest rates, which could be expected to fall sharply in view of the amount of foreign exchange being converted locally into Australian cash, and by inflation, which would be stimulated by unplanned increases in the money supply.

A new crisis unfolded on the last parliamentary sitting day of the year, 8 December, just as most inhabitants of the parliamentary village were letting their hair down. Hawke and Keating were not celebrating; they had heard from the RBA early in the evening that its New York office had reported a likely inflow of many millions of dollars the following day. Hawke and Keating spent the evening talking to one another, and to their economic advisers, about how they might avert this latest threat. At 10 pm, Keating told Stone over the phone that 'we are probably facing a float or something else'. Stone understood that the RBA favoured a float 'to get the politicians out of their hair', but he was nonetheless fiercely opposed, predicting that the dollar would rise by at least 5 per cent. This would reduce the international competitiveness of the Australian economy and bring 'an end to recent euphoria about economic trends'. In the current bull market 'we could afford to allow inflows to continue'. According to the Treasury record of the conversation, Keating 'seemed convinced by all this but noted that the Prime Minister had "bought in"', and he rang Stone back a little later to add that 'he was "afraid" that the matter was getting away from us'. A cabinet Economic Policy Committee (EPC) meeting was scheduled for the following day and with rumours running rife around Parliament House that something was up, closing the market on Friday seemed to Keating now to be the only feasible option. Stone argued against such a meeting of the EPC but agreed that if Hawke insisted it be held, the markets would indeed have to be closed, and they could only be reopened on the basis of a very different set of arrangements.[50]

Around midnight Bob Johnston, the RBA governor, received another alarming report from New York, news which he relayed to Keating by phone in Canberra: $800 million was expected to flow into the country on Friday

9 December, a sum amounting to 1 per cent of the entire Australian money supply.[51] Hawke and Keating now agreed to a full float. Keating consulted key ministers – Bill Hayden, as a former treasurer; John Dawkins, the finance minister; and Ralph Willis, shadow treasurer in opposition, now in charge of industrial relations. All agreed.[52] He also phoned Johnston, telling him the float was on, and asking him and his senior officers to come to Canberra on the first flight in the morning. Dealing in foreign currencies by Australian banks, except in small amounts for travellers, would be 'suspended for the time being'.[53] A series of morning discussions between politicians and officials culminated in a gathering of all the key players – Hawke, Keating, Stone, Johnston and various deputies, staffers and public servants. But in practice, the decision to suspend foreign currency dealing meant that there was no turning back. If the markets had reopened on Monday under the old rules, the government would have looked indecisive and foolish, its economic credentials shattered. The government had either to float or impose capital controls, and the latter solution would have issued a message about the Labor government's attitude to markets that it was quite unwilling to send.

The positions occupied by the various participants at the meeting were predictable enough. Only Stone and Treasury opposed the float, no doubt encouraged by Johnston's laconic admission that 'he did not know what would happen' after it. Stone thought *he* did, warning that the currency appreciation was likely to result in the kind of 'major shock' that would be produced by a 20 per cent tariff cut. The Whitlam government had cut tariffs by 25 per cent in 1973, with Hawke among its most vociferous critics; Stone was clearly playing to his audience, but he overreached when he went as far as to suggest 'an embargo on short-term capital flows'. Hawke and Keating, committed to 'the desirability of allowing market forces to have more rein', dismissed the idea.[54] So the decision taken was not only to float the dollar, but also – of at least equal import – to abolish most exchange controls. The horse had bolted; Stone and his officers retreated to Treasury to continue preparing the paperwork for the EPC. After it had applied its rubber stamp, Keating held a press conference to announce what had been done. He had Johnston, not Stone, at his side. On Monday, in an uneventful day of trading, the markets began dealing in Australian dollars for the first time. The sky remained in place.

★

The government attracted much praise for its courage, especially as journalists knew the decision to float had been accomplished in the face of Treasury opposition. The *Australian* headed its enthusiastic editorial on the float 'The Nation Has Now Come of Age' but the *Australian Financial Review*, while no less supportive of the float in its editorial, appeared a little more apprehensive in proclaiming on its front page the arrival of 'A Brave New World'.[55] A few years of hindsight did not cause journalists to alter first assessments of the decision's importance. In 1989 Greg Hywood declared that the float's effect had been to 'reshape the political and economic direction of the nation'.[56] For Paul Kelly, the float 'signalled the demise of the old Australia – regulated, protected, introspective', a judgment delivered in 1992.[57]

It has become common to attribute Australia's economic success since the early 1990s to this decision above all others. Floating the dollar has resulted in the usual fate of success: it has acquired more than its due share of fathers.[58] During the early years, the dominant narrative suggested that the float was the result of the flowering Hawke–Keating partnership, the growing authority in matters of economic policy of the Reserve Bank, and the eclipse of John Stone and Treasury as the main source of economic policy expertise. A biography published in 1988 by financial journalist Edna Carew with Keating's cooperation reported that 'Keating says he and Hawke took the view after the 10 per cent devaluation in March that the system of managing the exchange rate was finished'. Carew's phraseology is telling: 'he and Hawke'.[59] And as late as 1990, by which time his relationship with Hawke had broken down, Keating was still willing to discuss the float as a decision he and Hawke had made together.[60] Stone's opposition was always central to this narrative, allowing Labor to place its own political brand on the float: it became a bold and farsighted government, willing to make innovative and market-orientated policy in the national interest, unlike its political opponents and notwithstanding bureaucratic obstruction. Here was a potent political legend and one that served Labor's purposes well. The government's credibility among the financial markets and the business commentators in the media rose accordingly, even as many of its own supporters – especially once the dollar fell through the floor in 1986 – wondered what it had unleashed.

In the years since, the waters have been muddied by the bitter public feuding of Hawke and Keating, with Stone a late entry into these controversies. When he published his memoirs in 1994, Hawke proudly claimed the mantle of the float's architect: 'In this, as with so much else throughout that first year in government, the engine room driving economic change in Australia was my personal office.'[61] The claim is far from implausible. Hawke had formal training in economics, had served on the Reserve Bank board in the 1970s, and was surrounded by economic advisers such as Ross Garnaut who shared his perspective on the need for financial deregulation, fiscal discipline and lower tariff barriers. While Keating, too, had able economic advisers in his own office and in the bureaucracy, he was less well placed. His seven years as Opposition spokesman on minerals and energy, in which he had developed a close working relationship with mining industry leaders, had disposed him to support a loosening of government controls. But having left school at fifteen, unlike almost everyone who surrounded him in his new working life, he lacked formal economic training. Moreover, he had taken on the shadow Treasury role only at the beginning of the year. Early on, some of his public performances as shadow treasurer and treasurer were less than sparkling and, lacking confidence in his mastery of a complex portfolio, he leaned heavily on his department for advice. Yet Keating was also a gifted man with an unusual capacity to absorb, understand and communicate complex information, and he maintained a cordial relationship with the formidable, self-assured Stone. Until the very day of the float, the treasurer was hearing from Treasury and the RBA, from Stone and Johnston, two rather different stories about the best way forward.

Keating, said Hawke, 'was learning to swim'. He 'wished to take hold of the rope we were holding out, but ... John Stone had grabbed his legs and was holding on for grim death ... Paul would not kick free.' In October, recalled Hawke, 'Stone's vociferous opposition and Paul's obvious reluctance were at odds with the desire of my office to float the dollar immediately.' And even on the night before the float was announced in December, each time Keating 'mounted the stairs' in Parliament House to Hawke's office 'with the worry of Stone's opposition to a float etched on his brow ... he had to be coaxed and talked along'. Eventually, said Hawke, in the early hours of 9 December, he sent a staffer, Peter Barron, down to Keating's office with the message: 'We've just got to do it.' In this way, while conceding the difficulty of Keating's position in view of Stone's opposition, Hawke asserted his ownership of the ultimate decision.[62]

Keating has responded in kind with his own version of these events. Several published versions of the float from 1992 onwards – all indebted to Keating's testimony to some extent – place him, rather than Hawke, front row and centre of the decision. Keating has on several occasions nominated May 1983 as a critical month in the journey towards the float; apart from the appointment of the Martin inquiry, he claims to have asked the RBA at this time to prepare a 'war book' on the steps to be taken in the event of a float. The preparation of a war book does not, however, signal an intention to go to war; it merely recognises its possibility. Keating has also indicated that it was in May that he persuaded Hawke that the dollar should be floated: 'As often was the case with him after I had sold him on something, he became an enthusiast for it.'[63] Keating called the discussion with Hawke and his advisers 'good therapy, if all too often tedious'; that is, it was his investment in getting the support of Hawke's office for a policy that he already knew was right. The decision to float, in this version, was Keating's.[64]

How valid are Keating's claims? That he wanted to move in the direction of a less regulated foreign exchange market is beyond question. On 9 September, in a conversation with Bob Johnston at which the governor told him the RBA was leaning towards a 'dirty float' – meaning greater flexibility but with a significant level of central bank intervention – Keating did not demur, while explaining that he 'did not pretend to have a deep understanding of the matter but felt that that was the way to go'.[65] As it turned out, Keating was unimpressed with the results of the partial float that emerged the following month as a compromise between the positions of the RBA and Treasury. On 23 November – about a fortnight before the full float – he wrote to Johnston with his concerns about the recent upward movement in the dollar. While the October changes seemed to have had a pleasing initial impact of reducing capital flows, these had since resumed. He continued:

> I consider the almost unbroken upward crawl ... re-established in the market punters' minds the view that the only way our currency would go was up and, in this way, stimulated the resumption of unwanted flows. In short, I am concerned that the daily management of the rate effectively blew the opportunity provided by the changes to the system to break the vicious circle of capital inflows speculating on upward movements which were being forced on us by the inflows themselves.[66]

This appears to be a significant letter which has not so far figured in the continuing controversy about who floated the dollar. It looks remarkably like a declaration of independence, suggesting that Keating regarded the October reforms as a promising failure. While in his reply Johnston sought to allay the treasurer's concerns by playing down the role of speculative flows in dollar appreciation, it was clear that any further surge of capital, especially if it looked like it was coming from the 'punters' rather than long-term investors, was certain to prompt a renewed push for a float from Keating.[67] Indeed, by the end of November, it was clear that Keating anticipated a float sooner rather than later when his adviser, Tony Cole, informed John Phillips of the RBA 'that the Treasurer and the Prime Minister had had a discussion about rate management and the Treasurer had been given the "green light"'. It seems highly likely that the subject of this green light was a float.[68]

A third story – based on a mixture of recollection and personal papers – has come from John Stone.[69] Stone has positioned himself as a critic of Keating's version of events even more than of Hawke's, and he has contested the impression that Treasury was opposed to the float 'root and branch'.[70] On the face of it, his would appear to be an uphill battle. Yet by the spring of 1983 Treasury was indeed moving – albeit hesitantly and reluctantly – towards an acceptance of the float's inevitability, being willing to support an 'evolutionary' approach to liberalising the foreign exchange market. But senior officials recognised that any decision to withdraw the RBA from setting forward rates and to relax exchange controls was likely to increase the pressure for a floating spot rate, so 'the Government would need to be reasonably sure that this is the way they eventually want to go'.[71] Stone thought 'change ... should be undertaken in stages. A complete and wholesale leap to a full market system overnight would be an act of faith to which the Government has no need to commit itself at this time and the consequences of which cannot be clearly foreseen.'[72]

What is at stake in these disagreements? Hawke and Keating each wish to take the largest share of the personal credit for the float. But Keating could not have taken a decision as momentous as to float the dollar without Hawke's support, while Hawke could not have driven such a policy so successfully from his own office without the relationship that Keating had built up with Johnston and perhaps even that with Stone.[73] In terms of the politics, a divided house would have been disastrous; the change needed to be sold to party and public, not least because the Martin review would be recommending other changes that would require a reversal of Labor policy. The float needs to be seen in the context of the successful political relationship that was developing between Hawke and Keating by the end of 1983, and not through its later acrimony. Stone's preoccupations in the controversy are different. He wishes to suggest that there was a gradual evolution taking place towards a floating exchange rate, and that he and his subordinates provided their minister with advice about proceeding more slowly that would have been well heeded. While he and Treasury would pay the price for finding themselves on the losing side on 9 December, the basic thrust of his advice to Keating appears to have been sound. Keating's caution was also sensible in light of the advice he was receiving and the politics of the float. The consequences of a quick float could not have been foreseen, and none of the participants in the decision knew what would happen when the markets opened on Monday.

The float revealed some of the best features of the Hawke Labor government, as well as the traits that quickly came to worry its critics on the left. There was a boldness about it, a determination – as Hawke would say in another context – to '[f]uck the past', a refusal to be bound by established practice or tradition.[74] Exchange rate management was an arcane matter, understood even in its basics by relatively few people. It was easy, therefore, to carry one's views with minimal consultation beyond the experts. Its implications might have been far-reaching – the value of the dollar would increasingly serve during the decade as a proxy for the state of the economy, if not of the nation – but it did not immediately affect the interests of any of Labor's core supporters. Indeed, it was difficult to identify any vested interest worried by the float, and there was little criticism of what had been done, even from the Opposition.

Yet the float was also the ultimate top-down kind of reform that became synonymous with the Hawke government, and it has been celebrated in large part as a triumph of strong and decisive leadership – something about which the Labor Party has always been ambivalent. Of course, there was a need for secrecy in decisions about the exchange rate because of the dangers of currency speculation; it was simply not the kind of matter that lent itself to wide consultation. Yet it is both striking and symbolically powerful that most of cabinet and all of caucus were excluded from considering an issue that would matter so much for the nation's future. There is a retrospectively humorous set of documents in the Treasury files regarding a request of 8 November from Alan Griffiths, the caucus secretary, asking that Keating contribute a paper 'outlining the issues relating to the exchange rate'.[75] The request kicked around Treasury for a few weeks, and a paper was prepared and being checked by officials in the week leading up to 9 December. But it was destined not to leave the building, being made redundant by the dramatic events of that Friday. The story speaks eloquently of the irrelevance of caucus to what has come to be regarded as the most significant policy decision of the era.

The float, however, was just one of several government initiatives at this time that reshaped the financial order. Another was the simultaneous abolition of most foreign capital controls.[76] The Martin committee, moreover, gave the government the political cover it needed to present the Campbell report reforms as 'Labor' through and through.[77] One of the most important of its recommendations was that to allow the entry of foreign banks, a matter Hawke and Keating handled with considerable political dexterity. Keating's own family background and political lineage bestowed on him a rich store of opinions, emotions and rhetoric that could easily be turned to the uses he now required. His father's small engineering business had, by Keating's own account, suffered from its inability to raise the loans it needed to expand from Australian banks because they would only let his father borrow against his assets. Keating was also a protégé of Jack Lang, Depression-era scourge of the 'money power'. So when Keating 'sold' the foreign bank policy to the public and especially to the party, he emphasised the anti-establishment angle: allowing greater foreign competition would shake up Australia's banking industry, disturbing its cosseted dominance of the Australian financial world. The policy would also stimulate the economy. As he told the Labor Party's national conference in July 1984, 'Banking is the artery of the economy and we have had hardening of the arteries for too long in this country. It is time we unclogged a few.' Keating pointed out that international banks were already active in the Australian economy, operating as finance companies, helping to fund takeover bids, or operating out of a merchant bank or through an office in an Australian city. 'If it was not for the merchant banks here, for fifteen years gingering them up, we would still be back with quill pens and ledgers, up at the high tables making the folio entries.'[78] The Labor Left faction opposed foreign bank entry but without effect; the Right and Centre Left waved it through.

At the national conference, Keating had received strong backing from three Labor state premiers (the fourth, Wran, was chairing the conference). Much has been made of the divergence that supposedly emerged between the 'Keynesian' economic policy of the Victorian Labor government of John Cain and the 'economic rationalism' of Hawke and Keating. 'Ours was a Keynesian welfare state model,' recalled Cain, just as he recalled how much it was loathed by his federal counterparts.[79] The Victorian government was certainly more inclined to an expansionary economic policy than federal

Labor, and more confident of the capacity of public authorities to pick business 'winners'. To pursue this goal, the Cain government upgraded a body created by the previous government – the Victorian Economic Development Corporation – so that it became the 'principal agency for the provision of targeted loan and equity funds to business'.[80] But Cain's government also saw opportunities in financial deregulation, hoping that foreign banks might elect to set up in Melbourne, and that they would compete successfully with the existing trading banks which, in Cain's opinion, had 'shown a great lack of initiative'. He felt that manufacturing exporters had been especially starved for cash.[81]

In 1984 the Bannon government merged the local state and savings banks to create the State Bank of South Australia, which combined traditional retail functions such as home loans with markedly more ambitious lending and acquisition. The State Bank of South Australia was the centrepiece of its economic strategy: a cash cow for government, the driver of local business development and a source of local pride as it expanded beyond the state's borders. Adelaide might not have been able to attract the big global financial players but it had its own – or so the story went.[82]

Meanwhile in Perth, the Burke government hitched its wagon to Laurie Connell's Rothwells, which was a bank in name only, more a racket designed to finance Connell's expensive taste in Thoroughbreds and other forms of extravagance. The government's own Western Australian Development Corporation was wheeling and dealing with the best of them, in a state whose normal exuberance had received an additional boost from the America's Cup victory of its latest favourite son, Alan Bond, and from the much-anticipated cup defence in 1987.

Labor's enthusiasm for financial deregulation delighted, as it surprised, the markets, and it represented a major departure from its traditional suspicion of finance capital. Keating was rewarded in 1984 when the magazine *Euromoney* judged him Finance Minister of the Year – which translated locally into his being 'the world's greatest treasurer'.[83] The party that under one of its most revered prime ministers, Ben Chifley, had tried to nationalise the trading banks now took pride in the praise it received from local and international financiers. But at the party's grassroots, some very angry people found it difficult to square the direction of the ALP with what they thought it stood for. Some of their anger was aroused over issues of uranium mining policy, foreign policy and defence, a matter to be taken up in chapter 4. But the shift towards economic rationalism, as the free-market approach was increasingly called, was also a major grievance. A resolution of the party's North Sydney branch conveyed this growing disillusionment, expressing its:

> profound disappointment in the direction taken by the Biennial Conference. In particular, we are appalled by policy changes on the mining and export of uranium, East Timor, and foreign banks. The present policy of the A.L.P. in Government would have drawn howls of protest from the A.L.P. in opposition. The price of Madison Avenue politics is the long term loss of credibility on the part of the Party, and alienation of rank and file members.[84]

There was disgruntlement in the unions too. Financial deregulation was one thing. But Hawke had hinted that tariff protection was also in his sights – and that, they could not abide. John Button, as industry minister, was signalling that protection needed to come down, that industries needed to think in terms of better planning, improved skills, new technologies and superior products. 'There is a great unwillingness in this country to take risks,' he commented in an interview, as he bemoaned the habit of both manufacturers and unions begging government for handouts. But when Labor came to office he faced a more urgent problem than weaning industry off the government breast: the crisis in the steel industry. There was an international steel glut and BHP, the country's biggest company and almost its sole producer of steel, had already sacked thousands of workers. There was even talk of the company ceasing to produce steel entirely, a decision that would create economic and social chaos in Wollongong and Newcastle in New South Wales, and Whyalla in South Australia, the cities where steel plants were located. During the election campaign Hawke had promised a solution in his first hundred days in office. Now he – or rather Button – had to deliver. Hawke offered up his trusted economic adviser, Ross Garnaut, to work with the industry minister and his officials on what would become known as the steel plan. It was a five-year scheme, based on bounties aimed at encouraging investment and productivity improvements. That the plan did not guarantee BHP market share was telling; it reflected the government's developing challenge to protectionist solutions.[85]

Steel had long been regarded as providing 'the muscle of an industrial economy'. If so, perhaps the car industry represented its bone and sinew. Concentrated in Melbourne, Geelong and Adelaide, it was also heavily protected.

Behind a formidable tariff wall, quota restrictions and local content rules, five car producers turned out thirteen models, several of them with low production runs. Quality was variable; few cars were exported. The Button car plan, which was released in May 1984, envisaged reduced protection for the industry, and that manufacturers would be reduced to three and the number of models to six. When unions and firms later came to Canberra, and one manufacturer complained that if the number of cars flooding into the country continued 'like this we'll soon all be driving Daimler Benz', Paul Keating's eyes smiled: 'If that happens,' he said, 'we'll all be much better off.'[86]

Button had visited Europe early in 1984, where Sweden most impressed him as a source of ideas and inspiration for Australian manufacturing; on the left in the 1980s, there would be incessant talk of the attractions of the 'Swedish model'. Sweden, Button informed Hawke in a letter in February 1984, had already restructured its industry, the Social Democrats having eliminated 'hand-outs' to flagging industries. Button continued: 'The point should also be made, in the context of the endless debates in Australia, that the Swedes believe in the free market. They do not believe in bailing out weak industries, but their industry policy is based on deciding in broad terms what part of the market they want to be in ... they then direct government resources' to that part of the market to encourage research and development, venture capital and exports. Australia, thought Button, was reaping the consequences of its long-term protectionism in support of manufacturing – protection had cultivated 'a sort of Banana Republic mentality' – as well as its 'penchant for selecting a panacea for all the woes of Australian industry, such as the mining boom and, more recently, our colleague's repeated promises of the sunrise industries solution'. The 'colleague' here was Barry Jones, the science minister; 'sunrise industries' were new, clean, high-technology and capital-intensive, and Jones saw them as the path to a reinvigorated Australian manufacturing sector. Button, however, had been confirmed in his scepticism by visiting Europe: 'there is no talk of sunrise industries in Europe as providing any sort of panacea. What they are talking about is, if I may modestly say so, what I have been talking about for the last year ... the relevance of new technologies to existing industries in improving their capacity and performance.'[87]

A fight was brewing, and many observers thought that on the issue of protection, the 1984 national conference in Canberra would turn out to be a bloodbath. In the Labor Left, and among union leaders, protectionist sentiment remained strong. Unemployment was falling but only slowly – it was still, in mid-1984, almost 9 per cent and much higher in cities and regions of manufacturing concentration. With many of their members out of a job, few union leaders thought the time opportune to be reducing protection – although it is doubtful they would have seen any time as opportune – and one prominent left-wing official, the Amalgamated Metal Workers' Union's Laurie Carmichael, had instructed colleagues to go to Canberra to 'get rid of Button'. While they were unlikely to be able to do that, union leaders met with the industry minister in a hotel suite ahead of the conference debate. They wanted the party platform altered to conform with the Accord's commitment to protection; Button said he 'was not happy with the accord commitment to maintenance of high tariffs'; Ray Piriam of the Electrical Trades Union replied pointedly that 'he was not happy with [the] commitment to wage restraint in the accord' and Button ought to think about that. It 'was all pretty heavy going', the minister recalled. But they hammered out a compromise, and conference warfare was averted. In 'a short but acrimonious debate', speakers from the unions and the Left had made their point, but Button still felt it worth asking conference: 'why can Sweden make a car like the Volvo, and why can't we?'[88]

*

The Hawke government seemed to many commentators a new type of Labor government: men and a few women whose education had aroused a mixture of envy, suspicion, hostility and admiration as they had risen through the state Labor parties during the 1960s and 1970s. Union leaders had not disappeared, but neither were they any longer the 'typical' Labor parliamentarian.[89] The sociologist Sol Encel thought he was witnessing the effects of the 'managerial revolution' on politics, the rise of the 'information specialist' and the 'professional manager'.[90] It was certainly harder than ever before to spot old-style trade unionists in the ministry, although they were there. Stewart West, a former wharfie, was immigration minister, while Mick Young, an ex-shearer from South Australia who had distinguished himself as a gifted campaign organiser, unfortunately turned out to be an accident-prone cabinet minister. More common than the working unionist was the tertiary-educated professional who had come through the ranks of the union movement as a researcher, an official or both. Hawke had been a very early member of the species, while Ralph Willis, the industrial relations minister, was a later one. Both came to politics from the ACTU.

The Oxford connection was strong in the ministry: Hawke himself, Neal Blewett, the health minister charged with the job of setting up Medicare, and Kim Beazley, who would distinguish himself in the defence portfolio, were all Rhodes scholars, while Gareth Evans was also a graduate of the ancient university. Chris Hurford, like the fictional Jim Hacker in the British television comedy of the 1980s *Yes Minister*, was a graduate of the London School of Economics. Blewett, Beazley and Evans had all worked in universities, as had Barry Jones, though he was better known to Australians as a TV quiz champion. Lawyers – especially industrial lawyers – were prominent, in both federal and state governments. Even those federal government members with farming backgrounds, such as John Kerin, the primary industries minister, and Peter Walsh, initially in resources and energy but from 1984 in charge of finance, had attended university as mature-age students. Other ministers, too, had studied as adults, in some instances after they had been elected to parliament; Hayden was one of these and Barry Cohen, who held portfolios in the arts, environment and heritage in the early years of the government, was another. Keating was a notable exception to the trend towards academic credentials, but his taste for classical music and expensive antiques was, to say the least, unusual among the working-class communities of western Sydney among which he had been raised. The only woman in cabinet, Susan Ryan, was a former teacher active in the women's movement. Raised as a Catholic and with her eye on an education portfolio which Hawke initially seemed reluctant to give her – he was apparently worried about how Catholics would react to her feminism – Ryan 'enlisted the good opinion of Archbishop James Carroll', a politically astute prelate who chaired the NSW Catholic Education Commission. Ryan had been raised a Catholic, but was now – as Mick Young put it – 'a non-financial member'. She was also the first ever female federal Labor minister.[91]

The government was divided according to factions – Left, Right and, from early 1984, a Centre Left which included Hayden and many of his supporters along with an assortment of others who, for one reason or another, did not slot readily into the two larger factions. Factional leaders played a significant role in managing conflict and ensuring an acceptable division of the spoils of office, contributing powerfully to the government's stability. Yet there was also an emerging esprit de corps among ministers that transcended such factional divisions. It was captured well in a letter written by John Dawkins, the finance minister and a member of the Centre Left, to the prime minister in 1984 when the Hawkes were dealing with their daughter's drug addiction: 'My respect for you and your gift for leadership have grown continuously since we set out on this great venture – the cause and course of which remain absolutely correct.'[92] The Left was initially rather remote from the centre of power, as well as from the emerging orthodoxies in economic, defence and foreign policy, but these differences would decline after 1984.

The Hawke government's enthusiasm for 'reform' was rather less effusive outside the favoured field of finance. There was little interest in constitutional reform; a proposal for a bill of rights championed by the young attorney-general, Gareth Evans, floundered, and eventually died. Yet the show held together in large part because the government combined an economic policy increasingly geared towards the financial markets with a social policy that was recognisably Whitlamite – at least if you were prepared to squint a little while contemplating it. Above all, there was Medicare. After an arduous battle under the generalship of Bill Hayden, the Whitlam government had finally succeeded in establishing Medibank in 1975, just in time for the Fraser government to begin dismantling it. The Accord committed Labor to a replacement scheme of universal health insurance when it came to office in 1983. ACTU support was critical in Medicare's success, but so was the weakness of the opposition to Medicare from doctors, private health funds and even the federal Coalition. It also helped that the responsible minister, Blewett, was highly competent, and that Medicare would reduce inflation by flattening out medical costs.[93]

Another area in which the government quickly chalked up a major achievement was the passage of the *Sex Discrimination Act* in 1984, which aimed to remove the disabilities under which women laboured in connection with employment, education, housing and provision of services such as access to credit. It, too, experienced only a muted opposition in the parliament but there was a hard core of conservative MPs in each house – a few of them blatantly misogynistic – who saw the proposal as 'great load of nonsense'.[94] Senator Brian Archer, a Tasmanian Liberal, declared that no 'amount of legislation' would 'change the fact that most ordinary, natural women are homely and caring, that they are not wildly ambitious, that they are not naturally dominating ... Men, by nature, are most likely to be leaders, providers and protectors.'[95] Politicians such as these had the support of a noisy minority of moral conservatives outside who lobbied hard against the bill, professing to see in it a threat to the family, an effort to lock women out of the home and into the workforce, even a measure to facilitate abortion. A group known as Women Who Want to Be Women was prominent in stoking fears about the end of civilisation, claiming that the government was seeking to create 'a unisex society'.[96] They asked for divine help in dealing with the minister responsible for the bill, Susan Ryan: 'Please pray that God will restrain Senator

Ryan from devising more policies against the traditional family and schools where Christian principles are adhered to. A "disillusioned" Catholic, she needs a revelation and an infilling of the spirit of God, or to be removed from office before she has a chance to do any permanent damage.'[97]

In response to more considered criticism than that offered here, the government accepted amendments which provided reassurance to the nervous. Independent schools and religious bodies were permitted a wide field of exemption, and the bill was amended so that it covered only services available to both men and women – thereby taking some of the heat out of the abortion issue. Nonetheless, the Act was a major practical and symbolic achievement. Ryan had introduced the bill in the Senate, and there was a small number of women in each chamber of parliament able to speak from their own experience in support of a bill that the Australian Democrats senator, Janine Haines, praised for acknowledging that 'women are born with both a brain and a womb'.[98] The Labor Party's Senator Rosemary Crowley thought it would help challenge stereotypes that enchained not only women but also men who felt stuck in the 'perpetual position of breadwinner'.[99] There was no more reassurance here to determined critics of the bill as a home-wrecking instrument than there would be in lower-house Labor MP Jeanette McHugh's testimony that as a mother, there were times when she had felt 'imprisoned', with 'no outlet at all'.[100]

These achievements in health and women's rights nonetheless reassured some of the doubters that this was truly a Labor government, not a bunch of 'Tories in Labor drag'. But some critics on the left were not so sure, failing to see much recognisable as a link 'with traditional Labor views or practices', or a record as a 'reformist government' in the social democratic sense.[101] In seeking to place so much distance between its own performance and the legacy of the Whitlam government, had Labor thrown the baby out with the bathwater? In the mid-1980s, as the party retreated from its commitment to Aboriginal land rights, confirmed its commitment to the Western nuclear alliance, slashed its spending and deregulated the financial system, the government's standing dropped among both its declining core of traditional supporters and the middle class, whose support it needed to stay in power.

Popular memory of the Hawke government has given too little attention to the erosion of its electoral standing, even as its economic policy won over the financial journalists, corporate bosses and foreign exchange dealers. Commentators have conflated Hawke's personal popularity with attitudes to his government, and they have mistaken a preference for the Labor Party over its opponents – one that was never overwhelming in any election except that in 1983 – with a resilient enthusiasm for the ALP and all its works. Yet the increasingly dominant understanding of modernity found among its leaders – one focused on the creative and liberating power of markets – never quite won over the hearts and minds of Australian voters. Given the kinds of economic problems the government faced, and its determination to make difficult decisions to turn around the country's economic fortunes, none of this is so very surprising. But having abandoned the most significant weapon in its armoury – the ethical critique of capitalism – Labor now had to resort to maintaining a fragile, shifting alliance of voters that seemed forever in danger of falling apart under the impact of the latest economic crisis or policy disappointment.

*

The two landmark events of 1983 explored in this chapter – the America's Cup victory and the dollar float – could each be reconciled with the nation's traditions and history, as well as with the new visions of its future beginning to take shape in the early 1980s. Each was in its own way a gamble in a country that had often made a hero of the betting man. Better still – for Australians loved winners – the gambling had paid handsome dividends or, in the case of the float, had seemingly done nothing to hinder the economy's return to buoyancy. The America's Cup and the float had elevated the bold risk-taker – the male warrior prepared to 'fuck the past' – to the status of national hero; Bond, Bertrand, Lexcen, Hawke and Keating had, in just a few weeks, set the tone for an era. Yet glittering surfaces can be deceptive, and they are especially liable to deceive those responsible for creating them. Bond remained reckless, Hawke proud and self-righteous, and Keating – for all his growing confidence – could only guess at where the 'brave new world' of deregulated financial markets would take the country. The ordeals ahead suggested that while Australians could admire boldness, they yet harboured a suspicion that if things went badly wrong, they would end up having to pay the price.

3
'Vanishing Aussie'?

Seen in Fairfield: three boys on one bike. The steerer was of Middle Eastern extraction, on the crossbar sat an Aboriginal youngster, and an Asian boy clung on behind.

SYDNEY MORNING HERALD, 21 SEPTEMBER 1984

On 17 March 1984, speaking at a Rotary conference in Warrnambool, the renowned historian Geoffrey Blainey ended a speech concerned mainly with the theme that Australia had 'nearly always been a multi-cultural society' with a criticism of the present level of Asian immigration. Blainey alleged that recent policy gave a 'powerful preference to Asian migrants'; they had become the 'favoured majority' in Australian immigration policy. 'The pace of Asian migration', he argued, 'was well ahead of public opinion', and especially in those suburbs where Asian migrants were settling in large numbers and economic distress was considerable, people's tolerance and understanding were being sorely tested.[1] His comments caused a media and political storm that would continue for months and reverberate for years.

Australia in the late 1970s and early 1980s was experiencing its first wave of large-scale Asian migration since the Chinese rush to Palmer River goldfield in Queensland a century before. As late as 1975 there were fewer than 1000 Vietnamese living in Australia; five years later, this population had grown to 41,000; by the mid-1980s the number of Vietnamese-born people in Australia had doubled again, with the overwhelming majority settling in Sydney and Melbourne.[2] Suburbs such as Richmond and Springvale in Melbourne, and Cabramatta and Fairfield in Sydney, emerged as major areas of Indo-Chinese settlement. The changing ethnic profile of Richmond was clear enough when the Que Huon Vietnamese restaurant set up on Bridge Road where the Casa Viva Italian restaurant had traded just a few years before: 'Tam Pham is running the restaurant now – several cultures removed from Peppe's pastas and home made cassatas – but closer to Richmond's current ethnic make-up.' Victoria Street, reported the *Richmond Times* in 1984, 'grows daily more like a slice of Saigon', the Vietnamese shoppers outnumbering 'their Australian counterparts' among the Asian supermarkets and eateries.[3]

Multiculturalism, a concept borrowed from Canada, emerged in the 1970s as a new way of imagining and celebrating this diversity. The theory was that migrants would no longer be expected to assimilate to 'the Australian way of life' – as defined and practised by the dominant population descended from the British and Irish – but rather that the many cultures making up society would enrich the whole, offering cosmopolitan variety where there had once been only drab uniformity, tolerance in place of racism and conformity. Yet paradoxically, advocates of multiculturalism also claimed that the country had *always* been multicultural – by which they meant not everyone had been British or Irish – and they searched old convict lists for signs of the first Italian or Greek, celebrated the Eureka Stockade uprising as a multicultural affair, and looked for Chinese among the Anzacs of the First World War.[4] Multiculturalism sought legitimacy by giving itself deeper roots in the country's history.

Yet by the early 1980s multiculturalism's enthusiastic ideological embrace of ethnic diversity had acquired critics on both left and right. On the left, there were claims that it valued the superficial manifestations of cultural identity – like 'spaghetti and polka' – while doing little to counter social inequality.[5] But it was the attacks on multiculturalism from the political right which, once they became entangled in criticism of Asian migration, had the most far-reaching consequences for public debate. In 1980 Lachlan Chipman, a conservative philosopher, dismissed Australian multiculturalism in the magazine *Quadrant* as 'a threat to Australian society, and a racket to boot'.[6] Supporters of multiculturalism, by assuming that all cultural values were equally valid, promoted oppressive practices within ethnic groups. Multiculturalism, claimed Chipman, encouraged disintegration and hostility. Another conservative critic, the Melbourne academic Frank Knopfelmacher, was concerned that multiculturalism would result in separatism, civil strife and rancour, even 'urban terrorism ... possibly directed by hostile foreign powers and organizations'.[7]

These rather abstract if not paranoid arguments conducted among academics in publications read by few seemed a long way from the realities of life for migrants in Australian suburbs. Here, people were managing to get along with one another, rather as they had done in the 1940s, 1950s and 1960s when Australia had experienced its first mass migration from other than British sources. 'The Australian style is to keep differences quarantined,' the historian John Hirst has argued, 'and not to let them rampage in the world at large.'[8] In the early 1980s there was no reason to believe that the new story of Indo-Chinese migration to Australia would be much different from the older European one. The country would welcome Asian migrants in the same spirit as it had Balts, Italians, Yugoslavs and Greeks but without the heavy baggage of the White Australia Policy. It was just a matter of tinkering here and there to smooth over minor hitches and misunderstandings. 'You can't serve a Vietnamese chops and mash,' declared the convener of the Labor Party's ethnic affairs group in Richmond, but '[u]nfortunately a lot of the services have traditionally been biased towards [A]nglo-Saxon communities'. Such neglect of migrant needs, he added, encouraged separatist feelings and behaviour, as well as racism – presumably on the part of white Australians who resented ethnic enclaves.[9] Yet there was nothing here that suggested a profoundly different set of problems from those experienced by postwar European migrants and those who had tried to ease their passage into Australian society. And one did not need to look hard to see evidence of Indo-Chinese doing their best to fit in. In 1984 the Cambodian community in Sydney's Fairfield formed a Red Cross branch, and the Vietnamese community in the same area would have been pleased to attach their mixed-sex scouting organisation to the Scouting Association except that the Australian body refused to accept girls; it insisted that they maintain a separate organisation of Guides. The newcomers must at times have become confused when they were censured for their attachment to traditional mores and their failure to adapt to modern, and obviously superior, Australian ways.[10]

Vietnamese migrants had acquired the reputation – whether good or bad depended on your perspective – of being willing to take 'work nobody else wants at rates nobody else will accept and producing output nobody else can match'.[11] Still, unemployment rates among them were high, and economic competition in difficult times probably increased the likelihood of strains between the newcomers and those they encountered in their daily lives. There were tensions in early 1983, for instance, among white Australian and Vietnamese migrant fishermen at Newcastle. A few Vietnamese men had bought boats from fishermen leaving the industry, leading to complaints from the white fishermen that the industry remained 'overcrowded', that the industry could not 'settle'. The state Labor government refused to agree to requests for a three-year moratorium on licences and accused the white fishermen of racial discrimination, but the 'Australians' in any case met with the 'Vietnamese', asking them 'not to encourage friends or relatives to become professional fishermen'.[12] A couple of months later Tim Duncan in the *Bulletin*, responding to a recent brawl between Vietnamese and Lebanese migrants at housing commission flats in Melbourne, described the Vietnamese community as 'isolated, exposed and vulnerable'. Commentators recognised high unemployment, as well as the trauma associated with flight from Vietnam and the culture shock of arrival in a strange land, as reasons for a resort to violence.[13] But racist policing was also a problem. In Cabramatta in Sydney's western suburbs, relations between police and the Vietnamese community were 'extremely strained' following armed police raids of several homes in July 1983. Police blamed the language barrier and Vietnamese fear of uniforms for bad feeling; perhaps that was why the police conducting the raids had worn plain clothes, but they did not produce identification or search warrants, nor did they go to any trouble to explain why they were holding the residents at gunpoint. It was presumably not to look for heroin, because it had not yet come to police notice as a major problem in the area.[14] The migrants complained of rough treatment, property damage and '"racial" language', and no charges resulted from these raids.[15]

There were already vocal public critics of Asian migration to Australia before the eruption of 1984. Bruce Ruxton, the president of the Victorian branch of the Returned and Services League (RSL), had emerged as a loudmouthed opponent of Asian immigration. If Ruxton had not existed, any satirist charged with creating a returned digger for 1980s popular consumption would surely have come up with someone rather like him. Forty years after his service in Borneo and occupied Japan, he still looked the part of the digger, wearing a haircut that would have passed muster in Morotai back in 1945. Ruxton did 'angry' well, but an impish grin hinted that the mischievous impulse to offend rivalled in its strength his attachment to many of the outlandish attitudes he espoused.[16] He was an essential port of call for any journalist who wanted an outrageous quip on topics such as immigration, Aboriginal people, the monarchy, homosexuality or apartheid in South Africa. The Victorian branch of the RSL, under his influence, favoured a migration policy 'consistent with the recognition of our Anglo-Saxon heritage and traditions'; one that was therefore 'predominantly British, Irish or European'. It opposed multiculturalism in favour of a stringent policy of assimilation.

Ruxton himself was unusual among Australian public figures in the early 1980s in being prepared to call publicly for an end to Asian immigration.[17] But the federal Coalition's spokesman on immigration and ethnic affairs, Michael Hodgman, had also begun sniffing around the issue by early 1984. A long-serving Tasmanian politician whose mouth often seemed to run some way ahead of his mind, he criticised 'the Hawke socialist Government' for having slashed the number of arrivals from Britain, Ireland and Europe, which, he said, reflected the government's 'profoundly paranoid anti-British/anti-European bias'. Hodgman professed to be concerned about this 'radical and dangerous turn to the left in immigration and ethnic affairs' but it was obvious that his remarks, contained in a letter to the *Australian*, were a thinly veiled attack on Asian immigration.[18] The uproar around Blainey's comments in March 1984 would give Hodgman the opportunity to remove that veil.

In 1984 Blainey was in his mid-fifties and one of the country's most widely admired intellectuals. Uniquely among academic historians of his generation, he began his career as a freelance author, writing a series of well-regarded commissioned histories – mostly in mining and banking – before taking up an academic appointment at Melbourne University in the early 1960s. It was in this period that Blainey assumed a national profile, as the author of a series of groundbreaking books, the best known of which, *The Tyranny of Distance: How Distance Shaped Australia's History* (1966), also gave Australian English a phrase that would live on. By the mid-1970s he had an international reputation largely as a result of an influential book on *The Causes of War* (1973). A fine teacher, superb writer and media star who maintained an 'artlessly dishevelled' appearance, Blainey was, along with his former teacher Manning Clark, one of the few genuinely popular academic historians in the country;[19] he even had his own television series, *The Blainey View*. When the storm over Asian immigration broke around him in 1984, Blainey was also a university administrator, the Dean of Arts at the University of Melbourne, and he had held many senior government appointments. The 'Blainey debate', as it came to be called, would end any pretence that race could be kept clear of mainstream political argument. One of Blainey's most persistent critics, the historian Andrew Markus, judges him as having played a critical role 'in breaking taboos' over race in Australian politics, with consequences that are still being felt.[20]

Blainey professed to be surprised by the response his comments on Asian migration evoked – he had scribbled them hastily just before he left by plane for Warrnambool: 'I was just looking for an ending to my speech.'[21] He also claimed to have spoken as a historian. In this guise, Blainey was able to point to conflict between Europeans and Chinese on the nineteenth-century goldfields, but precisely how this past could guide the present was a matter of opinion.[22] Some commentators saw such evidence as an indicator of Australia's racist history, the legacy of which meant that the issue of race needed to be treated with the greatest sensitivity. But the Blainey view was different. Economic competition, he suggested, had led to European attacks on Chinese goldminers in the 1850s and 1860s; similarly, in the working-class suburbs of Australia's cities of the early 1980s, with unemployment persistently high, there was a danger of racial violence. But could the colonial 'lessons' of Buckland River and Lambing Flat be applied to Richmond and Cabramatta?

As the media publicity intensified, and Blainey began to feel besieged, his language became more belligerent. He was quoted in the *Age* as having suggested that 'if we gave $1000 to each of these refugees to go to a place further away it may be more beneficial', although he later denied having made any such comment.[23] He began referring to the government's 'Asianisation policy' – apparently on the basis of a passing comment from an unnamed spokesman of the immigration minister, Stewart West, on recent trends in the composition of the migrant intake to the effect 'that the increasing Asianisation was inevitable'.[24] The reason for this trend was that the intake of skilled migrants had been cut as a result of the recession, but the refugee and family reunion schemes – those most likely to be used by Asians – had been expanded by the Fraser government, a pattern continued under Labor.[25] There had also been a decline in European interest in migration to Australia during hard economic times, but Blainey insisted – without evidence – that prospective British and European migrants were subject to official discrimination. Ever the wordsmith, Blainey started referring to 'Third World immigration', as if to try to soften the racial basis of his campaign – for a campaign it had become. The government, he alleged, had introduced a 'new Surrender Australia Policy'.[26]

For an economic historian, Blainey used numbers in a way that was haphazard and tailored to suit his arguments. In his Warrnambool speech, he claimed that '[m]ore than half' of Australia's migrants now came from Asia, which was the basis for his claim of a 'favoured majority'. A few days later, he seemed to accept that the figure was 40 per cent, but even then he gave no recognition to the diversity of 'Asia' in such accounting, which included much of the Middle East, Turkey, India, Pakistan and Sri Lanka along with the east Asians and especially Indo-Chinese who were mainly in Blainey's sights. Blainey's 40 per cent, moreover, was based on a single quarter; the proportion of Asians for the nine months from July 1983 to March 1984 was well under one-third. And he offered no recognition that the overall number of Asians entering the country in 1983–84 would actually fall.[27] The Asian proportion of the population was tiny: 2 or, at most, 2.5 per cent. The distinguished demographer Charles Price, who expressed sympathy with some of Blainey's views, suggested that this proportion would on the present figures reach 7 per cent by the end of the century, a change amounting to something rather more modest than 'Asianisation'.[28]

A myth has grown that Blainey was persecuted for his views on Asian immigration, even that he was driven from his job for his beliefs. It is true that some staff from the history department at Melbourne University wrote a letter to the *Age* in May dissociating themselves from his views on immigration, emphasising that Blainey spoke for himself and not for historians at the university, and criticising him on the grounds that 'raising such an issue in racial terms (however much it is couched in the language of reason) becomes an invitation to less responsible groups to incite feelings of racial hatred'.[29] Some members of the wider historical profession also published a book critical of Blainey's use of history to support his attitude to Asian immigration.[30] All of this activity created an impression of historians hunting in packs, and of one of their number being persecuted by his academic colleagues for daring to question conventional left-wing pieties.

Blainey, however, was not required to play the martyr; he retired from the university of his own accord in the late 1980s and was still, in my own recollection of that time as one of his students, a popular and well-regarded teacher. It is also hard to see him as having been ostracised for his views. Especially early in the controversy, media commentators and conservative politicians were falling over one another to pay tribute to 'the valuable service' he had performed in raising this vital issue of public concern.[31] Enthusiasm for a debate over Asian migration – a reasoned debate, naturally, in the best traditions of John Stuart Mill's liberalism – flourished as never before among affluent, white opinion-makers; men, that is, who were unlikely to be called 'slants' or 'slopes' in the schoolyard or street, or to have their neighbourhood daubed in graffiti telling them to leave the country.

Meanwhile, the editors of newspaper correspondence columns almost disappeared under the avalanche of letters from readers on the issue, covering almost every conceivable angle.[32] In an unusual and probably somewhat optimistic projection of the likely effect of the newcomers on white Australia, one correspondent with the Melbourne *Age* thought Asians' 'gentle, patient natures' might in time 'bring about a slight amelioration of our brashness'.[33] 'Stem the Flow' and 'Racist and Proud' in the Melbourne *Sun* hardly needed to add anything to the pseudonyms behind which they hid in order to give the flavour of their opinions.[34] But Alexander Psalti, a Victorian National Party member, was out and proud when he warned in the *Age* against 'knaves' and 'useful idiots' who were 'trying to create racial havoc by forcing together unassimilable ethnic communities from radically different cultural backgrounds' in 'a policy of national suicide'.[35] His contribution was notable only because he followed it up a few weeks later with the still more remarkable claim, made at his party's state conference, that there had been a sighting of seventy Vietnamese people armed with M16 rifles in the forests near Charlton in central Victoria. Bill Hayden later reported in the federal parliament that this fanciful story had been invented and put about by the racist League of Rights, which was active in the Victorian countryside in fostering fear and loathing of Asians and Aborigines.[36]

The debate soon spilled over into party politics at the national level. There are good reasons to consider the symbolic end of bipartisanship over race and immigration in modern Australian history as having occurred on the afternoon of Tuesday 8 May during question time in the House of Representatives. The debate over Asian immigration had momentarily become entangled in a government decision to withdraw its financial support from the Big Brother Movement, which over many decades had been responsible for bringing thousands of male British youths to Australia as migrants, effectively operating outside the government's ordinary selection procedures. The organisation's role in British migration was an anomalous legacy of empire living on borrowed time, and the government had decided to end its privileged status. Here was a subject with an obvious appeal to Hodgman, who had been attacking the 'socialist' government over its supposed republican tendencies, and he used the decision on Big Brother to argue that the government's 'vicious attack on this organisation' was 'dramatic evidence' of its 'mean minded paranoia' and 'continuing anti-British bias'.[37] The Big Brother organisation, for its part, did nothing to win friends in the government after it intervened in the Asian migration debate by commissioning a poll which underlined opposition to Asian migration.[38]

Members of the Opposition directed a series of questions to Stewart West, the immigration minister, many of them coded to support Blainey's contention that government immigration policy had a pro-Asian, anti-British and anti-European bias. At one point early in the proceedings Lewis Kent, a Yugoslav-born Labor backbencher from Melbourne who had lived through the Nazi occupation, decided that he had heard enough and yelling, 'You are racist bastards!' began climbing over the seats in front of him towards the Coalition frontbench in the quest for a more physical confrontation than was usual in the federal parliament. He had to be restrained by other members of his party. Some more experienced members of parliament seem to have quickly realised that the country's progress in its relations with Asia since the end of the White Australia Policy was now at risk. Hayden, reflecting later in the day on the bitter exchanges that occurred during question time, recalled that 'for a few moments I was absolutely apprehensive. Something ugly flared for a few moments. This place is a microcosm of the community ... If we explode like that, imagine how the rest of the community can explode if it is misled as a result of some sort of misunderstanding'.[39] Liberal Party deputy leader John Howard later reflected: 'I, along with many other members of this House, was frankly frightened by the atmosphere that was created on 8 May.'[40]

There was more to the fissures opening up in parliament, and in the country at large, than a mere 'misunderstanding'. Historians have argued that in the 1960s the status of 'British race patriotism' as the dominant form of Australian nationalism rapidly declined. Yet even as references to Australia as a British nation became increasingly rare, there was no sharp break with the past. The country might no longer be essentially British and the intellectuals could have their fun playing with words about the country's Asian future, but this future was still to be white.[41] In any case, not everyone agreed that the country had ceased to be British in any fundamental way. The immigration debate of 1984 suggests that especially on the conservative side of politics, the British character of the country was something that was not to be surrendered lightly. One of Blainey's many accusations against the government was that its immigration policy was anti-British.[42] And in parliament Michael MacKellar, a former immigration minister and Liberal moderate, goaded the government to state openly that it wished to change 'the traditional population composition of this country' – an obvious euphemism for whiteness – as well as offering the view that Australia was:

> a basically British and European based society. ... The great institutions of this country have been handed to us because of our predominantly British tradition. This Parliament in which we stand, and in which we are proud to stand, is a British tradition. The British

concepts of law apply in this country. If the Government intends to attack those traditional institutions ... there will be problems.[43]

Even in the absence of the old racial language of 'blood and soil', the assumption that whiteness remained the foundation of Australian national identity had survived the passing of the White Australia Policy. What had changed was the disappearance of an acceptable language for stating such a preference openly. One attempt to find the right words lay in the federal Opposition's call for 'balance' in the migrant intake which, as the journalist Max Walsh rightly remarked in the *Age*, was really a way of 'saying that there are too many Asians coming in'.[44] Andrew Peacock, the Opposition leader, was concerned that 'the Caucasian component has dropped and the proportion of Asian intake has risen': the journalist Michelle Grattan described his solution – to increase those parts of the migration program that would lead to the entry of a larger proportion of Europeans – as 'a neat – but cheap – ploy, a way of trying to keep yourself clean while you hope the political dirt will hit your opponents'.[45] While some Asian-Australians did contribute their views, on both sides of the debate it was a European community being addressed, a white nation that was being enjoined to consider what to do about a non-white, Asian outsider.[46] The controversy crystallised many of the anxieties that white Australians had experienced in coming to terms with a post-imperial order in their region, and the implications – for their own sense of self, home and nation – of the rapid transformation of Asia since the 1960s. This was a country far from comfortable with an Asian destiny. The *Australian* worried that 'a deliberate program of mass Asian migration would fundamentally change Australia's character', meaning that 'Australians and Australian society should be systematically submerged into Asia'.[47]

The Coalition's effort to exploit the immigration debate largely backfired, and it soon retreated from its threats to emphasise the issue of Asian immigration as central to the next election.[48] Part of the problem was the sheer unattractiveness of Hodgman, whose references to the votes that his side of politics could gain from the government – he thought they might pick up twelve seats at the next election on the back of the issue – made the Coalition appear to be cynically stoking racism for electoral gain.[49] (When the Opposition later launched an innocuous immigration policy that largely signalled a retreat from its flirtation with racial politics, Peacock seemed noncommittal about retaining Hodgman in the portfolio after the election: 'I might wish to use his considerable talents elsewhere.'[50]) There was also condemnation of the Opposition in the press, especially in the wake of the parliamentary debacle of 8 May: 'cheap and nasty', 'the politics of desperation' and 'A disgraceful debate' were among the judgments delivered on the Liberal Party's performance that day.[51] Hawke had the best of it when he referred to the surgeon Victor Chang, then in the news for his work in saving the life of teenager Fiona Coote through a heart transplant operation: 'I ask Australians to remember who is leading that fight to save her life. It is a Dr Chang. I do not know the antecedents of Dr Chang but I am sure it was not Gundagai or Tallarook; it was somewhere in Asia.'[52]

Blainey became harder to defend as time went on. First, there was his claim that Asian migration threatened Australia's democratic institutions because Asia lacked freedoms taken for granted in Australia. And then later in 1984, he published an unpleasant book with the title *All for Australia*, recalling the name of a conservative political movement during the 1930s Depression. In it, while still claiming the 'middle ground' in the immigration debate, Blainey alleged that a covert plan had been hatched in a 'secret room' in the immigration department to change the ethnic composition of Australian, to 'Asianise' the country. He also claimed, on the flimsiest basis, that Vietnamese applicants were getting preferential treatment for government jobs.[53] Blainey attacked not only Asian migration but multiculturalism more generally as emphasising the rights of ethnic minorities at the expense of the majority of Australians, and encouraging social divisions while weakening national cohesion. Multiculturalism, in its supposed favouring of 'ethnics', was anti-British, and societies which attempted to encompass many cultures had failed. The key to maintaining tolerance was a sensible immigration program which, for Blainey, meant a much lower number of Asian migrants. While some of Blainey's critics thought his views a faithful reflection of conservative middle-class opinion, he presumed to speak on behalf of 'Old Australians' disturbed by Asianisation:

> In the Sydney suburb of Campsie are many Vietnamese, Chinese, Arabs, as well as the more traditional assortment of Greek, Italian, British and other peoples. To one woman, the suburb as she knows it has vanished:
>
>> Can I tell you what we have to put up with? Pavements are now spotted with phlegm and spit because they think it is OK to spit everywhere and spread germs. They are noisy and entertain late,

> way past midnight. They cook on their verandahs, so the sky here is filled with greasy smoke and the smell of goat's meat.

> Everywhere she sees babies and, as a taxpayer, she thinks to herself, I am helping to pay for their child endowment. She sees new migrants driving big cars: 'I resent seeing Ethnics flying around in flash cars while I have to walk all the time.' She dislikes the strange smells from the cooking and the smell of the garbage, and she names the nationalities who in her view produce the worst garbage ...

> This block of flats has turned into a slum. Downstairs live, I do not know how many, Vietnamese in the two flats. They are noisy and park their cars in inconsiderate places ... At one stage, they were even drying noodles on the clotheslines in the backyards.

'There will be bloodshed in this country,' the woman predicted, and so did Blainey.[54]

The reality was less dramatic. Public opinion polling did indicate some hardening of opinion against Asian migration.[55] Yet when the *Bulletin* sent reporters into Cabramatta and Springvale in the spring of 1984, they found 'some hostility toward the Vietnamese, much dull resentment, some complaints about irritations' – these included the Vietnamese being bad drivers and haggling in shops – but little to suggest the boiling white anger the media debate might have led one to expect. In Cabramatta, a retired army nurse and resident of twenty years told the reporters:

> They're very nice when you get to know them ... We've got Asian families on both sides of us and we natter over the fence the way you would with dinkum Aussies. They're very clean and tidy. They are polite and quiet. They mind their own business ... It's just the numbers; there are so many of them and they came so suddenly ... We're Australians: we believe in a fair go and we're prepared to give it to them. God knows, they deserve at least that after what they've been through.[56]

Several residents were unimpressed by politicians and academics who never came anywhere near their communities posing as experts on them, underestimating the ability of working-class people to get along with one another, exaggerating the racial tensions in daily life. The manager of the local ex-servicemen's club in Cabramatta looked out his office window each morning to 'see the little Asian kids toddling off to school across the park hand in hand with the little Aussie kids'.[57] But 'the Blainey debate' had given the rabid, the resentful and the plain racist licence to air their opinions and feelings. 'Vanishing Aussie' poured out his feelings in a letter to a paper in Sydney's Fairfield in June 1984, complaining about the tendency to pander to minorities such as the Vietnamese. Instead, 'we should be ... "Australianising" them':

> I realise drinking in a hotel or playing rugby league or cricket or having barbecues is not everyone's idea of a good lifestyle. But if you don't like it there are plenty of planes at Mascot to take you to whatever other lifestyle you like.
> I am sick of the word 'Cosmopolitan'.
> ...
> This is a country with its own culture, not some tourist resort where we jump to attention every time there is a new arrival.[58]

The issue would not go away; Australians of the 1980s would live in a society transformed both by Asian migration and a new, ambivalent white politics of race that followed in its wake.

★

The debate over Asian migration ran alongside another that raised the politics of race: a bitter national controversy over Aboriginal land rights. Paul Keating has recently said of Bob Hawke that he 'always cried for Aborigines, but of course he wouldn't do anything for them.'[59] When asked about the issue in an interview in 2009, Hawke blamed uncooperative governments and especially the WA premier Brian Burke: 'I would have liked to have done more. But I established personally a very close working relationship with the Aboriginal people.'[60] This idea of a 'close' personal relationship with this or that group of Australians was, for Hawke, a sustaining personal myth, but it should not be allowed to obscure the reality that Aboriginal people rightly felt betrayed by the failure of his government to deliver on its promise of national land rights. Imagining that they were working with a sympathetic government, they instead found themselves fighting a rearguard action: attempting to defend rights in the Northern Territory that were already enshrined in federal legislation, in the face of racist campaigns to foster the ill will of white Australia and belittle Indigenous culture.[61]

When Labor came to office in March 1983 committed to national land rights, it almost certainly underestimated the level of hostility its proposals would generate. Clyde Holding, the minister for Aboriginal affairs, correctly divined that he would receive no assistance from conservative governments in Tasmania or Queensland – Bjelke-Petersen worried about creating a 'class of black sheiks' – although the minister indicated that the federal government would be prepared to use its powers to create uniform national laws.[62] What he appears not to have anticipated was the opposition he encountered from Brian Burke, especially towards Aboriginal control over mining. Burke had little interest in Aboriginal rights, disliked the impractical idealism of white do-gooders, and lacked any rapport with Aboriginal people themselves.[63] Some of his critics thought that he persistently exaggerated the political threat of national land rights to his government's electoral standing, but Burke's fears were far from baseless. The WA branch of the ALP had arranged polling in Perth in mid-1984 which suggested that land rights were 'causing real electoral problems among middle class voters who have recently supported Labor'.[64] The situation in the bush, however, was likely to be even more hazardous, for the nature of Western Australia's electoral system would compound the effects of a rural white backlash; malapportionment gave country voters considerably more clout in parliament than their numbers warranted. The state's economy, moreover, was heavily dependent on the mining industry, which had recently been more aggressive in asserting its worth in the face of public attacks from Aboriginal people and environmentalists. It soon flexed its muscles in a manner that would have done nothing to assuage Burke's fears.

Hugh Morgan, the Melbourne-based executive director of Western Mining Corporation (WMC) and president of the Australian Mining Industry Council (AMIC) in the early 1980s, played a critical role in shifting the industry nationally to more forcefully defend its image and interests. Morgan was a neat, brilliantined man who looked like he had been born a mining executive. That was very nearly true; his father had also been WMC's managing director. Mining bosses frowned on national land rights legislation that would result in substantial Aboriginal control over mining being applied not just in the Northern Territory, as under the existing federal Act, but across the whole country.[65] In May 1984, in an explosive and widely publicised speech to an AMIC conference, Morgan quoted from the Book of Common Prayer and the New Testament in condemning critics of the mining industry as akin to Manichean heretics from Christianity who regarded the material world as 'inherently evil'. Indigenous control over mining, he argued, was de facto Aboriginal sovereignty, while legislative recognition of the spiritual claims of Aboriginal people implied acceptance of infanticide, cannibalism and 'cruel initiation rights'. He wondered whether in view of the supposed 'partiality of the Aborigines' to Chinese flesh in the nineteenth century, the recently arrived ethnic Chinese from Vietnam might be able to claim compensation from Aboriginal people who had devoured their ancestors.[66]

A fellow conservative who was present, Gerard Henderson, thought Morgan's effort 'perhaps the toughest speech I have ever heard' and judged that it 'played an important role in bringing about the Hawke Government's decision to back down on its commitment to introduce national land rights legislation'.[67] This claim cannot be substantiated, but Morgan's cruel denigration of Aboriginal culture was nicely calculated both to offend Aborigines and to exploit white racial prejudice.[68] His intervention certainly signalled to politicians of all parties a new political aggression, and not only on the part of mining industry leaders; both Blainey and Morgan would soon be identified with a broader political tendency called the New Right. Migrants, blacks and their tender-hearted, soft-headed supporters were the principal targets in mid-1984. But the New Right would soon turn its attention to a wider array of enemies.

During 1984 the WA Chamber of Mines and Energy ran an aggressive advertising campaign against the federal government's land rights proposals. The main burden of its message was that far from being opposed to land rights, it simply wanted 'equality'; that is, like other Australians, Aboriginal owners should not be permitted to prevent mining on their land. It was a potent call. Just as Blainey appealed to Australians' support for equality by claiming that Asian migrants were getting more favourable treatment than Europeans, the industry claimed that it, too, wanted nothing more than equal treatment for everyone, which would ensure that mining could continue to do its public-spirited work for the good of all. But just in case this message was not strong enough to persuade Western Australians of the danger that the federal government posed to the welfare of their state, it ran television advertisements in the second half of the year that showed a black hand building a brick wall across a map of Western Australia containing the sign:

KEEP OUT
THIS LAND IS UNDER
ABORIGINAL
CLAIM[69]

The miners' campaign did not so much shift public opinion on land rights – for a majority of voters were already quietly unsympathetic to that cause – as raise the issue's profile, and thereby persuade politicians of the presence of a white backlash. Their efforts were assisted by a campaign being conducted in Victoria by the racist League of Rights, under the guise of the Save Victoria Committee (which later became Save Australia 1984). During 1983 Save Victoria had been agitating among rural local councils against draft state land rights legislation and in the following year, it extended its campaign to the Hawke government's proposals.[70] These campaigns helped inflame smouldering hostility to Aboriginal land rights and to the protection of sacred sites.[71] As one Lowan Shire councillor remarked in response to a communication received from the Save Victoria organisers, 'Aborigines should not have land if they were not prepared to use it – this legislation was all part of the "handout" syndrome.'[72] Polling commissioned by the Department of Aboriginal Affairs and conducted in September 1984 found considerable opposition to land rights in 'middle Australia', and it was used subsequently in public debate to indicate the existence of a white 'backlash'. A careful study of this poll has suggested that the conclusions drawn from it ought to have been more tentative and less gloomy about white opinion. Much depended on the language used in debate: when opponents claimed that land rights offended the equality principle by giving Aboriginal people special privileges, it was easy enough to stir up opposition.[73]

Hawke met with both the Chamber of Mines and the AMIC twice during September 1984, on the first occasion requesting that they pull the 'black hand' advertisement. They agreed, but had already scheduled the campaign to end in mid-September, so were not being asked to concede much. Hawke would have been worried about land rights, possibly twinned with Asian immigration, becoming a federal election issue, especially in Western Australia. The miners, for their part, were concerned that if they were unable to get ALP policy reversed before the election, they would lack the clout to do so afterwards, when Labor would be able to claim a stronger mandate for acting; few doubted that the Labor Party would indeed be re-elected. Burke made a deal with the Chamber of Mines in his state on 22 September which gave them much that they wanted, especially with respect to continuing crown ownership of minerals and denying Aboriginal owners veto rights. He was also present in Canberra for the federal cabinet meeting on 24 September which, in a weakening of the principle of Aboriginal control over mining, adopted the mechanism of a tribunal to deal with differences between mining companies and Indigenous owners.[74] Holding's cabinet submission on this occasion was correct to predict that Aboriginal people and their supporters 'will claim a major retreat by the Government from the ALP's platform. The Government's credibility, particularly on the question of mining on Aboriginal land, will be questioned and I anticipate emotive and active public criticism.'[75]

A few days after his meetings in Canberra, Burke publicly repudiated key findings of a land rights inquiry by Paul Seaman QC. After detailed investigation, Seaman had recommended that legislation should include Aboriginal control over mining. When Burke released the Seaman report in September, he also issued the government's own principles which, among other things, overruled the suggestion of a mining veto. Burke then persuaded miners, pastoralists and Aboriginal representatives to assist in drafting a WA Aboriginal land bill in accordance with the government's newly announced policy.[76] But he soon ejected the National Aboriginal Conference (NAC) and its dynamic young chairman, Rob Riley, from the drafting committee, accusing Riley of having leaked confidential information to the press. Riley and the NAC subsequently campaigned against the bill.[77]

There had never been much pretence on the part of the WA Labor government that it would allow either state or federal ALP policy to hamper its actions, but Burke and some of his ministers were now increasingly brazen in their defiance of the official line. When federal minerals and resources minister Gareth Evans asked his WA counterpart, David Parker, whether ALP policy would play any part in his government's approach to land rights, he answered with a completely straight face: 'none whatsoever'.[78] Nor did the senior WA ministers in the Hawke government, notably Kim Beazley, Peter Walsh and John Dawkins, give an indication that they regarded anything short of a total capitulation to Burke's demands as an acceptable course.[79] The bill that went before the WA parliament in 1985, although offering Aboriginal people nothing on mining, did make a large amount of land potentially available for claims, but that only gave Liberal and National Party opponents a further peg on which to hang their criticisms.[80] It may be doubted whether Burke lost any sleep over this prospect. One of the wiliest politicians in the country, he had not only managed to divide Aboriginal opinion but driven a wedge between the conservative parties and their habitual supporters in the pastoral and mining industries who had helped him draft the bill. Given his lack of interest in land rights, Burke could not lose, however members of the conservative-dominated Legislative Council chose to vote on his bill.

The Opposition's contributions to the WA parliamentary debate over the land bill provide a revealing compendium of the common sense that informed conservative attitudes to race, Aboriginality and Australian history in the mid-1980s. There was much speech-making about members' deep concern for the welfare of Aboriginal people – all could agree it would not be served by 'the world's largest land grab' – and many a paean to equal opportunity and anti-discrimination, principles they claimed this 'racist' bill offended.[81] The proposed legislation, argued a couple of its parliamentary opponents – whether or not with a straight face *Hansard* does not record – would establish a system of 'apartheid', favouring the black millionaire over the most impoverished white: conservative MPs were unmoved when Labor members pointed out that black millionaires were rather thin on the ground, in Western Australia as elsewhere.[82] Instead, Opposition MPs taunted an Aboriginal Labor parliamentarian, Ernie Bridge, as well as a white Labor member whose first wife had been Aboriginal, Peter Dowding, that in supporting the bill they were claiming special rights for themselves or their children.[83] One member thought that if land rights were going to be given to Aboriginal people, then white farmers 'who also have an affinity with the land built up over generations' should receive similar legislative protection.[84] Land rights, said a member, would create two nations in one continent, or a state within a state: the Aboriginal one 'a stone age mendicant State'.[85]

Members' understandings of history were no more subtle than their claims concerning equality. Liberal parliamentarian Jim Clarko's reading of world history told him that 'land belongs to the last victor', and there were many expressions of certainty that Western Australians in 1985 had no reason to feel guilty about anything done in 1788 or 1829.[86] The Liberal Party's Reg Tubby declared of Aboriginal people, 'They are very lucky we came!' while another Liberal, Peter Jones, ridiculed the idea that land rights would 'either wholly or in part expunge the guilt we are all supposed to feel because we robbed the people when we landed here 200 years ago'. 'What gibberish!' he continued. 'Fancy saying that we dispossessed the people who were here, and therefore we have to do something about giving the land back.'[87] To the extent that they recognised racism, it was a phenomenon of the distant past, rather than a blight WA Aboriginal people still experienced in their daily lives.

The WA bill was defeated in the Legislative Council in April 1985, ending any immediate prospect of land rights legislation in that state. And although the federal government remained formally committed to a national model for almost another year, there was now little prospect of achieving it. Mungo MacCallum judged in May 1985 that 'for the first time in a great many years a large number of white Australians – perhaps even a majority' – saw Aboriginal people 'as posing a genuine threat to the system under which they live'.[88] But Aboriginal people themselves also now opposed what was on offer, not least because Labor's preferred national model would involve not the extension of land rights but their erosion, taking away control over mineral resources in the Northern Territory. In May 1985 they descended on Canberra to make their feelings known, protesting outside Parliament House and the British High Commission and occupying the Department of Aboriginal Affairs, whose permanent secretary was the veteran Aboriginal activist Charles Perkins. During the Parliament House protest, police prevented Aboriginal people from rushing through the front doors while Rob Riley and the Opposition spokesman on Aboriginal affairs, Roger Shipton, had a fiery argument which culminated in Shipton being led away by police because they considered his presence likely to lead to a breach of the peace. The protesters wanted to speak to Shipton's leader, Andrew Peacock, but neither Peacock nor Hawke would come out of the building.[89]

In January 1986, in the lead-up to the state election, Hawke provided a public assurance that the federal government would not override any WA land rights legislation. Burke won comfortably, but the Labor Left remained angry at the manner in which he, with Hawke's support, had been able to ignore party policy. With the prospect of an angry brawl at the forthcoming national conference, the ALP factions hammered out a compromise in the first half of 1986. There would be no national land rights but Aboriginal people would retain the power of veto over mining in the Northern Territory. The ALP's federal platform would remain unaltered; Burke dropped his threat to try changing it. Canberra promised his government $100 million over five years to buy land for Aboriginal people.[90]

The failure of national land rights followed the logic of Hawke's consensus style. Economic interests were to be consulted conscientiously and taken seriously as partners in a grand national enterprise; Aboriginal people were entitled to the crumbs that remained once these great interests had done their deals. No wonder Riley condemned the Labor Party's 'hypocrisy', arguing that it lacked 'political will and commitment'.[91] Aboriginal leaders especially resented the government's failure to conduct a publicity campaign in favour of land rights, which had been recommended by Australian National Opinion Polls. The government, said one leader, Pat Dodson, had 'done absolutely nothing to counter the racist and divisive campaigns waged against Aboriginal people by vested interests'.[92]

The accusation that it had betrayed Aboriginal people in 1984–85 would cling to the Hawke government down to the present day. Aboriginal leaders, meanwhile, looked forward to using the forthcoming Bicentenary of Australia as an opportunity to assert that the British had invaded their country and stolen their land, and that despite the many ordeals their people had suffered, they had never conceded their sovereignty.[93]

★

Ayers Rock – or Uluru, as it was increasingly called – occupied an uncertain place in the white Australian imagination in the 1980s. Its overpowering presence was a permanent temptation for any tourist business or government agency seeking to attract foreign visitors to Australia. Ruby Langford, a Bundjalung woman from coastal New South Wales, was profoundly moved when she saw the Rock for the first time on a visit in 1985:

> I sat completely still. It was like a huge animal that was asleep in the middle of nowhere. We came closer and I could feel the goosebumps and the skin tightening at the back of my neck ... It made me think of our tribal beginnings ... Time was suddenly shortened to include all of history in the present, and it was also stretched to a way of seeing the earth that was thousands of years old.[94]

In this way, Uluru was through tourism becoming a 'pan-Aboriginal sacred site' and an 'example of cultural convergence between Aborigines and white Australians'.[95] It was the place chosen for a series of television advertisements in 1986 to promote the Bicentenary; sixty celebrities – mainly but not exclusively white – were flown to central Australia to perform what looked rather like an extended Mexican wave while singing a catchy jingle, 'Celebration of a Nation', devised by an advertising firm. Uluru was their backdrop. The song began to the strains of didgeridoo, as if to signify the convergence of white and black cultures. Nature, however, seemed almost to mock the idea of Uluru as a place to celebrate the nation when a fierce storm broke just as the shooting finished. 'Oh, darling,' cried out Jeanne Little, a larger-than-life television personality of the period. 'The real Australia's quite frightening, isn't it?'[96]

Indeed it was. In August 1980 the camping ground at the base of Uluru had been the place of a great tragedy, one more in keeping with the sense of mystery associated with the Rock. Lindy and Michael Chamberlain, a couple holidaying from Mount Isa in Queensland, were cooking a barbeque while their two boys and young baby girl, Azaria, waited in a nearby tent. The Chamberlains claimed that a dingo took Azaria from the tent – a reasonable explanation, as there had been several recent attacks on visitors by the native dogs. Azaria would never be seen again, but her torn and bloodied jumpsuit was found nearby.

Rumours soon abounded that the Chamberlains had been responsible for the death of their baby daughter. They belonged to the Seventh Day Adventist Church, of which Michael was a pastor. Most people knew little about this small Protestant sect despite a history in Australia stretching back to the 1880s, and it was readily translated by increasingly fevered imaginations into a bizarre cult distinguished by its practice of child sacrifice. There were claims that Azaria meant 'sacrifice in the wilderness', not the benign 'blessed by God' claimed by Michael Chamberlain, and some attached significance to Lindy having on occasion dressed the baby in black.[97]

Despite swirling innuendo of more or less uniform implausibility, the coroner endorsed the claim that Azaria was taken by a dingo. But he also found that someone had disposed of the body, and he criticised park authorities for failing to deal adequately with the menace posed by dingoes to tourists, and police investigators for their lack of objectivity. The coroner cleared the Chamberlains of any blame in connection with Azaria's death. Smarting from this criticism, police continued investigating, applied successfully to have the original coroner's verdict quashed, and then charged Lindy with murder and Michael as an accessory. Despite the absence of a body, a confession or a motive, Lindy, by now heavily pregnant with another child, was found guilty at trial and sentenced to life in prison.[98]

The case had by this time become the subject of national hysteria, a rich body of urban myth and many, many tasteless jokes about dingoes and babies ('How should you bring up children? Kick a dingo in the guts').[99] Parts of the media treated Lindy as a witch, with male journalists lusting after her body – Lindy was attractive and dressed well in clothes that she made herself – while feeding opinion that she lacked the proper feelings of a mother. Her 'strong-faced look' – the sense that she was able 'to detach herself from reality' – infuriated many, and to some, this alleged failure to reveal her feelings in a proper motherly way was a firm indication of guilt.[100] Reporters read her emotions while she was on trial with the intensity, although certainly not with the skill, of a learned rabbi untangling the meaning of the Talmud.

Lindy Chamberlain was released from prison in 1986 and her unjust conviction was overturned in 1988; in the meantime, the stories told about the Chamberlains drew freely on the gothic image of the Australian desert as a place of mystery and horror.[101] But it was part of the changing mental landscape of white Australia that Aboriginal lore now provided much of the content of this mysticism. Dingoes rarely figure in Aboriginal belief, but there were stories circulating of a 'devil dingo' being one of the many beings associated with the Rock; his spirit sometimes inhabited living dingoes, causing them 'to act with uncharacteristic malevolence and ferocity'.[102] At the time when the issue of handing back Uluru to its traditional owners was in the news, a Sydney woman wrote to the *Australian*: 'Anyone who has visited Ayers Rock and has any feeling for atmosphere soon realises that its inherent mysticism is of purely Aboriginal origin.'[103]

Such arguments carried little weight with those who opposed the Hawke government's decision to hand Uluru and its surrounding country back to its traditional owners. In November 1983, when after more than a decade of discussions between Aboriginal people, politicians, officials and anthropologists the Hawke government announced that it would hand the Rock back, the conservative Northern Territory government of Paul Everingham responded by fighting an election on the issue, which it won in a landslide.[104] In the weeks leading up to the handover ceremony scheduled for October 1985, Everingham's successor, Ian Tuxworth, launched a national campaign against the decision. Tuxworth said that the day of the handover was a 'national tragedy' but even the *Northern Territory News*, not known for its radical views on land rights or anything else, seemed aghast at the chief minister's cynicism, explaining that 'only a month ago, the Government decided the Rock "belongs to all Australians" and that Aborigines should receive title only to living areas in the national park'.[105] The full-page advertisements that the Northern Territory government took out in newspapers also revealed that it had learned much from the anti-land rights campaigning of the previous couple of years. Describing the Rock as 'the heart of the country', these announced that 'The Rock Belongs to All Australians! (And Always Has)'. The federal government was handing over the Rock and its surrounds 'to fewer than 100 Australians', and would then pay 'these special Australians $75,000 a year to lease it back from them', as well as 20 per cent of admission fees from the national park. And in a message designed to help Queenslanders make up their minds about the matter, it warned that the Great Barrier Reef might follow.[106]

Opponents of the handover suggested that the Rock was being handed over to the 'wrong' Aboriginal people who had no special connection to Uluru; the campaign extended even to a plane pulling along a banner declaring, 'Ayers Rock should be for all Australians', which flew noisily over the 26 October ceremony. Both Tuxworth and the new leader of the federal Opposition, John Howard, boycotted the ceremony presided over by the governor-general, Sir Ninian Stephen. Howard, condemning the occasion's 'flamboyant symbolism', said that the federal Coalition would explore the feasibility of taking the Rock back.[107]

The handover was a rare triumph for Holding as Aboriginal affairs minister, and one of the few tangible achievements of the Hawke government in the field in its early years in office. Holding was an experienced political operator – he had led the state Opposition in Victoria for a time – and a well-meaning minister, but he increasingly found himself unable to manage the fervour aroused on each side of the land rights debate. His position was not unlike that of Stewart West in immigration. A hulking and slightly stooped ex-waterside worker, West was from the Left, a point that increased his vulnerability to attacks from the Opposition and other critics of immigration policy. He was a principled man but certainly not the cabinet's sharpest mind, nor its most polished performer. Like Holding, he was unable to comprehend what seemed to him a barrage of irrationality.[108]

In the eyes of these two ministers, opponents of government policy were uninterested in facts, in the habit of painting extravagant scenarios and irresponsible in their indifference to the dangerous passions unleashed by their overblown rhetoric. The pair sometimes called their opponents 'racists' but it was easy for those who rejected biological racism, and supported 'equal rights' rather than 'special rights', to respond that they were liberals or even socialists. That the effect of their support for 'equal rights' was simply to reinforce white domination and entrench inequality – in effect, to uphold the privileges of other 'special groups' – could be conveniently left aside. Mal Bryce, the WA deputy premier, cut through such rhetoric when he recalled of the colony's origins that 'Governor Stirling looked after his mates extraordinarily well. He did it on the basis of race ... because their skin was white.'[109] But proponents of land rights who made such arguments could be dismissed as guilt-mongers. Guilt, in fact, emerged in 1984 as one of the key emotions at stake in the Australian political process. The right claimed the left had too much of it, and that it was disfiguring the political process, threatening to wreck the economy and sapping national confidence. The left saw in the right's claims to blamelessness a form of psychological denial, a habit of protesting just a little too much about how little guilt anyone need feel about Asians and Aboriginal Australians.

For this reason and others, the almost simultaneous explosions over immigration and land rights in 1984 were a critical moment in modern Australian history. They ended the fragile bipartisanship over race that had emerged in the 1970s as Australians sought to come to terms with the implications of their colonial history. But the powerful impact of 'equal rights' talk in stoking resentment of Asian migration and killing national land rights ensured that the same language would be available in the future to any politician who felt that the advantages of its use would outweigh its risks. In the years ahead, the language of equality would be put to work against successful Aboriginal litigants, migrant welfare-recipients and queue-jumping refugees. The Coalition parties learned to their cost in their response to the Blainey debate that the risks of such political rhetoric were real enough, but politics is about the calculated gamble.

It has become customary to look back on Asian migration in the 1980s and the fear and hostility it generated with an air of condescension; to imagine that these anxieties were just a passing phase – a reprise of those which had initially been aroused by non-British migration – and that the Vietnamese migrants ultimately settled into Australian society, achieved material success, got their children into university and ceased to worry anyone except the hardened racist, who in any case soon moved on to the Muslims.[110] Where differences from earlier phases of migration are conceded, they are attributed to the decline of the traditional manufacturing economy in the 1980s, which denied many recent Asian migrants the opportunities that had been taken up by Italians and Greeks in the earlier period, and therefore exacerbated the sense of economic competition with members of the host society. Meanwhile, the fears generated by Aboriginal land rights are seen to belong to an old pre-Mabo politics, a time of grand symbolic gestures rather than the more recent hard grind of creating economic opportunity and alleviating resilient social problems. Aboriginal leaders who, with good reason, once looked on Hugh Morgan as a bitter enemy, now walk arm in arm with mining companies.

These ways of remembering the racial anxieties of the 1980s as either a silly panic or a response to economic crisis are each flawed. It is true that hostility to Vietnamese migrants would eventually decline, and equally so that the downturn in Australia's economic fortunes had contributed something to unease about Asian migration. Polling found that few wanted a return to a racially discriminatory immigration policy. But some Australians were seemingly glad the embarrassing White Australia Policy was dead and buried, while hoping they might commit it to the earth without having to allow *actual* Asians and Aboriginal Australians to live among them – other than in small numbers that posed no challenge to their sense of national selfhood.

The race debates of the mid-1980s exposed the limits of white Australia's adjustment to the world left behind by the retreat of the European empires after the Second World War. Australians had formally abandoned the White Australia Policy and recognised the need for a renovated relationship between black and white Australia. These were significant changes and they reflected Australians' talent for settling large numbers of migrants permanently, with minimal conflict or disruption. But such changes had occurred in a manner that minimised disruption to the *idea* of Australia as a white nation. The growing visibility of Asians in the nation's streets, workplaces and classrooms, and the new self-confidence of Aboriginal people combined to pose a more confronting challenge to white Australians' sense of who they were and what they might become. The stage had been set for a most lively Bicentennial year.

4

Power and Passion

Oh the power and the passion, oh the temper of the time
Oh the power and the passion
Sometimes you've got to take the hardest line.

'The Power and the Passion', Midnight Oil

The summer of 1982–83 might have been a time of heat, dust and fire for many Australians, but not for the thousands of protesters who descended on the remote south-western corner of the island state of Tasmania in December. For the next few months, their lives would be dominated by rain, mud and leeches. The Tasmanian premier, Robin Gray, had called the Franklin River 'nothing but a brown ditch; leech-ridden; unattractive to the majority of people'. Sensible protesters would have accepted parts of this unflattering assessment. But by the time their blockade of the Gordon-below-Franklin dam project was lifted in the early autumn, 1300 of them had been arrested, and 450 had done time in Hobart's Risdon Prison. On 16 December Bob Brown, the director of the Tasmanian Wilderness Society (TWS), was among those taken away. He would spend Christmas in jail where, among other diversions, he spent time reading *The Diary of Anne Frank* as well as a continuing flow of hate mail.

The protesters had come from all over the country, some the veterans of battles for the forests in northern New South Wales, others joining a demonstration for the first time. The TWS's strategy was to use the arrests to garner national and international publicity, an effort in which the police – some of them sympathetic to the 'no dams' cause – were complicit. They allowed protesters to make their gesture for the benefit of the media before taking them away; on at least one occasion, police were overheard asking demonstrators how many arrests they wanted that day. But the relatively benign character of law enforcement should not detract from the courage and conviction the protesters displayed. In the nearby town of Strahan, the threat of violence always hung over them; Brown himself received a bashing. And through their campaign of civil disobedience, protesters were the vanguard of a radical challenge to the way Tasmania had done business for generations.

In the politics of the island state, the Hydro-Electric Commission (HEC) stood like a colossus. For decades 'the electric Kremlin', as it was dubbed by its opponents, floated above the political fray as the vehicle of the island state's aspirations to industrial modernity. But the rise of a conservation movement in the 1960s brought with it more troubled waters. During the 1970s the HEC had managed to drown Lake Pedder in the quest for cheap power, but not without having to see off an anti-dam campaign that was a pointer to the future. In 1979 the HEC announced its next victim, the Gordon River below the Franklin, a project that would have destroyed a vast area of what was increasingly being called 'wilderness'. The campaign to save the Franklin was coordinated by the TWS. Its leader, Brown, was a tall, shy medical doctor who had come across from the mainland in 1972, a man of great courage who had publicly outed himself as homosexual in an intensely conservative community. He had found his way to environmentalism through a love of nature and bushwalking, which extended to eccentric participation in the quest to find a surviving Tasmanian tiger. After a rafting expedition with a friend on the Franklin River in early 1976, Brown committed his life to saving the south-west wilderness from the further depredations of the HEC.[1]

The victory of the Labor Party in the federal election of 5 March 1983 was bad news for the HEC for, in accordance with party policy, Hawke had vowed to stop the dam. When the Tasmanian Liberal government of Robin Gray challenged the constitutionality of the new government's anti-dam legislation, the matter went to the High Court. There was further controversy in April after the new attorney-general, Gareth Evans, requested that an air force flight photograph the site in preparation for the case. Although it was supposed to 'attract as little attention as possible', the day was cloudy, so the pilot flew just a few hundred metres above the site to allow the photographer a better view; the plane was about as conspicuous as it could possibly have been. Evans for his troubles earned the nickname 'Biggles' and later accounted for his actions with what he called 'the streaker's defence': 'It seemed, your worship, like a good idea at the time.'[2] The evidence so gathered was not tendered by lawyers for the Commonwealth, but nor did the court wish to see photographs of the threatened area taken in a more orthodox manner, which counsel for the Wilderness Society sought to present. These, said Chief Justice Harry Gibbs, 'could do no more than inflame our minds with irrelevancies'.[3] In a four–three decision on 1 July 1983, the court ruled in favour of the federal government, largely on the grounds that in halting the dam's construction, it was fulfilling its international obligations under the World Heritage Convention, which had listed the south-west wilderness area in December 1982.

The minds of many Australians had already been inflamed with Gibb's 'irrelevancies'; without them, there would have been no High Court case to be heard. The TWS understood the power of the visual image from the outset, and had cooperated in the making of documentaries whose emotional force was partly conveyed through the arrival of colour television in 1975. The wilderness photography of Peter Dombrovskis, especially his sublime *Morning Mist, Rock Island Bend*, was reputedly influential in bringing to a national audience a sense of the south-west's wonder. The symbol of the movement – a yellow triangle containing the simple but striking message 'NO DAMS' – started appearing on cars all over the country, while the folk-rock group Goanna had a surprise hit song with 'Let the Franklin Flow': it became the anti-dam movement's anthem.

The battle for the Franklin remains the single greatest environmental struggle in Australian history. It signalled for white Australians a new way of relating to place, a love of country that amounted to something more complex – and attractive – than classical nationalism's appeal to 'blood and soil'. It was a fundamentally visual and emotional appeal, one driven by a sense that the future of humanity required a new and more spiritually meaningful way of relating to the environment; that the country was something other than a resource to be exploited for material gain. Yet this remained a fundamentally white and European vision. There were Aboriginal sites of great significance on the Franklin and, although they were part of the reason for the World Heritage listing and the High Court decision, they barely figured in the mainstream campaign to save this 'untouched' or 'pristine' wilderness from destruction. That, too, might mark this moment as a product of the late 1970s and early 1980s, rather than of the different world made by the cultural politics of the Bicentenary.

Meanwhile, pragmatic politicians took note of the already stunning career of Dr Bob Brown. The wisest recognised that they had witnessed something other than a flash in the pan in this plain-speaking man who dressed in conservative dark suits like the respectable suburban doctor that he was, while living on the generosity of friends and supporters. National politics would never be quite the same again. Brown himself explained that his fight had been not only 'to preserve a beautiful wilderness area' but also 'against technological overkill'.[4] A man who would prove himself one of the truly great politicians of his age had arrived on the national scene.

*

Great politicians were sorely needed at a time when the world would come closer to nuclear war than at any time since the Cuban Missile Crisis of 1962. Both superpowers were armed to the hilt, having modernised their arsenal of weapons. The Soviet Union, led in 1983 by former KGB chief Yuri Andropov, had enough warheads to wipe out more than half the population of the United States and 70 per cent of its industrial base in the first twenty-four hours of a nuclear war. It would then have plenty left over to deal with its other enemies, as well as 360 new shorter-range ballistic missiles aimed at Western Europe, each with thirty times more explosive power than the bomb dropped on Hiroshima.[5] Meanwhile, even a single submarine in the American fleet contained enough warheads 'to destroy every Soviet city with a population of more than 150,000'.[6]

The Soviet Union faced not only a superpower, the United States, but also the nuclear weapons of Britain, France and China, a situation that contributed to its sense of encirclement. On 8 March 1983 Reagan famously referred to the USSR in a speech as 'the evil empire' and a fortnight later he announced the Strategic Defense Initiative, or 'Star Wars', a research program that aimed to surround the United States with a missile shield. In September, the Soviets shot down a Korean Airlines passenger jet, probably mistaking it for a reconnaissance plane that had been in the area earlier in the day, but Reagan proclaimed this incident 'an act of barbarism'. Then, in November, the Soviets became worried that a major NATO exercise was a prelude to a first strike on the USSR, leading to preparation across the Soviet military establishment for the outbreak of nuclear war.[7]

The Australian peace movement's activities and beliefs in the mid-1980s, as well as the responses they evoked from the Hawke government, need to be seen against this background of intense Cold War conflict. Changes in nuclear technology and doctrine were of particular concern. Through the 1950s and much of the 1960s, atomic weaponry was cumbersome and inaccurate, meaning that for each side the enemy's possession of nuclear weapons was a deterrent to any serious contemplation of their use in a war. This situation gave rise to the concept of mutually assured destruction (MAD): each side could be confident that an attack on the cities of the other would be returned in kind, with disastrous results all round. But the nuclear weapons of the 1970s were more accurate, and planners began to contemplate their use against the weapons and communications of the other side rather than against its cities – an approach that gave rise to the possibility of fighting and winning a nuclear war by developing a first-strike capability. While MAD had always raised the danger of brinkmanship, it had at least offered some rough sense of balance and stability. Talk of a first-strike capability upset such calculations.

These developments had significant implications for Australia because of its alliance with the United States and its hosting of joint defence facilities. A culture of secrecy had since the 1960s surrounded the three major installations – North West Cape, Pine Gap and Nurrungar – but by 1983 there was greater public knowledge about the purposes of US bases in Australia, which tended to stimulate greater concern. Left-leaning journalists and newspapers regularly published articles about the bases, while the Australian National University researcher Desmond Ball played an important role in disseminating information about their contribution to global security. Ball was critical of the excessive secrecy which veiled the activities of the so-called joint facilities.[8] A 'Preliminary Appraisal of the Effects on Australia of a Nuclear War', secretly prepared in 1980 by the Office of National Assessments, recognised that the bases 'might be targeted relatively early in a strategic nuclear war'. With half of the US nuclear warheads carried by submarines, North West Cape's contribution to naval communications seemed to make it the most attractive target from a Soviet perspective.[9] Experts considered that other bases in Australia were less likely to be attacked, but might well become targets if US forces were making significant use of them. Attacks on Australian cities looked less likely again, considering the availability of much more enticing targets elsewhere in the world.[10] But such calculations were, at best, informed guesswork, based on publicly available knowledge of Soviet military doctrine and what could be gleaned about the purposes of the bases.

If anyone had been inclined to take comfort from such expert opinion, projections of the likely loss of life in the event of attacks on Australian bases might have prompted them to think again. A nuclear attack on Nurrungar, for instance, if carried out during a north-westerly, might have killed about 10,000 people in SA cities such as Port Augusta, Whyalla and Port Pirie, as well as making many in Adelaide very ill. The less likely event of an attack on the naval base at Cockburn Sound in Western Australia could have caused

100,000 fatalities in Perth and Fremantle, while a similar attack on the air force base in Darwin would have killed or injured almost the entire population of the city. Nuclear attacks on a major Australian city such as Sydney or Melbourne would have produced hundreds of thousands of fatalities, with people being killed either by the blast or fallout.[11] One scenario had a nuclear attack on Australia leading to 1 million deaths from the blast and another 3 million from the fallout, accompanied by a dystopian nightmare in which people with access to fallout shelters may have needed to repel or even kill their neighbours to survive.[12] Book titles such as Jim Falk's *Taking Australia Off the Map* (1983) and Christopher Forsyth's *Can Australia Survive World War III?* (1984) spoke to the anxieties of the era. Falk, a physicist and anti-nuclear campaigner, began his with a vivid account of the effect of a hydrogen bomb explosion over the University of Sydney:

> As the shock wave hits the ground, the University is crushed as if by a giant sledge hammer. In central Sydney some tall buildings are smashed to the ground. Others are picked up and hurled into the sky. The wind builds to over 650 kilometres per hour, four or five times the speed of the worst hurricane. Within the entire central city all buildings collapse into an uneven plane of rubble. Whether in the open or inside, all the people within a 3 kilometre wide circle centred on the university are either killed outright or entombed. The swathe of destruction, however, extends well beyond this 'small' inner circle.[13]

In *Can Australia Survive World War III?* Christopher Forsyth, a journalist, concluded that it could and recommended civil defence and Eastern mysticism as preparation for the ordeals ahead.[14]

The huge crowds that attended the Palm Sunday peace rallies of the mid-1980s provide one indication of the fear aroused by the threat of nuclear war. These were occasions for rituals such as the 'die-in', when marchers responded to a whistle by falling to the ground, and for dress-ups and street theatre. Masks inspired by Edvard Munch's *The Scream* were popular; nuclear warfare among Ronald Reagan, Margaret Thatcher and Mikhail Gorbachev on stilts – for control of a papier-mâché earth – kept Melbourne crowds entertained in 1985. The 1983 marches attracted about 140,000, with the crowds in Melbourne (70,000) and Sydney (60,000) accounting for most of those attending. In Sydney the leaders of the march were Tom Uren, the left-wing Hawke government minister and Second World War prisoner of war, and

Patrick White, also a war veteran as well as a Nobel Prize–winning novelist. In Brisbane the state Labor leader, Keith Wright, explained that while he had always been opposed to nuclear weapons, he had refrained from associating with the peace movement 'in such a way that I could cause political harm to those I represented'. There was a pointed reminder of the repressive nature of the state's political climate in the conspicuous presence of a police photographer, taking pictures of every group as they passed him from his perch on top of an unmarked car.[15]

The Palm Sunday marches attracted a broad cross-section of participants. Alongside the silver-haired pensioners, married couples and children 'marching' in prams or on the shoulders of their parents were Sydney's 'Perverts for Peace' and 'Dykes for Disarmament'. Well-known public figures participated. Among the speakers at the 1983 rallies in Melbourne, Sydney and Canberra were, respectively, the novelist Helen Garner, playwright David Williamson and historian Manning Clark. The 1984 marches were even bigger than those of the year before – the *Australian* estimated that a quarter of a million took part, numbers that the Labor government could no longer afford to ignore. Bill Hayden began a tradition of issuing a message to the marchers expressing the federal government's shared commitment to peace and disarmament. The marchers, for their part, responded by inaugurating a tradition of their own; they jeered and hissed at the foreign minister's friendly statement.[16] There would be more of that to come.

★

Bob Hawke was the most strongly pro-American Labor leader of the postwar era, an attachment indebted to political calculation – his dependence on the pro-US Labor Right and his sensitivity to public support for the alliance – as well as to political conviction. He had come to office over the 'body' of a rival, Bill Hayden, who while also pro-American was (in his own words) 'less flexible' with them than Hawke was.[17] While still Labor leader in 1982, Hayden had declared that nuclear-powered and -armed ships would not be welcome in Australian ports under a Labor government. Subsequently, after pressure from within the party and from the US administration, he had to make a humiliating retreat.[18] And in the following month, Hayden reversed a party decision to support a moratorium on uranium mining made in 1977.[19] This amendment provided not only for the continuation of mining in the Northern Territory but also for its commencement at South Australia's Roxby Downs. On 31 October 1983 the federal cabinet decided to allow this venture to go ahead, a decision that created a major problem for the only Left member of the Hawke cabinet, Stewart West, who tendered his resignation in protest.[20] Unheard of in our own times, resignations of this kind were extremely rare even then – a fair indication of the intensity of feeling in the ALP around the issue of uranium. When the matter came before a special caucus meeting on 7 November 1983, Gerry Hand on behalf of the Left introduced an amendment reaffirming the party's 'total unequivocal commitment' to phasing out Australia's participation in the industry. He sought a comprehensive public inquiry into the Roxby Downs proposal and, subject to its findings, a prohibition on any further mines or new contracts for existing mines. But the cabinet decision was accepted by fifty-five votes to forty-six, a comfortable victory for pro-uranium MPs and a clear indication, as if any were needed, that the issue of uranium would be bitterly contested at the ALP national conference in July 1984.[21]

When that conference met, it did so in the shadow cast by a resurgent peace movement. The Lakeside Hotel in Canberra, the setting for the conference, was besieged by 1000 demonstrators, and during the debate on uranium they enthusiastically booed their enemies and cheered their friends.[22] The din and interruption during the prime minister's pro-uranium speech prompted party president and conference chair Neville Wran to threaten to clear the gallery. Hawke and Wran's factional colleague from New South Wales, Graham Richardson, described the issue accurately enough as 'the most difficult and emotional ... that we have looked at in the last 10 years'. On this point at least, he and left-wing NSW state government minister Frank Walker could agree: uranium, said Walker, was 'an issue which creates extremes of emotion', and he warned that those the party was alienating over it were 'the same people that came out in their thousands to support us in our marginal seats last federal election over the Franklin issue'. But supporters of mining pointed to polls that showed a clear majority of both overall voters and Labor supporters in favour of uranium, and they denied that there was anything especially 'Labor' about opposing it. Peter Walsh, who as the minister for minerals and energy was lead speaker, pointedly reminded delegates it was not so very long ago that the darling of the Left, Jim Cairns, had travelled to Iran to try to sell uranium to the Shah while 'another folk hero of our party', Rex Connor, was developing plans for a government-owned uranium industry. Walsh closed the debate by adding that he had originally joined the ALP because he saw it as 'the party of reason' but after listening to his opponents, he now wondered whether his original judgment had been correct, or if it had been, whether it was 'correct still'. Hawke, meanwhile, in a message directed at the protesters, declared that he would ignore intimidation but would be 'moved by reason ... by the processes of rational thinking'.[23]

That the uranium issue aroused emotions was undeniable. Disagreement over the issue had divided Hawke's own family, becoming the subject of strong disagreement between him and his two elder children, Steven and Susan, in the 1970s. What was more questionable was the Right's insinuation that the emotions were all on the Left side. Pro-uranium MPs were also 'emotional', for the issue of uranium had been inflated by MPs still haunted by the Whitlam era into a key test of Labor's fitness and capacity to govern. How the cards fell on uranium would determine whether Labor still belonged to those who believed that it was a pragmatic party of jobs and development committed to winning office, or a vehicle for middle-class 'trendies' who thought there was 'something obscene or immoral about attempting to find what is possible ... and not what one can simply airily talk about', as SA premier John Bannon declared.[24] After a fifty-five to forty-four vote in favour of the three-mines policy, the prime minister avoided a confrontation with protesters by leaving the hall via an internal exit, but other pro-uranium delegates were jostled as they sought to descend a flight of stairs lined with demonstrators holding candles.[25]

The Left fared no better on the future of ANZUS and the joint facilities, or on East Timor. In defence of the US alliance, Hawke appealed to 'Labor tradition', with the Curtin legend once again doing some heavy-lifting work for the prime minister, and he condemned the 'violent anti-Americanism' of the Left. A self-deprecating Hayden, who was again jeered by protesters, told delegates that he had no intention of repeating his 1982 gaffe over nuclear ships, but the conference did accept a proposal that US ship visits needed to be limited so that Australian facilities were not, in effect, home ports for such vessels. On self-determination for East Timor, which had been under Indonesian rule since 1975, Hayden regretted the impractical and emotional arguments of the Left.[26]

★

On Sunday 17 June 1984, sixty people assembled in the Canberra Peace Centre in the suburb of Kingston to form a new political party, the Nuclear Disarmament Party (NDP).[27] The inspiration came from a local anti-nuclear campaigner and academic from the Australian National University, Dr

Michael Denborough. To set up a party, 500 members were needed. Denborough knew where to find them: the NDP set up a table in the foyer of the Lakeside Hotel during the ALP conference and immediately signed up 200 members. There was no shortage of dissatisfaction within the left wing of the ALP for a new force such as the NDP to exploit, but the NDP also recruited more widely. Among its older members were Ted St John, who had been a fractious Liberal member of the federal parliament for a time in the late 1960s – he would become the party's NSW campaign director – and the eminent historian Russel Ward, an ex-communist and author of the classic work *The Australian Legend* (1958), who appeared on the party's Senate ticket. Patrick White helped in the early stages with money and lustre. But it was to the young that the NDP would need to appeal if it was to enjoy success; it could not afford to confine itself to tweedy academics, doctors' wives or serially disappointed baby boomers. In its quest for a 'glamour' candidate, the party's NSW committee approached the rock star Peter Garrett, the tall, shaven-headed frontman of the band Midnight Oil. Garrett agreed to come on board if he was nominated first on the Senate ticket, the only candidate with any prospect of being elected under the Senate voting system. Denborough – who as the party's founder had seen himself in this role, because a Canberra Senate seat was unwinnable – was furious, but the NSW people selected Garrett. Denborough and his supporters walked out of the meeting in disgust.[28]

Garrett was already a nationally recognised figure in 1984, but his association with the NDP would raise his profile considerably outside the ranks of the young people who admired his music. Midnight Oil, originally called Farm, had emerged on the pub rock scene in the 1970s, establishing a loyal following especially among surfies on Sydney's Northern Beaches. Garrett, then a law student at the Australian National University, joined the three original members, James Moginie, Andrew James and Rob Hirst, after answering an advertisement placed by the band. A charismatic man and distinctive physical presence with his lofty height and billiard-ball head, Garrett in his vigorous stage performances as the group's lead singer helped Midnight Oil to earn a reputation as one of the country's finest live acts. Their breakthrough album came in 1982 with *10, 9, 8, 7, 6, 5, 4, 3, 2, 1*. Songs such as 'Short Memory', 'US Forces', 'Power and the Passion' and 'Maralinga' were in the best traditions of protest music, yet married the Oils' distinctive political message of opposing imperialism, US domination, nuclear war and political apathy to the energy of Oz rock. The group tapped brilliantly into the fears and ideals of many young people who felt completely alienated by Reagan,

Thatcher, Fraser, Hawke and a succession of arthritic Soviet rulers. *10, 9, 8, 7, 6, 5, 4, 3, 2, 1* reached number three on the Australian album charts in December 1982 and remained in the top twenty for most of 1983, selling about a quarter of a million copies.[29] In February of that year, alongside Goanna, folk group Redgum and the rising new-wave band INXS, Midnight Oil performed in Melbourne at the Stop the Drop concert, organised by People for Nuclear Disarmament.[30] On meeting Garrett for the first time in 1984, Ted St John recorded in his diary that he was 'highly intelligent' and 'well-informed': 'He is dedicated to the cause, has been for years. He may do very well. I am impressed by his grip of the issue and his political acumen.'[31]

★

Another early 1980s rock band, Painters and Dockers, took its name from a union that would soon become synonymous with corruption in Australia. In 1980, as a result of media reports about the Federated Ship Painters and Dockers Union, the Fraser government appointed a royal commission to be conducted by Francis Xavier Costigan, a Melbourne QC. With his Jesuit education, proud Irish-Australian identity and strong identification with the underdog, Frank Costigan would turn out to be one of the most influential figures in transforming the handling of crime and corruption in late twentieth-century Australia.

There have been many tough trade unions in Australian labour history, but the Ship Painters and Dockers must surely remain unique in the role that murder played in its internal affairs. A number of officials had been killed 'in the line of duty' during the 1970s, raising the suspicion that there was something more going on than an ordinary struggle for factional advantage. Early in the royal commission's inquiries, a witness being interrogated about a company supposedly engaged in ship repairs produced files that contained evidence of a cheque for $1.5 million having been paid into the company's accounts. This seemed to Costigan inconsistent with a small outfit involved in ship repairs, so he subpoenaed an associated company's bank records and found that in just three months, $250 million had passed through one bank account. The royal commission, recalled Costigan, uncovered 'dozens of such accounts'.[32]

While finding that the Painters and Dockers Union was thoroughly corrupt and violent – its federal secretary had notoriously but accurately declared 'we catch and kill our own' – Costigan also discovered that it was 'an organised criminal group following criminal pursuits' such as fraud, theft, extortion, illegal gambling, drug trafficking and much else.[33] Most seriously for the ailing Fraser government, the commission found widespread tax evasion that came to be known as 'bottom of the harbour' schemes. These usually involved a company with a large tax liability being sold on to a tax promoter who would strip it of its cash and then send the company to the 'bottom of the harbour'; that is, hide it from the tax office. The shady and violent waterfront was useful to the promoters of such schemes, for companies with large tax liabilities and no assets could be sold for a fee to criminals in the Painters and Dockers Union, men sometimes living under a false identity, and thereby buried forever. The commission claimed to have identified one man, a bankrupt, who was the secretary of more than 2000 companies.[34]

The effect of Costigan's reports was sensational. His lapidary prose owed something to tabloid reporting and the royal commission gave unprecedented exposure to the problem of organised crime. But Costigan's methods were not to everyone's taste. As the inquiry drew to a close in 1984, Gareth Evans complained to his diary of 'the outrages ... perpetrated ... by Frank Costigan and his Savonarola-like Counsel Assisting, Douglas Meagher QC, who have been writing thoroughly irresponsible penny dreadfuls at vast public cost, disguising their obsessions beneath a mask of phony probity'.[35]

The occasion for Evans's exasperated diary entry was the Goanna affair. The Costigan commission had by this time been operating for about four years but was never intended to act as a permanent body. After he came to office, Hawke asked Costigan to concentrate on drug trafficking in the few months remaining while his government created the National Crime Authority to continue the investigation of organised crime. Costigan, however, became unhappy with the arrangements for the transition, concerned that several unfinished inquiries would not survive the end of his own investigation – particularly one involving a businessman the royal commission had codenamed 'Squirrel'.[36] Unfortunately for Squirrel, forty-two case summaries that Costigan wanted to be taken up by the new crime-fighting authority were leaked to the *National Times*. One was of particular interest. 'Goanna', according to the report, was a wealthy businessman with a 'flamboyant and very expensive' lifestyle and a 'gambling habit'. He was engaged in drug trafficking and pornographic video importation and distribution, and one of his business partners might also have committed a murder.[37]

The *National Times* had in its report changed 'Squirrel' to 'Goanna' – another creature known to climb trees – for good reasons. Kerry Packer, the media magnate who soon outed himself as the Goanna of the *National*

Times story, had told the royal commission in a public hearing that he had 'a squirrel mentality' about cash.[38] If the *National Times* had retained Costigan's original codename, Packer would have been readily identified. In any event, that Packer was the Goanna quickly became one of the country's worst-kept secrets. Evans reported an apocryphal interview with a senior politician: 'Have you ever to your knowledge met the Goanna?' 'No, but I knew his father, Sir Frank Goanna.'[39] (Packer's father was Sir Frank Packer.)

Packer, deeply upset by the accusations, would eventually be declared innocent of them by the federal attorney-general Lionel Bowen, acting under strong pressure from Hawke, on the floor of parliament in March 1987.[40] But in the meantime he had to endure a *Gillies Report* comedy sketch on the ABC, in which he was portrayed as a goanna, complete with explosive temper and massive tail – an uncannily accurate cross of man and beast. The accusations against Packer of drug trafficking and involvement in murder were scurrilous, implausible and, as became increasingly apparent after the commission closed, inadequately supported by evidence. But after almost four years of chasing corrupt and violent crooks, elusive money trails and ingenious schemes to fleece the public, Costigan understandably looked with intense suspicion on Packer's blatant obstruction of his inquiries and, when finally compelled to appear before the commission, his evasive testimony. That Packer was involved in shady tax schemes partly uncovered by the commission is beyond doubt, but that did not make him a drug dealer.

The Goanna affair added fuel to a firestorm of stories of organised crime and political corruption. Much of the attention centred on New South Wales, whose citizens sometimes seemed unsure whether they wished to eliminate or revel in the corruption that formed so salient a part of the state's cultural identity. To call a man a 'prominent Sydney racing identity' in the 1980s was to signal something more than that he was well-known and interested in horses. The assumed Mafia assassination in 1977 of Liberal Party candidate and anti-drugs campaigner Donald Mackay in the Riverina town of Griffith was a milestone in the emergence of organised crime as a matter of pressing national concern. Then, in 1981, a *National Times* report following the death of former Liberal premier Sir Robert Askin which claimed he was corrupt brought accusations of crookedness to the commanding heights of the state's political system. By this time, Neville Wran had been Labor premier for five years, and in 1982 he had to endure the exposure of the second-most senior police officer in the state, Deputy Commissioner Bill Allen, as hopelessly compromised by an impressive array of corrupt activities. The manner in which Allen's career had advanced reflected badly on the premier's judgment, and Wran later considered the affair decisive in wrecking his federal political ambitions.[41]

A landmark in the history of organised crime came with 'The Big League', an incendiary ABC *Four Corners* investigation by reporter Chris Masters and producer Peter Manning concerning corruption in the NSW Rugby League, which went to air on 30 April 1983. Masters, the brother of St George Dragons coach Roy Masters, knew something of the world of Sydney Rugby League and became aware of rumours that the game's chief, Kevin Humphreys, had embezzled more than $50,000 from Balmain Leagues Club to pay his gambling debts and then avoided punishment through the exercise of corrupt influences. Masters had testimony that the then chief stipendiary magistrate, Murray Farquhar, had in 1977 placed pressure on the presiding magistrate, Kevin Jones, to dismiss the charges. Farquhar claimed to have been acting on Wran's instructions, a suggestion that, if proven correct, would not only have ended Wran's career but would probably also have destroyed his government.

The dramatic force of 'The Big League' came, in part, from innovative use of actors and dialogue, which lent colour and authority to the allegations, including those against the premier.[42] Wran denied that he had been involved in having the case dropped and sued for defamation, but he eventually agreed to stand down while the matter was investigated.[43] A subsequent royal commission headed by Sir Laurence Street, the chief justice, found that Wran could not have made the alleged telephone call, but Humphreys was retried and found guilty, while Farquhar received a gaol term. A furious Wran alleged a media conspiracy against his government spearheaded by Fairfax and the ABC, considered himself vindicated by the finding and resumed as premier. But when his corrective services minister Rex 'Buckets' Jackson lost his job and eventually his freedom after federal police taps found that he had accepted bribes in return for the early release of prisoners, few were inclined to see it as an isolated case of a weak man using his office to pay his gambling debts.[44]

Wran's notion of a conspiracy can be readily dismissed, but it is true enough that some journalists, particularly in the Fairfax press, had little regard for the Labor government of New South Wales and believed that it was implicated in the continuing problem of organised crime. Many had earned their stripes around the time that the *Washington Post*'s Bob Woodward and Carl Bernstein had exposed the Watergate scandal. Their success in uncovering the corruption of Richard Nixon's White House has served as the nirvana of investigative reporting ever since, but it was an especially powerful exemplar for journalists who began their careers in the 1970s and early

1980s. Ordinary career ambition mingled with a conviction, widespread among Western journalists in the post-Vietnam War and post-Watergate era, that governments were by their very nature self-serving cabals that would lie and deceive as required. It was the role of journalists to expose this grubby business, in the interests of free, democratic and open society. Especially at Fairfax, journalists also influenced by the radicalism of the 1960s and 1970s were instinctively hostile to the machine politics of the NSW Labor Right, with its conservative Catholic strain, its cynicism about power and its culture of mateship. The vicious 1980 bashing of a left-wing ALP activist, Peter Baldwin, at his Marrickville home left the faction in particularly bad odour, while the Wran government's award of the contract for Lotto in 1979 to a consortium that included both Kerry Packer and Rupert Murdoch seemed typical of how Labor political business was done in New South Wales.

The decade and a half between 1975 and 1990 was a golden age of Australian investigative reporting. For the Fairfax press, advertising revenue was sufficient not only to sustain the efforts of investigative journalists at the *Age* and the *Sydney Morning Herald* but also to cross-subsidise the loss-making weekly the *National Times*. The Fairfax board and management allowed editors a long leash; editors, in turn, afforded their journalists a similar latitude. Other newspapers, such as the Adelaide *Advertiser* (on British nuclear tests) and the Brisbane *Courier-Mail* (on police corruption) also carried out influential investigative reporting from time to time. At the ABC, managers were prepared to permit producers and journalists considerable leeway in pursuing their inquiries. Governments and citizens under investigation could and did respond with libel actions – the Burke and Bjelke-Petersen governments were notorious for their use of government-funded writs to strangle criticism – and while these were to be avoided where possible, they were also seen to come with the territory.

In the particular case of New South Wales, it was obvious that there was a major problem with organised crime, one which allowed illegal gambling, drug dealing and prostitution to flourish under police protection. Masters has recalled 'the tawdry façade of governance and rule of law' in Australia at that time, when corrupt behind-the-scenes influences in the practice of politics and the administration of justice were taken for granted and tolerated by most Australians. 'I did not so much find the subject of corruption as it found me,' he explained.[45]

★

The long-running Lionel Murphy affair would capture the most sustained public attention to the Labor Party's contribution to official corruption. And while one of the issues at stake was again judicial corruption in New South Wales, in this case the implications were far wider. The Murphy affair was a major Australian constitutional crisis, involving a man who inspired affection, admiration and loathing in both greater quantities and more unusual patterns than most public figures of his time. The social and legal reforms for which Murphy had been responsible as attorney-general in the Whitlam government were arguably its greatest legacy. Most importantly, there was the *Family Law Act*, the subject of both admiration and a revulsion that, in a few sad cases, spilled over into murderous attacks on Family Court judges and their families. Murphy had as a minister sometimes shown a want of political judgment, as in his notorious 'raid' on ASIO headquarters in Melbourne, and his appointment to the High Court in 1975 was predictably condemned by Labor's opponents as a political move. But on the bench, Murphy distinguished himself as a capable and reforming judge who, by the early 1980s, was being spoken of as a possible future chief justice. In private life, women found him attractive, despite his lack of conventional handsomeness and a nose of gargantuan proportions. 'He had the gift of making you feel that you were the most interesting person in the room,' recalled Gillian Appleton, the wife of one of Murphy's close friends.[46]

The chances of Murphy becoming chief justice were shattered by the publication of the so-called *Age* tapes in February 1984. The *Age*'s story, which focused on the telephone conversations between an unnamed judge and an unnamed solicitor, purported to reveal a 'network of influence'. Most of the conversation reported by the paper, while of a knockabout variety, was fairly innocuous and even without context seemed a long way from indicating corruption on the part of either interlocutor. What was for the judge potentially damaging, or at least highly embarrassing, turned out to be rather the result of a sloppy error on the part of the *Age* which it took a fortnight to correct, by which time the damage was well and truly done. The article had managed to confuse the two speakers and so reported that 'the judge talked of his drunkenness and sexual achievements and the solicitor said he could arrange girls for the judge'. The solicitor was supposed to have asked about one particular occasion: 'Did you have a good time?' to which the judge replied, 'If you can call getting tired and drunk and f— ... everything a good time.' In fact, it was the judge who had asked the question, and the solicitor who had replied.[47]

The *Age* was vague about the source of the material, which bore on the question of its reliability. The recordings, transcripts and summaries had been illegally created by NSW police and come to the paper from Bob Bottom, an independent crime reporter, but he had refused to tell the editor, Creighton Burns, of his source. The *Age*'s reporting of conversations between the solicitor and the judge had depended on written transcripts and summaries and in only one instance on an actual tape, which was in any case found to be a copy that might have been edited. The material had been collected by police for intelligence purposes only and its accuracy could not be tested. The usefulness of the summaries seemed even more dubious. All of these considerations had led the *Age*'s Fairfax stablemate, the *Sydney Morning Herald*, to decline to use the material when Bottom offered it.[48]

The identity of the judge and the solicitor did not remain a secret for long, with Murphy being named in the Queensland parliament by one of its most corrupt politicians in a highly competitive field, Don Lane.[49] The solicitor in the story turned out to be Morgan Ryan, a friend of Murphy's since the early 1950s and a man whose friends, associates and clients tended to figure whenever a royal commission or a muckraking journalist was reporting on the seamier side of Sydney life. The federal attorney-general, Gareth Evans, handed the *Age* material over to the federal police and the incoming Director of Public Prosecutions, Ian Temby. Neither could find anything suggesting that Murphy had committed a criminal offence, nor that he had engaged in 'proved misbehaviour' of the kind provided for in section 72 of the constitution as being grounds for the parliament to remove a judge. The federal Senate, however, where the Australian Democrats held the balance of power, decided that a committee of inquiry was in order. When it reported five months later, the committee agreed that the *Age* material was of dubious reliability and contained nothing that would suggest Murphy should be removed from office. But it was divided over another issue. The committee had heard evidence from Chief Stipendiary Magistrate Clarrie Briese that Murphy had tried to influence him in connection with a case involving Morgan Ryan's alleged participation in an immigration racket. When Briese's secret evidence leaked, the result was electrifying, not least because he recalled that Murphy had asked him in a phone conversation: 'And now, what about my little mate?'[50]

Murphy denied that he had used these words but the question immediately entered Australian folklore and has remained there ever since. As evidence of wrongdoing on his part, the 'little mate' reference was about as useless as the *Age* material. It proved nothing. But in the context of the public debate over corruption in Australian life in the 1980s, it was like a match to dry grass. The tradition of mateship had come under sustained attack since the 1970s by critics who associated it with the exclusion and oppression of women, gay men, Aboriginal Australians and ethnic minorities, and a blind loyalty between men that was careless of ethics and the law. Corruption's bedfellow was mateship. Mateship could help explain the ties between gang rapists, between corrupt police, between Labor politicians and their rich friends – and in the case of Murphy and Ryan, it accounted for the strange bond between an eminent judge and a somewhat less eminent solicitor.[51] The critics allowed for sentimentality playing a role in such relationships, and it was difficult even for mateship's harshest critics to present loyalty as an unalloyed evil. But where such concessions were made, they were leavened by the awareness of self-interest, the sense that mateship ultimately depended for its survival on a mutual back-scratching by those inside the fraternity. Steele Hall, the SA Liberal MP and former premier, connected corruption, mateship and the culture of the Labor Party itself when speaking to a censure motion in September 1984: 'Are Labor Party governments organically deficient in their capacity to fight crime and overcome the criminal element in this community? Is there a structure within the Labor Party, or is it built in such a way that it is unable to resist the claims of mateship?'[52]

The Senate committee divided over the Briese allegation but Murphy's refusal to be questioned – he submitted an unsworn statement instead – suggested to the casual observer that he had something to hide. A second Senate committee was formed in an effort to end the stalemate, but when it reported at the end of October, like the first it failed to achieve unanimity. Four of its members believed Murphy could not be found guilty of a crime on the basis of the evidence available to them, but five out of six thought it possible that the parliament could conclude that 'proved misbehaviour' had taken place and thereby remove Murphy from the bench. Murphy now took leave from the court and soon afterwards, Temby decided that although a conviction was improbable, in order to clear the air of increasingly wild innuendo, Murphy should be charged with two counts of attempting to pervert the course of justice, one concerning the Briese allegation, and a second arising from an allegation by another judge, Paul Flannery. Temby had determined that the considerations which would apply to a normal citizen – that there had to be a reasonable prospect of a conviction – need not hold in the case of a public official at the centre of widely circulated allegations. His reasoning – which was not released publicly until 1986 – although defensible, raised serious questions about the civil rights of public figures.[53]

On 5 July 1985 Murphy was acquitted of the Flannery charge but found guilty in connection with the allegation that he had tried to influence Briese. Some of the jurors subsequently made known their concerns about Murphy's fate, for having requested guidance before they delivered their verdict, they believed they had been misdirected by the judge. In November the NSW Court of Appeal agreed with them when it quashed the Murphy conviction and ordered a second trial. In April 1986 Murphy was acquitted of the Briese charge, but his ordeal was still not over. New allegations against him emerged in the press and in a separate inquiry into the *Age* tapes, and a majority of the judges on the High Court bench indicated to the government that they would be unprepared to sit with Murphy in future cases. They rested their objections partly on Murphy's failure to subject himself to cross-examination under oath at his second trial.[54]

The government now had the makings of a full-blown constitutional crisis on its hands. Senior ministers hoped that Murphy might extract it from its growing difficulties by resigning and they enlisted the governor-general, Sir Ninian Stephen, to try to persuade him to do so. Murphy, however, dug in and made clear his intention of returning to the bench. Amid a confusing series of exchanges between the government and the judges, who now retreated from their earlier apparent belligerence, the government decided to appoint a parliamentary commission of inquiry to investigate whether Murphy's behaviour would justify the parliament removing him from the court.[55]

No one could have predicted how the crisis would be resolved: Murphy was dying of cancer and had only months to live. When at the end of July he informed his fellow judges at their regular meeting that he was gravely ill and wanted to return to the bench for a while before the end, William Deane, a future governor-general, broke down but Harry Gibbs coldly replied: 'Can't you wait until the inquiry is finished?'[56] The government, however, terminated the commission of inquiry and Murphy returned to the bench on 1 August 1986 in what one of his supporters, Professor Tony Blackshield, called 'an unforgettable symbol of judicial independence'.[57] He died on 21 October 1986, on the same day his final judgment was handed down in court.

That Murphy did in fact seek to use his influence to help Morgan Ryan in his troubles with the law seems likely. Gillian Appleton, who was married to one of Murphy's closest friends, the former Whitlam government minister and judge Jim McClelland, reports that Murphy made at least two phone calls to McClelland seeking to influence him in connection with Ryan's problems. On the second occasion, after McClelland asked, 'Are you trying to get me to put the weights on a judge?' Murphy replied sarcastically: 'Oh we wouldn't want to do that, would we?' McClelland testified at trial but was only asked about the first phone call. Appleton reflects: 'Clearly Murphy thought that the old mates' network would override any considerations of propriety. Over the years I came to realise that attempts to exert influence were an integral element of this network, and one well understood and used by its members.'[58] But on his death in October 1986, it was easier to make a martyr of Murphy. Neville Wran, who had recently resigned as premier, delivered the eulogy at a packed memorial service in Sydney Town Hall. He knew that Murphy was no saint: 'The very richness and zest of his humanity ensured that.' Wran had not been especially close to Murphy, but he appears to have identified strongly with him as a fellow sufferer at the hands of the media. The moving conclusion to his eulogy prompted a standing ovation:

> There used to be a good Australian word for the value of openness and equality in our society.
> I am proud I can still use that word for Lionel Murphy.
> He was my mate.[59]

*

By September 1984, and with a federal election likely before the end of the year, the stories of corruption emanating from New South Wales became too great a temptation to resist for Andrew Peacock, the federal Opposition leader. The economy was continuing its improvement and Hawke remained a popular political leader. The immigration issue having proved too hot to exploit for electoral gain, Peacock turned his attention to corruption. On 13 September, he moved a censure motion against the government for its failure in combating organised crime. One of Peacock's purposes was to insinuate that the closing down of the Costigan royal commission had been the result of a desire on Hawke's part to protect his power base in the NSW branch of the ALP. But early in his speech, Peacock overstepped the mark in calling Hawke a 'little crook', 'a perverter of the law of this country' and 'one who associates with criminals and takes his orders from those who direct those criminals'.[60] There was no evidence to support any of this, and Peacock appeared to have blown the Opposition's chance to exploit the issue.[61]

A week later, Hawke issued a statement condemning Peacock and denying his claims. The prime minister was particularly vehement about the issue of the drug trade, a 'subject in respect of which I have to fight to retain my rationality when contemplating what should be done to those who endanger the lives, particularly of our young'. At the accompanying press conference, he added: 'There is no matter which, for intimate reasons, I feel more strongly about than this.'[62] Many of those present interpreted this as a reference to his older daughter, Susan. A few weeks before, the *National Times* had published an article which questioned why convictions against her for cultivating and possessing Indian hemp had been overturned in the appeal court by Judge John Foord without any legal reasons being provided for upholding the appeal. The judge concerned, as the article explained, had recently spent some time off the bench after Clarrie Briese had accused him of attempting to influence the outcome of committal proceedings in the Morgan Ryan case.[63] But Hawke's oblique reference was not to Susan; it was to his younger daughter, 23-year-old Rosslyn, who with her husband was addicted to heroin. The Hawkes had become aware of this recently when Rosslyn had given birth to a child, because she had so wasted away that her life was in danger. When pressed by journalists about whether he would be suing Peacock, Hawke broke down and wept, explaining: 'You don't cease to be a husband. You don't cease to be a father.'[64] Hawke wept again the following day on radio while being interviewed by John Laws.[65] A few days later, Hazel Hawke explained on television what had caused her husband's tears, and the heartbreak that the news about their daughter had caused her family.

The Hawkes were far from alone in having to deal with the problem of drug addiction. The media regularly carried sensational reports of the lives of the drug barons and those who pursued them, the murder of couriers, the occasional bust, the detective caught dealing, the politician calling for a harder line or – much less often – a softer one. But behind the headlines was another more elusive and tragic story of the effect of heroin on Australian society. A 1985 article in *Business Review Weekly* declared that '[t]oday's executive package often includes a child with a heroin habit', a subject, said the article's author, 'that strikes more fear into the hearts of parents than any other'.[66] The danger of finding your children addicted to heroin was actually rather small, but the number of 15- to 34-year-olds whose deaths were related to opiate abuse climbed from less than 100 in 1979 to more than 160 in 1983 – when a new danger emerged for users through HIV, the antigens of which could be spread by the common practice of sharing needles.[67] Neville

Wran's successor as premier, Barrie Unsworth, and federal industry minister John Button had each lost a son to a heroin overdose, as did the Sydney Rugby League legend Jack Gibson. Parents of children who died in this manner might carry with them a sense of guilt for the rest of their lives.[68] Many more families lived for years with the problem of drug addiction. Frank Costigan's son was just one among many children of the middle class who battled heroin addiction in the 1980s.

Illegal drugs pervaded the world of popular music. The global triumph of INXS during the 1980s occurred amid a whirl of cocaine and speed. When they toured in the wake of their spectacularly successful album *Kick* (1987), they kept on staff a roadie whose job it was to keep them efficiently supplied, as sure a sign that they had made it big as lead singer Michael Hutchence's parallel success in wooing starlets and supermodels.[69] In both 1987 and 1988 Nick Cave, then based in Berlin and enjoying an extraordinary burst of creativity with his band the Bad Seeds, appeared in court in London for heroin possession.[70] Grant McLennan, a member of another group achieving critical acclaim in Britain at this time – Brisbane's The Go-Betweens – was also a user. He introduced Steve Kilbey of The Church to the drug, an attraction that sent Kilbey on a rapid downhill slide.[71] Others, however, managed to combine their drug taking with a burgeoning career. The singer and songwriter Paul Kelly called heroin in his memoir 'the one for me, the recreational drug of choice'. But where the cliché had heroin users as hopeless addicts seeking to exorcise some demon or other, Kelly 'didn't take heroin because I felt bad or because I had an unhappy childhood. I just liked it.'[72]

Many more used marijuana than other illegal drugs; almost three in ten of the population had tried it in the second half of the 1980s, although far fewer were regular users.[73] Some graduated from other illegal drugs to heroin but found that it was not for them. Nikki McWatters, an adventurous young Gold Coast women who had moved to Sydney in search of fame, fortune and sex with rock stars, also found cocaine. On one particular evening, however, when it was not to be had, she and a friend used heroin instead. 'I had never tried heroin and the very word seemed poisonous as a scorpion.' But she decided to give it a try: 'She injected me and the rush almost knocked me down. I shut my eyes and swooned into a chair, then stumbled down the hallway to the bathroom. Heroin did not agree with me. I spent the rest of the night vomiting, retching until there was nothing left to expel but air and noise and the aching in my ribs.'[74]

Estimates vary and need to be treated with great caution, but there were perhaps 35,000 regular users of heroin in Australia by 1986, with possibly another 75,000 having used the drug occasionally.[75] If these figures are accurate, it means that about 4.5 out of every 1000 Australians between fifteen and forty-four were regular users of heroin, and about ten in 1000, or 1 per cent, had experimented with it at some time or other. The number of Australians using heroin was therefore very small. According to one study, nineteen out of twenty Australians had never tried either heroin or cocaine and of the very small number who had, three-quarters had not done so during the previous year. Public concern about heroin in the mid-1980s, then, greatly exceeded the actual danger it posed. In 1985, that more than one in six Australians saw illicit drugs as the country's greatest problem says much about the effect of sensational media coverage.[76] Yet by the late 1980s, the rate of heroin use had probably climbed, cocaine was spreading beyond the affluent, amphetamines were in growing demand and ecstasy had arrived on the party scene.[77] Meanwhile, in some remote Aboriginal communities, petrol sniffing was a common practice among young males, and one that seemed to be both spreading and growing in intensity.[78]

There were also a few areas in Australia's largest cities where drugs formed the very fabric of the community. Kings Cross in Sydney was probably the country's most lucrative corner for drug dealing,[79] but the Vietnamese centre of Cabramatta, with its large black-market economy and high youth unemployment, was increasingly associated with heroin trafficking by the early 1990s. In Melbourne, bayside St Kilda remained the focus of the drug trade where, as in Kings Cross, it was in an unholy alliance with prostitution. Trading in sex was for many the most convenient way of raising sufficient funds to pay for a heroin habit of $300 to $600 a week. The need for heroin bound a sex worker to a pimp or brothel as securely as any alternative form of coercion.

Yet if panic about illegal drugs was waning by the end of the 1980s, or at least becoming more concentrated on well-known trouble spots, concern about legal drugs such as alcohol and tobacco was heading in the other direction. The 1980s saw a growing emphasis on a long and healthy life among the population that led to vigorous and effective anti-smoking campaigns. The activist group BUGA-UP defaced billboards advertising cigarettes while governments stepped up their public health campaigns, restricted advertising of tobacco products and mandated health warnings on cigarette packets.[80] In 1985 they launched the National Campaign against

Drug Abuse.[81] Meanwhile, new research in the mid-1980s drew attention to the dangers of passive smoking which, in combination with the spread of open-plan offices and air-conditioning, raised growing health concerns.[82] Unions demanded 'the right of non-smoking members to work in a smoke-free environment'. 'There is no civil right to assault a fellow worker,' declared Paul Munro, national secretary of the Administrative and Clerical Officers Association in 1985, and 'increasingly the dispersal of tobacco smoke in confined working spaces must be recognised as a form of assault'.[83]

During 1987 and 1988, Telecom, Australia Post and the Victorian government all banned workplace smoking, while the chairman of the Public Service Board, Peter Wilenski, announced that all federal office space would be designated non-smoking from 1 March 1987, which meant that if there were to be any exceptions they would need to be agreed by a workplace consensus. A full ban would begin in 1988. Unions, however, were of more than one mind when it actually came time to lay down rules, for they worried that smokers might find themselves victimised by employers and excluded from work. And even at the end of the 1980s, very few private employers had banned workplace smoking. Anyone who spent more than a few minutes inside a pub, nightclub or restaurant – and that of course included those who worked in one – still had to wash their hair and clothes to remove the smell of tobacco smoke.[84]

In Canberra, outside any public service office, there was often for many years to be seen a rather pathetic crew taking a smoking break – in some ways, a return to an older blue-collar tradition of the smoko. The journalist Tony Wright reported in March 1988 that a young woman with frizzy hair complained to him of being made 'an outcast'; another felt like 'a leper'.[85] Some doubted whether public servants were made of sufficiently stern stuff to continue this practice, at least during a Canberra winter. When I visited Canberra in early 1990, there was a story in circulation, probably apocryphal, that foreign tourists visiting the city were surprised at the ubiquity of sex workers waiting outside public service buildings for their clients. Although smokers were a declining proportion of the population, the number of young female smokers was increasing; possibly a hint that the threads connecting cigarettes, sexiness and sophistication were, despite the growing concentration of cigarette smoking among poorer and more marginalised groups, still far from being severed.[86]

*

Hawke's tears over his daughter's drug use sparked a public debate about the phenomenon of a politician weeping in public. And because the politician was a man – as most politicians were – the debate had larger implications for what such behaviour meant for Australian masculinity. It was not the first time Hawke had broken down in public. It had also happened in 1981, in the parliament, when he was accused by the Opposition of having sold out Israel over Labor opposition to sending a peacekeeping force to the Sinai.[87] Australians might not quite have adopted the stiff upper lip as a mark of their national character in the manner of the mother country, but the dominant style of Australian masculinity up to the 1960s had been stoic and phlegmatic, leavened by the sentimentality associated with mateship. The dominance of this style had been challenged by the social revolution of the 1960s and 1970s; a more androgynous performance of masculinity could be discerned among younger men, some of whom had even taken to wearing an earring, previously the habit of only a somewhat eccentric bohemian minority. But the implications of this transformation for politics, the commanding heights of which were dominated by men who had reached adulthood by the early 1960s, remained largely untested. Liberal Party strongman Wilson Tuckey was a former publican from the WA outback, where there was little evidence of a new and 'softer' masculinity; he thought Hawke's behaviour intolerable, declaring that 'Australians are entitled to the guarantee that their national leader has the moral fibre to carry the pressures of national calamity. After the Prime Minister's "I want my mummy" performance today, it is clear that Australia has no such leader at present.'[88] The elegant and tanned Peacock responded more sympathetically but his deputy, John Howard, condemned Hawke for his 'appalling double standards' and 'fragile glass jaw'; the context of Hawke's tears had, after all, been his own talk of suing Peacock.[89] An Adelaide publican was unsure whether it amounted to 'a tremendous case of acting or a terrible case of weakness – either way I can't accept it'.[90] Press gallery reporters, however, agreed that the tears were both genuine and unlikely to do Hawke any damage politically – indeed, that as a combination of genuine emotion and 'devastating politics', they had turned the debate about organised crime in the government's favour. Journalists considered that women voters might especially sympathise, a supposition that appeared to be supported by ALP focus-group research that was being conducted at the very time the incident occurred. 'Last night, it was the Opposition that was crying,' *Age* journalist Michelle Grattan concluded.[91]

Hawke's family anguish and tears elicited kind notes from friend and foe alike. The Liberal Party's Tony Staley wrote that he was 'very moved on seeing your emotions about your family surface'. He hoped that it would not only draw attention to the pressures under which politicians worked but also 'help to turn around that appalling Australian proposition that "grown men don't cry"'.[92] John Dawkins, then finance minister, wrote that '[a]s one who has a great but occasionally inconvenient talent for involuntary displays of emotion I have felt deeply for you during the last week', while Ian Leslie, the Channel Nine reporter, said that 'as a father, may I say it gives me a certain warmth to see a man capable of some emotion ... despite the importance of his office. May we give you a fair go.'[93] Journalists, as well as some of Hawke's opponents, debated just what a 'fair go' might entail. Some considered that it involved toleration of a single outburst, but not a second one, as occurred on radio the following day. 'After Thursday's lapse into humanity,' Paul Ellercamp of the *Australian* suggested, 'what people were looking for ... was reassurance of Mr Hawke's strength.'[94] Graham Little, a Melbourne University political psychologist, judged that Hawke's strength lay in just this combination – his capacity to combine a 'masculine' power with values more commonly associated with the 'feminine', such as compassion and cooperation; 'that Hawke's particular gift' was 'to attach virility to compromise, or consensus', to negotiate without appearing to lack male potency.[95] The Melbourne trucking magnate and ex-footballer Lindsay Fox put it well in a letter he addressed to Hawke 'man to man': 'You are a natural leader and a strong man. Only a strong man will cry in public.'[96]

*

There was an oblique connection here with the world of sport. In 1984 Australian cricket was still bearing the wounds of the Kerry Packer World Series Cricket (WSC) revolution. The cricket establishment and WSC had come to an accommodation in 1979, one that greatly favoured Packer's Channel Nine, which acquired the rights to broadcast the game that he had now done so much to commercialise. But among the players, there remained tension between those who had joined the rebels and those who stayed behind to continue playing official Test matches.

Kim Hughes, who as a promising rookie had remained with the cricket establishment, was now Australian captain, but his relations with several of those who had joined the Packer-led rebellion, notably Ian Chappell, Dennis

Lillee and Rod Marsh, were rancorous. All had retired but their criticisms of Hughes's captaincy continued in the media and through the rumour mill. The blond, curly-haired Hughes was a skilled and courageous if impetuous WA batsman whose misfortune it was to have taken on the captaincy during an era when the wounds from the split of 1977–79 remained unhealed, the Australian cricket team was in decline, and the West Indies – with their frightening fast-bowling and talented, hard-hitting batsmen – were nearly unbeatable.[97]

When Australia played the West Indies in the first Test in Perth in November 1984, the latter managed 416 runs in the first innings compared with Australia's 76. By the time of the second Test in Brisbane, even the prime minister felt justified in handing out advice to Hughes. Hawke, ironically, had almost lost the sight in one of his eyes a few weeks before when hit by a short ball while wearing glasses during a 'friendly' game between his staff and the press gallery. But even with Hawke's advice, the Australians fared only a little better in Brisbane than they had in the west. Hopelessly outscored in the first innings yet again, they at least made a spirited fightback in the second that forced the great Caribbean team to bat a second time to win the game. Sections of the Brisbane crowd booed the Australian captain when he came out to bat. Before the game was over, Hughes had decided to resign his captaincy.[98]

At the post-match press conference, Hughes announced that he had a statement to read. But after three sentences, 'There was a poignant pause as Hughes's lips quivered.' After an effort to resume reading, he 'rose from his chair and in a high-pitched broken voice' said to team manager, Bob Merriman: 'You read it.' Hughes immediately walked out to tell his players of his decision. Again he broke down before he could get much out, sat down on a bench with a towel over his head and then, according to one teammate's recollection, 'sobbed for over half an hour'.[99]

Many sports commentators who had witnessed his anguish were inclined to treat Hughes's weeping sympathetically and he apparently received 1700 goodwill messages in five weeks. A cartoon in the *Australian* was somewhat backhanded in its praise; in a reference to Hawke's recent tears, it had one man saying to another on observing a bawling Australian captain: 'Fancy quitting just when he's showing a leadership quality.' But the veteran Australian commentator Alan McGilvray described Hughes as 'a little boy who hasn't yet grown up' while Rugby Union coach Alan Jones declared that while there was nothing 'unmanly' about crying in private, the Australian captain 'should have been able to control himself'. Sections of the

British press were less kind again. The *Daily Express* proclaimed it 'very sad to see our rough, tough Foster-swigging cousins reduced to blubbing. Their Prime Minister started the trend. Their cricketers are continuing it.' Headlines screamed 'Struth it's sad', 'Weeping Matilda' and 'Why are the Aussie men such cry babies?' A cartoon in a quality broadsheet had an English woman complaining to her husband: 'You never show any emotion – I think I'll leave you for an Australian sheep farmer.' Barry Humphries consoled English readers that '[c]rying on the telly is so much better than the old days when they would simply chunder'.[100]

Hughes suffered in comparison with Hawke because he had failed to combine his tears with strong leadership – rather he seemed 'a born loser'[101] – and because the occasion of his weeping was less grave – defeat in a game of cricket – than the devastating circumstances with which Hawke had to deal. Yet what is striking in each case was the debate that ensued about how men should manage their emotions in a public forum. In retrospect, the public weeping of two of the nation's leading men in two of its most significant spheres – politics and cricket – is a notable landmark in the history of Australian masculinity and the evolution of its emotional life.

*

In late 1984 Hawke's tears were not enough to reassure the most committed Labor supporters that his political messages were resonating with the wider voting public. Lola Brooks from Cremorne in Sydney had in 1983 queued for hours and then, lacking a ticket, had talked her way into the Sydney Opera House for the launch of the party's campaign. But eighteen months later, a few weeks before the beginning of the 1984 campaign, she wrote to Hawke: 'I believe Australians need to see more of Bob Hawke the man as opposed to Bob Hawke the Prime Minister. I'm aware that facts about the recovery have to be hammered home but can't it be done in a way that is not just quoting statistics?'[102]

Hawke had called an early election to take advantage of the economic recovery and his personal popularity. At any other time in the history of the Labor Party, a second comfortable win at a federal election – as the ALP achieved under Hawke's leadership on 1 December 1984 – would have been considered a triumph. But after the many political and economic successes of the government during 1983 and 1984, its high standing in the polls and the extraordinary personal standing of the prime minister himself, the result was a disappointment. The swing away from the ALP was almost 2 per cent, and the government's majority declined from twenty-five to sixteen seats in a House of Representatives that had been enlarged from 125 to 148. The adoption of 'above the line' voting for the Senate undoubtedly confused some voters, and might have worked against the government, for the rate of informal voting for the lower house more than tripled from 1983.

A post-election internal review by the party identified other problems: at over seven weeks the campaign had been too long; the Peacock Liberal Opposition had been able to set the agenda; the Labor campaign had lacked strategic direction; the party should not have agreed to the innovation of a televised debate; the government was seen to lack a vision and, as Lola Brooks's letter hinted, it had failed to arouse enthusiasm or excitement; expectations of a landslide led some voters to switch sides so as not to encourage adventurism on the government's part and to teach it a lesson. The review also recognised that the ALP's support among younger voters had fallen since 1983, a trend it connected with the nuclear issue.[103] The NDP had, in fact, performed creditably – with a primary vote in the Senate of just over 7 per cent – but Garrett narrowly failed to get elected in New South Wales. Its only breakthrough was in Western Australia where Jo Vallentine, a Quaker, won a seat. But December 1984 would turn out to be the high-water mark of the nuclear issue's impact on mainstream electoral politics. After the election, the NDP disintegrated in the face of an effort by the Socialist Workers Party to steer it in the direction of a policy of unilateral disarmament.[104]

Some Labor Party members and supporters were, by the final months of 1984, deeply unimpressed by what seemed to be happening to their party. The secretary of a small branch in a Victorian coastal town complained to national secretary Bob McMullan that his members were 'downright wild and unhappy':

> The rank and file have had no say for many months and this debacle is one of the results ... The A.L.P. is our party no one member is above it, we are not happy with Bob Hawkes [sic] domination of it, if elected members are not strong enough then rank and file will have to look more closely at preselection. Bob Hawke never mentions the A.L.P. but my party, my government.[105]

Worse followed the election. During 1984 and 1985, three issues of foreign and defence policy drew attention to the nuclear issue. All emboldened the anti-nuclear left, both within and outside the ALP. One of them, the MX missile affair, was deeply damaging to Hawke's prestige.

The first was the ANZUS crisis. On 14 July 1984 the jovial and portly David Lange led the New Zealand Labour Party to a resounding victory in a snap poll. In contrast with its counterpart across the Tasman, New Zealand Labour policy opposed the visit to their country's ports of nuclear-armed or -powered ships. From the moment he took office, Lange faced the unenviable task of managing the crisis that this policy inevitably provoked, and his often inept handling of it only made things worse. In January 1985 New Zealand declined to permit a visit of the USS *Buchanan*, an obsolete ship that was almost certainly non-nuclear, and which Lange had earlier given every sign was likely to be acceptable to his government. The Americans felt as if they had been deliberately humiliated, but the issue of ship visits mattered to the Reagan administration primarily because of the potential of New Zealand's 'nuclear allergy' to spread to other, more important allies, such as Australia and Japan. New Zealand's example seemed likely to prove attractive in these and other countries where public opinion had already been ignited by the threat of nuclear weapons.[106]

While New Zealand public opinion was firmly in favour of ANZUS, a large majority of voters also supported an anti-nuclear policy. But opinion in the electorate at large was not Lange's main problem. Unlike Hawke in Australia with his base in the party's powerful pro-US Right, Lange lacked sway over the New Zealand Labour Party, which in any case harboured much stronger anti-American sentiment than the ALP did. And as time passed, Lange also seemed to enjoy his growing international celebrity as an anti-nuclear statesman, just as the nuclear ships issue became a focus of nationalist pride for New Zealanders.[107] Even in late 1984, some Australian commentators believed that the days of ANZUS might be numbered, for the United States was committed to a policy neither to confirm nor deny that its ships were nuclear-armed or -propelled. None of this was good news for Australia, and especially not for Hawke. If the United States allowed New Zealand concessions that were not available to its other allies, the pressure from within the ALP for Australia to demand a similar dispensation, if not more, would be hard to resist. If, on the other hand, New Zealand's position resulted in the complete collapse of ANZUS, there was little prospect that either the US Congress or the ALP would allow a new treaty to replace it.[108]

The lack of personal rapport between Hawke and Lange was also a factor in these events.[109] From their first meeting as fellow prime ministers, Hawke felt that he 'was dealing with a buffoon' and even in public, his contempt for the NZ prime minister was all too obvious. Hawke was especially hostile to what he considered the devil's pact that Lange had made with his Left, the trade-off between dry economics and a radical foreign policy.[110] But Australia wished to preserve both its alliance with the United States through ANZUS and its close relations with New Zealand. Accordingly, it went out of its way not to be seen to be taking sides. Bill Hayden, as Australia's foreign minister, had a far better relationship with Lange than Hawke did. He declared publicly that Australia would not be acting as 'a messenger boy' for the United States, and he worked hard to maintain Australia's formal neutrality in the dispute.[111]

New Zealand's stand angered the Australian right, emboldened the left, and worried those in the centre. The New Zealand–born Queensland premier, Joh Bjelke-Petersen, provided a lighter note with the kind of political quackery for which he was notorious when he used an obscure health regulation to impound a shipment of NZ chocolates and beer, and added for good measure that he would stop New Zealanders getting jobs in Queensland. He beat a hasty retreat only when it was pointed out that said chocolates were made with Queensland sugar, and that the value of his state's exports across the Tasman far exceeded the traffic in the opposite direction.[112]

For the Australian left and peace activists, the NZ path was an enticing one. Lange reported to Hayden as early as September 1984 that 'he had received hundreds of letters from Australia which left him with the impression that' they were 'trying to use events in New Zealand as leverage for their position in internal ALP fights'.[113] Peter Batchelor, the secretary of the Left-dominated Victorian Labor Party, sent a telex to the ALP's Canberra office in March 1985 on behalf of his branch supporting New Zealand's anti-nuclear policy and condemning US efforts 'to bully New Zealand'. 'Far from uncritically accepting every demand that comes from the United States,' his message continued, 'we should formulate our own independent foreign and defence policies, objectively evaluate the increasingly high costs of the American alliance, and determine whether ANZUS is compatible with a non-nuclear defence policy for Australia.' Batchelor pointedly added that the Victorian party would invite Lange to speak at its state conference in June.[114] NZ Labour Party speakers were prominent at the 1985 Palm Sunday peace rallies – future prime minister Helen Clark addressed the assembly in Sydney – while in Canberra marchers 'formed a human chain between Parliament House and the New Zealand High Commission'.[115]

The second nuclear issue that concerned the Hawke government in the aftermath of the 1984 election was the MX missile affair, a legacy of the Fraser government. The MX was a ten-warhead intercontinental ballistic missile that could be launched at short notice and was sufficiently accurate and powerful to destroy an enemy's nuclear silos. It was one of the new generation of weapons designed to contribute to a first-strike capability.[116] In 1982 Fraser had agreed to provide support for the US testing of these new missiles off the eastern Australian coast, a commitment Hawke reaffirmed to the Americans without going to the trouble of consulting his cabinet or party room.[117]

When the party did eventually hear of the decision, while Hawke was in Brussels and on his way to the United States in January 1985, there seemed to be the possibility of a cabinet revolt or even of a party split. There was no question on this occasion of Hawke simply sneering at the nonsense being peddled by his opponents about the US alliance and then doing as he saw fit. Hosting of joint facilities and US ships could be represented as a contribution to nuclear deterrence, but such arguments did not readily apply to helping test such an aggressive weapon of war as the MX. Moreover, the whole scheme seemed to fly in the face of Australia's formal commitment to disarmament.[118]

Faced with a cross-factional revolt back in Australia, Hawke reluctantly asked George Shultz, the secretary of state, and Casper Weinberger, the defense secretary, to absolve him of the commitment. The Americans were amenable – they had enough on their hands in dealing with New Zealand – but the episode was deeply embarrassing to Hawke. Paul Kelly of the *Australian* newspaper called the backdown 'the most important victory so far won by the anti-nuclear movement' and 'a humiliating retreat' for Hawke.[119] There is still a thick file in the records of the ALP national office of resolutions from state branches, sub-branches and members around the country condemning Hawke and his government over the MX missile affair.[120]

The third big nuclear issue of the mid-1980s was the Royal Commission into British Nuclear Tests in Australia. Between 1952 and 1957 there were twelve explosions at the Montebello Islands off the WA coast, and Emu Field and Maralinga in the SA desert, as well as a series of minor trials that continued through to 1963. Stories concerning the damage done by the tests to the country and to the health of ex-servicemen and Aboriginal people had circulated for many years but, due in large part to investigative reporting by the Adelaide *Advertiser*, they acquired a new piquancy in the early 1980s. The issue brought together three prominent concerns: the danger of nuclear weapons, Aboriginal rights, and a desire on the part of white

Australians for emancipation from a British imperial past. All of this was magnified by the showmanship of the commission's president, Justice James McClelland, or 'Diamond Jim' as he had long been known on account of his flashy taste in dress.

With a dubious regard for the subtleties of Australia's relationship with Britain during the 1950s, McClelland, another product of the Irish-Australian rebel tradition, saw the issue in terms of a conflict between a perfidious Britain and an Australia ruled by sycophantic Anglophiles such as Robert Menzies.[121] When his inquiry travelled to Britain in early 1985, he criticised the alleged obstruction he encountered, which he portrayed as a clash between straight-talking, no-nonsense Australians and a 'lick-spittle' British bureaucracy. Even some sections of the British media accepted this idea – they didn't much like the excessive bureaucratic secrecy either – but for sections of the Australian media there were great attractions in simplifying a complex issue as a national contest between a hidebound mother country and a cheeky larrikin judge from Down Under.[122] As McClelland later explained to the Australian satirical magazine *Matilda*:

> When we got there, their attitude was that we'd find it too cold and if it was hard to get what we wanted, we'd pack up and go home. Frankly, my attitude was 'fuck you bastards, we'll get what we can out of you, even if we have to shame you into it by going public and showing what you're about'.[123]

While the royal commission investigated the claims of British and Australian servicemen who believed their health had been damaged by the tests, it was the inquiry's exposure of a cynical and callous disregard for the safety of Aboriginal people that attracted the most notice. McClelland was particularly galled by a remark the commission found in one document, a criticism by the chief scientist in the Australian Department of Supply, William Butement, of a native patrol officer's unbalanced outlook in 'apparently placing the affairs of a handful of natives above those of the British Commonwealth of Nations'.[124] The commission investigated stories told by Aboriginal inhabitants of the SA desert of a 'Black Mist' which one Indigenous man, Yami Lester, reported had caused sickness and left him temporarily blind in one eye and permanently blind in the other. It told the story of an Aboriginal family found wandering in the prohibited zone, whom the authorities seized and showered, with no sensitivity to their culture or feeling for their dignity. And it suggested that authorities had, in their efforts to move one group of Aboriginal people away from the bomb testing area, sent them into the desert where they subsequently perished. It was stories of this kind that figured in the media, and which attracted the notice of songwriters such as Paul Kelly:

> First we heard two big bangs
> We thought it was the Great Snake digging holes
> Then we saw the big cloud
> Then the big, black mist began to roll
> This is a rainy land[125]

The report of the McClelland royal commission was a significant document marking the arrival of a post-imperial Australia, for it identified Britain as a foreign country – an idea that would have been incomprehensible to Australians of the 1950s – and it presented the British as prone to manipulating and exploiting the Australian people, with the assistance of a local class of conservative Australian Anglophiles and expatriate Britons. The result of this positioning was to displace responsibility for the treatment of Aboriginal people onto another country – the report recommended that the British should have to pay for the site to be properly cleaned up – as well as onto conservative forces in Australia. Yet atomic testing in the SA desert could not have happened unless white Australians held Aboriginal people in low esteem, while the Labor Party when in government in the 1940s had been as enthusiastic about opening up the Australian desert to British weaponry as Menzies would prove to be a few years later.[126] Official Australia, it seemed, was still not ready to own up fully to what it had done.

5
The Deal-Makers

Too good to be true
Mirage
Too good to be true
Mirage
This is too good to be true.
        Television advertisement for Sheraton Mirage Resorts, 1988

In the American film *Wall Street* (1987), the corrupt and super-rich anti-hero, Gordon Gekko, declared that 'greed is good'. No Australian entrepreneur was quite so succinct, but neither would any have quibbled. The entrepreneurs might have owed their first duty to their shareholders, but they also saw themselves as public benefactors of the front rank – men who were remaking not only the economy, but the culture itself. Australians wedded to a moribund collectivist ethos needed to learn initiative. Capitalists and workers long accustomed to being coddled by government should acquire self-reliance. Old money – 'The Establishment' – needed to be confronted in its complacency. Australians should celebrate excellence – especially when embodied in its most successful capitalists – rather than knocking it. The tall poppy should not be cut down, but admired for its beauty.

There was a simple way of stating these ideas: Australians needed to become more like Americans. The social-democratic thinker Hugh Stretton condemned 'the cult of selfishness' that he viewed as the product of this marriage of 'the old capitalist greed' and 'the new self-indulgence'. Stretton described 'The New American Man':

> He's commonly a small affluent male, aged between 30 and 49 with the lines of his face set permanently in a relaxed sneer. His sex life has always been so coolly predatory and emotionally unrewarding that

he's beginning to need commercial aids and diversifications to keep it interesting. He sincerely desires to be rich. He has the standard reactionary rhetoric about leaving economics to the market, though he's not usually taking market risks himself, or not with his own money – he's more likely to be in Personnel or PR or Management Education or Financial Journalism. He's into the tax revolt and supply-side incentives boots and all. He's against welfare. He's against environmental protection. He wants strict air safety because he's nervous flying, but he's against most other health and safety regulations.[1]

Almost as if to announce the advent of this new world, the *Business Review Weekly* (*BRW*) published a Rich List (of 144 individuals and 21 families) for the first time in November 1983 to promote to its readers the wealthy and successful as models of 'inspired striving'. *BRW* noted that the average wealth of its 1983 rich was $32.2 million, in a nation where the average net personal wealth was about $28,000 and the average adult male income $9656 per annum. Nevertheless, *BRW* considered that its list revealed 'a relatively wide distribution of wealth in Australia' as well as 'a preponderance of "new" fortunes rather than inherited wealth', the latter resting on 'a very multicultural base'.[2]

The last claim was certainly true. The earliest *BRW* Rich Lists are testament to the extraordinary success achieved by many European migrants to Australia in the decades following the Second World War, with Poles and Hungarians – many of them Jewish refugees from the Nazis, others fleeing communism – being especially conspicuous. The financial journalist Ruth Ostrow would later write a book called *The New Boy Network* which celebrated the achievements of these migrant entrepreneurs. Initially excluded from the centres of wealth and power by their status as new arrivals, they relied on other migrants, family connections and their own wits to make their way in the world. Wartime deprivation had fuelled an intense desire for the security promised by wealth, accompanied by an iron determination to make the most of their second chance.[3] Many would vastly increase their fortunes in the 1980s. A few, who entered into the gambling spirit of the 1980s with an excess of enthusiasm and a dearth of prudence, would lose everything.

Yet these were not the very wealthiest Australians. At or near the top of the Rich Lists of 1983 and 1984 were media barons such as Rupert Murdoch, Kerry Packer and the Fairfax family. In these cases, dynastic wealth had formed the basis for extensive and – by the 1980s – highly profitable media companies. Empires built on meat were also prominent: the Ingham brothers ($220 million in 1984), who supplied much of the nation's poultry, and the Smorgon family ($180 million), who began as Russian migrant butchers in the Melbourne suburb of Carlton in the 1920s but had since diversified into a manufacturing congomerate, rivalled the media bosses in their wealth. But Murdoch, with extensive media interests in Australia, Britain and the United States, was in 1983 and 1984 judged the nation's wealthiest man. The Fairfax family, the oldest of Australia's media dynasties, also enjoyed a highly profitable era in which their company, based on the *Sydney Morning Herald*, the Melbourne *Age* and the *Australian Financial Review*, was valued by *BRW*, itself a Fairfax publication, at $175 million in 1983 and $300 million in 1984. It is little wonder that Packer, Murdoch and many others looked enviously on Fairfax's 'rivers of gold' – its lucrative classified advertising – but the firm was also seen as impregnable in view of the extensive holdings of the Fairfax family.[4]

Another widely coveted company was BHP, the nation's largest, with its extensive mining and manufacturing interests. Robert Holmes à Court, a Perth-based lawyer and brilliant corporate raider, mischievously claimed that his ambition was to turn it into a subsidiary of a firm he controlled, Bell Resources. By the time the 1984 Rich List appeared, Holmes à Court was said to have already amassed a personal fortune of at least $165 million. In an era when bankers were falling over one another to offer loans to ambitious entrepreneurs of this kind, public companies – especially when cashed-up or undervalued – were vulnerable to raiders. Beginning with a failing WA wool knitting company as his vehicle for expansion, Holmes à Court took over many firms at home and abroad during the 1970s and early 1980s on his journey to the commanding heights of the business world. In 1982 he gained the ailing entertainment empire of British impresario Lew Grade, which included the Beatles' song list. But failed takeover bids were also profitable. If a target company took defensive action by offering to buy shares at a greatly increased price, or a rival wanted control of the company desperately enough to offer to buy his shares for more than Holmes à Court considered they were worth, he would offload his stock. He made $11 million when defeated for control of Ansett Airlines in 1979 by Rupert Murdoch and Peter Abeles.[5] Where selling up in this manner was part of a deliberate strategy, the pejorative American term 'greenmail' could be applied, but Holmes à Court always denied that he was aiming merely to generate cash profits from his share-buying.

By 1985 the effects of an already impressive bull market were apparent in *BRW*'s list. With a fortune of $300 million, Holmes à Court was now judged the country's richest man; in the previous year alone, his wealth had increased by $135 million, or $2.6 million per week. The Murdochs, however, were still the richest family, with $400 million. Large personal profits were being made from media and retailing empires but the fortunes of developers such as George Herscu, Frank Lowy, Ted Lustig and the Grollo brothers – all European migrants – were also growing quickly on the back of a buoyant market in commercial property. The Grollos – in close cooperation with good friends like Norm Gallagher in the leadership of the Builders' Labourers' Federation – were erecting Melbourne's massive $350 million Rialto Tower, the tallest building in the Southern Hemisphere when completed in 1986. Larry Adler, another Hungarian migrant who had started the insurance company FAI, was also rising fast, having in a single year managed to triple a fortune now estimated at $100 million.[6]

By the time the 1986 Rich List was published in August of that year, the era of the entrepreneur had well and truly arrived, as had 'the Takeover Revolution'; among the more significant of the mergers at this time was that of the large and venerable Melbourne-based businesses Coles and Myer.[7] The Myer family thereby relinquished control of a retailing empire that had its origins in an emporium established in Bendigo on the eve of federation. But there were large compensations: $72 million in cash and 40 million shares in Coles Myer, as well as two seats on the new company's board, and *BRW* esti mated the family's wealth at $330 million. Another fabulously rich Melbourne clan, the Murdochs, were also flourishing in the bull market, with an approximate wealth of $700 million on the back of a massive increase in the price of their News Corporation's shares.[8] Rupert himself had, however, disappeared from the Rich List to become a citizen of 'the richest, most free and happiest country in the world' – as he called the United States.[9] US law prevented foreigners from taking up more than 20 per cent of a broadcasting licence and Murdoch wanted to buy a suite of American television stations. In a ten-minute citizenship ceremony in New York City in September 1985, he 'absolutely and entirely' renounced 'all allegiance and fidelity to any foreign power, potentate, state or sovereign of whom or which' he had 'heretofore been a subject or a citizen'. The foreign power in question was Australia, the sovereign Queen Elizabeth II. But put this way, Murdoch was surrendering very little: he was in all but name already a potentate in his own right, a 'Multinational Man ... by choice, a man without a country'. The judge who administered the oath of allegiance told Murdoch and the other 185 aliens in the ceremony that they now had the same rights as every other citizen of the United States; if they had something to say, he added – possibly with tongue in cheek – they could write to the newspapers.[10]

While he had given up his right to cast a ballot at Australian elections, Murdoch's wants were rarely permitted to slip from the forefront of political consideration. In 1986 Hawke and Keating consulted their cabinet colleague Gareth Evans on whether he thought Murdoch could legally hold dual citizenship, as he had requested, and which was permitted to Australians provided certain criteria concerning residency could be met. Evans thought not, unless the existing legislation was amended. Unsurprisingly, the matter appears to have been taken no further, for many Australians already believed the government to be working too hard to make life easy for big business, and especially for media bosses such as Murdoch.[11]

★

Hawke, Keating and their closest allies and advisers in the ALP favoured Packer and Murdoch over the two other major media companies, the Herald and Weekly Times (HWT) and Fairfax. The right wing of the NSW Labor Party, which formed Hawke and Keating's power base, was now especially close to Packer. His father, Sir Frank, had been a dogmatic opponent of the Labor Party, but this matey Labor fraternity and the macho, sports-mad, knockabout businessman were simpatico. Some right-wing Labor politicians were infatuated with those who had enjoyed material success, and they relished the generous hospitality Packer laid on for them. Packer, for his part, enjoyed exposure to successful politicians who understood the media and would be willing to do him a good turn when the need or opportunity arose.

If Hawke and Keating had a less warm personal relationship with Murdoch than with Packer, they nonetheless hoped that any favours in their power to give would be returned in kind. All remembered the mess he had made of Whitlam in 1975, and they were aware of his partisanship in favour of Thatcher and Reagan. Hawke and Keating's loathing for HWT, which Murdoch had in his sights, was predictable, since it had never been a friend of the Labor Party. But their hatred of Fairfax had different roots. It too had once been a formidable opponent of the party, but its journalists' attitude was generally favourable to the key policies of the Hawke government. Hawke and Keating's antagonism to Fairfax had more to do with recent exposés and investigations, which all too frequently seemed to be concerned with Labor luminaries or businessmen who would increasingly be dubbed Labor 'mates'. Fairfax had published articles alleging improprieties or worse on the part of Hawke's close friends Peter Abeles and Kerry Packer, as well as Keating's friend and fellow antique collector Warren Anderson, a property developer who became caught up in the bottom-of-the-harbour tax controversies of the early 1980s. Fairfax papers had also been responsible for the corruption allegations against Lionel Murphy; in short, the company had allowed its journalists a long leash, and this was offensive to politicians who saw 'the deal' as at the heart of political, as of business, life. In the case of Fairfax, they had no one with whom they could clinch 'the deal' that would ensure their problems went away.[12]

All of these likes and dislikes came powerfully into play when the federal government considered media ownership in the mid-1980s. The issue arose in part out of the manifestly inadequate provision of television services to areas outside the major cities. In the early 1980s, 35 per cent of homes with televisions received only one commercial station and the ABC. The Fraser government's decision in 1979 to invest in a satellite opened up the possibility of better services in the regions, but with the danger of centralising power over programming and eroding local production. However, the two-station rule adopted by the Menzies government still prevailed as general policy: no one could own more than two television stations, with a limit of one in any metropolitan market. An owner with stations in Orange and Cairns reached their limit at the same point as Kerry Packer, with his Channel Nine studios in Sydney and Melbourne. This traditional structure could not sustain an expansion of services. Yet when the federal government considered its options, it was faced with a number of contending interests. The big players in the metropolitan television industry – Packer, Murdoch, Fairfax and HWT – would benefit from being able to establish national networks that could beam programs directly via satellite into the regions. But the result would be the consolidation of their dominance. Newer players wanted to be able to expand in ways that the present two-station agreement made impossible. Meanwhile, existing small regional players worried about surrendering their monopoly in a limited market.[13]

Keating would eventually play the decisive role in providing a solution. Late in 1986, after sometimes bitter internal argument arising from a concern that Hawke and Keating were bending over too far to help Packer and Murdoch, the government announced the new arrangements. In future, a single owner could have as many television stations as they wished – although no more than one in any city or region – so long as they did not exceed a national audience reach of 75 per cent (a figure whittled down to 60 by the time the legislation was eventually passed). Alternatively, a company could own newspapers – but it could not own both a television station and a newspaper in the same market. Keating memorably warned that you could be 'queen of the screen' or 'prince of print' but not both. Yet what the government spun as an even-handed policy aimed at preventing media concentration was really nothing of the kind. Not only would it place control of Australian television in fewer hands, it was also highly suited to the government's favourite media moguls. Packer did especially well out of it, for he was primarily in television. His print media interests were concentrated in magazines, which were excluded from the cross-media laws. Murdoch was a little more awkwardly placed, since he retained a 15 per cent share in Network Ten. But he was likely to have to relinquish it in any case, since foreigners were not permitted to own more than 5 per cent of an Australian television station. The effect of the new laws was not merely to minimise harm to the favoured ones, however. The ability to create a national network greatly increased the likely sale value of Murdoch's and Packer's TV assets; it was estimated that the government's decision had put a billion dollars in their pockets. And it was clear to everyone concerned that Packer and Murdoch had also been informed well in advance about what the government was up to, whereas HWT and Fairfax seemed rather in the dark. Murdoch, in fact, launched a successful $1.8 million bid for HWT a week after the new media laws were announced, fighting off a rival bidder, Holmes à Court, and buying out the share raider Ron Brierley.[14] When added to his existing holdings centred on the *Australian*, his new print acquisitions would deliver about 60 per cent of the audience for daily newspapers in Australia. None of the other great takeovers of the 1980s would have such lasting consequences.[15]

*

The new laws combined with the takeover revolution and then, from October 1987, with more turbulent market conditions, after which some media companies went into receivership. The troubled Network Ten – controlled for a brief period by Frank Lowy's Westfield, primarily a developer of shopping malls – looked for a time as though it might not survive at all. One of the key players in the media pass-the-parcel of the late 1980s was Christopher Skase, who in 1987 bought Channel Seven in Sydney and Melbourne from Fairfax.

Of the new breed of entrepreneurs, Skase, a former financial journalist, was perhaps the most dazzling. Not for him the manufacture of steel or the processing of poultry, nor even the brewing of beer. Skase's fare was more glamorous – jewellery retailing, electronic media, resort development. His name and image were tied irrevocably to the luxurious Sheraton Mirage resorts that his Qintex group was building in Hawaii, on the Gold Coast and, most spectacularly, at Port Douglas in northern Queensland, where the buildings seemed to float on top of magnificent saltwater lagoons.[16] His opulent Brisbane office, built in 1986 and paved in 'vivid blue and white quartz', was described by one architect as a 'post-modernist Roman bathhouse', the stone having been 'mined in Brazil, polished in Italy and imported especially for Qintex'. The reception area included a waterfall and an assortment of antiquities including an Egyptian mask said to be over 3000 years old, a Greek vase and 'the marble torso of a muscular, Roman warrior', perched 'on a slab of dark blue sandstone quartz'.[17] Skase seemed to be placing his own empire in a distinguished lineage. He appeared in the Rich List for only the first time in 1986, with an estimated net worth of $35 million, but a year later his wealth was said to have doubled. More significant was his personal control of a company which by 1987 had assets approaching $1 billion, but, alarmingly, debt of over $500 million and shareholder equity of less than $400 million.[18] The spectacular expansion of Qintex was built on Skase's hard work, his bankers' generosity and the public boosting offered by admiring business reporters in awe of the rapid rise of one of their own.

Skase had begun his career in the early 1970s, first as an employee of Melbourne stockbroking firm J.B. Were, then as a financial journalist with the *Sun* and the *Australian Financial Review*. His corporate empire he built entirely from scratch. But Skase was unpopular with the Melbourne business establishment, which some blamed for the scuttlebutt that he was gay. Or perhaps it was the other way around, and the rumours of homosexuality contributed to his unpopularity. In the macho world of Australian business, that the handsome, olive-skinned Skase had been in an early and short-lived marriage, later wed an older woman, produced no children of his own and took a little care over his appearance combined to produce the only possible conclusion.[19] Skase certainly resented the Melbourne establishment, which might help explain why he moved to Brisbane in the mid-1980s, where he took up residence in a massive, new $4 million home overlooking the Brisbane River, built inside a compound created by the purchase and demolition of two historic homes. As at Qintex's offices in Creek Street, there was much exotic fare; the Roman theme was continued, with 'a life-size marble statue of Julius Caesar'.[20]

With his lively wife, Pixie, Skase threw the very best parties. At the 1984 Christmas party in Melbourne, scantily clad 'rein-dears' – said to be models – handed out presents to guests.[21] In 1985, having moved north, Skase chartered a plane to bring his Melbourne friends up to Brisbane for the Qintex annual Christmas gathering. When they arrived twenty-seven white limousines were waiting to take them to their hotel. The marquee on the banks of the Brisbane River was 'a wonderland of fairy lights' hosting fifty white snowmen decorated with silver and gold ribbons, as well as 450 guests who partied until dawn. Premier Bjelke-Petersen, fresh from an assault on striking electricity workers, was there to enjoy the hospitality.[22] By the time of the 1986 party the Skase guest list had grown to 540 and the gathering was held in the Brisbane Sheraton ballroom. Skase walked in accompanied by smoke and ticker tape. As in 1985, the Krug – champagne that usually sold for over $100 a bottle – flowed freely.[23] The Skases were the business world's glamour couple, Skase himself the epitome of the new entrepreneurs with his private jet, luxury yacht and homes around the world. And in 1987 he was not yet even forty.

★

Alan Bond, valued at $25 million when he appeared in the 1983 Rich List soon after his America's Cup success, was said to be worth $200 million in 1986 and $400 million in 1987.[24] While his reputation for financial brinksmanship remained, he had also taken on good businesses – especially in brewing – that seemed to provide his empire with an unaccustomed solidity. In 1985 he made a successful $1.2 billion bid for Castlemaine Tooheys, to add to his Swan brewery. It was widely believed that one could not go broke selling beer to Australians – but Bond was already a man famous for flouting received wisdom. In any case, the Castlemaine Tooheys deal ran into immediate problems because Bond's debt refinancing, a condition of the deal, was based on a plan to evict the publicans who held the leases on hotels owned by the brewer. The hotels were then to be sold to generate cash to help finance his acquisition of the company.

Here, the best-laid plans of the America's Cup hero ran into the quicksands of local custom and loyalty. It had long been taken for granted that the signing of a lease in New South Wales gave a publican security of tenure and that the lease's value was based, in part, on a component called 'goodwill'; that is, an intangible quality that was the true worth of the business. Goodwill included the loyalty that a publican built up with customers; it was value not found in bricks and mortar but which had a real price attached to it when a business was transferred to someone else. In the case of the Tooheys hotels in question, the total goodwill was estimated as being worth $30–40 million, and hotel lessees had sometimes paid $500,000 or more for a single pub. If Bond threw the 130 publicans out of their hotels without recognising the value of this goodwill, they each stood to lose a vast sum.

Some lessees received eviction notices but refused to move, resisting the effort to strip them of their property. Others would eventually be robbed of the value they had built up in their businesses. The publicans established a $2 million fighting fund and, not for the first or last time, Bond appeared to be something other than a popular hero when his business ambitions were thwarted. Reg Lynch, a battling Sydney publican and family man who had made a success of his Pymble hotel and feared that Bond was about to take it, killed himself by suffocation with a bag. His distraught wife remarked of Tooheys before the Bond takeover: 'If you had any problems, there was always someone you could ring who would help you out. It was like being part of one big family.' Here was a common refrain of the mid-1980s: of a society in which the bonds of custom and mutuality were being destroyed by greed and individualism. Eventually, in August 1987, the NSW Supreme Court ruled that the publicans could be evicted only if they were paid compensation for the goodwill in their businesses. But Bond still managed to cheat some of them, and he welched on a deal that they would be turned out only in the event of misbehaviour or if they fell behind with their rental payments.[25]

In 1987 Bond bought Channel Nine from Kerry Packer for over a billion dollars, a deal that was part of the increasingly frantic trade in media assets. It was even more foolish on Bond's part than indicated by the massive price tag. While he had to hand over $800 million to Packer, the deal also left the happy vendor with $200 million in preference shares in Bond Media and another $50 million in options. If Bond was unable to redeem the preference shares with cash on 31 March 1991, Packer would be able to take back his television stations. In the meantime, Packer was receiving $12 million a year of Bond Media's profits.[26] When the dust settled on the 1980s boom, this deal came to be seen as perhaps the decade's grandest folly, with only 'Young' Warwick Fairfax's attempt to take control of the Fairfax media empire providing serious competition.

★

When the *BRW* Rich List announced Australia's first two billionaires in 1987, it unsurprisingly included the cashed-up Packer, along with Robert Holmes à Court: the 'patrician and the punter', as Les Carlyon dubbed them. '[I]t was the age of the entrepreneur, just as surely as 1847 was the age of the squatter,' he declared.[27] 'Only the 1851 gold rush could rival 1987,' added *BRW* business editor Robert Gottliebsen, grasping for another historical comparison.[28] But there were really no comparisons that quite worked. Mergers and acquisitions alone accounted for over $11 billion in 1987; Australia had never seen anything like it.[29] Yet while recognising that 'eventually the stockmarket will take a tumble', Gottliebsen was optimistic: not only had unprecedented wealth been created, the foundations of even greater wealth were being laid.[30] That the entrepreneurs' castles had been built of sand seemed to elude even the most experienced business journalists.[31] As on the occasion of every previous boom, there was something deeply alluring in the idea that this one was different from all the others.[32] A recognition that 'many of the new men were essentially traders, buying other people's assets rather than creating new ones' was leavened by the 'aggregations of substance' that they had supposedly assembled.[33]

The boom, however, was in its essentials a familiar enough beast, being fuelled by sharply rising prices – especially of shares, which quadrupled in value between 1983 and 1987 – combined with the banks' willingness to risk large sums of money. The tax deductibility of interest payments encouraged a preference for taking out loans over issuing shares. Higher share prices and increased company valuations stimulated by takeover activity could then be used as security against the next loan, much as rising land values had fuelled Melbourne's famous boom of a century before.[34] But interest rates remained high and climbed further in response to the plunging dollar in 1986, while profits were often too low to absorb the obligations incurred through massive borrowing and capital issues. Asset sales were one way of dealing with the problem of a lack of cash, a solution that sometimes motivated more borrowing for the sake of acquiring more cash and assets buried in takeover targets. These could be deployed to deal with problems elsewhere in one's sprawling empire. Within groups such as Bond and Qintex, assets and money were shuffled among companies in ways that obscured the financial situation of any particular part. Meanwhile, armies of lawyers and accountants advised on how these businessmen could organise their affairs so as to pay tax of five and ten cents in the dollar – as Ron Brierley's Industrial Equity Limited (IEL) and John Elliott's Elders IXL did respectively in 1986 – rather than the official company rate of 49 per cent.[35] The ease with which money could be taken out of the country encouraged the use of tax havens such as Liechtenstein, a Bond favourite, or the Bahamas, Packer's refuge of choice.

Above all, there was naïve optimism that values would keep climbing, even if subject to the occasional market 'correction'. Financial deregulation was a contributor to this dangerous cycle because corporate regulation largely failed during the 1980s. New government agencies such as the National Companies and Securities Commission and the National Crime Authority were ill-equipped to deal with the scale and complexity of the transactions that became standard fare. Entrepreneurs maintained teams of professionals who were skilled in finding legal loopholes, creative accounting and opinion-shopping among auditors, who mysteriously failed to report adversely on companies teetering on the brink of collapse. The knack of burying inconvenient detail in company annual reports advanced in leaps and bounds. The most successful Australian novelists of the period, such as Thomas Keneally and Peter Carey, had talented rivals in the corporate world in the art of imaginative fiction.

Deregulation had increased the international mobility of capital and the competition among banks for local business, providing borrowers with considerable market power. That was one of its aims. The result, however, was not lower interest rates and easier credit for enterprising small and medium-sized businesses, but a scramble among the banks for market share. The interest rate for housing loans, for instance, was 15.5 per cent in 1986–87. Such rates were in part the result of inflation which, although lower than in the 1970s, never dropped below 7 per cent after 1984 and in 1986–87 climbed above 9 per cent – at a time when US inflation rates bobbed around between 2 and 5 per cent.[36] Inflationary expectations encouraged businesses to borrow heavily, since the value of both the principal and interest payments would decline with rising prices. Profit margins on such lending were slim, which encouraged high levels of risk-taking among financiers sometimes inclined to equate caution with a deficiency of masculinity.[37] All of the chatter concerning a new and softer masculinity engendered by feminism seemed rather irrelevant when one contemplated the world of big business, since each corporate boss had a team of executives – almost exclusively male – who resembled nothing so much as a football team preparing for a big game. The media responded by reporting business affairs as if they were indeed sporting contests.[38]

The greatest of them in the 1980s was between John Elliott and Robert Holmes à Court over control of BHP, Australia's largest company. It would have been hard to conjure two men less alike. The chain-smoking, football-loving Elliott's public persona was that of the rugged Aussie bloke without polish or pretension, one with the tastes and manner of an ordinary working man.[39] 'In an era when males are tending to become effeminate, he is the opposite end of the graph,' wrote journalist Keith Dunstan in 1985.[40] A comedy program that used rubber dolls to satirise Australian public life presented a beer-swilling, fag-smoking Elliott, whose nose resembled more an elephant's trunk than the admittedly ample version on his face. The Elliott doll's verbal signature was to exclaim 'pig's arse!' often backed by a thunderous belch. But in important ways Elliott epitomised a new breed of Australian businessman. A scion of the Melbourne middle class rather than the establishment – to put him through a private school, his parents ran a milk bar on top of his father's day job as a public relations man – Elliott was among the first to complete a Master of Business Administration (MBA) at Melbourne University. From there, he went to work for the consulting firm McKinsey, including eighteen months in its Chicago office, returning to Australia determined to apply American management know-how to the local scene.[41]

Elliott was a planner, a businessman who believed that a gut instinct and dogged determination were of no use without a clear strategy and a talented team of executives. Having set his sights in the early 1970s on an old and underperforming Tasmanian jam company, Henry Jones IXL, Elliott gained the critical backing of powerful members of the Melbourne business establishment for a takeover bid. Sir Ian McLennan, the chairman of BHP, was a supporter, as was Sidney Baillieu Myer, of the namesake retailing firm, and Roderick Carnegie, Elliott's boss at McKinsey and later managing director and chairman of the giant mining company Conzinc Riotinto of Australia. Elliott assembled a team of smart young men who, from their modest offices in South Yarra near the old IXL Jam Factory – redeveloped as a collection of posh shops and boutiques – went on to take over the old SA pastoral company Elder Smith Goldsbrough Mort in 1981. McLennan, at seventy-two, emerged from retirement to become chairman of the company being run by his forty-year-old protégé, identifying the company more closely than ever with the Melbourne business establishment. The spectacular acquisition of Carlton and United Breweries (CUB) for almost $1 billion followed two years later.[42]

Elliott's move on CUB, coming at it did in the very week the Australian dollar was floated, might be construed as cutting the ribbon on the age of the 1980s entrepreneur. The chain of events was triggered by another takeover specialist, Ron Brierley, who had built up a stake in CUB, to which its board and chairman, 71-year-old Sir Edward Cohen, responded with something less than a vigorous defence. Elders IXL was already effectively a subsidiary of CUB, which owned just under half the company, so Elliott was deeply interested in any attempt by an outsider to accumulate a large parcel of CUB stock. Cohen dithered over legal technicalities; Elliott and his advisers, by way of contrast, had a contingency plan for just this kind of eventuality. Having decided that only a full takeover of CUB would work financially for Elders IXL, the nimble Elliott raised the $700 million cash he needed from three foreign banks in just a couple of days, thereby incidentally contributing to the federal government's decision to float the dollar. *BRW* declared the rapid-fire Elders takeover of CUB a 'victory for the smart, fast-moving, MBA-style business breed over the entrenched traditionalist'.[43] CUB's board would not be the last to find itself unable to withstand the pressures of the new kind of corporate life that emerged in the 1980s.[44]

By early 1984 Elliott led one of Australia's largest and most successful companies. He was powerful and well-paid but not personally wealthy by the standards of the era's really big men, since he owned only a modest stake in the company he led.[45] He was also unusual among the major entrepreneurs of the period in wearing his political allegiances on his sleeve, eventually becoming federal president of the Liberal Party in 1987 after an earlier stint as treasurer.[46] His supporters in the Liberal Party talked of him as 'the rich man's Bob Hawke'[47] – to which an obvious retort might have been that Bob Hawke was the rich man's Bob Hawke – and he had publicly expressed political ambitions as early as 1973.[48] As the Liberals floundered under the leadership of Andrew Peacock following the 1983 election, and again under Howard after the 1987 defeat, Elliott emerged as one possible answer to their problems.[49] The talk about a transfer to politics continued through the 1980s, a further destabilising factor for the party, as if it did not already have enough to contend with. Yet Elliott often gave the impression that he regarded the current crop of politicians – on both sides – as a collection of mediocrities, and that all the country really needed was to hand over the reins to a successful businessman – that is, to someone just like him. He repeatedly revealed an absence of political finesse, publicly criticised the policies and leadership of his own party, and made a habit of impugning the very vocation that he claimed to be interested in practising. His policy ideas were also frequently impractical, while his understanding of history, to which he made frequent allusion, was embarrassingly shallow. Churchill and Thatcher were his heroes: John Dorman Elliott would, like them, save his ailing country from the squabbling, weak-kneed bunglers.[50]

Holmes à Court cut a very different kind of figure: aristocratic in bearing, prone to long and seemingly thoughtful silences, carefully chewing over his words, dry in wit, polished in manners, refined in taste. Distantly related to Lord Heytesbury, a nineteenth-century British politician and diplomat, Holmes à Court called his private company Heytesbury Securities and used the family insignia as his own.[51] He had garages full of classic cars and studs of valuable Thoroughbreds, but did not bet. And when his horse, Black Knight, won the 1984 Melbourne Cup, Holmes à Court was a long way from Flemington, tucked up in his bed asleep in London where he was doing business.

While he was not given to advertising his political allegiances, his wife Janet was left-wing and his own loathing of racism as a young man appears to have been one of the reasons he decided to live in Australia rather than Rhodesia or South Africa. The financial journalist David Uren noted that Holmes à Court 'never indulged in the union-bashing oratory or monetarist pontificating common among his peers in the business world'.[52] When unions worried about a possible threat to the Button steel plan expressed opposition to his bid for BHP, he had little difficulty reassuring them that they had no cause for alarm, and he similarly managed to charm powerful members of the Hawke government.[53] All the same, Gareth Evans, federal minister for resources and energy, confessed in his diary in March 1986 after a dinner at his place for the Holmes à Courts that he was becoming irritated with the entrepreneur's 'absolutely unashamed arrogance – if that's the right word: maybe it's better to say "supreme self-confidence"'. Yet Evans remained impressed with 'the sheer class of the man ... which is manifestly in a category above and beyond any of his competitors, and light years beyond that which BHP itself can muster'.[54]

Holmes à Court launched his first bid for BHP in 1983 using a tractor distribution company called Wigmores. Few took the bid seriously and Holmes à Court was able to acquire only a small number of shares. A second attempt in 1984 was a more serious proposition: this time he built up a 4.5 per cent stake. His masterstroke, however, was to enter into an options agreement with another aggressive share raider, John Spalvins of Adsteam, which in essence allowed Holmes à Court to continue secretly building his stake through Spalvins while BHP thought he was actually offloading its shares. In October 1985 it came to light that Holmes à Court owned an alarming 11 per cent of the company.[55]

With a share-market value by 1986 of around $10 billion, and more than 60,000 employees and 180,000 shareholders – many of them in for the long haul – BHP would be a glittering prize for any entrepreneur with the wit, resources and luck to gain control of it. When the social researcher Hugh Mackay investigated Australia's attitudes to big business in 1985, he found that BHP had 'a special status in that many people appear to feel themselves qualified to comment' on its performance and management. He attributed this specialness to BHP's dominant position and corporate advertising in which it had deliberately placed itself in a close relationship with the community, with the result that the community felt that it had a right to criticise as well as to praise.[56] BHP mattered to government for these kinds of reasons, for its role as a major producer of what had become the country's most lucrative export commodity, coal, as well as for the $3.4 billion in tax, royalties and levies it delivered every year.[57]

The Hawke government did flirt with the idea of a national-interest test in connection with Holmes à Court's ambitions. BHP, for its part, wanted the government to use a *Trade Practices Act* provision prohibiting the transfer of monopolies to block him. In early March 1986, Hawke government ministers heard each side in the struggle make its pitch, BHP executives first, led by their managing director Brian Loton, and then the lone figure of Holmes à Court addressing them the following day. When Keating told Loton that they would also be seeing Holmes à Court, the BHP man replied: 'I know, Paul, I've got to tell you he's fantastic; you know he's his own financial adviser, his own lawyer, his own analyst and his own operator. He's phenomenal.' Holmes à Court did not disappoint, easily outshining the BHP team. Cabinet, after reassurance from Keating, rejected the idea of interfering in the matter. When Stewart West, the only minister to put up any resistance, predicted 'a great unity ticket in Caucus against the Cabinet's proposal', Keating replied: 'It won't be the first time that Caucus has leapt to the defence of the Melbourne Club.'[58]

Keating and almost everyone in cabinet had again signalled sympathy with the risk-takers against the establishment. The free market and the national interest were now one, so far as big takeover bids were concerned – and this idea would increasingly overtake the government's attitude to the economy as a whole. While attracting much less attention than the decision to float the dollar, the government's hands-off approach to the struggle for BHP was hardly less significant. The reasoning was simple, and based on the very same assumption as the decision to float: the market knew best. If the financiers were prepared to bankroll a bidder, and a company's shareholders were willing to sell at the price being offered, that provided the most rigorous national-interest test available. As a critic of the government, Brian Toohey, put it in 1987: 'The market is always right. It commands respect, because, behind its apparent volatility, it makes impersonal, objective judgments ... What would have been dismissed a few years ago by Labor advisers as an ideology of unswerving self-interest is now accepted as "market sentiment" faithfully reflecting some undefined, but greatly revered "fundamentals".' Here was indeed a new way of thinking, especially for Labor; to question the market was now to risk being 'branded a fossil from the Whitlam era'.[59] But this economic rationalism also hitched the government to a wagon that would provide a wild ride in the years ahead.

Markets, as Toohey suggested, were not impersonal things. They were made of people, and the Melbourne establishment showed that it was still capable of closing ranks against a raider from the west. When Holmes à Court looked likely to take control of BHP unless a third player intervened decisively – and it was clear it would not be the federal government – Elliott was able to repay some old debts to the Melbourne establishment that had long backed him, while using the threat to strengthen the company he led. In January 1986 Holmes à Court announced a bid of $1.295 billion that would have given him 39 per cent of BHP: given the spread of small shareholders, quite sufficient to control it. Talks between Elliott and BHP about defensive action began; Elliott saw BHP as a potential backer of the international expansion of his brewing interests, and he did not want the company to fall into the hands of an interloper. But there was no agreement between the two companies about how to deal with the threat from Holmes à Court, and BHP looked like it might suffer the same fate at his hands as CUB had suffered at Elliott's.[60]

Elliott decided to take action without BHP knowledge or cooperation, in the hope of getting the Big Australian to the negotiating table. Elders would acquire just under 20 per cent of BHP. Ideally, that would force the company into a billion-dollar investment in Elders IXL, in a defensive cross-shareholding arrangement. On 10 April 1986, having lined up a couple of billion dollars from bankers, stockbrokers operating for Elders were offering to buy BHP shares for seventy-two cents more than the closing price of the previous day. There was much excited speculation that Elliott was behind the $10 million per minute splurge on the Melbourne Stock Exchange, and just before two o'clock he called BHP's Brian Loton to confirm the rumours.

After more buying on overseas exchanges overnight and in Melbourne the following day, Elders had a stake of almost 19 per cent of BHP, close to the maximum permitted without announcing a formal takeover bid.[61]

It had been a frenzied day of trading, the boom's emblematic moment. BHP responded quickly by taking out a $1 billion shareholding in Elders IXL, a prudent measure since anyone who now gained control of Elders would, as a result, also win a large stake in BHP. But Elliott did not enjoy negotiating with his rival Holmes à Court. They met over two-and-a-half hours on the Saturday morning following the Elders raid, each refusing to sell his stake to the other. Holmes à Court offered to take over Elders on terms he thought might be attractive to Elliott: 'We'd get control and you'd get to be Prime Minister.' There were, as was common in negotiations with Holmes à Court, long periods of silence. Elliott recalled: 'We spent a lot of time just looking out of the window, which pissed me off because I was anxious to get away to the footy.'[62] By the end of May Holmes à Court would own about 28 per cent of BHP's shares – not enough to control the company, but too many for him to be ignored indefinitely.[63] Both Elliott and Holmes à Court would be appointed to the BHP board in a peace deal agreed later in 1986, although no one imagined that either of these ferociously competitive men could remain content with this arrangement for very long.

*

Elliott was at the centre of the other great battle of the era: that between CUB and Bond for beer sales at home and abroad. With its ambition to 'Fosterise the World', CUB would do for beer what McDonald's had done for hamburgers and Colonel Sanders for fried chicken – but not if Bond had anything to do with it. Bond, like Elliott, was determined to increase his sales in the British and US markets with his Swan Premium Lager and Castlemaine XXXX. The companies controlled by Elliott and Bond both launched aggressive overseas advertising campaigns, with Paul Hogan featuring in Foster's commercials and Bond's using images of matey outback types; nobody's stereotype of Australia was too radically challenged. But closer to home, the battle was even more intense. Beer-drinking was one of several popular Australian activities in which regional and state loyalties were resilient. In this field, as in so many others, entrepreneurs believed they could remake the culture; by creating a national market for their wares, they would complete the nation-building that federation-era politicians had begun in the 1890s. By 1986, after his group acquired Castlemaine Tooheys in 'the largest takeover in Australian corporate history', Bond controlled almost half the Australian beer market, with his strength being in Western Australia, Queensland and New South Wales.[64] CUB, which controlled much of the remainder, had its heartland in Victoria, but it had taken over Tooths and so, like Bond, had a foothold in the Sydney market. Sydney became the key battleground; the intensity of this struggle gained something from beer's declining sales in the face of the challenge offered by wine.[65]

Advertising executives, like producers of armaments in wartime, rubbed their hands with glee at the lucrative accounts gained from these battles. Swan was marketed through a series of advertisements designed by the firm Mojo, famous for its ocker ads and catchy jingles. The Swan commercials featured various well-known Australians accompanied by a song containing the refrain, 'They said you'd never make it.' Drinking Swan was for those who did things the hard way but finally 'came through' – just in time to celebrate their success with a long, cold beer. But the results of all this activity must have been disappointing to the Perth entrepreneur, for drinkers remained notably loyal to their favourite brands. Queensland drinkers and publicans proved especially resistant to an interloper from the west – and Bond's beers even lost market share.[66] CUB, meanwhile, put the Foster's label on the country's great sporting events, including the Victorian Football League (VFL) grand final, the Adelaide Formula One Grand Prix and the Melbourne Cup. Elliott cut a dashing figure chatting with Princess Diana in the official party in 1985. He had apparently made it – and without the assistance of Swan Lager.

★

These businessmen could not have plied their trade without willing bankers, and of the major trading banks, Westpac – formed by a merger of the Bank of New South Wales and the Commercial Bank of Australia in 1982 – was the most 'willing', handing over vast sums to some of the nation's most reckless buccaneers.[67] Banks now sometimes found themselves lending hundreds of millions to an entrepreneur aiming to take over the business of one of their longstanding customers: Westpac lent money to Holmes à Court in his quest to acquire BHP, which had itself previously used Westpac as its banker.[68] The practice of stitching together loan finance from a variety of sources, at home and abroad, also made the calculation of risk on the part of the lender more difficult than ever. Westpac, for instance, handed over large sums to George Herscu for his madcap American adventures. Herscu's 1985 takeover of Hooker Corporation, Australia's second-largest property company, was the prelude to an ambitious course of speculative investment in Australia and especially the United States that eventually destroyed the company and sent Herscu bankrupt. When the company collapsed, its debts to about seventy-five banks amounted to $2 billion; Westpac alone was down $200 million. But Herscu's disastrous shopping mall projects in the United States reflected the extravagance of his personal taste. The lavish opening of the massive Forest Fair mall outside Cincinnati in March 1989 was attended by 70,000 people, with Herscu's favourite singer, Marie Osmond, providing the entertainment. A band played 'Tie Me Kangaroo Down, Sport'. George Herscu, too, was in his own way taking Australia to the world.[69]

ANZ, which had lost its exclusive status as the Fairfax banker in 1983, may well have provided the 26-year-old business novice Warwick Fairfax with a vast loan as a way of restoring its standing with the great company. It is otherwise difficult to explain the bank's apparent madness in funding the young man's takeover of the family business. Warwick, fresh from Oxford, Harvard Business School, the Chase Manhattan Bank and the *Los Angeles Times*, was determined to take control of a company he believed to be his rightful inheritance. Sir Warwick, his father, had died earlier in 1987 and Young Warwick's shy older half-brother James had for a decade been a fine chairman of the board.

Young Warwick's interests, according to his mother, Lady Mary, were Jesus and journalism; he had a close relationship with a number of other earnest young Christians whom he had met at Oxford.[70] His head full of the latest business management theories, Warwick had quietly devised a scheme to seize control of the company in collaboration with his mother and a coterie of public relations men, advisers to the family and plausible deal-makers – the most plausible of them all being the WA banker Laurie Connell, who was promised an astronomical fee of $100 million in return for his dubious services. Even as originally devised, the deal was risky, since it assumed that members of the Fairfax family with shares in the company would hold on to them and willingly accept Warwick's control. Instead, they sold their shares at the high price being offered through the bid, which meant Warwick needed additional finance to buy them out. Meanwhile, even before the takeover was accomplished, the stock market collapsed in October 1987, slashing share prices across the board, but Warwick persisted in the bid, therefore paying pre-collapse prices. ANZ eventually lent him $2 billion. Those who sold their Fairfax shares made a killing in a depressed market, and Warwick had to start selling off assets in the very same depressed market to refinance the bid. Young merchant bankers getting their start such as Malcolm Turnbull hovered around the dying elephant, collecting millions of dollars in fees as they helped it over this or that hump by locating emergency finance.[71]

Australia's oldest and greatest media company spent the early 1990s in receivership, a century and a half of Fairfax family control coming to an end. While the poor judgment of Warwick and his mother was primarily responsible, without the acquisitive takeover culture of the 1980s, and without a lender such as ANZ being willing to hand over such a vast sum, Warwick may well have been content to join his friends on a Christian commune and live off the dividends from his shareholding. At the very least, he might have spent a decade learning a little about the family business; the chairmanship of the company was likely to have eventually fallen to him given the structure of the family's share ownership. A joke that did the rounds asked: how do you create a small business in Australia? Answer: you give a large business to Warwick Fairfax.

Fairfax was perhaps the most prominent example of an 'establishment' business destroyed in the new economic climate of the 1980s, although it was not unique in this respect. Adsteam – the venerable Adelaide Steamship Company, established in 1875 – which was run by a Latvian migrant named John Spalvins, experienced a period of massive expansion in the 1980s before falling apart in the wake of the 1987 stock-market crash. Spalvins, who had married into the Adelaide establishment, borrowed heavily in building up a company that included such businesses as Woolworths and David Jones as well as large shareholdings in the trading banks. The various entities in the Adsteam group were buying shares from one another, pushing up the share price, paying each other dividends recorded as profits, and then borrowing heavily on the increased paper value of the stock. Spalvins's gambling on the options market against Holmes à Court also led to huge losses, contributing to the eventual collapse of his group.[72]

While the big banks were more than pleased to compete for the business of corporate adventurers of this kind so long as the boom lasted, at the riskier edges of the financial market there were the cowboys such as Connell – called 'Last Resort Laurie' on account of his reputation for lending money to unfortunates refused by everyone else – and the Melbourne merchant bank Tricontinental's brash young chief, Ian Johns. Owned but not controlled by the State Bank of Victoria, Trico deliberately courted riskier lenders on a course of rapid growth. Its stated assets grew by 101 per cent in the year to 1986 and a further 32 per cent to 1987, by which time they stood at $2.6 billion, making it officially the country's largest merchant bank. Trico's apparent success won for Ian Johns the Young Businessman of the Year Award in 1986. One of the award's judges was Christopher Skase, a favourite client.[73]

*

The blinking computer screens in bank offices across the country hinted at a mathematical sophistication in assessing risk; the reality was very different. Banks lent millions of dollars to a non-government organisation in Victoria, the National Safety Council (NSCV), on the security of empty crates that its chief had managed to persuade bankers were full of expensive equipment. The NSCV, founded in 1927 to promote road and industrial safety, was led by a shadowy figure who called himself John Friedrich. He later turned out to be an illegal immigrant named Friedrich Johann Hohenberger, who had arrived by plane in January 1975 after faking his death when caught embezzling from his employer in his native West Germany. After spending time working in Aboriginal communities, Friedrich applied successfully for a position with the NSCV. He quickly rose through the organisation to become its chief in 1982. His salary eventually climbed to $130,000, although he lived a modest lifestyle with his Australian wife and children on a property near the NSCV's base at Sale in Gippsland.[74]

Friedrich, described later as 'an affable, motivated workaholic', was able to transform his sleepy outfit into a sophisticated search-and-rescue organisation by fraudulently borrowing hundreds of millions of dollars and eliciting the assistance of a few friendly businesses that helped him cook the books.[75] His frauds were intended to build up the NSCV and so feed his narcissism; they were not for his personal financial benefit.[76] Partly organised on paramilitary lines, the NSCV at the time of its collapse in 1989 had assets including a fleet of 22 helicopters, 10 fixed-wing planes, a 42-metre flagship, a midget submarine, search and rescue boats, a vast array of vehicles, decompression chambers, computer equipment, an infra-red scanner and much else that was shiny, flashy and expensive. Pigeons were being prepared for search-and-rescue missions, dogs to be parachuted with their handlers into remote areas to look for missing people. Friedrich enjoyed surrounding himself with fit young men – some of whom he rewarded with expensive cars – and he was especially proud of the elite para-rescue group, or PJs (parachute jumpers), as they were known. The NSCV's macho image was cultivated partly for the consumption of suggestible bankers, but after the collapse, rumours abounded, predictably, that Friedrich was homosexual and, equally predictably, that the organisation was a CIA front. The NSCV did have prestigious clients such as the defence forces, and it would not be surprising if one of the Australian intelligence services had at some time called on its vast expertise and expensive equipment. Charles Blunt, the federal National Party leader, wrote to Friedrich to compliment him on 'a true example of private enterprise in action' – as it unquestionably was.[77] Meanwhile, its staff had grown from 100 in 1984 to 450 in 1989. When the organisation finally collapsed, these people lost their jobs, in a regional centre on the cusp of a recession.

Friedrich's own memoir is often unreliable, but his account of the manner in which bankers pushed money on the NSCV has about it a ring of authenticity: '[We] never once had to approach anyone to ask for money. They came to us every time and asked us if we wanted money ... They made much more effort to sell their product to us than we did to buy it.' Friedrich used the millions he borrowed as cash flow to keep his organisation running. The NSCV's debts on collapse amounted to $258 million, with the State Bank of Victoria the biggest loser at $103 million. When in March 1989 Friedrich's chairman eventually got around to asking him to explain some financial anomalies in the accounts, Friedrich disappeared, becoming the target of a police manhunt that attracted frenzied media attention. There were reported sightings in the most unlikely of places, but after a couple of weeks the police picked up the fraudster near Perth. Friedrich committed suicide by shooting himself in the head near his home in 1991, shortly before he was due to stand trial for his misdeeds. After his death, it was discovered that he had been perpetrating another fraud while on bail.[78]

The scandal at the NSCV was bound up with the influence exercised by a charismatic and driven man, who was notably successful in persuading others to trust in his ability and integrity. Friedrich resented comparisons with the likes of Bond and Skase, but there were nonetheless resemblances between the NSCV's collapse and other corporate disasters of the era. They too were based on the power that could be wielded by a strong, well-connected and often charismatic chief. And just as the distinction between gambling on horses and gambling on the stock market could be obscure to the uninitiated, so the line between the conman and the merely persuasive entrepreneur usually seemed clearer before, than after, corporate collapse. Everyone could agree, for instance, that the handsome Gold Coast entrepreneur Peter Foster was a conman because he had attempted to fix a boxing match, sold 'slimming tea' and somehow managed to instal himself as the boyfriend of Britain's most famous 'page-three girl', Samantha Fox.[79] But Kerry Packer also became involved in a madcap scheme with some of his shadier mates to market an elixir of youth. Drug lords, too, were obviously crooks, although it was considered likely that several of them, such as Griffith-based Mafia boss Robert Trimbole and the 'colourful Sydney identity' Abe Saffron, would have qualified for the *BRW* Rich List if the scale of their riches were public knowledge.[80]

In Friedrich's case, the accumulation of support from bankers, politicians, police, public servants, military officers, his own staff and Gippsland worthies protected him from serious scrutiny until there was substantial evidence of suspicious behaviour. Similarly, it was a major coup for Skase when his already tottering empire gained the usually cautious Australian Mutual Provident (AMP), with its vast superannuation funds, as an investor in 1988. Anyone inclined to ask difficult questions about Skase or Qintex was likely to be discouraged by the fact that he so obviously had the confidence of a major Australian company, formed in 1849, which had been sufficiently careful with its shareholders' money to avoid Bond, Bell and Hooker.[81] Yet it was one of the features of the 1980s boom that those institutions – often in life insurance or superannuation – which had traditionally provided share registers with their stability, were now more willing to shop around for places to invest the $80 billion or so that this industry controlled.[82]

AMP also invested in Westmex, a company run by another and even younger entrepreneur, Russell Goward. The curly-haired and cherub-faced Goward was a bonsai graft of Skase and Bond; in his person he embodied almost every cliché imaginable about Australian 1980s entrepreneurs in their purest form.[83] Goward grew up in Brisbane and Canberra, where he claimed to have known poverty – but this appears to have been part of the personal myth he built around his 'rags to riches' story for the consumption of suggestible financial reporters and investors. After leaving school as a teenager, he worked at the National Library and in Treasury before taking up a position with the merchant bank Hill Samuel, which would later become Macquarie. He then went on to work at Ron Brierley's IEL, where he was appointed chief executive before the age of thirty. Brierley appeared to be grooming him for succession but that was not how things worked out. The two fell out – probably over a disastrous exercise in property development for which Goward was held responsible.[84]

In 1986 he bought a 'cashbox' oil and gas exploration company called Westmex for $2.4 million and set out on a buying spree in Australia and Britain. 'I always borrowed as much as I could,' he later explained. 'Contrary to the thinking of my parents' generation, whose ethos was to buy their house and spend the rest of their lives paying it off, I've always believed that if you've got the right investment philosophy you can make a lot of money on banks' money.'[85] And having applied this 'investment philosophy', Goward turned Westmex into Australia's largest wholesaler of stationery, as well as a major retailer of shoes in the United Kingdom. His acquisitions appeared to have neither rhyme nor reason, but he made a virtue of buying unglamorous companies producing essential goods. By late 1989 Goward's personal wealth was estimated at $50–55 million, while his company's value was around $580 million. But its accounts were so remote from reality that Westmex gave rise to one of the very few occasions during the 1980s when an auditor of a major company felt compelled to resign in protest. Nonetheless, the media were mesmerised. Goward's mansion had a miniature rainforest complete with 200,000 specially bred earthworms; there was a $350,000 Bentley in the garage; he had even hired a jumbo jet to fly deer from New Zealand to his farm, north of Sydney. Goward commuted between Sydney and London, leaving his wife and three children in their Wahroonga mansion, and his mistress – who happened to be his wife's sister – in another mansion just up the street.[86]

Goward claimed to spend most Sundays with his family: '[b]ut as soon as there is a quiet moment, my mind slips back to making money.' 'Hobbies that don't make money', he explained, were 'a waste of time'. His was studying the lives of self-made businessmen.[87] But despite this improving reading, an economics degree and part of a law degree, he later tried to persuade a court that he did not understand the distinction between 'debits' and 'credits'.[88] By early 1990 Goward's business was in receivership with $100 million in debts in Australia, and another $160 million in Britain. It turned out that Goward's 'personal' belongings were in most cases owned by the companies he controlled, but his personal debt was still $36 million, and in early 1991 he entered into voluntary bankruptcy. Goward's marriage had broken up in 1989. His assets – the mansions, the Bentley, the deer farm – were sold to pay his creditors, who received about one-tenth of their money back, but despite his ordeals Goward still seemed able to live comfortably with his new eighteen-year-old wife. His bankruptcy was extended on the grounds that he appeared to have assets, and possibly an offshore company, that he had not declared. Goward, his gorgeous curly locks long gone and his beatific looks faded, would spend the late 1990s in prison. But the thousands of shareholders who lost everything – many of them 'mum and dad' investors attracted to the whiz-kid image in the media and its popularity among stockbrokers – are unlikely to have gained much satisfaction from this inglorious end.[89]

In the decades after the Second World War, some sociologists considered that business would in future be run by anonymous managers, ownership was becoming irrelevant and the age of the robber baron was over. The highly personalised business world of Australia in the 1980s largely confounded such predictions, with the most prominent entrepreneurs conforming to familiar stock types, as in a bout of professional wrestling. Rupert Murdoch was the ruthless genius, Kerry Packer the gambling plutocrat with an instinctive sense of the common man's tastes because he so largely shared them. Alan Bond was the cheeky larrikin, the Pommy migrant who had made good and stuck it up the Yanks. His mate Laurie Connell was the wily, shady dealmaker with the impeccable political connections and a strong liking for the horses. But Robert Holmes à Court was presented in a very different vein: the enigmatic genius with the mysterious African past, the elegant man of culture more interested in the game itself than the vast riches that came from his skilful playing of it. His rival for control of BHP, John Elliott, was the rugged, football-loving, beer-drinking Aussie bloke; soaked in a wash of Foster's, it was easy to overlook the university qualifications, the years as a consultant at McKinsey. Ron Brierley, a New Zealander based in Sydney, was the cricket-loving, stamp-collecting and chess-playing bachelor who shunned the glitter associated with the era's high-flying businessmen and made his millions while everyone else was too busy to notice what he was up to. Warwick Fairfax, having lost the media empire controlled by his family for a century and a half, was presented as the nerd, possibly a religious nut, and eventually the idiot son. Christopher Skase was the glamorous whiz-kid, the driven workaholic, and Goward the same but in miniature.

Through media representation of this kind, a world that was strange to people who could not tell the difference between a share option and a bond issue was subjected to the familiar disciplines of character and plot. Hugh Mackay commented that in business as in politics, people yearned 'for "stars", for leaders, and even for larrikins', welcoming 'the cockiness of an Alan Bond, the suave success of a Holmes à Court or the cheek of a Murdoch'. But this was decidedly a spectator sport, not one in which most Australians felt able to participate themselves. 'I don't know the first thing about trading on the stock market, but you get really involved when you hear about some of these mergers and takeovers,' remarked one of Mackay's informants. Another wondered whether he might be able to get in on the action: 'Can ordinary blokes like us buy shares in some of these big outfits like Coles and Woolies and Ansett and everything? Or would they just laugh at you?'[90]

*

Scott Whybin was twenty-seven as the 1980s boom reached its climax. A Newcastle boy, he had already enjoyed a highly successful career in advertising, working in Sydney, London, Melbourne and San Francisco. His career plan was to have his own agency by the time he reached thirty, and to retire at thirty-five. 'I do worry sometimes about losing touch with reality,' he told the author Anne Coombs:

> because of the amount of money I earn. When I go back to Newcastle it's like coming up for fresh air, but it's difficult ... how do I tell my mates, some of whom are mechanics and the like, about what I do, about what I earn? Well, I just don't ... I don't tell my family what I earn anymore either. They're proud of me, but they can't comprehend it ... You get to the point where you go into a shop and see a jacket with a price tag of a couple of grand on it, and you walk out with it.

Whybin had worked on his agency's Swan Lager advertisements; in this manner, Bond's riches, taken largely from his bankers' vaults, flowed down through Whybin's employer, Mojo-MDA, to support the young man's impulse buying.[91] The very wealthy – men like Bond – rushed around the world on private jets, holidayed on luxury yachts and mixed with the global super-rich with whom they increasingly did their business. But as vast riches washed through the top end of town, they also flowed in mere millions and hundreds of thousands to the ranks of the sharebrokers, lawyers, accountants, merchant bankers, foreign-exchange dealers – and to admen.

Those who sold expensive real estate, antiques, clothing or luxury cars added thousands of newly rich to their familiar clients. By 1987 Australia was said to have 30,000 millionaires and 6600 multimillionaires, as well as the two men with a billion-plus each, Packer and Holmes à Court.[92] The flamboyant display of wealth followed new money even more readily than it had the old. The rich built imposing and luxurious mansions, or renovated old ones, with columns, arches, marble and high ceilings providing the setting for heavy furnishings and fabrics. A tennis court and a swimming pool were essential, a water view nearly so. Marble and oak at home became both a means of displaying success and perhaps a form of psychological compensation for the houses of cards being built in the nation's boardrooms. Laurie Connell was in the process of building a $30 million home when his particular house of cards, Rothwells, collapsed. He had spent $8 million buying and then demolishing seven homes along the Swan River to achieve his heart's desire.[93]

The rich filled their homes with expensive things, both old and new. One enterprising Brisbane couple took advantage of the Bjelke-Petersen government's habit of allowing the demolition of historic buildings in the name of progress to build up a magnificent collection of materials from wreckers' sites, which they then used to create their luxurious home. In the years leading up to the Bicentenary, Australiana – such as silver-mounted emu eggs – became increasingly popular among the rich. As the driven and ambitious in politics and business did their best to destroy the old Australia, they also seemed to place 'a greater value on things past ... reminders of the good old days'. Australian art did well, as did Australian wines, but champagne had to be French.[94] The most expensive and therefore most desirable art was also to be acquired abroad. Alan Bond's purchase of Vincent Van Gogh's *Irises* in November 1987 for almost US$54 million was then a record, but in accord with the general pattern of his activities, Sotheby's, the auction house, had lent him half the purchase money. After Bond's success in the America's Cup, ocean-going yachts also became popular among the very wealthy, who were able to reproduce in miniature on deck the structures of authority to which they were accustomed in the boardroom. Those they hired to do the skilled or hard work of sailing their yachts were known, respectively, as 'jockeys' and, astoundingly, 'niggers'.[95] Real jockeys were needed for those partial to Thoroughbred racing, another favourite hobby. Connell was reputedly the largest racehorse owner in the country with 400 Thoroughbreds, thereby providing one piece of the puzzle concerning what happened to the hundreds of millions of dollars that disappeared into his failed businesses.[96] George Herscu, whose pleasure in the conspicuous display of his riches matched Connell's, owned Hyperno, which won the Melbourne Cup in 1979. Herscu lived in a grand Toorak mansion in Melbourne, modelled on 'Tara' in *Gone With the Wind*. His instructions to the builder had been to give him two of everything, including indoor and outdoor jacuzzis. At his son's 1985 wedding the 650 guests were able to enjoy the seven-tiered wedding cake.[97]

Marriages and other festive occasions among Australia's super-rich during the 1980s were important for the display of wealth, because they were bound to attract considerable publicity. The 1985 wedding of Alan Bond's daughter Susanne reputedly cost $400,000, involving the restoration of a Fremantle church and the erection of a dance floor on the Swan River. Gretel Packer's twenty-first birthday in 1987 caused her father to dip into his small change to the tune of $200,000, a sum unlikely to worry a man capable of betting – and losing – several million dollars on a bad day in a casino or at the track.[98]

Some businessmen, including Bond and Packer, kept mistresses. Each summer during the 1980s, Packer paid to have a couple of houses in Palm Beach, north of Sydney, filled with French champagne, food, flowers, furniture, art – and high-class prostitutes, the latter brought in from overseas as one might import any other luxury item but without the expense of customs duties. Packer in this manner rewarded some of those in business and politics who had helped him become one of Australia's richest men.[99]

Australia's rich ate in the best restaurants, such as Chez Oz in Sydney. Perth's Mediterranean, half-owned by Laurie Connell, became a famous venue for the deal-making of that city's new rich; diners there were known to make their way through four cases of Dom Pérignon in a day. Restaurateurs were reporting by 1986 that the fringe benefits tax had reduced lunchtime trade but not evening dining, where the well-heeled expected to enjoy their meals with silver, not stainless steel.[100]

If fine dining was too effete, rich men could turn their attention to football, where they could both shape and share the triumphs of the fit lads with whom they gained the right to fraternise through their wealth and connections. In Victoria, John Elliott was president of the glamorous Carlton Football Club, trucking magnate Lindsay Fox was in charge of the battling St Kilda, and Budget hire-car boss Bob Ansett was the North Melbourne chief. These men often sought to import the very same methods they used in their business dealings to football administration, a field that they believed had too long been the preserve of the worthy former players whose skill with a leather ball was not matched by business nous. The 1980s became a critical period in the transformation of the main football codes, Australian Rules and Rugby League, into big businesses organised to tap into national markets.

Played mainly in New South Wales and Queensland, Rugby League was by the early 1980s in a state of crisis. Several clubs were heavily in debt and in danger of collapse. The NSW League suspended for the 1984 season one financially troubled club, Newtown – it would never reappear in the big league – and tried unsuccessfully to get rid of another, Wests. The competition had by this time expanded beyond Sydney, taking on teams from Canberra and the Illawarra in 1982, and then further 'franchises' – as they were becoming known – from Newcastle, Brisbane and the Gold Coast in 1988. In the following year, the Canberra Raiders became the first of these new teams to win a premiership. By this time, the competition was in better financial shape and from 1989 it conducted a highly successful advertising campaign that drew on the talents of the American singer Tina Turner. A further boon for League was the newly minted tradition of State of Origin football, which began in 1980. Within a few years, the annual series of matches between New South Wales and Queensland – in which players represented the state from which they came rather than where they presently lived – was attracting huge interest, attendances and TV audiences. That the first decade of the competition was dominated by the less populous and more parochial of the two states, Queensland, did much to stoke interest.[101]

Australian Rules – like Rugby League, a game traditionally rooted in local loyalties and an intense emotional attachment to one's club – became similarly swept up in the new corporate spirit.[102] Yet probably half of the Victorian Football League (VFL)'s clubs were on the brink of insolvency in the early 1980s as a result of rising player payments, transfer fees and poor management.[103] In 1984 Elliott led an initiative to form a breakaway league; one result of this secession threat was a change in the VFL's governance and a renewed drive to corporatise the sport.[104] There were strong pressures to close grounds and merge clubs, or move them interstate to tap into new 'markets'. Fitzroy – rather like Newtown, a team based on an old but now gentrifying inner suburb – enjoyed fair success on the field in the mid-1980s but only narrowly averted an attempt to move it to Brisbane in 1986 (a move that would eventually be forced in 1996).

Such efforts cut across a resilient culture in which team loyalties were inherited like genes. Efforts to merge clubs or move teams elsewhere in Australia provoked lively grassroots resistance on the part of supporters for whom the Saturday afternoon ritual was a link not only with a loved place – the home ground – but also a connection to a way of life pursued by their parents and grandparents before them. The defiant and successful movement in late 1989 to save the struggling western suburban Footscray from a merger with Fitzroy drew on loyalties to class, club and community, a sense that others looked down on the western suburbs, a feeling that malign forces were trying to destroy something precious and loved. The campaign also attracted supporters of other teams fed up with the corporatisation of their game. Car stickers that declared 'Up Yours Oakley' – naming the VFL's chief, Ross Oakley – turned up on cars all over the city, while Footscray's Vietnamese traders were among those who offered financial and moral support. 'I guess some of their kids'll be playing for us one day,' remarked one middle-aged woman during a celebration of the victory.[105] For those who fought to save Footscray, one of the problems was the VFL's obsession with creating a national league, one that would extend the code – or 'product' – to Sydney and Brisbane as well as encompassing the major football-playing states of South Australia and Western Australia. By 1991 what was now called the Australian Football League (AFL) included clubs from all five mainland states.

It also looked for a time as if rich men would become not merely the presidents, but also the owners, of Australian professional football teams. The major experiment of this kind involved the Sydney Swans, a club which emerged from the relocation of the unsuccessful South Melbourne team in 1981. The effort to place the Swans on a secure financial base and promote the game to a Sydney audience flushed out a 'medical entrepreneur', Dr Geoffrey Edelsten, then unfamiliar to most members of the public but better known to the Australian Tax Office. Since graduating in medicine from Melbourne University, Edelsten had enjoyed a colourful if rather chequered career as a medico, businessman and playboy. He had produced pop records, owned a nightclub, established his own flying doctor service, run health studios, set up a high-tech pathology laboratory in the United States, and offered a Family Health Plan in Sydney – which looked to police rather like a medical insurance business, minus the licence required for operating one. He had even sponsored the Bluebirds – a troupe of dancing girls whose presence at Carlton home games was intended to add an American-style razzmatazz and sexiness.

By the mid-1980s his hair was grey but he was nonetheless still skilful in attracting female talent – he had married a professional model, Leanne, more than twenty years his junior. By this time Edelsten was best known for operating a chain of Sydney surgeries that, in their decor and design, had more in common with brothels than most people's image of a humble general practitioner's rooms. But then Edelsten was no humble general practitioner, even if all his patients needed to do to enjoy the luxurious facilities provided by 'the Hugh Hefner of medicine' was to flash their green and gold Medicare card.[106] 'His surgeries are decked out in gold, with salmon pink velvet couches, enormous chandeliers and mink-covered examination tables,' reported one journalist. 'Gold-clad hostesses and a small robot offer refreshments and educational advice to patients, who are told that if they wait more than 10 minutes to be attended to they are entitled to a free Instant Lottery ticket.'[107] The surgeries also came with white baby-grand pianos; a pianist was sometimes paid to entertain patients while they waited.[108] The glitz of the surgeries matched that of the Edelstens' private lives. There was the $6 million home in Dural and luxury cars with numberplates that said 'Macho', 'Spunky' and 'Groovy'. And there were the gifts to Leanne, which supposedly included a pink helicopter – that it was pink Edelsten always denied, but many people swear that they saw it – and 'a $100,000 pink Italian sports car lined with white mink'.[109]

In late July 1985 the VFL agreed to award the licence for the Swans to Edelsten in preference to the bid of another businessman, Basil Sellers, one 'of much more conservative bearing'.[110] The league needed to get the Swans noticed in a tough market, and Edelsten appeared to be just the kind of showman capable of helping it out. Indeed, the syndicate to which he belonged played up the glamour as a means of distinguishing itself from the other bidders.[111] It promoted the Edelstens as embodying Sydney's colour, playfulness and hedonism in contrast with the sober restraint of Melbourne. Edelsten exuded flamboyance, wealth and success, and Leanne – present when her husband learned that his Swans bid had been successful and wearing 'a sequined white jumper, red leather pants and wetlook white thigh-length boots' – was central to his image. Media reports said the price was $6.3 million, a figure that casual observers assumed had been carved out of a much greater fortune, but it soon became clear that the deal was a rather more tangled one.[112] Edelsten eventually handed over about $3 million, mainly other people's money.[113] It looked increasingly as if Edelsten was really a frontman for other interests, but there was no denying his ability to attract notice.[114] He was helped by a spectacular, long-maned, blond full-forward named Warwick Capper, who wore striking white boots and shorts even tighter and more revealing than the usual skimpy kind. He, too, briefly became an image of Sydney spunkiness and flamboyance.

Edelsten's association with the Swans gave his surgeries publicity that allowed him to evade the prohibition on doctors advertising their services, but it was the doctor's business interests outside football that caused him problems soon after the award of the licence. A Labor senator, George Georges, alleged under parliamentary privilege that Edelsten was the 'Dr X' named in a parliamentary committee report as being investigated for medical fraud.[115] Edelsten took out a full-page advertisement in the *Sydney Morning Herald* declaring his innocence. An exposé of Edelsten's business methods in the satirical magazine *Matilda*, which imputed various forms of lurid criminality, added further damage and provoked a lawsuit.[116] Worse followed: Edelsten soon stood accused of having hired the notorious hit man Christopher Dale Flannery to assault a patient who had given him trouble.[117] He had already stood aside as Swans chairman but still had a long way to fall. Edelsten subsequently became bankrupt, divorced, was struck off the medical register and sent to prison.[118] And as the 1980s passed into mythology, his and Leanne's lifestyle was seen to epitomise the era's excesses.[119]

This AFL experiment with private ownership was short-lived, being abandoned in 1993, but the corporatisation of the sport was relentless. The conflict between old and new came to a head in the 1986 grand final, played between Carlton and Hawthorn. While both teams were successful and well-managed, Carlton's reputation under Elliott was that of a wealthy, prestigious and blue-blooded club; Hawthorn cultivated a reputation as family-minded, homespun and old-fashioned. The Carlton stereotype had recently received powerful reinforcement through the expensive recruitment of several high-profile players from other clubs in Victoria and interstate, and football writers promoted the match as a clash of cultures in which the soul of football – or perhaps something even greater – was at stake. The press noted that Carlton had a $50,000 celebration – or wake – planned at the plush Southern Cross Hotel, whereas Hawthorn's would cost just $15,000.[120]

Hawthorn was already dominant at half-time, when the entertainment included children unfurling an enormous banner that had an Australian flag on one side and a Foster's logo on the other.[121] After Hawthorn ran out easy seven-goal winners, one commentator registered a 'feeling among more disenchanted football fans that the game is fast becoming a glorified commercial for Foster's Lager', while another managed to discern in Hawthorn's victory the lesson that 'breweries are more readily obtainable than premierships and that Carlton doesn't own football'. The Hawthorn president, Ron Cook, made the victory sound like a factory Christmas bonus: 'Today was a reward for the workers at the club.' 'In a humble club like Hawthorn,' he claimed, 'you make it, not buy it.' This was quite disingenuous – Hawthorn bought players like everyone else and, no less than Carlton, was being reshaped by the game's commercialisation. Carlton in any case turned the tables in the following year's grand final, played between the same teams.[122]

By the mid-1980s, there was a strong sense of an old order passing. 'It's all about big business and big money,' complained one commentator, 'and very little to do with the bloke in the outer.' A perceptive observer of the 1986 grand final also noticed that the old post-match tradition of players from opposing teams swapping their jumpers as an expression of good sportsmanship was almost dead; only one pair did so. On the other hand, Prime Minister Hawke was loudly booed at the presentation ceremony, as if he embodied much that was wrong with the game and the nation, as well as with the wider world that was doing so much to reshape the destinies of each.[123]

*

Alan Bond was full of bright ideas about how the Hawke government could help him keep the America's Cup. It could buy *Australia II* – which it did; it could permit tax-deductible donations – which it didn't; it could run a lottery – an activity which, being a money-spinner for state governments, it could not countenance.[124] But when it finally came time to defend the cup, Bond had fallen by the wayside, defeated for the right to defend it by a rival WA syndicate headed by businessman Kevin Parry. There was a lot of money in Perth in the mid-1980s: Parry had reputedly plunged $28 million into the effort, which had seen his *Kookaburra III* outshine Bond's *Australia IV*. But Parry lacked Bond's personal magic; reflecting on the response of the crowd in Fremantle, one commentator thought *Kookaburra*'s victory 'had as much emotion and excitement to it as a day at the Colosseum without the lions or the Christians'.[125] Nor was Bond gracious in defeat. '[W]e won it for Australia,' he declared in a post-race speech, 'now don't you lose it ... if Kevin doesn't defend it, we'll go and get it back for him.' Parry was furious, and he made his feelings known in an angry rejoinder. But the same front page of the *West Australian* that reported these exchanges also carried the story that Bond had bought Channel Nine from Kerry Packer. He was already moving on.[126]

It is not quite true to say that anyone who was anyone found themselves in Fremantle in the summer of 1986–87 – that final golden time before the stock-market collapse changed everything for Australia's super-rich. There was minor royalty, the occasional international celebrity, foreign businessmen by the score, and Australian VIPs such as Joh Bjelke-Petersen – who explained that he had come for the *Melbourne* Cup – were at '10 cents a dozen'. Rumours abounded of celebrity sightings: Joan Collins, Sylvester

Stallone, Jacqueline Onassis, her former brother-in-law Ted Kennedy. None showed; nor did anyone claim to have seen Elvis. But thousands of tourists descended on Perth and Fremantle and, according to one estimate, 500 prostitutes accompanied them in the expectation of an increased demand. Luxury yachts and charter boats crowded the harbour. The Burke government hired a luxury launch, at a cost of $300,000, to entertain VIPs; even the premier conceded that John Curtin was probably turning in his grave.[127]

The Americans won the series 4–0. A banner welcomed the victorious US skipper back to shore: 'Well done Dennis, you bastard!'[128] But even before Dennis Conner's decisive victory over the Australians, Alan Bond – the hero of Newport – had announced that for the 1990 cup he would be throwing his weight behind a syndicate being organised by a Japanese billionaire. He was disarmingly frank in explaining why: 'Our sponsorship of the syndicate will greatly assist our brewing and other business aspirations in Japan.'[129]

6
Taking Credit

Imagine working in a factory. That would be hell.
RUSSELL GOWARD, SYDNEY MORNING HERALD, 3 MAY 1986

Science fiction is often set in a distant time and place. It is a measure of the rapid, unsettling and, to many observers, disturbing nature of the changes sweeping over Australia in the 1980s that George Turner, the country's most successful science fiction writer, set much of his international hit *The Sea and Summer* (1987) in Melbourne only about sixty years into the future.

Turner's was a dystopian vision: a city blighted by global warming, unemployment and overpopulation, and divided socially, culturally and physically into a tiny elite of Haves – known as 'Sweets' – and the overwhelming majority of Have-nots, or the 'Swill'. The two classes – each instantly recognisable through dress, speech and smell – hold each other in mutual contempt. The Swill live in 'the towers', a group of massive derelict high-rise apartments, each housing 70,000 or so people stuffed into cramped and filthy rooms, the upper levels no longer serviced by lifts – the government having realised long ago that it could save a packet by simply leaving them broken – the lower floors subject to regular flooding, the result of the rising sea levels associated with the greenhouse effect, the 1980s term for global warming.

Corruption is rife and society consumed by fear. The Sweet especially fear the Swill: they fear that the squalor, violence and disorder of the towers might consume the whole city; they fear losing the privileges of Sweet life, and so having to move into the towers or, at best, into the Fringe – a grubby liminal zone inhabited by the downwardly mobile who have not quite fallen all the way. But the Swill do not pose a revolutionary threat; they are preoccupied with the daily struggle for survival and are controlled by the tower bosses, who cooperate with the police and the army to ensure that the ailing society does not collapse entirely.

Turner's message was that governments were busy 'preserving and continuing their own power' while the dangers of overpopulation, starvation, unemployment, financial collapse and environmental catastrophe loomed.[1] The novel was deeply coloured by the present: a mid-1980s economy which delivered great privileges to a few and uncertainty to many, while unemployment and poverty continued for a large minority. Melbourne of the 1980s had real towers – its high-rise Housing Commission flats – so obviously the model for the much larger, more hopeless examples in *The Sea and Summer*. In 1984 residents of the North Richmond high-rise estate staged a rent strike to persuade the state government to improve the security of their building. In the previous three years, the estate of 6000 people had seen three murders, twenty-five assaults and many more violent incidents. Over seven weeks, striking residents paid their rent to the Tenants' Council rather than the government, which was losing $55,000 a week while the action continued. Seventy per cent of residents participated; the strike ended only after the government agreed to spend $950,000 on better security.[2]

The decay of traditional manufacturing undermined the material well-being and security of people such as these. Manufacturing employment dropped in absolute numbers as well as relative to the overall workforce in the decade between 1974 and 1984, and it contributed little to employment growth during the 1980s. In 1984–85, 1,023,000 men and women were employed in manufacturing, which had only increased to 1,064,000 by 1987–88. Nonetheless, as a share of exports, manufacturing increased from under 19 per cent in the period 1984–86 to over a quarter by the end of the 1980s, assisted by the lower value of the dollar.[3] And although it came down from around 10 per cent in 1982–83, unemployment remained high. The official figure was around 8 per cent or more until the end of the decade, when it briefly dropped to about 6 per cent. For the young, the unemployment rate was higher – about a third of all unemployed were teenagers in the mid-1980s – but it was older workers who were likely to experience the most difficulty finding a new job once they became unemployed. In 1987 the average period out of work for an unemployed person between the ages of thirty-four and fifty-four was well over a year – sixty-two weeks – and the median duration about six months. While there were some improvements after the 1982–83 recession, structural changes that included the decline of manufacturing and agricultural work ensured that long-term unemployment remained a serious problem across all age groups.[4]

For many young people, being on the dole was accepted as a way of life and resented for the stigma attached to it, as well as the limits it imposed on one's choices, pleasures and opportunities. The unemployment benefit – at about $50 a week in the mid-1980s – could underwrite a fairly bare existence punctuated by the occasional treat if you were able to find a large share house to live in. A continuing high rate of unemployment made it a little easier for those without a job to rationalise life on the dole. As one young women explained, 'There's no reason why everyone in Australia shouldn't work if they want to, but I don't think you should have to. I think it's really good if people enjoy being on the dole; then other people who are unemployed and looking for a job should thank those people.'[5] Many young people turned to friends for short-term credit or a meal, or they approached a charity for help.[6] Life – even one's mood – revolved around dole day, which at least opened up the possibility of temporary pleasure and freedom – perhaps a 'rage' at the pub, or a new item of clothing – and a little relief from anxiety about debt.[7] The unemployed complained of being bored and depressed. Many coped by relying on soft drugs. As one young Perth woman said in 1985, 'Life's fun when you're stoned ... you go out to the kitchen and get a packet of Sao crackers and vegemite, and you all have a feast ... [Pot] was a saviour when I was unemployed.'[8]

Above all, unemployed people resented being looked down on by those with jobs and especially by the officials they had to deal with: 'they're fakes, they're frauds, they try to be up here, and they try to put you down there.'[9] The dole bludger stigma, which gathered powerful momentum in the 1970s, might have intensified during the 1980s given the greater premium of money and success. One young unemployed Perth man was unimpressed by Alan Bond: 'We're all expected to think that this guy is so great because he's rich ... our whole lives are based around materialistic values. You know, you've got to get more, you've got to have a house, a boat, a car to be successful. You've got to go out and make money ... that makes not having a job and not living that way, so much worse.'[10]

Even for many of those in employment, money remained a constant worry. 'Sometimes I go to sleep at night just wishing that I could wake up in the morning and find that all our money worries had gone away,' commented one informant of social researcher Hugh Mackay in early 1984, 'It'd have to be by winning the lottery, though. There's no other way.'[11] A 1988 survey of 1800 people found that almost 40 per cent of people indicated that at some time in the last year they 'had been unable to make ends meet', while over 10 per cent sometimes went without food and more than a quarter without buying clothes that they needed.[12] Life cycles remained critical. Those with a job yet without dependents usually coped, but once people married and had children, there was often little money to spare – life was arranged around the arrival of the next pay packet, mitigated by the use of credit cards. Once children had reached adulthood and were capable of providing for themselves, there would normally be less financial pressure, although the growing tendency for children to leave home in order to establish their independence – rather than to marry – could be a source of disappointment for some parents, if a relief to others. Yet leaving home was not necessarily a final decision; well over half the men and almost two-thirds of the women who first left to establish their independence would return to live in the family home some time afterwards. For many middle-class Australians, retirement could be a comfortable time, although some complained that they achieved a desirable level of affluence only when it was too late to enjoy it. And when the government in 1985 introduced an assets test for the old-age pension as well as a 30 per cent tax of lump-sum superannuation payouts, some believed that they were being penalised for a life of hard work and self-denial.[13]

In 1985 and 1986, a deterioration in Australia's economy led to cuts in government spending and threatened living standards. The dollar's value dropped by 40 per cent between February 1985 and August 1986, reflecting a decline in the value of Australia's exports. Australians were buying more goods from the rest of the world than they could afford, on the basis of what the country's farmers and miners were selling in the world's markets.[14] The key moment in bringing home this sense of crisis was Paul Keating's 'banana republic' remark – made in a radio interview on 14 May 1986 with veteran Sydney announcer John Laws from a phone in a restaurant kitchen in Melbourne. Alarmed by the announcement the day before of a gap of almost $1.5 billion between export earnings and the value of imports, Keating told Laws that 'we must let Australians know truthfully, honestly, earnestly, just what sort of an international hole Australia is in'. Unless the government could get the country to make the necessary adjustments, Keating warned, 'then Australia is basically done for. We will just end up being a third-rate economy.' The fallback position, if nothing were done, would be 'to slow the growth down to a canter':

KEATING: Once you slow the growth under 3 per cent, unemployment starts to rise again.
LAWS: And then you have really induced a depression.
KEATING: Then you have gone. You are a banana republic.

Seeing selected lines from the interview on their screens when they returned after lunch, foreign-exchange dealers nearly went berserk in their efforts to offload Australian dollars. Never had there been a more vivid illustration of the new entanglement of politics and the market, as 'the herd mentality of the traders' responded to the interview by pushing the Australian dollar down three cents. Yet they were operating on the basis of a misapprehension. Keating was not proclaiming Australia's inevitable decline into a Third World economy, but issuing a warning about 'what would happen if nothing was done'. Michael Stutchbury in the *Australian Financial Review* speculated – with deadly accuracy, as it turned out – that the 'episode could prove a big bonus for Mr Keating in his political campaign for spending cuts'.[15] But that was not how it initially appeared; Keating had been a victim of his own considerable eloquence, of wanting to create a sense of urgency, but not intending to go so far.[16]

The sense of crisis continued into the winter of 1986, culminating in an even more wild ride on the foreign-exchange markets on 28 July – described by Paul Kelly as 'probably the single worst day in the first three terms of the Hawke Government'. The Australian dollar that day fell to 57.10 US cents, breaking what government ministers considered a sixty-cent 'psychological barrier'.[17] With the floating of the dollar, the performance of the currency had become a litmus test for the state of the nation. As the government's Expenditure Review Committee met, Keating had in front of him a portable screen on which he could keep himself – and his colleagues – up-to-date on the state of the currency as they made their decisions about what to cut and by how much for the following month's budget. Peter Walsh, the finance minister and an ERC member, 'was closer to despair than I had been even in 1975. We had not been a bad Government, certainly not by Australian standards, and we did not deserve the catastrophe inflicted on us.' But as Walsh knew only too well, since the float 'Australian standards' no longer counted for a hill of beans. After a break, the ministers went off to speak on the phone to the equally worried Reserve Bank governor, Bob Johnston. In a reminder that a floating dollar did not mean that the bank was prepared to leave the fate of the nation's economy to the tender mercies of young men in Armani suits, the RBA intervened at 12.30 pm by raising short-term interest rates from 14.6 to 16 per cent to steady the currency.[18]

Further developments in Canberra during the afternoon would have reminded dealers of the dangers of gambling in a game in which one of the parties could change the rules at a moment's notice. When the ERC reconvened, it made two decisions. One was to get rid of a tax on 'widely held debentures' – or bonds – 'issued overseas'. These were a popular instrument in corporate takeovers, and the tax had only been reintroduced earlier in the month. The ERC then decided to rewrite the budget so that instead of the $5 billion deficit widely anticipated, there would be no real growth in expenditure.[19] At four o'clock, Keating announced not only the decision to abolish the tax but also a rash of measures that drastically reduced the restrictions on foreign investment in the Australian economy. These had been in the pipeline and Treasury officials had the paperwork ready, but the announcement's timing seemed designed to reassure to the markets.[20]

For the Labor Party, the decision on foreign investment was a turning point. Keating had been a protégé of the party's most celebrated – and reviled – economic nationalist, Rex Connor, the Whitlam government's minister for minerals and energy, whom the *Australian Financial Review*'s Greg Hywood now imagined turning in his grave. Labor's 'sense of tradition and the core of Labor thinking has come under intolerable pressure from economic realities', Hywood added, for the crisis was pitting the government not only against 'the major players in the economy but against its own ranks' conception of what the Labor Party stands for'.[21] But the run on the dollar in July 1986, and the response it had evoked from government, already suggested that Labor's economic nationalism was redundant, its economic rationalism ascendant. Nostalgic appeals to a 'lost' national sovereignty would in future carry little weight in the face of such overwhelming financial power.

*

As the economic crisis of 1986 unfolded, right-wing ideologues immediately reached for their typewriters so as not to miss this once-in-a-lifetime opportunity to sheet home to the public the dismal failure of 'socialism' and the urgent necessity of destroying unions, cutting wages, dismantling industrial arbitration and slashing government spending. An *Australian* editorial warned that it was 'no use attacking the government of the day because we, as a people, have been enjoying the excesses in which we have been indulging'.[22] But in the real world, many Australians might have questioned the proposition that they had been living a life of indulgence. 'The greatest humiliation I ever suffer,' explained one of Mackay's focus-group members when he asked them about the subject of money in 1984, 'is having to ask one of the kids if they can lend me a couple of dollars out of their money box to see me through to the end of the week.'[23]

One factor that allowed many Australians to mask the effect of the wage squeeze on their living standards was the burgeoning dependence on personal credit. While the use of credit cards had become widespread in the 1970s with the development of the popular Bankcard, it was in the following decade that Australians overtook Americans as the largest per capita users of consumer credit.[24] For those surviving from one pay packet to the next, a credit card might also help cover emergencies. 'I completely forgot about new school shoes,' said one informant in 1984. 'Major things like that hit you out of the blue, and that's when you're so grateful for Bankcard. You've still got to pay it off ... but at least you buy some time.' For others living even more precariously, credit cards were crucial to keeping afloat: 'We've gradually got all the credit cards – Bankcard, Diners, American Express, Mastercard. What we do is go to the limit on each one when times are tough, and then gradually pay them off over the maximum period.' And like the entrepreneurs, people were prepared to 'shop around'. Those who had been raised to look on the local bank manager as a man of substance whose opinion mattered now felt that they held the whip hand.[25]

Between 1983 and 1991, the average debt per head in Australia increased from $3191 to $7162, while between 1980 and 1996, average indebtedness soared by over 11 per cent per annum – all at a time when earnings grew by an average of only 5.6 per cent each year. Although most debt arose from housing loans – Australians owed four times as much on their homes in 1991 as in 1980 – the overall increase in other forms of personal debt more than tripled in the same period. By 1988–89 Australian households were spending more than they earned, but the gap between income and spending was increasing fastest among the poorest fifth of households. In 1988–89, they were, on average, spending 80 per cent more than they earned. Unsurprisingly, personal bankruptcy was increasing markedly.[26]

Deregulation of the foreign-exchange market led to unanticipated financial embarrassment for some borrowers. Between 1982 and 1985 lenders persuaded some 3000 to 5000 clients that it would be in their interests to take out loans in a foreign denomination, with Swiss francs often the currency of choice.[27] The attractions were obvious. Late in 1984 Australian

180-day bank bills cost a borrower 12 per cent; their Swiss equivalent, just 5 per cent. At a time when it was widely believed that the Australian dollar would appreciate, few saw any need to hedge their borrowing; indeed, to do so would have negated the advantage of borrowing in a foreign currency. But following the plunge in the dollar in 1985–86, many borrowers found themselves in severe trouble. A Perth hotelier, having taken out a loan for $2 million in 1984, now owed more than $4 million, and many farmers had the banks breathing down their necks. Some lost their properties.[28] Joh Bjelke-Petersen was another to become entangled in Swiss franc borrowing. As would later become a little clearer when the media and a royal commission turned closer attention to his business affairs, these losses probably lent an urgency to Bjelke-Petersen's need to supplement his legitimate earnings with money from other sources – such as a series of large bribes from businessman Sir Leslie Thiess and $400,000 from Alan Bond supposedly in settlement of a libel action.[29]

It was bad enough that the principal owed had blown out so drastically for such borrowers, but the more immediate problem was that interest payments had also doubled, thereby swallowing an increasing volume of their cash flow. In some country towns, a network of 'brokers, accountants and solicitors' had encouraged borrowers to take up Swiss franc loans. The resulting effect on particular regions of defaults was potentially devastating. Banks, in their defence, claimed that clients had been warned about the risks, but many borrowers denied that they had received any such warning. By 1989, 300 had taken legal action but the cost of litigation acted as a strong deterrent.[30]

The idea that there was a personal relationship between customer and bank manager was widely recognised as being in decline. Deregulation upheld a different kind of model, that between 'a vendor and purchaser of a commodity – money', but there was a massive imbalance of knowledge, power and resources between a bank and a small borrower. The belief that banks had a particular duty of social responsibility had not died easily and many borrowers were still inclined to assume that the bank knew what it was doing when it offered a loan, an impression that gained greater weight from new-fangled technology and terminology. In reality, many bank staff lacked even a rudimentary understanding of how the foreign-exchange market worked.[31]

★

A *BRW* report of September 1986 judged that 'Swiss franc borrowing' was 'the final debilitation for many on the land'.[32] By the mid-1980s, the growing atmosphere of crisis was especially evident in the bush. Simmering rural discontent had been behind the formation of the National Farmers' Federation (NFF) in 1979. There followed a dispute with the Australian Workers' Union that began in 1980 and climaxed in 1983-84, over the use of wide combs in shearing which the union opposed – ultimately, in vain. In 1984 Ian McLachlan, an SA grazier from a pastoral family wealthy enough to appear on the *BRW* Rich List, became president of the NFF. A Cambridge graduate and former first-class cricketer, McLachlan was in many respects the unlikely leader of a populist campaign. As a staunch advocate of the free market, he had no truck with the state interventionism – sometimes dubbed 'agrarian socialism' – connected with the old Country Party. Indeed, one expression of the rural revolt of the mid-1980s was dissatisfaction with the established political leadership. At Werris Creek in the New England region of New South Wales, a young farmer named Tony Windsor was the leader of a group of producers who called on National Party leaders to lift their game or else find themselves the targets of preselection challenges for their blue-ribbon seats.[33] Old divisions between large and small farmers, which went back to the days of free selection in the nineteenth century, were behind some of the fissures in rural politics, but the NFF would prove itself remarkably successful in persuading all that they shared a common interest as men and women on the land.

McLachlan's ambitions for the NFF extended beyond farmers; it would stand apart from the consensus and reshape the national economic and industrial agenda in a free trade and free market direction.[34] He was sometimes touted as a future conservative prime minister. McLachlan's ascendancy in rural politics in the mid-1980s signalled his determination to confront both government and unions in the interests of his members. Yet precisely what was in farmers' best interests was no easy matter to discern, for inequalities in rural Australia increased markedly during the 1980s. Taken as a whole, farming seemed in poor shape. Incomes declined by 45 per cent between 1980 and 1987, with thousands of producers barely surviving. In 1985 the average farmer earned around $7000, roughly a third of what his or her wage-earning counterpart could expect. Indeed, many supplemented their inadequate farm income with wage labour; it was joked that a definition of a 'viable farmer' was one married to a teacher or a nurse. The use of new technology and chemicals boosted output and productivity but also flooded the market, raised costs and damaged the environment. In 1985-86, the period when rural militancy exploded, 55 per cent of farmers on family farms growing wheat and other crops, and 30 per cent of all kinds of farmers, spent more on their business than they earned. Farmers, to remain competitive, were forced into relationships of growing dependency on agribusiness, banks and expert advisers. Meanwhile, four out of every ten Australians looking for a job lived outside the major metropolitan areas. Unemployment rates in many rural areas were at Depression-era levels and businesses dependent on farmers' custom were under growing pressure. More stress, family conflict, poor health and suicide were among the progeny of rural poverty.[35]

Yet this was not the whole story, for wealthy farmers and major commercial concerns were still doing well. The average income for woolgrowers in 1986–87, for instance, a time of good prices, was a very healthy $35,600, with the wealthiest 12.5 per cent having incomes of over $83,000. And agribusinesses such as John Spalvins's Adsteam and John Elliott's Elders IXL, which incidentally had Ian McLachlan on its board, were recording healthy profits. It was in this context that the NFF was arguing that lower taxes, free markets and government deregulation would solve farmers' problems. But there was a distinct disinclination on the part of NFF leaders when addressing angry rallies to explain that the logic of the free market was that small and inefficient producers went to the wall while the already successful grew at their expense.[36]

It was a part of the genius of McLachlan and the NFF to draw on Australia's rural myth and the resilient individualism of farming people to persuade them that everyone on the land shared a common interest. The wealthy grazier and Elders board member could join hands with the struggling wheat farmer, for they were really fighting the same battle. During 1984 and the first half of 1985, there were rallies in several regional towns and metropolitan centres. A protest in Melbourne attracted an estimated 30,000 marchers – described as 'lots of men with red, round faces' – who chanted that they wanted a 'fair go' and held signs announcing 'Farmers: The New Poor' afflicted by a disease called 'Agricultural Income Deficiency Syndrome' (AIDS). They ended their protest with 'Waltzing Matilda', a song honouring the exploits of a swagman who stole a sheep from a farmer and then drowned himself to evade capture by the police. Farmers laid blame for the problems of rural Australia at the feet of unions and governments, animal liberationists and greenies. They had little to say about the trade war between the United States and the European Economic Community, or the declining viability of the family farm in an international agricultural system based on ever larger aggregations of land and capital.[37]

Such complexities were similarly absent from discussion outside Canberra's Parliament House on 1 July 1985 when a crowd variously estimated at between 25,000 and 40,000 – said to be the largest ever brought together for a rally in the capital – gathered on the opening day of the national tax summit. McLachlan addressed the assembled farmers in aggressive rhetoric, complaining about the cost of fuel and, like the Melbourne protesters, demanding a 'fair go' for farmers who, he said, were subsidising the rest of Australia to the tune of more than a billion dollars a year. Buckets circulated, and an Australian Farmers' Fighting Fund was launched. The prime minister, one of the likely targets of this fund, was 'greeted with derision' when he addressed the crowd, with one theatrical protester waving a 'huge cow pat in the air whenever Mr Hawke said anything disagreeable'. Some farmers called out, 'We want Joh', but the NFF pointedly refused to allow Bjelke-Petersen or other conservative politicians who were present to speak at the rally. The NFF was asserting its independence, the farmers' determination to help themselves. The *Canberra Times* proclaimed 1 July 1985 'the day when Australia's rural community re-emerged as a crucial political force'. Farmers heralded the arrival of the new year in 1986 by dumping wheat on the steps of Parliament House in Canberra, and at its conference held later in the year, the NFF voted to boycott the paperwork required by the new fringe benefits tax. A $200 million relief package announced in April by the federal primary industries minister, John Kerin, only led to further protests. SA farmers went so far as to picket the homes of state Labor ministers.[38]

*

The NFF argued a free market agenda in which relief for farmers would be paid for by lower tariff protection for manufacturing and lower wages for workers.[39] It had lobbied the government in favour of floating the dollar in 1983.[40] Now, it lobbied for a free labour market, but it also took matters into its own hands. Even today, 'Mudginberri' is a word that evokes feelings of warm nostalgia among Australia's political right. A small and isolated abattoir in the Northern Territory, Mudginberri was owned by Jay Pendarvis, an American who had lived in Australia since 1967, running a business that captured, slaughtered and exported feral buffalo. In this respect and others, Mudginberri was an unusual operation. The dependence on feral animals meant that the supply of stock was unpredictable, and the operation was conducted not under an industrial award but a contract system. Pendarvis would engage a contractor at an agreed seasonal price per carton of meat, and the contractor would then employ the labour required to carry out the work. Pendarvis thereby neatly avoided a direct employment relationship with much of the workforce. The arrangements appear to have been informal and the work practices flexible, to use a euphemism, allowing him to avoid pesky inconveniences like workers' compensation and penalty rates. It suited a certain kind of employee: an individualist determined to make a large sum of money as quickly as possible before leaving the industry.[41]

The prospects for those who intended staying were not so bright, as the meat industry had been in decline since the mid-1970s. Many abattoirs had closed and thousands of workers found themselves without jobs. In these circumstances, the industry's main union had every reason to ensure that work was shared widely while pay rates and working conditions were protected. All the same, it was a conflict-ridden industry in which strikes were frequent.[42]

The powerful Australasian Meat Industry Employees Union (AMIEU) was hostile to the kind of contract labour used at Mudginberri. It favoured a tally system, whereby workers would be paid at a certain rate for an agreed output, at a higher rate for additional production up to a certain maximum, and at a higher rate again for any work over that figure. There were also complex variations on this system for different kinds of tasks. For the union, the system had the advantage of imposing a certain pay rate as well as influencing the size and nature of the workforce required for a job. Importantly, the wage rates were also used to determine conditions for the majority of the workforce – probably about 80 per cent – who did not directly participate in the tally system.[43]

The system had its critics who thought that it undermined output and productivity, but it was not the racket that union-busters claimed. From 1981 the AMIEU sought to extend the Meat Industry Award, which included the tally system, to cover the Northern Territory. Employers opposed this, so the matter had to be dealt with by the Arbitration Commission. In September 1984 the commission indicated that while it would not apply the system, there were other benefits in the award that should be enforced. When the new award was announced in April 1985, it included a clause that effectively allowed workers to agree piece (or result-based) rates with their employer, with or without the involvement of the union. So far as the union was concerned, this permitted employers to make an offer on a take-it-or-leave-it basis, which they suggested was already Pendarvis's practice. Unfortunately for the union, it was unable to get the support of Pendarvis's workers for industrial action and a picket was manned by workers from other abattoirs. It was peaceful and no one was prevented from entering the abattoir, but meat inspectors refused to cross the picket line, with the result that meat could not be exported from Mudginberri. Since the abattoir was primarily an exporter, Pendarvis could not conduct his usual business.[44]

The dispute took on wider significance for three reasons. First, the NFF decided to turn it into a casus belli. It raised a $1.5 million fighting fund, and Mudginberri became the arena on which it chose to extend the rural revolt into the field of industrial relations. Second, Pendarvis and his supporters successfully used the secondary boycott provisions of the *Trade Practices Act* in a damages claim against the union.[45] They could do so because the picketers were not Mudginberri employees, and therefore had no protection under the act. The result was an award to Mudginberri's owner of $1.76 million. Third, on all sides the dispute came to be seen as carrying a wider significance. As the *Australian* commented, 'There are many more Mudginberris in Australia, where, if workers were to get rid of restrictive practices and demarcation rules, they could receive higher rewards and the economy would benefit from the increased efficiency.' The paper even made Pendarvis its Australian of the Year for 1985.[46] When he heard of the award, a worried Pendarvis rang editor Les Hollings, a vociferous supporter of right-wing political causes, to let him know he was an American citizen. Hollings reassured Pendarvis that he did not need to be an Australian to receive the award; he might have added that, as a Murdoch publication, the *Australian* was the very last newspaper in the country likely to object on that score.[47]

Pendarvis was a convenient figurehead for the NFF and its allies, an outback battler supposedly persecuted by a greedy and militant union. He was even mentioned as a possible conservative candidate for the NT seat in the 1987 federal election. But nobody doubted that McLachlan and the NFF's industrial officer, Paul Houlihan, were really running the show and that the show in question was a war on trade union power, not the future of an obscure meat-exporting business.[48] The NFF, the NT government and the Westpac Bank provided the necessary cash to prosecute this campaign. The territory government handed over almost the entire annual budget of its Agricultural Development and Marketing Authority – nearly $1 million – while the bank provided a $2 million line of credit, for which the government went guarantor. Then, in what the bank assured everyone was the purest coincidence, the government shifted its own $1.3 billion account from the Reserve Bank to Westpac.[49]

Pendarvis's health was broken by the dispute, and he had to be talked into continuing the fight on more than one occasion. Eventually, he came to realise that he was being used as 'a tool of the NFF'.[50] In 1988 Mudginberri was closed as a result of a shortage of buffalo induced by the NT government's campaign to reduce brucellosis and tuberculosis, but for the New Right, Pendarvis had served his purpose.[51]

★

The media discovered the New Right in 1986, in the midst of rural revolt, the Banana Republic panic and a series of well-publicised industrial conflicts that signalled a new resolve on the part of some employers.[52] Its emergence cannot have had much to do with actual strike activity, since the number of working days lost through industrial disputes had fallen from 4,192,000 in 1981 to 1,256,000 five years later.[53] Rather, the New Right's emergence represented a revolt against the consensus politics of the Hawke government. Business organisation was fragmented in the mid-1980s – a disunity skilfully fostered by Hawke almost from the moment he came to office – and there was nothing even approaching agreement about the best way of organising industrial relations.[54] The New Right focused attention on the damage wrought by excessive government regulation and tariff protection but most of all by union power and the arbitration system. For eighty years, they said, Australia had been penalising its highly efficient export industries – pastoralism, agriculture and mining – to prop up the manufacturing industry and urban wages. Two articles in the right-wing magazine *Quadrant* early in the Hawke years crystallised attitudes. The first was by a middle-ranking public servant in the Department of Employment and Industrial Relations, Gerard Henderson, who had earlier been on the staff of Bob Santamaria's right-wing Catholic National Civic Council (NCC). Henderson produced an article in September 1983 called 'The Industrial Relations Club', in which he presented Australian industrial relations as fundamentally an exercise in mutual back-scratching. A coterie of Melbourne-based commissioners, union leaders, business representatives, industrial lawyers and public servants operated 'in a club-like atmosphere' surrounded by 'an ethos of complacency and self-congratulation' in which economic realities took second place to deal-making.[55] A second contribution to *Quadrant* in October 1984 came from the Treasury secretary, John Stone. Stone had already announced his intention of resigning from the public service when he delivered '1929 and All That' as the Edward Shann Memorial Lecture at the University of Western Australia.[56] Now, he was launching a career as a right-wing activist. Like Henderson, he had the wages system in his sights – 'a crime against society' – but Stone developed a more ambitious argument that 'the spirit of enterprise is shackled and weighed down by the dead hands of governments'. He appealed to the spirit of achievement represented by Gallipoli, Kokoda, Douglas Mawson, Charles Kingsford Smith, Howard Florey – and Geoffrey Blainey.[57]

Stone and Henderson had one thing in common, apart from their right-wing politics. As civil servants, neither had themselves been much subjected to the rigours of the market. Indeed, it was a feature of the New Right revolt that it tended to bring together aspiring politicians, political staffers, speech-writers, academics, public servants, consultants, lawyers, journalists and industrial relations practitioners. People risking their own money were not only inconspicuous, they were frequently berated as being part of the problem on account of their cosy deals with government and unions. Yet it was critical to the New Right's campaign to reshape Australian public policy that conventional ways of thinking about both the resolution of industrial conflict and the public service needed to be discredited. Industrial arbitration had to be stripped of its remaining judicial dignity, the public service of any residual status it enjoyed as a patriotic institution connected with a nation-building project. Henderson took to this task with relish, opening a 1986 speech by ridiculing the department that had once employed him for the number of refrigerators it provided its staff. His former colleagues, he indicated, were stupid and self-serving, overwhelmingly concerned with their pleasures and perks. At the lunch held to mark his departure from the Department of Employment and Industrial Relations, he 'ruefully reflected' that during his four years in the public service he 'had lost more brain cells than any of my senior officers were born with. This comment was not appreciated by some senior officers. Some others, fortunately, could not comprehend it.'[58] By the time he made this speech to a group of like-minded right-wing activists, Henderson was exercising what were left of his brain cells as chief of staff to the Opposition leader, John Howard.

These activists drew on a particular understanding of Australian history, a melodrama of 'goodies' and 'baddies' in which the 'baddies' – Alfred Deakin's Liberals and the Labor Party – had triumphed over a few economically literate souls who recognised that the laws of supply and demand could not be lightly brushed aside. They reserved a particular venom for Henry Bournes Higgins, the pioneering Arbitration Court president and architect of the living wage. Higgins, in arguing that industries must either pay their workers a living wage or cease to trade, was responsible for the gross inefficiencies that had sent Australia into inexorable national decline.

In short, he was 'a nut ... who, to the great detriment of his country, found himself able to give legal form and substance to his fantasies'.[59]

The response of those who wished to deal with 'our Higgins problem', as they called it, was to establish the H.R. Nicholls Society in early 1986. Henry Nicholls had been an English radical, a Chartist who came to Australia during the 1850s gold rush. Many decades later in 1911, in his dotage as the editor of a Tasmanian newspaper, Nicholls found himself charged with contempt of court after writing of Higgins as a 'political Judge'.[60] Ray Evans, who had himself once been a Labor man but was now an assistant to Hugh Morgan at Western Mining, was impressed by Nicholls's defiance when he encountered the story.[61] Along with John Stone, Barrie Purvis, the director of the woolbroking employers' body, and Peter Costello, a young barrister and Liberal Party activist, Evans wrote to interested parties in January 1986 proposing the formation of a society 'to give new impetus for reform of the present labour market and to provide a forum for discussion of alternatives to the present regulation of industrial relations'. It suggested that the stakes were high. The outcome of the present debate over industrial relations would have 'great significance ... for Australia's future economic growth, political development and ultimately, perhaps, territorial integrity'.[62]

Costello had recently become a figure of some national repute on the back of a legal battle in Victoria. The Dollar Sweets case arose from an industrial campaign run by the Federated Confectioners' Union (FCU). As in other famous industrial cases of the mid-1980s, the situation was peculiar. The union concerned, led by Carlo Frizziero, was militant, hostile to the Accord, and on the far left of the Victorian Labor Party. In April 1985, just a few weeks before the Dollar Sweets strike, the small group of left-wing unions with which he was associated had suffered a major defeat at the Victorian Labor Party's annual conference, when they failed to prevent the readmission to the party of four conservative unions that had left during the split of 1955 and had subsequently been associated with the Democratic Labor Party: the Clerks, Shop Assistants, Ironworkers and Carpenters and Joiners.[63] The party conference damaged the far left's image, and did little to enhance that of the Victorian Labor Party generally. The wild melee that occurred at Coburg Town Hall recalled the physical combat and bitter passion of the episode to which this Sunday morning was a tragicomic postscript: the Labor split of 1955. It was one thing to issue black armbands to delegates entering the hall, and for the president of the Musicians' Union to play on his clarinet 'a mournful refrain of The Last Post'. It was quite another for left-wing activists to hurl abuse, punch and jostle delegates, and throw overripe tomatoes at their opponents as they tried to enter the hall. Once they were inside, fights broke out, and tomatoes started raining down from the balcony on selected targets; old left warriors such as George Crawford, the state president, and Bill Hartley, former party secretary, raged against their enemies.[64]

The Dollar Sweets dispute added to the reputational damage incurred by the far-left unions. A small family business with twenty-seven employees operating in suburban Glen Iris, Dollar Sweets was even better suited to an anti-union propaganda blitz than Mudginberri. Here was another case of 'the little man who stood up to trade union bullies and thugs'.[65] The boss, of Austrian descent, was Fred Stauder, and among the firm's products were Hundreds and Thousands, as seen and admired on fairy bread and birthday cakes at children's parties. The FCU, having achieved a reduction of working hours to thirty-six per week in the larger firms, had now moved on to the likes of Dollar Sweets. But Stauder replied that the business could not afford any additional reduction in the working week. In July 1985 the FCU called a strike and established a picket: fifteen of the company's employees stopped work. After Stauder told them that they would either have to sign a no-strike agreement or face dismissal, he terminated their employment and replaced them.

The strike was not good-humoured. Telephone wires were cut and locks filled with glue. There was a bomb threat, an arson attempt and a physical altercation between Frizziero and a truck driver delivering sugar to the factory.[66] The union dropped its claim for reduced hours, but demanded that the striking workers be reinstated. Stauder turned to senior business leaders for help – they directed him to Costello, a 28-year-old barrister, who offered as a long shot the possibility of a successful common-law tort action. With the Melbourne Chamber of Commerce providing the money, in November Dollar Sweets issued legal proceedings against the union. In the following month, a decision of the Supreme Court called the union's behaviour 'stupid and nihilistic' and ordered that the picket be lifted. The parties later settled for a union payment of $175,000 in damages.[67]

A much bigger strike during 1985 also helped place a spring in the step of New Right activists. The dispute occurred over the efforts of the South East Queensland Electricity Board (SEQEB) to use contract labour. The National Party government had introduced a regime of equalising electricity costs across the state, the effect of which was to deliver a large cross-subsidy to rural and provincial consumers at the expense of those living in the major centres. But the result – massively increased electricity bills for city-dwellers – was potentially damaging to the government at a time when Bjelke-Petersen's decision to sever his coalition with the Liberal Party demanded National Party electoral gains in the more populated areas.[68]

The dispute bubbled on for almost a year before exploding into a full-scale strike in February 1985. Efforts by the State Industrial Commission to settle the dispute were unavailing and on 7 February, with thousands of consumers already in the dark, the Bjelke-Petersen government declared a state of emergency. With the government's support, SEQEB management subsequently sacked 1000 striking linesmen, replacing them with non-unionists bound by contracts containing no-strike clauses. Solidarity strikes, pickets and protest marches were ineffective in countering Bjelke-Petersen's war against Electrical Trades Union members. Instead, the government introduced a series of laws intended to curb union power in the industry. And in a familiar move that reprised the ban on street marches in the late 1970s, Bjelke-Petersen transformed protest into a threat to law and order by strengthening the powers of police in a manner that outlawed pickets – anyone now deemed to be interfering with the power supply could be arrested. In August a handful of members of a group that called itself 'Concerned Christians' protesting near SEQEB headquarters were arrested under the *Electricity (Continuity of Supply) Act*.[69]

Most of the striking workers were left without jobs or hope but with a burning resentment of their treatment at the hands of SEQEB, the government, union officials and Labor politicians. Many thought they had been sold out by their leaders for the sake of career advancement and political advantage. There was particular bitterness over the abject surrender of the Trades and Labour Council.[70] Meanwhile the strike's undoubted victor, Bjelke-Petersen, reached his apogee as a hero of the political right.[71]

The growing aggression of a handful of employers in the mid-1980s saw a distinct reaction set in, based on the suspicion that industrial warfare incurred intangible social and economic costs along with the more obvious benefit of being able to pose, like an ancient ruler, with one's foot firmly planted on the neck of a vanquished foe. The tipping point was Robe River, the last of the fabled New Right industrial disputes of the mid-1980s. Of the four, it was the most ambiguous in its immediate politics and eventual impact. No dispute, however, better illustrates the apocalyptic strain in New Right industrial relations, a vision in which a period of intense conflict would give way to an industrial utopia in which bosses and workers would deal with one another as autonomous and rational individuals, free from the insidious interference of union or state. The lion would lie down with the lamb. But as always in such matters, opinions differed on who was the lion, and who the lamb.

Robe River was in the Pilbara, a remote region in the north-west of Western Australia that was a leading producer of iron ore. Robe had operated from 1970 as a joint venture under the management of the American firm Cleveland Cliffs, but in 1986 Peko-Wallsend, one of the partners, became the majority shareholder and took over the running of the company. Profitability had climbed rapidly in the first half of the 1980s. However, the Japanese steel industry, which was Peko's leading customer, entered a more difficult period after 1985, which reduced the scope for exports. Peko's new chief executive, Charles Copeman, blamed the company's problems on slack management and 'restrictive work practices' – a phrase that entered the political lexicon. After sending in a team of executives to investigate, Copeman sacked four senior managers and demoted the managing director, then declared existing industrial agreements null and void. Hypocritically – considering Copeman's contempt for the arbitration system – the company wanted to place all workers on the site under the federal award system, a move opposed by the state Labor government.[72]

To the extent that restrictive work practices were a problem at Robe River, they were the result not of the compulsory arbitration so hated by New Right ideologues but of the localised bargaining they wanted to replace it with. Robe River differed from other Pilbara companies in seeking to exploit the spot – or short-term – market in iron ore rather than long-term contracts. Spot prices were higher, but with this came an acute sensitivity to industrial disruption, which in turn encouraged a compliant response to union demands.[73] For the new management, it seemed that if local arrangements could be overridden, many of the practices that Peko believed were wrecking the operation could be removed.

Having announced its intention to remove restrictive work practices, the company conducted what many workers saw as a reign of terror. It transferred workers around the operation irrespective of previous arrangements, including a sixty-year-old tea lady who was 'reclassified as an ore handler and put out on yard duties'. While the company did its best to present its workers as the beneficiaries of a well-developed system of rorts, there was also sufficient adverse publicity about Peko's behaviour to prevent Copeman from becoming a popular hero. Peko's aggression and vindictiveness disturbed even those convinced that conditions at Robe River were on the soft side. Union representatives complained that management had targeted them for demeaning work in what they called 'punishment details', while the company introduced new tenancy agreements in the company towns of the north-west providing for a 400 per cent rent increase for workers who went out on strike. Wives feared being evicted from their homes, while work contracts now provided that 'any or all of the conditions of employment can be changed weekly at the sole discretion of the company'.[74] Most seriously for Peko's reputation, when the WA Industrial Relations Commission (WAIRC) ordered a moratorium on industrial action and investigation of work practices, the company sacked sixty-four employees who had resisted changes in their working arrangements. When the WAIRC ordered their reinstatement, Peko sacked its entire workforce of 1160; it looked like the kind of lawlessness of which H.R. Nicholls Society types had accused unions at Mudginberri and Dollar Sweets.

In Pilbara towns such as Pannawonica and Wickham, workers and their families were seething at the company's behaviour. They recalled with nostalgia the previous company at Robe River, Cleveland Cliffs, as one that had cared about its workforce. Some were prepared to acknowledge the 'rorts' and conceded that there were practices that could now readily be abandoned.[75] 'I know there's got to be changes,' commented one worker. 'I think most of us do. But the way the company's going about it. You know, just splitting the town, making people angry.'[76] An apocryphal story about a strike that had supposedly taken place in the distant past over the flavours of ice-cream available at the local store was disseminated to discredit the local unions. And Pilbara families especially resented the idea, current in the state's more closely settled south, that they were 'filthy rich' and living a life of luxury and comfort. Food, electricity and petrol prices were high, and holidays expensive because of the region's remoteness.[77]

Central to Peko's strategy for dealing with its workforce was to sow divisions between the white- and blue-collar employees, between 'staffies' and 'wages'. Staffies had to sign contracts agreeing to take the places of striking blue-collar workers or face dismissal. Previously, community clubs and organisations – indeed, Pilbara social life – had promoted an easy sociability between the two groups. As blue-collar workers and their families saw it, there was little consciousness of status difference between them: it was 'a close-knit community' in which people 'got on well'.[78] Hence, for blue-collar unionists, the failure of most clerical staff to support them aroused bitter resentment; they regarded them as 'scabs' and deliberately shunned them.

Those who turned up to take the places of striking workers were greeted at the security gate by a menacing banner that proclaimed: 'Scabs. Nowhere to run. Nowhere to hide.'[79] Staff who entered a local hotel 'soon left under a barrage of abuse from unionists'.[80]

The lockout ended on 3 September, after the Industrial Commission rejected Robe River's appeal against an order to reinstate sacked workers. But the company's refusal to enter into conciliation meant that there would be no quick end to the dispute. The commission eventually upheld the company's right to eliminate restrictive work practices. Union leaders had worked hard to restrain their members, preferring 'passive resistance' to a strike. But the company continued to carry out reprisals. In December 1986 a strike finally occurred over harassment of unionists, white-collar workers performing blue-collar labour, and staffing levels. Pickets were established and unionists showered abuse on strike-breakers as they arrived for work each day. Meanwhile, the company took its cue from Mudginberri and Dollar Sweets – Peter Costello was advising Copeman – and issued writs against individual union officials and conveners.

In the New Right industrial fable, Peko was a tower of strength. In reality, there were good reasons why it should now seek a compromise. Peko's Japanese partners had expressed concern about the company's manner of dealing with its employees as early as August, and the WA government was furious with Peko for the dispute's impact on the state's reputation as a reliable exporter of iron ore. Bob Hawke, equally unimpressed, had called employer militants of the Copeman type 'political troglodytes and economic lunatics'.[81] The ACTU had established a fighting fund and workers from other Pilbara mines had expressed a willingness to shut down the whole region's iron-ore operations. Even as it issued one legal writ after another, Peko could not be sure of how far the unions would be prepared to go. Early in 1987 negotiations between ACTU president Simon Crean and Copeman resulted in a peace deal, although not without some resistance from rank-and-file unionists. It was hard to miss the irony: Copeman, the scourge of arbitration and the unions, had relied on one to deal with restrictive work practices, and on the other to extract him from industrial chaos of his own making.

Peko was soon reporting a happy and productive workforce, which the company and its New Right supporters treated as vindication.[82] Sceptics, however, were unconvinced by claims of an outbreak of happiness, and pointed out that other companies seemed to have managed greater productivity, and probably greater happiness, without prosecuting industrial warfare on a grand scale. The federal government's move away from allowing price inflation to determine the level of the basic wage (a system called 'indexation') late in 1986 cannot be seen as a direct outcome of the New Right revolt. Hawke had been playing with the idea of linking wage levels to considerations of efficiency and productivity, in addition to price increases, for many years, and the government remained committed to an entrenchment of the award system and the role of unions within it.[83] And it is by no means self-evident that in the short term it became easier as a result of Robe River to imagine large workplaces across the nation full of employees on individual contracts, for the dispute was an illustration of the costs of open industrial warfare.

Robe River was also the occasion for the H.R. Nicholls Society coming to national attention as a mysterious and possibly dangerous cabal, contributing to New Right stridency – and a backlash against it that would soon have disastrous political consequences for opponents of the Hawke government. The Prices and Incomes Accord was based on a fusion of politics and industrial relations that eventually helped keep the Labor Party in office for longer than any previous ALP national government. By contrast, the political right's attempt at creating its own fusion, at Mudginberri and Robe River, would help keep the Coalition out of power for another decade.

★

The Labor Party's investment in the Accord was no better illustrated than in the destruction of the Builders' Labourers' Federation. In September 1985, in what became known as the Accord Mark II, the ACTU and the Hawke government agreed to a 2 per cent wage cut in return for income tax cuts and government support for superannuation.[84] None of this held much attraction for the BLF, which covered an industry whose dangerous and cyclical nature encouraged workers to 'make a killing' when times were good, rather than 'the slow drip-feed of benefits and tax transfers' implied by the Accord.[85] But the issue of the BLF's militancy was entangled in the personality cult surrounding its leader, Norm Gallagher, and his efforts to avoid prison for having taken bribes from employers. In June 1985 Gallagher received a savage gaol sentence of four years and three months. Considering the gentle treatment that the employers on the other end of these payments had enjoyed back in 1983, it was reasonable that BLF members should regard this result as an egregious display of the judicial system's class bias. In October, however, the Supreme Court quashed the conviction and ordered a retrial, having found that the judge in the original case had misdirected the jury.

The BLF had been deregistered in 1974 yet survived, and its leaders had no reason to imagine that this time would be any different. They misjudged their enemy. Bill Kelty and the ACTU had no use for a union that openly defied the Accord; the BLF's rivals, such as the Building Workers Industrial Union, had no reason to oppose its deregistration for they would be able to pick up new members; and the federal Labor Party, committed to the Accord as the key to political survival, would be delighted to see the back of a union whose behaviour grossly offended its principles. Meanwhile, governments such as John Cain's in Victoria, the heartland of BLF power, looked to the building industry as a driver of jobs and development, and to big metropolitan construction projects as a key to the future of the state. As shown by the BLF's disruption of the construction of light towers at the Melbourne Cricket Ground, a battle that Cain had won, the union did not regard itself as a compliant junior partner in this worthy enterprise. Governments moved to ensure that businesses were onside, introducing a code of conduct to be signed by each firm which, if breached, could result in the withdrawal of utilities or permits. By early 1986 all of the major firms in Victoria had signed up. Developers would no longer be able to enter into deals with the BLF, as they had in the past, and then pass on the costs.[86]

The union's enemies were closing in. Deregistration day was 16 April 1986. When they showed up for work, BLF members found the major sites swarming with police. Each received a document that gave them a choice between resigning from the BLF and joining an alternative union, or losing their job. Most chose resignation from the BLF, helped along by payments of up to $1500 represented as 'back pay' and other benefits. But some of these men were left broken-hearted by the destruction of a union that, for all its faults, had provided a lowly group of workers not only with better pay and conditions but also a sense of pride and belonging.[87]

*

The Liberal Party did not have formal factions in the manner of the Labor Party, but the industrial battles of the mid-1980s exposed a division between 'wets', who were industrial relations moderates sympathetic to the party's interventionist traditions, and 'dries', who favoured free-market policies more indebted to Margaret Thatcher and Ronald Reagan. Dries tended to favour John Howard as one of their own – although he was too much of a pragmatist to go all the way with them – while wets leaned towards Andrew Peacock. Ian McPhee, a Melbourne Liberal and Opposition frontbencher, was the party's leading 'wet'.

The Peacock–Howard relationship, never terribly happy, had disintegrated after the 1984 election. Howard regarded Peacock as a lightweight and refused to give an undertaking that he would never challenge for the top job. The simmering rivalry between them came to a head in early September 1985, when Peacock provoked a confrontation. Howard pledged his loyalty as deputy leader but refused to rule out the possibility that he might challenge for the leadership. Peacock then foolishly engineered a party vote for the deputy leadership, which Howard won. Peacock resigned and Howard was elected leader.

In mid-1985 the government held a tax summit in Canberra which debated a number of options for reform. Paul Keating and Treasury argued for a consumption tax, but opposition from the ACTU as well as key ministers prompted Hawke to force a retreat, for which Keating never fully forgave him. From this time, the deteriorating relationship between its prime minister and treasurer became central to the story of the Hawke government. But the government did effect changes to the tax system in the mid-1980s. It slashed the top rate of income tax from 60 to 49 per cent and introduced both a capital gains tax and a fringe benefits tax – neither of them loved by business – as well as increasing taxation of lump-sum superannuation payouts and imposing an assets test on the pension. The Coalition parties under Howard opposed all of these measures while promising to reduce income tax. Howard had long favoured a consumption tax and was unapologetic about reducing the 'progressivity' of the existing tax system – that is, its redistributive function – but his difficulty was that he was being outflanked on the right, where there was support for a flat income tax of about 25 per cent as well as opposition to a consumption tax.[88]

The rise of the New Right was at best a mixed blessing for Howard. He hoped to exploit for the conservative side of politics the sense of urgency created by economic difficulties and the iconic industrial disputes. Yet while he favoured a decisive move against the unions and the industrial arbitration system, and in favour of the privatisation of government assets, New Right political commentators invariably gave the impression that no policy the federal Coalition could conjure would ever be sufficiently hardline for them. Howard was nonetheless travelling well in the opinion polls as the government grappled with the economic problems of 1986, and there was every reason for him to look with optimism on the Coalition's prospects in the election that was due by early 1988.

*

Queensland's Gold Coast seemed to capture the very essence of the strange boom in consumption, investment and speculation that coexisted with the gathering sense of economic crisis in the mid-1980s. The old fibro shacks and modest holiday flats were fast disappearing, to be replaced by tall, glittering structures, the opulence of which added new allure to a magical place of sunshine and pleasure.[89] One of the most spectacular, the Conrad International Hotel and Jupiters Casino – named after an Aboriginal youth, Jupiter Mosman, who had discovered gold at Charters Towers – began operating late in 1985 and opened officially in February 1986. But after the novelty wore off, many Queenslanders returned to their more familiar and homely haunts: the poker machines just across the Tweed in New South Wales. Those unable to make that journey could enjoy the amusement machines installed in Queensland clubs that were being illegally used for gambling under the protection of corrupt police.[90]

Jupiters epitomised the paradoxes that were gradually undermining National Party dominance of Queensland. Alongside the austere Protestant morality associated with the premier and his wife, Flo, a federal senator best known for her pumpkin scones, there was a fast-developing glitzy leisure economy founded on tourism, drinking, gambling, sex – and corruption. Behind the impressive chrome and glass of the new apartment buildings and resort developments was an economy whose poor performance belied the boastful parochialism of the local political and business elite. Meanwhile, the Japanese business and tourist dollar was receiving a most cordial welcome from a political regime utterly dependent on the votes of a white conservative rural base, which had little time for foreigners and long memories of the Second World War. Finally, behind all the regime's empty talk of free enterprise lay the power of an authoritarian and interventionist government with its grubby paws all over the economy.

Sanctuary Cove, another major Gold Coast development of the mid-1980s, provided a neat illustration of how flexible was the definition of 'private enterprise' in the Sunshine State. The brainchild of former Datsun dealer Mike Gore, who had recently turned to the more lucrative business of property development, Sanctuary Cove would open in early 1988 amid much fanfare. The jovial, pot-bellied Gore represented a particular kind of Gold

Coast entrepreneur: exuberant, thrusting and uninhibited in cultivating the state government.[91] One result of this was the *Sanctuary Cove Resort Act* of 1985, which removed a piece of unpromising swampland from local government jurisdiction and provided the means by which Gore could create his ideal resort. 'An island of privilege in a sea of mediocrity', Sanctuary Cove would keep a dangerous world at bay.[92] As a publicity pamphlet explained: 'The streets these days are full of cockroaches, and most of them are human ... Every man has a right to protect his family, himself and his possessions ... Sanctuary Cove is an island of civilisation in a violent world, and we have taken steps to ensure it remains so.'[93]

While Gore's language – or, rather, that of his advertiser and mate John Singleton – provoked outrage, he also captured something of the new conservatism in the verbiage with which he surrounded his enterprise.[94] His elitism, however, was state-subsidised, for the government lent the cash-strapped entrepreneur $10 million during a difficult period, which helped save the floundering project.[95]

Developments such as Jupiters Casino and Sanctuary Cove were the glitzy facade of the Queensland economy, but there was also a less glamorous side that was nonetheless critical in underwriting the long rule of the state's National Party regime. By the early 1980s coal had overtaken the historically dominant wheat and wool as the country's most valuable export commodity, and Australia emerged as the world's largest trader of coal by sea. The following year it was announced that General Electric would sell to BHP the American company Utah, the owner of several Queensland mines, a major step by the Big Australian towards a heavier reliance on the resources industry – which is where it had begun before taking its detour into steelmaking in 1915. Japanese steel producers' success in exploiting slack demand to force down coal prices would contribute to Australia's economic difficulties in the mid-1980s, yet the coal industry had by the end of the decade succeeded in capturing a larger share of the global market.[96]

Coal mining deployed the latest technologies but remained a dangerous occupation for those who did its underground work. Even while the stockmarket heroes Elliott and Holmes à Court battled for control of BHP in Melbourne's boardrooms, the company's mine near the central Queensland town of Moura presented its 2500 residents with their second tragedy in a little more than a decade. Soon after 11 am on 16 July 1986, it was rocked by an explosion and a landslide. Twelve miners working 200 metres below the surface were killed. '[T]here is a strong spirit running through the township', explained a local resident, 'There's something in a miners' town that isn't anywhere else.' Whatever this 'something' was, the townspeople desperately needed it. A memorial service attracted 3000 people; it was held in a park behind a memorial hall built to commemorate an earlier disaster in 1975 which had killed thirteen men. 'The occasion was as unhappy as could possibly be imagined,' reflected the resources and energy minister Gareth Evans, who was there to represent the federal government, 'with nearly every one of the dead men having young wives and young children.' As the town mourned its losses, the men's bodies were still lying in the mine, where dangerous gases had so far made their recovery impossible. Evans handed over letters of sympathy from the prime minister and did his best to console the bereaved, 'but it was not an experience I would ever want to have to repeat.' The people of Moura were not to be so fortunate. In 1994 yet another disaster killed 11 men.[97]

*

Even allowing for the state's rigged electoral system, the victory of Joh Bjelke-Petersen's National Party in the Queensland election of November 1986 was an extraordinary and unexpected achievement. The ridicule of southerners seemed only to increase his support at home, and the Nationals actually managed to improve on their tally of seats from 1983. On the night of the election, as he watched the triumphant 75-year-old premier claim victory on television, the federal Liberal leader, John Howard, turned to his wife, Janette, and said: 'We'll have trouble with this lunatic now.'[98] He was right: Howard recognised that the Queensland premier was an utterly ruthless political operator who was nearing the end of his political career, one who had become ever less inhibited about expressing contempt for weak southern politicians of whatever stripe.

There had been talk during 1986 that Bjelke-Petersen's next move would be on Canberra: rumours that he would retire from state politics in 1987 in favour of one of his younger and more able ministers, Mike Ahern, and make 'a tilt at Federal politics'. The premier was said to be telling businessmen at National Party fundraising lunches that 'John Howard would never make a strong Prime Minister.'[99] The message, of course, was that Bjelke-Petersen had just the steeliness needed to sort out the nation's problems.[100] Precisely who first came up with the idea of a push for Canberra is unclear, but two Gold Coast businessmen, Brian Ray, a friend and associate of Kerry Packer, and the aforementioned Mike Gore – members of a group soon famous as 'the white-shoe brigade' in honour of their supposed partiality to snazzy light-coloured footwear suited to beachside informality – were involved from an early stage. One of Gore's aims was to instal as premier his mate Russ Hinze, a competent but morbidly obese and venally corrupt Gold Coast politician and minister, a plan whose realisation required Bjelke-Petersen's removal from the state scene.[101] So, well ahead of the state election, Gore hired and flew in a young Canadian political analyst named Allan Gregg who, as head of a company he had founded called Decima, studied past electoral results and arranged new polling.[102] Gregg is supposed to have concluded from his research that a Bjelke-Petersen–led Coalition could defeat the Hawke government. According to Gore, Gregg thought that 'if Joh didn't, the Liberals wouldn't and the Labor Government would be returned for at least two terms'.[103]

Gregg had already made a name for himself as a winner on the conservative side of Canadian politics, and Gore seems to have been in awe of him as 'the most astute political manoeuvrer in the world'. In appearance, the Canadian seemed an unlikely adviser to the Queensland Nationals, with his ponytail, diamond-stud earring, t-shirt and rolled-up jacket sleeves – all very stylish in a 1980s kind of way – along with his taste for American vulgarisms such as 'motherfucker' that were not in common usage among Kingaroy Lutherans or even Gold Coast car-dealers. Gregg later described to the journalist Paul Kelly his impression of Bjelke-Petersen as 'a mean Ronald Reagan', an assessment that might have been unjust to a distinguished US president.[104]

Armed with Gregg's research, Gore claimed to have won over a 'sceptical' Bjelke-Petersen to the idea of a national political crusade.[105] Like several other Gold Coast entrepreneurs, Gore disliked Howard, having criticised his efforts to close tax loopholes while treasurer in the early 1980s. And with a government as pro-business as Hawke's in power, it was not as if the world was going to come to an end if one's political meddling ultimately helped Labor retain office. This kind of calculation may well have been relevant to other players in the Joh-for-PM drama as well, including the NFF's Ian McLachlan and his sidekick, Rick Farley, who flirted with Joh's crusade only to abandon it at the very last moment.[106] And within the Queensland Nationals hierarchy, there was a complacency about the damage that a Bjelke-Petersen push might do to the Coalition in Canberra, since 'it wasn't as if there was anything down there that was really worth preserving'. Loathing of the Fraser government – and the conviction that if elected, Howard and Sinclair would do no better – were forceful drivers of the Queensland assault on the federal Coalition.[107]

At Liberal Party headquarters in Canberra, meanwhile, there was plenty of alarm concerning the premier's ambitions for a federal career. A 'Note for File' entitled 'The Joh Conundrum', produced on 21 December 1986, listed Bjelke-Petersen's possible motives for a move on Canberra, which included a desire to leave his mark on federal politics by getting rid of the Hawke government, pressure from Hinze and the white-shoe brigade armed with their encouraging research and piles of money, dissatisfaction with the federal Coalition and its leadership, and a desire to advance the vision and policies of the New Right.[108] It was thought to be 'dangerous and undesirable to try to arrange [a] formal meeting between John Howard and Joh'.[109] Everyone was waiting for a rally scheduled for Wagga Wagga on 31 January 1987, when it was expected that Bjelke-Petersen would make his plans clearer. He did, but not markedly so: Bjelke-Petersen declared that those who did not support 'me and my policies' would find their seats contested by one of his candidates at the next election.[110]

Liberal Party war-gaming yielded various conclusions about the gathering crisis, some reassuring, others more worrying. On the reassuring side, it was clear there were no circumstances under which Bjelke-Petersen could become prime minister. The Nationals' electoral prospects in the big cities were poor; even in Queensland, they held no federal seats in Brisbane or on the Gold Coast. Research also indicated that in the big cities 'support for the Queensland Premier was fairly superficial'. 'His status and potential as a Prime Minister' were 'diluted by his age, his rambling, raving and dithering, his often obvious senility, the gerrymander he has introduced into Queensland, [and] a belief that the Queensland economy is not all it is cracked up to be'.[111] But more worrying for the Liberals and Nationals outside of Queensland essentially in New South Wales and Victoria – was the effect on voters of division in the conservative ranks. Andrew Peacock, a friend of Russ Hinze through their mutual interest in horses, had allowed himself to be drawn into the Joh push without apparently making a definite commitment. Peacock mattered because some of the Allan Gregg–Mike Gore 'research' was based on the idea of a Bjelke-Petersen and Peacock team.

At first it was unclear whether Bjelke-Petersen intended working through the Queensland Nationals or going it alone and creating a new force. But once Queensland National Party president Sir Robert Sparkes reluctantly decided to support the Joh crusade, the pressure on the federal Coalition increased markedly.[112] A meeting of the Queensland Nationals' central council at Hervey Bay on 27 February agreed to back the 'Joh for PM' cause 'for Australia's sake', and requested that federal National Party leader Ian Sinclair withdraw the party from the Coalition or, failing that, Queensland National Party members leave the Coalition.[113] Howard and Sinclair worked hard to keep the show together, but the threat that the Queensland Nationals posed to the preselections of all of its federal members ultimately broke the Coalition. During a speech at a Canberra National Party federal council meeting in late March, Bjelke-Petersen had dramatically 'thrust both arms high in the air' before declaring, 'I have some very, very good news for you today – the Coalition is finished'.[114] A month later the federal Liberal and National leaders accepted that the Coalition was indeed 'finished', but Howard bitterly concluded of Bjelke-Petersen that '[h]e will clearly go down in history as the Coalition wrecker and he has no chance of ever becoming Prime Minister'.[115]

The Labor leadership regarded the civil war in conservative politics as a gift from the gods. On 27 May, buoyed by encouraging polling, an improving economic outlook and a well-received May Economic Statement delivered by Keating, Hawke secured a double dissolution and called an early election for 11 July 1987. Bjelke-Petersen was in California at the critical moment; some media reporting had him in Disneyland. It is a measure of the incompetence of the Joh crusade that Bjelke-Petersen was caught unawares by Hawke's announcement, for even a political novice should have recognised the temptation of an early election as overwhelming. He quickly returned to Australia and after a ham-fisted effort to enlist Ian McLachlan and thereby gain a running mate as well as access to the NFF's organisational structure and cash, Bjelke-Petersen announced that he would not, after all, be going to Canberra. In reality, he had little choice: there was no national organisation for a campaign, and in New South Wales the Liberals and the Nationals had agreed to an electoral pact in which each would direct preferences to the other and away from Joh candidates.[116] As the parties prepared for the third election campaign in just over four years, Howard flew to Brisbane, where he and Bjelke-Petersen issued a joint statement in which they agreed to work together to defeat the Hawke government. Such an outcome was still conceivable, if unlikely, in view of Bjelke-Petersen's surrender and Howard's courage and dignity under pressure. But there were still 'Joh Independents' in the race – with the Queensland premier's support – against official Coalition candidates in several lower-house seats, including against Sinclair himself in New England, and Joh Senate teams running in South

Australia and Western Australia. None gained election, but they did much to confuse further already confused voters.[117]

The Joh-for-Canberra crusade collapsed under the weight of the enormous deceptions, and self-deceptions, that it demanded of its proponents. The campaign depended in the first place on the myth of Joh Bjelke-Petersen's political invincibility, and in the second on the idea that Queensland's brand of authoritarian populism could be exported to the rest of the country. It also rested on the fantasy that an Australian federal government could perform the functions the public demanded of it with a 'flat tax' of just 25 per cent – Bjelke-Petersen's main policy. But his authority was already crumbling when he undertook his crusade – and the peculiarities of Queensland state politics which he had so successfully exploited were the product of a development-orientated economy based on resources and tourism, a rigged electoral system, and rampant cronyism and corruption. It is one of the era's ironies that the country's most rancorously parochial politician should also have turned out to be its most ambitious and deluded nationalist homogeniser. For Bjelke-Petersen believed that the rest of Australia should become like Queensland and that no mere state boundary could withstand the overwhelming force of his will to make it so.

*

Despite enjoying the Bjelke-Petersen farce, the federal government was facing serious problems of its own. As early as April 1986, Bob Hawke had told a television interviewer: 'The party is over. Finito ... We are now in a crisis which is as great as the crisis of war.'[118] A few months later, in October 1986, a document drafted for the party's campaign committee reported that '[i]n talking up gloom or supporting harsh and necessary decisions', the government had sometimes made it seem to traditional Labor supporters that it 'gets a sadistic pleasure out of their hurt or we make it seem like the electorate is getting deserved punishment'. There was even worse news about the electors who would actually determine the government's fate: the mood in the middle ground was 'seething anger and resentment' at the government's economic management. 'The Government is in serious trouble', it concluded, and would lose the next election unless the economy and the government's 'approach and application' improved.[119]

The government's problem lay in the perception that despite the rhetoric of sacrifice, a few Australians still seemed to be doing very nicely indeed. The 1980s are now recognised as the beginning of 'the great divergence': after several decades in which people had been growing more equal, Australia, like other Western capitalist states, entered a period in which inequality became more marked. According to one estimate, income inequality increased by between 5 and 9 per cent during the 1980s, with the richest 10 per cent increasing their share of net income from 23.1 per cent to 24.9 per cent. Indeed, on these figures, the income share of all groups except the top fifth declined. Thanks to careful targeting of those in the greatest need, old-age and invalid pensioners, sole parents and recipients of the unemployment benefit who were over twenty-one all enjoyed increases across the 1980s, and poorer families benefited from initiatives such as the Family Income Supplement (1983) and the Family Allowance Supplement (1987). But middle-income families with children who were largely outside the social security system suffered a fall in the real value of their disposable incomes.[120]

Two million Australians lived below the poverty line, and both the overall numbers of the poor and their size as a proportion of the population grew under the Hawke Labor government. At the beginning of the decade 10.7 per cent of 'income units' – essentially couples, families and individuals supporting themselves – were living in poverty, compared with 16.7 per cent at the end of the decade. But these figures were calculated using a relative standard devised by Professor Ronald Henderson in the 1960s, an approach that has been criticised as misleading during periods of strong employment growth because the effect is to raise the poverty line rapidly, thereby increasing the number of people said to be poor. In sum, while poor people often had more money to spend, they were unable to share fully in the benefits of a growing economy.[121]

Indeed, as the stock-market boom peaked during 1987, the paradox that many Australians appeared not to have much benefited was becoming harder to ignore. Researchers found that Australians were, by international standards, remarkably tolerant of income inequality but that most people grossly underestimated the differences between the earnings of ordinary wage and salary-earners and the very well paid. Australians, it appeared, had become victims of the myth that their regulated wage system had solved the problem of income inequality, rather as the New Right had managed to delude itself that this same system was the origin of most of the country's problems.[122] But those who were better informed about the obscene amounts that the super-rich actually earned could see danger brewing. The business journalist Robert Gottliebsen was excited about the booming share market in 1987, but worried that '[t]he great problem faced by entrepreneurs and senior executives as they become better rewarded is that the workforce will, understandably, want the same treatment. If that happens, inflation will once again go through the roof and our prosperity will end.'[123]

Australia's new rich and super-rich certainly had no reason to bemoan the political regime under which they had achieved their success. There was no shortage of businessmen prepared to sing the praises of the Hawke government, nor was Hawke himself coy about complimenting Australia's corporate leaders as public benefactors of the highest order. At a business awards ceremony during the 1987 election campaign, Kerry Packer and Alan Bond both endorsed the Hawke government. Bond said the 'the Government should be applauded for allowing Australian business to succeed', while the prime minister described Packer as a 'close personal friend'.[124] But mutual admiration of this kind was a double-edged sword, giving rise to increasing press coverage about Labor's relationship to big business. Soon after the election, Hawke praised Bond as 'one of the most outstanding exports from Pommieland':

> There is a lot of sloppy talk going round this country at the moment that there should be no place in the concerns of a Federal Labor government for the Alan Bonds of this world. I want to repudiate that nonsense unequivocally ... It would be a perverse sort of discrimination in our society in my judgment if we didn't recognise the enormous contribution of the Alan Bonds and the other great risk-takers and entrepreneurs of this country.[125]

An example of this 'sloppy talk' was to be found in Brian Toohey's blistering 'The Death of Labor', an article that appeared in his new magazine, *The Eye*, in July 1987 because his previous employer, Fairfax, refused to publish it. 'Hawke and Keating do more than enjoy the company of the new tycoons,' Toohey explained, 'they share their values ... The Labor Party is an irrelevancy – an embarrassment that can be explained away to the people who count; a vehicle to deliver votes from those who don't.'[126] It might have been the government's sensitivity to this kind of criticism that helped produce the only real gaffe of the 1987 election campaign, when Hawke committed his government in his policy speech to the proposition – so obviously unattainable – that '[b]y 1990, no Australian child will be living in poverty'. The phrase apparently remained in the speech by accident; Hawke had intended to say that with the government's new Family Allowance Supplement, there 'would be no financial need for any child to live in poverty'.[127]

Labor's decision to replace its longstanding advertiser, Forbes McPhee Hansen, with John Singleton Advertising was another indication of the party's hard pragmatism. In the folk memory of the Labor Party, Singleton was recalled mainly for his involvement in the right-wing libertarian Workers' Party in the mid-1970s and his role in running scurrilous anti-Labor advertisements in 1974. Often described as an ocker, a larrikin and, rather like Hawke, everybody's mate, Singleton was widely admired for having the common touch. His firm came up with a catchy jingle for the campaign – 'Together: Let's Stick Together, Let's See It Through' – which enjoined Australians to 'keep on holding tight / To that great Australian dream' while reminding them that 'Nobody ever got anywhere / Changing horses in mid-stream'.[128] Singleton also produced 'Whingeing Wendy', actually Wendy Wood, the wife of a friend and a woman who as 'Beryl Timms' had sometimes featured on his radio program as a rough-as-guts proletarian everywoman. Wood was a strongly committed Labor supporter who had complained to Singleton that he had to do 'something' about John Howard 'to get across that what he's saying is just bullshit'. The following week, Wood received a call from Singleton's ad agency asking her to come in to talk about the advertisement she was going to make. This was news to her – but the advertisement was brilliant, featuring Wood looking into a camera from a suburban kitchen, speaking to John Howard in her own broad working-class accent, animated by an authentic conviction that the Liberal leader was, indeed, a bullshit artist. 'Where is the money coming from?' she asked. What was Howard going to cut?[129]

The Liberals, already wounded by the Joh for Canberra push, committed a further gaffe when Treasury detected an accounting error in their tax policy. Howard admitted the mistake, but it reinforced a sense among political observers, and probably many voters, that the Liberal Party was not ready for office. In the end, there was a small swing in the overall vote to the Coalition but it was concentrated in safe Labor electorates. Meanwhile, the government's success in some marginal seats held by the Coalition allowed it to increase its tally from eighty-two to eighty-six. Perhaps a fifth of the electorate had switched sides since the 1984 election, but it is a measure of the confused character of the politics of the mid-1980s that the defectors from each side seem to have more or less cancelled each other out.[130] All commentators could agree that Hawke was still a major asset. According to one estimate, he had swung 1.4 per cent of the vote to Labor that would otherwise have gone elsewhere.[131]

The 1987 election was the last one of the 1980s 'boom', such as it was. By the time the party next faced the polls in 1990, the stock market had collapsed, the political agenda was being reshaped by environmental issues, and the country was well on the road to yet another recession. In the meantime, Australians grappled with the challenges of living in an era that brought together boom and crisis, nationalism and globalisation, confidence and anxiety, conservatism and exuberance, creativity and conformism. No period since the 1920s had seen such a confusing melange. Pessimists thought that this historical comparison was all too apt, being haunted by the thought that 1987 might be another 1929.

7

New Pleasures, New Dangers

The 1980s was a decade possessed by the idea of style, although it had little style of its own.

Edward Colless, Australian art critic

Australians of the 1980s understood that they were undergoing rapid change, yet change that was fundamentally different from 1960s permissiveness and 1970s disorder. When commentators discussed intimacy, for instance, their dominant theme was that the sexual revolution was over. As a long article published in *Time Australia* late in 1986 put it, Australia had performed 'a sexual somersault': 'It is as if, after a wild sexual binge, Australians are picking wearily through the post-party debris. There is some confusion about exactly what they are searching for, but it is more than just their underwear. Discarded values are being re-examined and tried on. New values are being sought and sampled.'

'The buzz words of the new sexuality', it continued, were '"caring", "commitment", "permanent", "sharing"'.[1] The sense that something had changed was not dependent on AIDS, because even in April 1983, when AIDS was not yet much of a local news story, the women's magazine *Cleo* was already asking 'Is Sex Dead? (Or at Least in Trouble?)':

> Is sex in trouble? Could be. In the wake of the sexual revolution there's a shift of values towards romance instead of lust, courtship instead of seduction. People don't feel happy any more about one-night stands or casual encounters. Singles bars don't do the business they once did. And we even hear that early promiscuity can lead to cancer of the cervix.

In the sexual revolution, '[t]here was nothing hidden, nothing forbidden, nothing sacred'. But *Cleo* author Julie Clarke thought that a combination of economic uncertainty, herpes and Lady Diana Spencer had prompted second thoughts. 'Because of herpes,' she declared, 'sex for some has reacquired the shades of sin and sordidness it had when *Lady Chatterley's Lover* was banned.' Meanwhile, virginity was making a comeback, thanks also, in part, to Lady Di: 'The Prince searched far and wide across an England cleaned out of virgins by the sexual revolution. But clever Lady Di, it is said, had her eye on a royal marriage all along. Ignoring social mores, she kept herself pure and her reward was a video wedding that had even punkettes in tears.'[2]

There was little evidence, however, of a major backlash to the sexual revolution. 'In my age group, sex is everyone's idol,' a fourteen-year-old boy told an interviewer in 1985. 'It's the go.'[3] Premarital sex had gained widespread acceptance; the journalist Adele Horin's assessment in 1981 that '[t]he virgin bride ideal had almost expired' was confirmed by a study conducted a few years later in Toowoomba, a conservative Queensland city, which found that while most people still opposed extramarital sex, a large majority approved of premarital sex.[4] A survey carried out by the magazine *Dolly* of its readers in 1983 – the 6500 respondents were mostly teenagers between fourteen and eighteen – yielded similar results. The sample was, of course, self-selecting, and skewed towards those more likely to experiment in personal relationships. More conservative and religious parents would surely have refused to allow their teenage children to have a publication in the house that advocated masturbation – 'It is not a good idea to put anything in the vagina unless it's a penis or a finger' – and openly discussed both sex and drug use.[5] Still, it is notable that of those surveyed, 85 per cent approved of sex before marriage and around half had already lost their virginity, of whom 46.7 per cent claimed to have done so at fifteen or sixteen. While an academic estimate from the mid-1980s suggested that only around 35 per cent of sixteen- and seventeen-year-olds had experienced sex, even this lower figure points to considerable experimentation. And of those in the *Dolly* survey who had experienced sex, almost half claimed to have felt guilty afterwards, but very few were worried by either religion or a belief that premarital sex was wrong. They were more concerned about their parents' views, or because they had been talked into it by a pushy boyfriend.[6]

Attitudes to abortion were also being reshaped by the greater permissiveness of the era, although here, religious beliefs continued to exert a clearer influence. About 70 per cent of Australians believed in God, two-thirds in an afterlife, and one-third in the devil and hell, and those with religious beliefs were more opposed to abortion than others were. A national survey found that the majority would allow abortion in most circumstances, but support was higher if there was a strong chance of a serious birth defect than merely on grounds of poverty or if a single woman did not want to raise a baby on her own. Among *Dolly*'s young respondents, three-quarters approved of abortion in general but less than half considered that an unwanted or unplanned pregnancy was a satisfactory reason for one. From the mid-1970s to the mid-1990s, however, mirroring a broad decline in religiosity, the proportion of Australians who supported unqualified abortion rights moved from less than a third to around half.[7]

None of this public opinion, of course, mattered to the Bjelke-Petersen government, and in May 1985 Queensland police raided abortion clinics in Brisbane and Townsville, seizing patient records and arresting doctors. But the Townsville charges had to be dropped when the women refused to testify, and a Brisbane trial ended in acquittal when the court judged that doctors had acted in good faith to save the mother's life – a common-law formula that had previously been used by courts in Victoria and New South Wales to liberalise abortion.[8] Sex education was still prohibited in Queensland schools at this time, and the government refused to permit condom vending machines in the state's universities. When the young Gold Coast schoolgirl Nikki McWatters – Catholic and fearful of approaching a doctor for contraception – found that she was pregnant, she took a bus across the border to Tweed Heads to have a termination. 'Cramping and stinging and feeling like a piece of meat carved up in a butcher's shop, I clenched my teeth and swore off sex for life,' she recalled.[9] Adele Horin found that many teenagers she spoke to in 1981 were, like McWatters, not using contraceptives, and she surmised that the lack of any explosion of teenage pregnancy was due to abortion.[10] A 1984 *Woman's Day* survey of more than 3000 single female readers found that over three-fifths had not used contraception the first time they had sex, and that three-quarters of those aged twenty-five or younger had taken their chances at one time or another.[11] The *Dolly* survey, meanwhile, found that almost 14 per cent of the sexually active said they had been pregnant, with about half of these claiming to have secured an abortion and over a quarter miscarrying.[12]

That the story of sex in the 1980s is more one of a revolution accomplished than one betrayed is underlined by the spread of de facto partnerships. Already in 1982, close to 5 per cent of couples were living in de facto partnerships, with more than two-thirds of those aged under thirty-five.[13] By 1986 the percentage of all couples in such relationships had risen to 6 per cent and by 1991, to 8 per cent.[14] 'Living together' was for most of these couples a 'trial marriage', an interregnum in which the partners postponed a permanent commitment until they felt economically or psychologically ready. The issue came under an unusual form of mass scrutiny in 1987 when on the popular television soap *Neighbours*, a female apprentice motor mechanic named Charlene Mitchell (Kylie Minogue) and her boyfriend Scott Robinson (Jason Donovan) contemplated moving in together. Both were eighteen and their parents did not approve, so they decided to marry. 'Scott and Charlene's decision to make their love official initially sent shockwaves through Ramsay Street,' reported *TV Week*.[15] It is easy to see why. At the 1986 census, the median age at first marriage for men was 25.6 years; for women, 23.5 years.[16] But in a program aimed in large part at the young, cohabitation remained sufficiently controversial to necessitate a teenage television wedding (no doubt the promise of stellar ratings was also a temptation). Still, Jason Donovan was more in tune with the times than his character, Scott: 'If I was that much in love with someone I would like to live together and see how it works and if we are compatible as a team it could be right to marry.' Kylie Minogue was no more approving: '[T]here is no way I would get married at such a young age,' she said. 'There are too many things I want to do.'[17] In choosing a church ceremony, however, Scott and Charlene were still among the majority of couples – just under 59 per cent – who opted for a minister of religion, although the figure was declining: it had been 86 per cent in 1972, just before the federal government authorised the appointment of private wedding celebrants. More generally, around 60 per cent of Australians reported attending church more than once a year in the 1980s, down from 70 per cent in the 1960s. But many, just like Scott and Charlene, only turned to religion as a source of dignified ceremony on the rare occasions when they felt the need for it.[18]

Declining church attendance sits comfortably enough with the impression that there was no mass backlash against moral permissiveness in the 1980s. The idea that there was appears to have been little more than a myth aimed at prescribing disciplined sexual behaviour and reinforcing familiar gender norms. An anti-feminist message was certainly discernible in the advice of Bettina Arndt, one of the most influential sexual revolutionaries of the 1970s, who was now worried that sex was fast becoming a 'battleground with women calling most of the shots': 'in our eagerness to achieve sexual equality for women, are we destroying the essence of sexual give-and-take?

Instead of revelling in our partner's pleasure, we seem constantly to be checking a balance sheet to make sure he doesn't draw ahead.'[19] Arndt was by no means the only woman to indicate that the sisterhood might be getting ahead of itself. Dame Leonie Kramer, a politically well-connected conservative and Australian literature professor, was adamant that 'it is very important for a man to feel the head of the household, someone whose basic responsibility is to take care of the family'.[20]

Others argued that if many women were still unhappy, it had more to do with continuing sexual inequality. Young women complained that the sexual double standard had shown a remarkable resilience: the guy who slept around was a hero but the girl was still a slut.[21] And despite their growing numbers in the paid workforce, married women largely shouldered the burden of domestic labour. Men's contributions were often confined to occasional outdoor work such as mowing the lawn or taking out the rubbish, or they might play with the children;[22] yet even some well-educated men experienced an ambivalence about having been drawn into the world of nappies and playpens. Richard Neville, a leader of the 1960s counterculture, thought he discerned the emergence of 'a new concept of fatherhood', one which he welcomed, if in a slightly baffled way, but thought might be 'bad for business'. Men who had traditionally 'valued worldly ambition above commitments to infants' now found themselves suffering 'bouts of resentment against the mothers' and '[s]craping the dried pumpkin soup off the ceiling'.[23] The conflict between the ideal of 'personal growth and fulfilment' – a powerful legacy of women's liberation and the sexual revolution – and the 'self-sacrifice' demanded by family life, remained a dilemma for both men and women.[24] But feminists suggested that when accounts were settled, women got a raw deal.

Still, some discerned the emergence of a 'new man', a more sensitive creature whose sensibilities had been reshaped by feminism. Perhaps he wore an earring – the code of the time was that in the left ear it indicated that you were straight. Men's groups emerged, some concerned with issues like custody rights, but others interested in exploring from the male perspective 'intimacy, awareness, emotional commitment, opposition to violence' and the like.[25] The young author Kathy Lette mercilessly satirised this by suggesting that such 'modern men' were 'just as pussy-struck as the yobboes and surfies you left behind in suburbia, but much more dishonest. They don't tool, root, poke, plug, meat inject or stab a "chick". They make her "aware of her sexuality"'.[26] And while in the age of Bob Hawke and Paul Hogan it was de rigueur for young middle-class surfer and footballer types to play the ocker, there were also signs of greater sensitivity. The history student and actor Alice Garner recalled of the boys she and her friends formed relationships with at Melbourne University that while 'they might talk too loudly after a few beers', they were mainly 'more enlightened than their fathers' generation', respecting their girlfriends' autonomy, living independently, learning to love cooking, and even – perhaps hardest of all for the Australian male – displaying affection.[27]

But there was still the problem of the boys talking 'too loudly after a few beers'. Early in 1984 a group of Canberra women, supported by a start-up grant from the federal government, thought they might have the solution when they set up a wine bar, performance venue and arts centre in the suburb of Lyneham. Their conviction was that 'women were wasting away' in the suburbs, and that they would appreciate 'an environment free from sexual harassment and aggression'.[28] They pointedly named their new enterprise Tilley's Devine Café Gallery, thereby honouring a ruthless Sydney crook of the mid-twentieth century named Matilda Devine, best known as a brothel-keeper. Tilley's, as the café became known, only admitted a man if accompanied by a woman. More controversially, it was given over to women-only nights on Friday and Saturday, which in order to get around possible legal difficulties were called 'private functions'. While some fulminated against such restrictions as discriminatory – a *Canberra Times* columnist called it 'the Martina Navratilova Café for Refractory Harridans'[29] – women defended Tilley's on the grounds that:

> many women ... enjoy each other's company without the unwanted attentions of predatory males. Obviously not all males are predatory but a sufficient proportion of them infest your average bar in Canberra and make the existence of Tilley's a necessity and a delight ... the house-trained man is welcome at Tilley's and to ensure that his habits remain tidy he is only admitted if accompanied by a woman.[30]

As the café's founder, Pauline Cardini, later explained, '[w]omen did not and do not have equal opportunity to social space'.[31]

*

Language was another battleground between genders. Government efforts to promote non-sexist language – including in the newly adopted national anthem 'Advance Australia Fair', which replaced 'Australia's sons' with 'Australians all' – often met with male ridicule. As feminist historian Bev Roberts pointed out, it was not the words that were 'being challenged but the particular forms of social change they represent' – notably 'the movement of women into the public sphere'.[32] The growing number of female professionals was indeed a conspicuous cultural change of the 1970s and 1980s as feminism marched through the nation's institutions, giving birth on the way to the 'femocrat', a peculiarly Australian usage for a feminist who works through the bureaucracy to advance women's rights. Perhaps 'marched', however, is too strong a term, for the changes wrought by feminism were not invariably welcomed. In 1983 a judge of the Family Court, Hubert Frederico, informed a female barrister wearing slacks that such attire was not permitted in his court and he was sufficiently petty to adjourn the case.[33] In the same year, the Cain Labor government in Victoria turned its attention to discrimination against women by sporting clubs which operated on crown land; nine out of ten golf clubs, for instance, refused women full rights.[34] But the hottest controversy concerned membership of the venerable Melbourne Cricket Club (MCC). Families put the names of their sons on the club's waiting list at birth; women could accompany their husbands to events, but were not permitted to enter the 'sacred' Long Room. A large majority voted at a meeting to end the discrimination, but it did not reach the two-thirds required under MCC rules. A subsequent postal ballot resulted in an end to the ban, and women were now permitted to place their names on the 28-year waiting list. One thorny question remained: what would women have to wear? Surely not the tie or cravat required of men? The club's secretary, Dr John Lill, explained that a skirt would be acceptable but slacks would probably also be all right so long as they were accompanied by a jacket.[35]

Clothing often figured prominently when women challenged men's public power. In popular memory, shoulder pads perform the same symbolic work for women's changing status in the 1980s as the bicycles and bloomers of a century before. Women dressed for success or, as it was now often said, engaged in 'power dressing', embracing styles inspired by male business attire.[36] Yet if they did so in the expectation that choosing the right set of clothes would puncture male dominance, they were surely disappointed. Power-dressing demanded of women gender performance of a complexity that no man was expected to negotiate. She should dress so as not to look like the secretary; she should not exaggerate her bust; she should be feminine but not too sexy: the rules were complex, the codes nuanced and changing.[37] *Women Australia*, a magazine aimed at professional women, declared in 1985 that 'the days of women dressing like pseudo-males to get ahead in business are long gone'. Here, there was an insistence on fashion as the preserver of a feminine look. 'Everything is prettier,' said a woman working in the fashion section of the Australian Wool Corporation. 'Bosoms and waists are obvious. Women no longer feel they have to look like men to compete.' Another expert agreed 'that executive dressing was generally softer and more feminine today'. Women in conservative fields like insurance and law were advised to splash a bit of colour into their 'black, navy, grey, white or cream suits' via a well-chosen shirt. In sum, women should look neither too masculine nor too feminine; they should be pleasing to the male eye, but not distracting.[38]

The 900,000 or so jobs that appeared in the globalising Australian economy of the period between 1983 and 1993 went predominantly to women – about two out of every three – and a majority were part-time.[39] Nursing, held in the strange mixture of veneration and disdain that society frequently reserved for 'feminine' occupations, was typical of the work being taken up by these women. The Florence Nightingale 'lady with the lamp' image still prevailed; nursing was considered a calling rather than a profession, conjuring images of devoted self-sacrifice that were in perfect harmony with traditional understandings of women's natural disposition. By the mid-1980s, however, many nurses not only recognised the sexist and self-serving nature of such imagery, they were prepared to act to improve their lot. The flashpoint for conflict was Victoria, where nurses were leaving the profession in droves and there was a chronic undersupply of qualified nurses – a problem not likely to be resolved while pay, conditions and career structures remained so poor. In 1984 Royal Australian Nursing Federation (RANF) members voted to get rid of their 'no strike' rule, which officials had come to recognise as a weakness in their dealings with employers who knew that however badly they were treated, nurses would in the last resort refrain from withdrawing their labour out of a sense of duty to their patients. Industrial action followed in 1985 when nurses refused to carry out 'non-nursing duties' in protest at understaffing. But this was a mere prelude to the explosive conflict of November and December 1986, when the Victorian branch of the RANF voted to strike in response to an award that left many of its members worse off than before.[40]

The fifty-day Victorian nurses' strike initially had considerable public support, not least because there was widespread dismay at the state of the health system and the incapacity of the state government to solve its major problems. Nurses were sometimes in tears as they left their patients behind to join pickets and, while hostile editorial writers casually likened the nurses' 'militancy' to that of the deregistered BLF, the public was under no such illusion. A skeleton staff remained in all hospitals, critical care wards were exempt from action, and the union succeeded in maintaining an impressive solidarity. This achievement was due in no small part to Irene Bolger, the recently elected Victorian secretary of the union. A socialist and feminist who made no effort to hide her radical politics, Bolger became the main public face of the strike. In many ways, her prominence was misleading, for the action's massive rank-and-file support was never in doubt. But Bolger's uncompromising language and powerful public presence encouraged opponents of the strike to present the nurses as naïfs who were unaware of the perils into which they were being led by their knowing and wilful secretary. 'Irene Bolger', declared the *Herald*, had 'led nurses into a confrontation not just with the Government, but with themselves and the principles they live and work by ... they put their own self-interest first'.[41] Nurses angrily denied such a characterisation which, although in line with conventional anti-union rhetoric, inevitably took on a gendered meaning when such judgments were delivered by men against women. Similarly, striking nurses regarded with contempt the premier's appeal over Bolger's head to their sense of a 'higher duty', not least because from the other side of his mouth Cain – echoed by his health minister, David White – darkly warned that they were laying themselves open to criminal and civil action. Cain also held over the union's head the possibility of using emergency powers to break the strike, but nurses knew that the government was hamstrung by the political and logistical difficulty of replacing them; Victoria was not Queensland, and nurses were neither electricity linesmen nor builders' labourers.[42] The government in any case knew that the award the union was striking against was a shambles, and while it maintained a cynical hardline opposition to the nurses' case, it worked behind the scenes with the ACTU to reach an agreement. After the RANF escalated the strike in December by withdrawing members from some critical care units, there were stronger signs of division among its members over methods, an apparent shift of public opinion against the union and a gradual drift of nurses back to work. But the union was able to call off the strike shortly before Christmas, its main claims having been conceded.[43]

The nurses' defiance was an emasculating experience for men unused to having their weakness so publicly exposed by women. Bolger was especially disturbing to their equanimity. Responding to intimidation from Cain and White, her rhetoric was more Margaret Thatcher than Norm Gallagher: 'The threats have not brought this serious dispute one step closer to settlement – and will not.'[44] But the growing presence of women in positions of power sometimes provoked more primitive displays of male chauvinism. This was certainly the case in one of the best-known instances of 1980s workplace harassment, that of Jane Hill and the NSW Water Board. Hill was a young, able and popular woman who was active in her union and whose social life largely 'revolved around office activities'. She worked in the commercial branch of the Water Board and was thirty-one when promoted to the role of supervisor. That was the beginning of her troubles, for the men she supervised made it clear they intended to get rid of her. Her phone would ring; she would hear a recorded message from a venereal disease clinic. While mail addressed to her seemed no longer to find its way to her desk, there was a generous flow of pornography, sent anonymously. An advertisement for a brothel was placed conspicuously on a noticeboard near her desk, as was a bikini-girl calendar and a magazine image of a naked woman with a boa constrictor around her neck. An anonymous letter warned her pointedly: 'You'll get yours bitch.' Management was inept in dealing with the men concerned, and the NSW Equal Opportunity Commission eventually awarded Hill $35,000 compensation in May 1985. The deputy secretary of the commission and director of affirmative action who had failed to take any action against her tormentors had already by this time been promoted to secretary.[45]

This case was unusually extreme, but a *Woman's Day* survey of single women found that one in seven had been assaulted, and one in three sexually harassed.[46] A study of the WA banking industry found that four out of five women said they had been sexually harassed and for most this involved personal comments about appearance, or lewd jokes or comments.[47] Many women probably endured various types of sexual harassment. A woman in her thirties complained that she had 'come to expect sexual harassment in the office. I've been subjected to it since my late teens, but I still haven't worked out how to deal with it – and keep my job.'[48] Joanne, a clerk who figured in a Brisbane *Courier-Mail* article, had a large bust and told a reporter that she had been subjected to regular comments and, in the case of one colleague, even to fondling. 'I've tried everything,' she reported:

> I've tried to laugh it off; I've dressed like my grandmother; I've asked him politely to stop; I've cried and I've threatened to tell the boss. But

I'm scared I'll look like a fool so I haven't.

But I feel tense and sick whenever he comes near me and I've never hated anyone like I hate him.[49]

Women Australia reported that 'small professional offices of doctors, accountants and lawyers' were 'prime spots for sexual harassment'.[50] Few such cases made it to a court or tribunal but even when they did, the bodies supposed to protect women were not always effective in doing so. In a notorious case that came before the Human Rights and Equal Opportunity Commission in 1988, Marcus Einfeld refused to award damages to several women who had clearly been sexually harassed because 'women with normal experiences ... know very well the various ways in which some men occasionally behave'. The women concerned should have been able 'to handle with confidence and equanimity, and without harm, the conduct of the respondent'.[51]

The transformation of the modern office into a cross between a tutorial room and a café might have encouraged harassment, especially banter, in an age when sex talk was more open and older restraints governing behaviour in 'mixed company' were breaking down. Work processes that involved regular and extended face-to-face discussion could also have been a factor, as in the clichéd 'butcher's paper and crayons' brainstorming or gatherings around new-fangled electronic meeting boards.

*

By the early 1980s, the situation for both gay men and lesbians in Australian society had improved markedly from just a few years before, when there had been doctors still treating homosexuality as a disease, and one or two carrying out brain operations to cure it. The gay radicalism of the 1970s had not quite revolutionised the law, politics and society, but homosexuals now resembled other recently established minorities in a multicultural society: they were a group to be tolerated rather than despised, a lifestyle accepted if not yet celebrated. Yet like those of other minorities, their freedoms remained precarious. Not everyone regarded homosexuality so benignly: many Christians still believed it a sin; 'poofter bashing' was claimed by gay men to be common; homosexual acts between consenting adults in private remained illegal until 1984 in the country's most populous state, New South Wales, and at the end of the decade were still outlawed in Queensland, Western Australia and Tasmania. In 1988 a gay couple of Nerang on the Gold Coast found themselves the subject of a front-page article in the local newspaper when they were discharged on good behaviour bonds after having had sex in their own home. One reader of the paper complained about its coverage of the case, for he had 'a lovely fifteen-year-old daughter' and did not want her corrupted by reading 'disgusting news about disgusting people'.[52]

In the larger cities, homosexuality was visible in the developing commercial precincts, such as Oxford Street in Sydney and, a few years behind it, Commercial Road in Melbourne's Prahran. Gay pubs, restaurants, saunas and porn shops opened; a three-part *Daily Telegraph* report in early 1983 claimed, rather implausibly, that Sydney alone had over 400,000 homosexuals, as well as 'dozens of clubs, 12 gay hotels, five gay bookstores, five gay restaurants, three newspapers and a gay counselling service', as well as its annual Mardi Gras.[53] Certainly, the area around Oxford Street had seen the development of a commercial gay world of considerable liveliness, but the activist and academic Dennis Altman thought the number of male homosexuals actively engaged in Sydney's political and commercial gay subculture was possibly as low as 15,000. The idea that Sydney rivalled places such as San Francisco and New York as a gay city he believed a myth.[54] Indeed, there was a reminder of continuing vulnerability to harassment when in January 1983 police descended on Club 80, a sex-on-premises venue, arresting five men and taking down the personal details of 200 others – in a manner that the men believed left them open to blackmail and discrimination.[55] But it was notable that a tabloid such as the *Daily Telegraph* should now report sympathetically on gay men. Its account might have been a little breathless, as it laid out for readers its astounding discovery that 'most Sydney gay men aren't limp-wristed or flamboyantly effeminate. They're ordinary office and blue-collar workers who travel to and from work with you each day.'[56] Yet at a time when homosexual acts in private remained illegal, it was hard to overlook how radically the climate had changed since the late 1960s.

It was on this world that the acquired immune deficiency syndrome (AIDS) landed like a bomb – if one with a fuse that at first burned slowly. The first Australian case appeared in 1982 – in Sydney – and it was reported publicly in May 1983. In the early days, some called AIDS the 'Gay Plague', a nod to the theory that it resulted from the homosexual lifestyle. Certainly, many of those afflicted in the United States seemed to be male homosexuals, but fears that the blood supply might be contaminated were realised in July 1984 when the first such Australian case came to light. Then, at the time of the 1984 federal election campaign, the Queensland minister for health announced that three babies had died after receiving infected blood and another was seriously ill. Cases such as these established a distinction in the minds of many people between gay and therefore 'guilty' AIDS victims – whose infection had resulted from their promiscuity – and 'innocent' sufferers such as children and haemophiliacs who caught the disease from blood products infected by reckless gay men.[57]

Moral conservatives and political opportunists now saw their opportunity to exploit others' suffering to make a point about God's wrath. The federal National Party leader, Ian Sinclair, blamed AIDS on the Hawke government's 'promotion of homosexuality as a norm'; Fred Nile, a clergyman and NSW parliamentarian, blamed 'the anonymous multiple nature of homosexual perversions'; and Hiram Caton, a philosopher and Queensland National Party member, blamed the 'extreme egotism and colossal impertinence' of gay men.[58] As late as 1988, the federal Coalition health spokesman Wilson Tuckey used the startlingly inappropriate forum of the third national conference on AIDS to declare that 'AIDS is very much a disease that results from deliberate and possibly unnatural activity'.[59] In the same year, in a flagrant homophobic stunt, members of a Gold Coast municipal council tried to make it compulsory for landlords to notify authorities if letting a house to someone with AIDS.[60]

Pressures for abstinence were one outcome of the AIDS crisis: Adele Horin suggested in a *National Times* article in 1985 that for many gay men, '[p]eriods of celibacy alternate with sexual binges, followed by misery and retreat'.[61] AIDS, however, did not start a sexual counter-revolution, either among gay men or anyone else. For the gay community, the right to anal sex had been at the symbolic heart of homosexual law reform since the 1970s, and any 'solution' to AIDS that involved its abandonment would have been a major defeat.[62] Instead, the concept of 'safe sex' was put to work to modify the sexual behaviour of gay men. Governments – and notably the federal government under the leadership of health minister Neal Blewett – worked with both doctors and the gay community to educate its members. They resisted calls for mandatory testing of high-risk groups, the closure of gay saunas and the isolation of AIDS sufferers. Condoms were distributed at gay venues, and sexually explicit government-funded information educated gay men on how they might keep themselves safe. Most quickly understood that unprotected anal sex was dangerous, but confusion prevailed in some other areas, such as oral sex.[63] The general picture, however, was of a shift towards safer practices that confounded the most alarming predictions, as well as common stereotypes of gay men as naturally irresponsible and lacking in self-control.[64]

Among gay men, fear and grief were widespread, as dozens, then hundreds and eventually thousands of men were diagnosed with the disease. Men watched their lovers and friends waste away as the human immunodeficiency virus (HIV) that caused AIDS attacked sufferers, making them susceptible to infections that usually took their lives. But gay men also organised against the virus, fought efforts to ostracise sufferers, told their stories in a manner that gave the virus a human face – and aligned their experience with the language of trauma increasingly prominent in public discourse. They resisted a sense that they were victims, not wanting to 'sit around in groups drinking out of polystyrene cups and talking about death ... we are not dying, we are living with the virus'.[65]

Governments extended the 'safe sex' message to the community as a whole, thereby breaking down the stigma of the disease by treating it as something every sexually active person should worry about. The most dramatic example of this was the Grim Reaper advertisement of 1987. With his creepy eyes, familiar scythe and the trusty bowling ball that he used to knock over a rather ordinary-looking group of men, women and children in a foggy bowling alley, the Grim Reaper would become one of the most memorable and instantly recognisable icons of the era. The ad's frightening voice-over warning that the disease, unless stopped, might kill more Australians than the Second World War, completed the sense of menace. The National Advisory Committee on AIDS, chaired by the magazine editor Ita Buttrose, certainly got its money's worth from Grey Advertising, as the campaign ran for only three weeks.[66]

Indeed, it might have been *too* successful. Focus-group research carried out during the first half of 1987 found that AIDS was one of the four issues ('crime', 'family breakdown' and 'community fragmentation' were the others) that came up spontaneously in every discussion, and that people feared the disease in both a 'personal' and 'general' sense. The authors of the report noted that these fears seemed 'to bear little relation to the actual risk' – it was small beer compared with road accidents and heart disease – and offered the explanation that the fear of AIDS might stand in for a broader sense that 'all was not right in their society'.[67] Certainly, the number of Australians prepared to nominate AIDS as the most serious problem facing the country jumped from 6 per cent in 1985 to 13 per cent in 1988.[68]

Safe sex usually meant condoms and the leading producer of them, Australian company Ansell, reported that its sales rose by 25 per cent between 1986 and 1988.[69] An effect of the AIDS crisis was to increase both the public visibility of gay men, and the legitimacy of homosexuality as a form of human intimacy. Community fears of the spread of AIDS among heterosexuals also legitimised the teaching of sex in schools, still a controversial issue in the 1980s. And there was a more explicit treatment of sexuality in public debate. We can see the wider effects of 'safe sex' talk in a humorous manual produced by Kaz Cooke for young women in 1988:

> There's nothing more likely to encourage a boy to wear a condom than telling him that's the only way you'll feel comfortable having sex. 'There'll be no bonking otherwise,' is the general line you may wish to run.
> One man I know said 'If it meant I was going to get a root, I'd put a kettle on the end of my dick.'
> And if you whisper in your friend's ear that you'll be happy to help him practise, I would imagine there's no real need to make other arrangements for Saturday night.
> No side effects, no unwanted pregnancy, no diseases. No wonder they're back in fashion.[70]

Here was a feminist message intended to empower young women in their dealings with men but also, as in the campaigns being directed at gay men, something more: a language of individual responsibility and choice that was in tune with the tenor of the age. It did something to undercut the sexual revolution's privileging of spontaneity, but not its emphasis on desire and pleasure.

*

At least at first, AIDS seemed to have closed off to a new generation the freedoms and pleasures associated with growing up as a carefree baby boomer. Yet technology was opening another door, promising the chance to live simultaneously in the private space of one's bedroom and as a global nomad, wandering the world with like-minded peers via the computer, the modem and the bulletin board. A youth living in the northern NSW town of Lismore in the 1980s apparently sensed these possibilities when he noticed a Commodore 64 computer in the window of a local shop. 'By the time I was sixteen,' he recalled, 'the computer had become my consciousness. It was the beginning of a new life.'[71]

The desktop computer has been one of the most influential and enduring of the technologies that came to prominence during the 1980s, although few lives would be so marked by its appearance as that of Julian Assange, the teenager who had looked longingly on the contents of that shop window. He recalled years later, after he had become one of the world's most famous men, that he belonged to 'a generation' that 'came of age in the late 1980s'. Entering the world of computers was 'a new way of being in the world' and 'a new way of being in your own skin'.[72]

But it was really, as he admitted, the modem that changed his life, for the young Julian Assange became a computer hacker calling himself Mendax (from Horace's *splendide mendax*, 'nobly untruthful'), part of a small global community of elite hackers who managed to penetrate the systems of corporations and government agencies. In his own way, the young Assange was showing that Australians could move in the world as the equals of anyone – and in his case, without even leaving his bedroom.[73]

If, as has sometimes been suggested, the microcomputer revolution began with the first IBM personal computer, it came rather late to Australia. The model was released only in January 1983, almost eighteen months after its American debut, and sold for around $1600.[74] But the first personal computer show had been staged in Sydney in 1979 and the earliest computer stores opened at this time.[75] When the magazine *Australian Personal Computer*, which began publication in 1980, organised its first show in Sydney Centrepoint in 1983 it expected a crowd of 10,000 but more than double that number showed, with exhibitors being 'particularly impressed by the quality of visitors, the majority being potential customers rather than casual browsers'.[76] A few months later a perplexed subcommittee of the East Lindfield Public School in Sydney could not decide from among the already bewildering variety of computers on the market which would be best for their school. Their solution was to invite suppliers to mount an exhibition at the school; it attracted 4000 people to see the twenty-five brands on display.[77] By late 1984, there were over 140 brands of computer available in Australia, and new software was arriving on the market at a rate of around 100 programs per month.[78]

Computers did not at first come cheap. A Panasonic JB-3000 cost about $6000 in 1982, the price of a new Datsun sedan, while the state-of-the-art Apple Lisa – 'the darling of the executive desktop' that introduced such novelties as the mouse, the icon and the drop-down menu – sold for $12,000 when it was released in the following year. If you wanted a very basic printer to go with it, you were up for another $695.[79] Clearly, only large businesses or the immensely wealthy could afford such a computer, and it was also a common complaint that personal computers all came with too little memory and no software, so that by the time you had bought everything you needed, 'the standard machine price has long receded into the distance and you really have made a capital investment'.[80]

When the Apple Macintosh appeared in 1984 as a 'little brother' to Lisa, it was considerably cheaper at $3445, but with a printer you were up for well over $4000.[81] Jonathan King, who organised the Bicentennial First Fleet Re-enactment of 1987–88 (see chapter 8), took advantage of the new technology, shelving his 'Luddite tendencies' in mid-1984 to:

> buy one of the new-fangled computers to develop the First Fleet operation in style. From that moment, the Re-enactment was programmed on the Apple Macintosh system that enabled the small man to compete with big government departments and corporations ... before long we were producing letters that looked as good, if not better, than those from the Chairman of Directors of BHP.[82]

Portable computers – the ancestors of today's laptops – also began appearing in the mid-1980s at between $4000 and $5000.[83] A Commodore 64 could be picked up in 1983 for just under $700, but that excluded the monitor and the cassette player required to use any of the programs. Originally 'a low-end business machine', it was taken up in many homes for other uses, and especially for games, allowing it to compete with the games-only units produced by Atari and Nintendo.[84] Parents who had absorbed the contemporary wisdom that computers were going to be essential to their children's future might well have wondered how their playing of Space Invaders and Pac-man on a Commodore or Atari was going to make all the difference. Still, by the early 1990s, about a quarter of all Australian households had a personal computer.[85]

Australians increasingly expected that the computer would play a critical role in their future, and especially their children's future. Barry Jones, a federal Labor MP, published a book in 1982 called *Sleepers, Wake!* which predicted Australia was about to pass into a post-service economy in which computers would take over many forms of manual labour. 'Computerization', he suggested, 'has the same aim as contraception – to eliminate people. The contraceptive pill has done for the birth rate what the silicon chip is intended to do for the labour force.' Jones predicted that without the right policy response, the rapid growth of computing technology would massively increase social inequality. Yet he was able to console his readers that for the time being, the incompetence of local management meant that Australia lagged well behind the United States in applying computer technology to manufacturing and business administration.[86] This must have seemed like a rather small mercy, and one unlikely to protect living standards for very much longer. When the Hawke government won office in 1983, it came bearing a policy for the teaching of computers in schools that imagined such education would make Australia more competitive and more equal. The computer was both an object of fear – pointing to the competitive world which the nation had to face – and a partial solution to the national economic malaise.[87]

The desktop computer, because it combined a range of functions such as typewriting and bookkeeping, offended some long-standing notions about how to organise the work of an office. Was it efficient to carry out word processing on expensive and sophisticated computers when there were cheaper, less complicated devices, such as electric typewriters and word processors, capable of doing just as good a job? As one expert pointed out to the trade journal *Office News*: 'what happens when a secretary or a typist needs to use it for 60–70% of the day? You effectively have a $10,000 machine being used for typing!!'[88] There were other difficulties, such as worries that computer illiterate executives were making their decisions 'on wrong figures ... produced by an enthusiastic executive punching a few keys – but not really understanding what the PC and its programme is doing to these figures'.[89] Managers worried over purchases, even hiring expensive consultants to get it right. 'There are processes more arduous than buying a computer for your office,' explained *Office News*, such as 'swimming the English Channel, writing the script for *Return to Eden*, [and] stealing a Picasso' yet 'few in which one is made to feel such a drip'.[90] Computers still had limited capacity for storing information, and there were concerns that such information could be too easily altered or manipulated. Accordingly, microfilm was marketed for its efficiency, durability and stability; it would ensure that valuable office space was not wasted on storing paper files. Electronic typewriters were also being aggressively marketed, even as they lost sales to personal computers. '[O]ne thing is certain', predicted the magazine in 1989: 'electronic typewriters will be around for a long time'.[91]

The intensification of office work had by the 1980s created major medical problems for the mainly female workforce of typists. Some were in agony. Yet there were claims from sceptics, who drew attention to a lack of 'objectively measurable symptoms', that the repetitive strain injury (RSI) of which many complained was a psychological ailment.[92] The greater susceptibility of women to RSI fuelled sexism, even misogyny. *Office News* published an unsigned article in February 1986 claiming that the condition was most likely psychological – the author compared it with an Aboriginal person being sung to death – and that it was benevolent employers who found themselves subject to the most claims of RSI – thereby suggesting that it was a form of malingering. Fundamentally, claimed the author, RSI was the result of 'boredom and disappointment':

> Nearly half a century ago someone said that most men lived lives of quiet desperation. Since that time many more women have come into the workforce and are staying in it through their adult lives and now they too will be leading the same lives of quiet desperation. Since women have had far less time to learn to live with that desperation, as opposed to housework desperation, their minds may not accept the situation and have started to rebel ... Are RSI sufferers the final casualties in the industrial revolution as it tapers off into the post-industrial society so beloved of Barry Jones? ... In short some of us, the majority, are going to be the chumps and a tiny few are going to be the champs. There is very little that anyone can do about it, except to redesign the systems to reduce the number of chumps at the VDUs [Visual Display Units].[93]

Between January 1983 and April 1984 in New South Wales, 284 cases of RSI were recorded, compared with 181 other cases of workplace accident and injury.[94] The Australian Public Service Association claimed in September 1984 that it knew of 3000 cases, and complained that 'the management response has been slow and in many cases totally unsatisfactory'. Interestingly, it recognised that factors other than actual 'keying and viewing' were undermining the health of office workers involved in repetitive tasks. 'For the keyboard/clerical worker', declared a union manual aimed at assisting workers to avoid or mitigate the effects of RSI, 'the lack of career advancement, poor salary levels, physical factors, noise, lighting, boredom, work routine, sexual harassment and machine-paced tasks' were combining to undermine workplace safety.[95] RSI seemed related to a wider sense of alienation.

Meanwhile, there were predictions that another revolutionary technology would soon make its way from the mail room to the office desktop and the home, thereby linking one and all to the world: the fax machine. Its expansion was spectacular: in 1984, there were only 8000 fax machines in the country but in the first four months of 1986 alone, 9000 units were shipped into Australia. In the 1985–86 financial year, almost 19,000 fax machines cleared customs, mainly from Japanese manufacturers, and there were perhaps 50,000 installed units in Australia by mid-1987.[96] At the beginning of 1986, Jonathan King was confused when an Australian public servant asked him to fax a draft letter to be transmitted to Britain. 'Righto,' replied King, 'I'll do that immediately.' 'As I hung up,' he recalled, 'I wondered exactly what a "fax" was.'[97] A couple of years later, when John Laws was interviewing John Howard, the Opposition leader explained that he had been able to keep up with news in Australia while travelling overseas 'because of the wonders of the facsimile machine' – the latest news arrived under his hotel door each morning:

Laws: How did we live without the fax machine?
Howard: I don't know.
Laws: I am damned if I know. Fantastic.
Howard: It is incredible. It's a bit like the time after phones were invented. It is quite extraordinary.[98]

Faxes nonetheless needed aggressive advertising because there were more than a dozen competing firms trying to sell them and they were far from cheap, costing between $3000 and $7000 in 1986. The cheaper models by the mid-1980s had a transmission rate of twenty to twenty-five seconds per page; top-end varieties could manage about ten seconds better and some could send a single document to multiple locations. But the fax machine's critical advantage over its older rival – the telex machine – was much cheaper transmission costs. One A4 page could be faxed to the United States from Australia for $1.32, compared with $5.60 for a telex.[99] Here was a powerful instrument of globalisation, and there were predictions of 100,000 installed units by the end of the decade.[100] In November 1988, an article in *Office News* headed 'E-mail Poised for Dramatic Growth in Australia' did not identify any likely threat to the spread of the fax machine.[101] At the end of the 1980s, the exciting new development was the laser fax, capable of using plain paper rather than the special shiny variety designed for fax machines.[102]

★

The home was also being transformed by technology. Families no longer had 'record players' so much as 'sound systems', with many upgrading to the new compact disc player even while most music was still also being released in older formats such as vinyl and cassette. Pre-packaged kitchens in new homes now sometimes came with a dishwasher and usually with space for a microwave, while laundries were built in the expectation that they would host a dryer. In more expensive new or renovated housing, bedrooms came with ensuites, bathrooms with spas and heated towel rails. Many homes had two or more colour televisions as well as a personal computer. And all of these shiny goods needed to be kept from the covetous who might be tempted to steal them for a quick and dirty sale in a hotel bar. Residents installed burglar alarms and formed Neighbourhood Watch groups to protect the valuable goods that their hard-earned money – or line of credit – had won for them.[103]

Easily the most significant of the new technologies of leisure and entertainment was the video cassette recorder (VCR): no new technology since the television had exercised such an influence over people's leisure. In 1982 just one in twenty Australian households had a VCR, yet within a little more than five years, this figure had risen rapidly to more than half. By 1988 $50 was the going rate for a 'hot' VCR on the black market; burglars were often leaving them behind and making off with the microwave and the computer instead.[104]

A visit to the local video rental store became a ritual for many Australian families, with evenings given over to the viewing of new releases or old favourites. Since many homes had more than one television but only a single VCR, this might have brought some families together at least occasionally, where once they scattered to the various corners of the house to watch their preferred programs or pursue other interests. Viewers were liberated from the programming of television stations because they could now record their favourite shows and watch them when they liked, pressing the fast-forward button when they came to the advertisements. No wonder there were concerns of 'a real threat to commercial television viewing'.[105] It might be imagined that cinemas also had reason to be concerned by the ubiquity of the VCR, but it did not kill them off since suburban multiplexes emerged to show the new releases before they made their way to the video store. Patronage actually grew as these cinemas showed a variety of films day and night, with better sound and picture quality than either drive-ins or independents.[106] Even in an age of nostalgia, the old theatres lacked an allure capable of withstanding the pressures of the market, and many staged their last picture show in the 1980s.

The VCR might, however, have contributed to a decline in reading. In 1978 one in five adults declared they had bought a book in the previous week, compared with just over half that number by 1989. Moreover, the proportion of people who said they had bought or borrowed books in the previous week declined from a third in 1978 to just over a quarter a decade later. More than half of all respondents declared that they were reading a book at the time they were surveyed, but this figure included students. The story was not a happy one for Australian fiction, long regarded as a litmus test for cultural vigour. Australian books accounted for just under one in ten fiction sales and an even smaller proportion of library borrowing, but almost half of the non-fiction books readers bought and nearly a third of those they borrowed. About one-third of the books being read by children were Australian.[107] The Literature Board of the Australia Council – the main vehicle for federal funding of books and writing – spent between $3 million and $4 million a year supporting literature in the second half of the 1980s;[108] yet the audience for the main genres that received support – fiction, poetry and drama – remained somewhat limited. The rise of multinational publishing placed considerable pressure on the small local publishing houses that had done much to promote a local literature since the 1960s.[109]

The existence of a flourishing national literature retained its status, alongside the newer and more popular medium of film, as a prestigious marker of cultural identity. 'It is curious that the idea of a national culture has such tenacity,' commented the academic Tim Rowse in 1985.[110] The 1980s saw the passing of an older generation of Australian novelists such as Christina Stead (1983), Eleanor Dark (1985) and Patrick White (1990), the rising fame at home and abroad of established authors such as David Malouf, Thomas Keneally, Frank Moorhouse and Peter Carey, and the emergence of a new group of writers, of whom David Foster, Elizabeth Jolley, Alex Miller, Amanda Lohrey, Peter Corris, Kate Grenville, Rodney Hall and Tim Winton were notable. Australia did not produce another Nobel laureate to follow White's triumph in 1973, but there were two Booker Prize winners: Keneally in 1982 with his Holocaust story, *Schindler's Ark*, later made into a multiple Oscar-winning film by Steven Spielberg; and Carey's *Oscar and Lucinda* in 1988, set in colonial New South Wales.[111] David Williamson remained the country's best-known dramatist, with plays such as *Sons of Cain* (1985), borrowing freely from colourful media reporting on corruption in Sydney, and *Emerald City* (1987), also set in Sydney, a rollicking story of the worlds of publishing and entertainment. Stephen Sewell and Nick Enright emerged as major figures during a decade of consolidation for Australian drama, with Enright displaying a notable versatility in his writing for theatre, musicals, television and film.[112] His comedy *Daylight Saving* (1989) – centred on the marriage of Tom, the manager of a tennis star, and Flick, the owner of a successful restaurant – explored the pressures that the busy careers of successful professionals were imposing on their intimate lives. Enright also at this time co-wrote the screenplay for *Come in Spinner* (1990), a polished TV adaptation of Dymphna Cusack and Florence James's 1951 novel about the wartime experiences of three women working in a beauty salon. In poetry, the literary critic David McCooey has suggested that there was a 'Generation of '79' – John Tranter, John Forbes, Laurie Duggan, Alan Wearne and John A. Scott – whose eclectic styles and use of everyday language signalled both their desire to create a recognisably Australian poetry and an engagement with the new intellectual fashion of postmodernism. But it was Les Murray who emerged by the end of the 1980s as the nation's most acclaimed poet; a writer of awesome linguistic facility, he identified with a rural and traditional Australia that many cultural sophisticates thought the country would do well to leave behind.[113]

The strength of Australian writing was also reflected in satire and comedy.[114] David Foster, a former research scientist, was a notable satirical novelist whose style sometimes recalled that of Joseph Furphy eighty years before, but it was in popular culture that we can most readily see a comedy and satire boom. Sketch comedy was dominated during the mid-1980s by the ABC's *Australia, You're Standing in It* and *The Gillies Report*, and later in the decade by *The D-Generation*, *The Comedy Company*, *Fast Forward* and *The Big Gig*. *Australia, You're Standing in It*, which had two seasons on the ABC in 1983 and 1984, relied on the comic talents of a married couple, Rod Quantock and Mary Kenneally.[115] Kenneally joined Stephen Blackburn to form the show's memorable Tim and Debbie. Always jumping on the latest bandwagon, they said 'amazing' and 'excellent' a lot, used strange legal-sounding phrases like 'adverted to', and were capable of extraordinary jumps in logic; most of their talk rapidly descended into nonsense. That Tim and Debbie were a satire on the pseudo-sophistication of young inner-suburban trendies did not apparently discourage schoolchildren from driving their teachers to distraction by imitating their bizarre speech, with its rising intonation at the end of each sentence. When Kenneally asked a teacher who was a fan if he taught children like Tim and Debbie, he replied that he taught *with* people like Tim and Debbie.[116]

The king of political satire, however, was Max Gillies, whose impersonations of the political leaders of the day – both local and foreign – disclosed a singular talent, one well supported by writers such as Patrick Cook, John Clarke, Wendy Harmer, Phil Scott and the historian Don Watson, later a prime ministerial speechwriter to Paul Keating.[117] Gillies did a fine Whitlam and an uncanny Bob Santamaria – the old Catholic anti-communist warrior – but Bob Hawke was his masterpiece. Not even death served as any defence against Gillies's biting satire. Sir Robert Menzies sang from heaven the glorious ditty 'I'm Glad I'm Not Alive Anymore', complete with angel's wings rivalled only by his eyebrows in their size and splendour.

Political satire never again reached such heights but sketch comedy remained vibrant. *The D-Generation*, like *Australia, You're Standing in It*, had its origins in Melbourne University revue comedy and provided the launching pad for almost an entire generation of young Australian comedians. Then, in the late 1980s, *The Comedy Company* introduced TV audiences to a new cast of comic characters that included Con the Fruiterer, a Greek greengrocer played by Mark Mitchell; Kylie Mole (Mary-Anne Fahey), a Melbourne schoolgirl who captured the idiom of the late 1980s schoolyard 'rooly' well; Uncle Arthur (Glenn Robbins), an accident-prone, organ-playing embarrassing relation; Col'n Carpenter (Kym Gyngell), a born loser – and many others. Created by Ian McFadyen, who also acted in the show and was then married to Fahey, the satire was less 'political' than Gillies's had been but sophisticated in its own way – and for a couple of years, immensely popular.

So too was another sketch comedy show, *Fast Forward*, produced by the lawyer Steve Vizard, and the ABC's *The Big Gig*, hosted by Wendy Harmer; both first went to air in 1989. *Fast Forward* emphasised media parody and continued the tradition of political satire via its 'Rubbery Figures' segments, which featured puppets depicting the major political figures of the time. *The Big Gig* had more in common with live stand-up comedy, recreating for the TV screen the setting and atmosphere of a major venue, and even coming with its own live audience. Among the acts that *The Big Gig* brought to national notice were the Doug Anthony Allstars, a talented musical comedy team consisting of Tim Ferguson, Paul McDermott and Richard Fidler. Named for obscure reasons after a leader of the federal Country Party, they had begun their careers as Canberra street buskers. Their ABC TV performances included the song 'I Fuck Dogs' ('You'll never be alone if you give a dog a bone') and they enjoyed testing – and pushing outwards – the boundaries of the permissible while also pricking the pretensions of the reflexively progressive.[118]

Situation comedy on the whole did less well than sketch comedy, which had natural roots in the live scene. One exception was *Acropolis Now* (1989–92), a sitcom set in a café and centred on the adult children of Greek migrants, which emerged out of the enormously successful stage show *Wogs Out of Work* created by actors Nick Giannopoulos and Simon Palomares.[119] Another ingenious and massively popular sitcom, *Mother and Son*, written by Geoffrey Atherden, concerned the relationship between a recently divorced journalist, Arthur Beare, played by Gary McDonald, and his mother, Maggie, whom the veteran radio and stage actor Ruth Cracknell turned into one of the greatest Australian comic characters of all. Maggie combined suspected dementia with an extraordinary talent for manipulating the long-suffering Arthur, and audiences loved the delicate balance between its black humour and absurdity.

*

Australians laughed at Arthur and Maggie's dysfunctional little household each week in homes that were growing larger. The average size of an Australian house increased by a third between the early 1970s and the late 1980s, partly through larger new homes, partly through a renovation craze that extended the size of old ones. Stephen Knight, a Melbourne academic, observed in 1990 that it seemed in Australia 'culturally impossible to live in a house and not do something to it'. Some streets in exclusive suburbs became perpetual building sites. Those with the money to do so often tried to give their new or renovated homes a 'historic' look, 'to alter a house to some basically fictional version of authenticity'. A.V. Jennings promoted its 'Australian Classic' as capturing 'all the style and individuality of the Federation era, while providing for all the amenities, comfort and luxury expected of a contemporary home of this class'. A taste for 'ornate, nostalgic design ... produced a bewildering blend of historical styles'. An award-winning project-home design of the period was 'based on late-19th century Italianate villas' while some advertising in the 1980s even reverted to using the term 'drawing room' when it meant 'living room'. Cottage gardens, too, made a comeback, in contrast with the fashionable 1970s preference for natives.[120]

The well-off also turned their attention to the restoration of inner-city houses – in keeping with the love of old things – which generated a minor industry in the materials and skills needed to recover their faded charm. Even the federal treasurer was not too busy to get in on the act, buying a former boarding house in Sydney's exclusive Elizabeth Bay, which he renovated room by room as a future home for his family and prized collection of antiques. This enterprise might help place in context Keating's having blamed the nation's increasingly unaffordable housing on those living 'in a house with a block of land, with the backyard swimming pool, the rotary hoist, the ground in front ... and insisting that no other form of development is AOK for Sydney'. His own tastes were clearly more European than Californian. Still, the growing diversity of Australian households such as those made up of just one person or of 'dinks' – double income, no kids – ensured that the old detached home on a quarter-acre block was not for everyone. Developers responded by offering expensive high-rise alternatives to those who wanted to combine modern luxury with the convenience of living close to the city. The Como development in Melbourne's South Yarra offered 'luxury New York-style apartment living', but almost four out of every five approvals in the late 1980s were still for a detached home.[121]

In 1985 the film *Emoh Ruo* ('Our Home' spelled backwards) satirised the suburban dream, following the trials of a young family after they abandon their caravan and seaside lifestyle for a dream home on Sydney's suburban frontier, a place that turns up many more sharks than the beach they left behind. While obviously exaggerated for comic effect, the difficulties the couple experienced in making ends meet would have been familiar enough to many first-home buyers in the mid-1980s, and especially in the Sydney market. The most popular of the project-home designs in Victoria in the late 1980s, a modest three-bedroom favourite among first home-buyers, cost $43,900, or around $80,000 on a block in an outer-western suburb. But anyone attempting to put together a similar package in outer-western Sydney would have been up for something like $120,000. Lenders tended to regard mortgage payments that swallowed about a quarter of a family's income as the benchmark for assessing their ability to meet their obligations, yet the national ratio of repayments to median family income by the late 1980s was 32 per cent nationally, and 38 per cent in Sydney.[122] For families dependent on the low income of a sole wage-earner, owning a home in a major city was now out of the question. Between 1980 and 1989, Sydney median house prices increased by 245 per cent at the same time as the basic wage rose by just 130 per cent, and by 1988 the payments on a standard loan would have accounted for 60 per cent of the income of a single breadwinner on the basic wage.[123] The proportion of owner-occupied dwellings actually declined between 1986 and 1991.[124]

At the same time as they upgraded at home, creating havens of leisured consumption, Australians were also upgrading away. The traditional January holiday in a beachside caravan park was giving way to a more commercialised, luxurious and expensive style of vacationing based on travel further from home for shorter periods. Resorts and theme parks proliferated – most obviously on Queensland's Gold Coast – and many families convinced themselves that their high-pressure lifestyles warranted an annual pampering of a kind that three or four weeks in a caravan or cabin had never delivered – especially to mothers who found themselves doing much the same kind of domestic labour as at home. That was now left to others – mainly cheap, casual labour – and not only in Australia but also abroad, for a week or so in Bali or Fiji was now within the reach of a growing number of Australians.[125]

Yet there was also a convergence between ordinary life and the holiday. Resort-style developments such as Sanctuary Cove on the Gold Coast presented life as a perpetual vacation.[126] Meanwhile, TV advertisements for Christopher Skase's Sheraton Mirage resorts – also opened in 1988 amid much extravagance – pictured men and women wearing evening dress for dinner, swimming pools that were larger versions of those found in the backyards of the well-heeled, and golf courses and luxury shops of much the same kind that they frequented when they were not on holidays.

*

For many young people the possibility of a job, let alone home ownership and a luxury holiday, seemed well out of reach. In an era when individual achievement and success were elevated, many found their satisfactions elsewhere, in the pleasures of popular culture and style, the joys of cheap technology, the role-playing of a game of Dungeons and Dragons, the mobility provided by skateboards and BMX bikes, the admiration of peers, a pride in demonstrating superiority over others. Some formed street gangs with other youths who shared their interests, prejudices and tastes: 'skinheads', 'surfies', 'breakers', 'writers', 'mods' (or 'trendsetters'), 'rockers' and 'punks'. They often self-consciously picked up these identities from overseas, adopting them as their own. For a mid-1980s Perth skinhead, demonstrating that one could be both an Australian and a skinhead was seemingly to be accomplished – like much else – with violence:

> There's a lot of English skinheads around and they say, 'Oh yeah, well you're not a Pom. You can't be a skinhead' and all this. I just turned around and said, 'You're in Australia.' And then they start pushing you and I said, 'Don't push me or I'll kick you in', or something like that, and then they just back off a bit.

His obvious loathing of 'boongs'[127] and Vietnamese – 'the refugees and shit, they're a waste of time' – suggested that he was the authentic article, if also a deeply unpleasant one.[128] Mods were equally indebted to English styles but in their case, with a dash of early-sixties nostalgia. 'Mods believe in style, sophistication', a Perth member of the species explained to a researcher in 1986. 'But it's away from society's accepted view of style. It's our own style that is sort of separate.'[129] In Melbourne the vibrant jazz scene to which the up-and-coming singer Kate Ceberano belonged similarly understood the pleasures of style and nostalgia. Young audiences turned up to her performances dressed 'in vintage clothing', having taught themselves 'all the old dances: the foxtrot, the samba, the Charleston, the cha-cha'. Ceberano 'sang in a kind of hybrid Ella Fitzgerald/Billie Holiday voice'.[130]

'Breakers' and 'writers' gained their inspiration from the New York hip-hop and breakdancing scene. Breakdancing, popular among a few young people – predominantly male youths – is a strenuous set of movements that require considerable strength and dexterity. Breakdancers with their baseball caps, sneakers and designer fashions would carry around a cassette player – 'boom box' – and set up on a favoured street, square or park, with the latest rap music accompanying their moves.[131] The 'writing' scene emerged out of breakdancing, initially as a sideline but by the mid-1980s as a subculture in its own right. Writers were graffiti artists, mostly male, who usually did their work with spray cans along train lines, sometimes on the carriages themselves, or on public buildings and walls. In a few cases, derelict commercial sites became informal galleries of colourful graffiti art. Each writing gang developed a recognisable style, sought to out-daub (or 'burn') the others, and some gained recognition in the art world as practising an innovative and legitimate form of artistic expression – a matter of some irritation to police, government, transport authorities and, no doubt, the railway employees handed the job of cleaning up after them. Graffiti art could also be dangerous: a Melbourne writer lost his legs and a Sydney writer his life in accidents on trains in the late 1980s. A 1989 cover story in the *Age* suggested that the scale of the city's graffiti plague indicated 'a deep teenage alienation'. Yet writing was also an expression of individual creativity and group belonging, a quest for recognition among peers and the public. 'We just want to be known to be good at something,' explained one young writer. When authorities began to open up legal spaces for graffiti art, the scene entered a period of decline.[132]

*

Music was central to the lives of the young. Their musical tastes – often displayed through t-shirts that announced whether one was into Michael Jackson or Iron Maiden – expressed identity and style. They read magazines such as *Smash Hits* and *Rolling Stone* and covered their bedroom walls with pictures of androgynous boy singers with mullet cuts and girl bands in dungarees with ruby-red lips and big hair posed as wild and unruly, while actually gelled strictly into place. They watched music programs on the television like Australia's own *Countdown* and *MTV* from the United States, and they listened to tapes on their Sony Walkmans and to FM stations such the ABC's Triple J – or, if they were from a country town, fiddled with the dial 'seeking out faint, scratchy signals of exotic broadcasts far away' while having to make do with a plain diet of top-forty 'hits' on the local station.[133]

From popular music, young people learned about love, sex and politics. Girls dreamed of romance and sex with rock stars and fantasised about becoming the next Madonna, Samantha Fox, Kylie Minogue or Chrissy Amphlett. Boys dreamed of becoming the rock stars with whom girls dreamed of sex and romance, and they fantasised about bedding their favourite Bangle, Chantoozie or Bananarama girl. Girls and boys saved up their pocket money to buy records, and they recorded their favourite songs on cassette tapes from the radio and their record collection, to be enjoyed whenever they chose. To create a compilation of one's favourite songs – a mixtape – and present it to a boy or girl one liked was as meaningful as a first kiss.[134]

The 1980s are usually associated in Australia, as elsewhere, with post-punk, funk and new wave, as the legendary pub rock tradition inherited from the 1970s was recast in the face of changing patterns of taste and new global – but really British and American – influences. INXS, the biggest Australian band of the era, formed a bridge between the old and the new. Tim, Andrew and Jon Farriss grew up in a solidly middle-class home, first in Perth and later in Sydney, where the family moved in 1971. There, they would meet Kirk Pengilly, a high-school friend of Tim's, as well as a rather intense young misfit with an interest in philosophy and poetry, named Michael Hutchence. He formed a friendship with the middle Farriss brother, Andrew, who shared his love of improving reading. The circle that would become INXS was more or less complete when a young bass player named Garry Beers, more sporty than the others, began jamming with a group of schoolboys that included Hutchence and Andrew Farriss. Inspired by an ad for IXL jam, they called themselves INXS and joined Sydney's exuberant pub rock scene at the end of the 1970s, one in which young men banged out loud music in heaving, smoke-filled hotels while their sweaty audiences of surfies, students and young workers got drunk on beer. Under the management of the enterprising Chris Murphy, they recorded a couple of albums, built up an Australian following and began looking for opportunities abroad.[135] By the time they had produced their first major local successes, *Shabooh Shoobah* (1982) and *The Swing* (1984), they were already gaining fans in the United States.

As the group's frontman, Hutchence emerged in the mid-1980s as INXS's most popular and recognisable figure. He departed not at all from existing scripts governing the behaviour of male rock stars of the vaguely arty and philosophical type: angst, drugs, booze, sex, a succession of beautiful girlfriends and a dash of the brooding poet and intellectual, the latter courtesy of Kahlil Gibran and Hermann Hesse. Indebted to the example of the Doors' Jim Morrison for his image of intellectuality and to the Rolling Stones' Mick Jagger for his uncanny ability to draw attention to his groin, Hutchence was in many respects a liminal, contradictory figure, perfectly matched to an era in which, as the cross-dressing English singer Boy George showed, there were rewards to be had for carefully tended ambiguity. Mesmerising in his effect on women, he was a somewhat androgynous figure with his shoulder-length wavy hair, a slightly pimply and pockmarked face, and a mild lisp.[136] Tall and lithe to the point of felinity and exuding a legendary sexual confidence, he was also shy and far removed from ocker masculinity. '[T]he least determinedly Australian member of INXS' spent his childhood and youth in Hong Kong and Los Angeles as well as Brisbane and Sydney.[137] It would be hard to imagine a young performer better prepared by his upbringing than Hutchence to make his way as an Australian in a global popular culture.

Despite their quiet cultivation of an image as easygoing Australians not given to airs or pretensions, INXS were at first thought to be British by some US critics.[138] They were certainly as slick and commercial as the best of the British new romantic bands, eclectic in their borrowing of styles – funk, rhythm and blues and heavy rock – and eager to take up the latest computer technology to achieve a product that could seem, to some critics, just a little too perfect. The British pop magazine *New Musical Express* ridiculed their sound as '[m]achine beats borrowed from black dance pop, but sugared for mass consumption', yet the effect on young American audiences was electric. 'The girls moon doe-eyed over Hutchence, wigging and pouting in a vain attempt to catch his eye,' reported a journalist of a concert in Seattle. 'The boys screw up their faces and punch the air a great deal.'[139]

INXS's international orientation belonged to the new wave, a more musically sophisticated evolution of punk that gained a global ascendancy over popular music in the 1980s. Their hit albums of the mid-1980s – *Listen Like Thieves* (1985) and especially *Kick* (1987) – turned them into global superstars. *Kick* reached number three on the American charts and sold about 9 million copies.[140] 'New Sensation', 'Devil Inside', 'Need You Tonight' and the romantic ballad 'Never Tear Us Apart' became the sound most associated with INXS and, through repetition on radio ever since, among the most recognisable sounds of Australia's 1980s. In this regard, the band's only serious rival was perhaps Midnight Oil, with whom INXS had sometimes performed early in their career. As we have already seen – and will see again in chapter 8 – the Oils were a decidedly more political band, more jealous of their artistic integrity and the purity of their message in the face of the temptations of commercialism. And although they engaged very directly with the local scene, Midnight Oil were a band of social-movement politics, which was by definition global – and they found an international audience for their music and message in the second half of the 1980s to complement their soaring popularity in Australia.

There were other international triumphs, too, such as the pop duo Air Supply, comprising Graham Russell and the spectacularly afro-ed Russell Hitchcock, who had a string of US hits in the early 1980s; and Men at Work, led by Scottish-born Colin Hay, whose album *Business as Usual* and hit singles 'Who Can It Be Now?' and 'Down Under' enjoyed spectacular chart success. 'Down Under' received a new lease of life from the America's Cup victory of 1983: its lyrics were hardly a celebration of national character – Australia was a place where women 'glow', and men both 'plunder' and 'chunder' – but no one let such complexities spoil the party. A subsequent hit by the group, 'Overkill', exposed their sensitivity to the darker side of celebrity and success.[141] Crowded House also did well in the United States, Britain and Europe, as well as closer to home – including in founding member Neil Finn's native New Zealand. Their ballad 'Don't Dream It's Over' (1986) reached number two in the US pop charts.

Post-punk bands such as Perth's The Triffids and Brisbane's The Go-Betweens won respect and credibility, but neither popularity nor riches. Grant McLennan, a member of The Go-Betweens, who based themselves in Britain for much of the decade, complained of the difficulties for such a band in the age of manufactured pop stars when he described the 'celebration of the ephemeral, music as supermarket trash. And we are not part of it.

I'm into writing classic songs that'll last forever and the notion of permanency is a terribly unfashionable one at the moment.'[142] But The Go-Betweens still craved the commercial success that forever eluded them, not just the critical acclaim they were offered by the musical press and appreciative fans. They came closest to a hit with their 'Streets of Your Town' (1988), a song which charted, albeit modestly, in both Britain and Australia, as well as superbly capturing the darkness in the heart of sunny Brisbane – their town – in the twilight of the National Party's long reign. The combination of bright, upbeat music and the darkest of lyrics – such as its reference to 'battered wives' – was a potent combination.

Nick Cave was another Australian expatriate performer. Growing up in a middle-class family with his father a teacher and his mother a librarian, Cave attended art school before emerging as an angry young man in Melbourne's post-punk scene as lead singer of The Birthday Party, who made a successful career in Britain and Europe in the early 1980s. The gaunt, dark-haired Cave subsequently based himself in Berlin; in 1987, a reporter from Britain's *New Musical Express* found him living in the corner of an office. 'Everything I use I borrow,' Cave explained. 'I've never had a flat.' Self-consciously playing the misfit, the scavenger and the scammer, Cave was a leading member of Berlin's artistic and bohemian underground as he forged a career as frontman for Nick Cave and the Bad Seeds. But like those of bohemians in other times and places, Cave's career aspirations were of the usual kind: '[r]ecognition, success, that sort of thing.'[143] There would be plenty of 'that sort of thing' to come, even if many of those in awe of Cave's immense talent and inventiveness fully expected that his chaotic life would end in a heroin overdose.

In the second half of the 1980s Cave experienced an extraordinary burst of creativity which included the albums *Your Funeral, My Trial* (1986) and *Tender Prey* (1988); an acting, scriptwriting and musical role in the Australian film *Ghosts ... of the Civil Dead* (1988); and a powerful gothic novel on which he worked for many years, *And the Ass Saw an Angel* (1989). Although he was the product of a country fond of thinking itself secular, Cave's vision was essentially religious, infused with biblical and apocalyptic imagery, and concerned with the grand themes of love, sex, suffering, death and evil. In this, he surely had as much in common with older compatriots such as Patrick White, Arthur Boyd and Manning Clark as he did with the obvious influences on his career: Bob Dylan, Leonard Cohen and Neil Young. The opening track of *Tender Prey*, 'The Mercy Seat', one of Cave's best, is a religious meditation of striking power and originality – an ironic juxtaposition of Old Testament justice of an eye for an eye with the merciful figure of Christ the carpenter, crucified 'like some ragged stranger'. In this terrifying account of a man facing the electric chair, Cave's raw vocals bring out in full force the song's haunting lyrics. When *Tender Prey* was released to critical acclaim, Cave was in rehab.[144]

The Oz rock of the 1970s – and the impression that every Australian band found it necessary to belt out their songs like AC/DC and Cold Chisel did – gave way to a wider spectrum of music as the transnational influence of post-punk, new wave, funk, hip-hop and much else reshaped popular taste. One measure of change was that the white male-dominated pub rock culture was becoming a little less so, with the mainstream success of some Aboriginal singers and groups such as Yothu Yindi, and the prominence of the Eurogliders, I'm Talking and Divinyls, all of which had female lead singers (I'm Talking had two). In 1990 Chrissy Amphlett of Divinyls, already famous for her wild stage performances, had a hit with 'I Touch Myself', a song in praise of female masturbation which, in the spirit of pleasure all round, also contained a couple of upbeat allusions to fellatio. But some bands such as the Choirboys – whose 1987 song about drug addiction 'Run to Paradise' was one of the biggest-selling Australian singles of the decade – continued the older pub rock tradition. So, in a manner, did Uncanny X-Men, a Melbourne group headed by the pint-sized, prancing former Catholic schoolboy Brian Mannix. Their 'Everybody Wants to Work' (followed, in the song, by 'No, no, not me') nicely captured a youthful cynicism about the 1980s premium on careers and money. Old pop stars revived. Johnny Farnham – now just plain John – left behind his 1970s hits such as 'Sadie the Cleaning Lady' and 'Raindrops Keep Falling on My Head' for the comparative sophistication of 'You're the Voice' and 'A Touch of Paradise'. His *Whispering Jack* (1986) sold a million copies and he was named Australian of the Year in 1988. Other performers, such as Jimmy Barnes, formerly of Cold Chisel, and Daryl Braithwaite, of Sherbet, forged successful careers as solo artists.

Some popular music barely disclosed any local influence at all. The Melbourne group Pseudo Echo could have walked straight out of a London club; with their blow-dried hair and modish fashions they were an echo indeed – of British new romantic bands such as Duran Duran and Spandau Ballet. Icehouse, led by classically trained oboe player Iva Davies, was also a polished act completely in step with international new-wave pop. Hunters and Collectors, by way of contrast, began as a rather arty Melbourne outfit that enjoyed limited popularity until their 1986 album, *Human Frailty*, which included the stunning love song 'Throw Your Arms Around Me'. Their songs oozed the atmosphere of their city. Paul Kelly similarly bombed in his early recorded work but his finely honed sense of place and storytelling in song won him a growing local audience and a steadily rising reputation in the second half of the decade.

*

The world of popular music was interwoven with other cultural forms. Richard Lowenstein not only made many of INXS's most successful videos but also a film about Melbourne's punk-drug scene of the late 1970s, *Dogs in Space*, starring Hutchence. Nick Cave, as we have seen, moved into film and literature while punk, post-punk and new-wave rockers frequently emerged from the art schools. Cave and Reg Mombassa (Chris O'Doherty) of Mental as Anything were examples, but unlike Cave, Mombassa continued to practise as an artist even after achieving rock fame. Cave took many years to get over the sense that rock music was among the lower forms of creative endeavour, yet rising young artists such as Howard Arkley, who would relax in his studio strumming the only chord he knew on a guitar, sometimes gave the impression that they would have been happiest as punk rockers.[145] Heroin and amphetamines certainly pervaded both worlds. The young rebels of punk and avant-garde fashion, such as Katie Pye in Sydney or those involved in Melbourne's Fashion Design Council, also commonly emerged from the art schools, and their creations could at times seem better suited to the inner-city gallery than the bodies of those who frequented such places.[146] Yet what drew all of these forms of creative endeavour together was a sense of style associated with new wave. The preferred image was that of the outsider battling the establishment, the bohemian on the margins, the 'white Aborigine',[147] or, as the artist Jenny Watson explained in 1984, 'a sort of *Mad Max* character, the nomadic warrior alone with him or herself against the Beckett-like dead landscape in a nuclear, post-Capitalist society'.[148] But capitalism was not quite over yet, and the market soon demonstrated that there was money to be made from being 'poor' and 'marginal', yet 'hip' and 'stylish'.

Artists and critics grappled with the old question of whether art in Australia needed to be recognisably Australian. A group of young Melbourne artists called themselves ROAR – a pun (on 'raw') that was also indebted to an old black-and-white film of an extinct Tasmanian tiger giving a silent roar – and set up a gallery in Fitzroy. They took much of their inspiration from the Angry Penguins artists of the 1940s, turning from the 1970s focus on conceptual art towards figurative painting in an expressionist style (which critics predictably dubbed 'neoexpressionism'). But where artists such as Albert Tucker, Arthur Boyd and Sidney Nolan had responded to the dark era of wartime Australia, the ROAR artists' often colourful work seemed a more joyful and optimistic statement about being young and creative in Melbourne's inner suburbs.[149] For the young Melbourne critic Paul Taylor, however, 'conformism' remained 'the flavour of the month' in Australian art, 'this month, every month, month after month'.[150] The ambitious and entrepreneurial Taylor, who died of AIDS in his mid-thirties, established a groundbreaking journal of art criticism called *Art & Text* in 1981 and curated the *POPISM* exhibition at the National Gallery of Victoria before heading for New York. Popism came to be treated by some critics as a school in its own right, an extension of the 1960s and 1970s practice of pop, minimalist and conceptual art. Rather than ransacking the national artistic past, Taylor prescribed photography and large doses of French post-structuralist theory as antidotes for what was wrong with the local art scene.

*

The 1980s now look rather like a hinge in twentieth-century Australian history, a moment of transition between old and new ways of living. Powerful technologies changed people's lives at home and work, yet they can seem modest compared with the more drastic transformation that the arrival of the internet would bring in the following decade. The sexual and gender revolutions that commenced in the late 1960s continued to reverberate through public and private life in the 1980s, but old masculinities remained in the bedroom as well as in the boardroom, and women had barely begun their conquest of the commanding heights of politics, society and culture. The AIDS crisis gave new visibility and legitimacy to gay life, yet it also mobilised old and dark fears.

Australian culture was perhaps less preoccupied by the end of the 1980s with questions of national distinctiveness than it had been a decade before, yet much cultural expression retained an intensely local flavour in its quest for universal themes. The troubled Melbourne artist Howard Arkley's paintings of suburban houses stand as some of the most recognisable images of the period. While so obviously influenced by international pop art, they also contained a powerful mythological and nostalgic quality, not least for the wealthy clients who bought up the lot at $6000 a piece during his 1988

'Houses and Homes' show. These were consumers buying memories of their childhood: of the simpler world of suburban Australia before their own lives were transformed by the money that came with success in a globalised economy.[151] Yet as the affectionate response to Arkley's images showed, globalisation did not erase local or national distinctiveness in the arts; it provoked a more intense preoccupation with what was most valuable in the Australian past and present, and a quiet hope that one need not adopt an anodyne international style in the quest for cultural recognition. These preoccupations would be woven into the politics of the Bicentenary.

Sheltering from the Ash Wednesday bushfires in an underground tunnel, Reefton, Victoria.

DAVID COMBE... THIS COURT FINDS YOU GUILTY OF THE CHARGES AGAINST YOU... (WHICH REGRETTABLY CANNOT BE SPECIFIED BECAUSE OF NATIONAL SECURITY)...... AND SENTENCES YOU TO LOSS OF LIVELIHOOD.....
PRYOR

Clockwise from top left: David Combe on trial but Judge Hawke has the case in hand.

Paul Keating explains how it is.

For Geoffrey Blainey the name-tag was already superfluous.

Bob Hawke and Alan Bond celebrate *Australia II*'s victory in Canberra.

The changing face of Cabramatta.

'I had my pride': Cliff Young waves to admirers.

Bob Brown gets together with some friends in Tasmania.

John Elliott reviews the game with Carlton captain Stephen Kernahan.

Russell Goward thinking about how to make his next ten million.

Elegant even in caricature:
Robert Holmes à Court.

Robert Holmes à Court
by Joe Greenberg (1923–2007)
watercolour, crayon, coloured pencil,
gouache and felt tipped pen on paper
Collection: National Portrait Gallery, Canberra
Gift of the artist 2001

A LOSER   A WINNER

Malcolm Fraser and Bob Hawke have a good cry.

Christopher Skase enjoys a well-earned break.

What you need: Michael Hutchence relaxing with girlfriend Michele Bennett.

Paul Hogan (right) and John Cornell living it up.

Howard Arkley's suburban houses are now among the most evocative images of the 1980s.

Howard Arkley, *House and garden, Western suburbs*, Melbourne 1988
synthetic polymer paint on canvas, 174.7 × 400 cm
National Gallery of Australia, Canberra: Purchased 1988
© The Estate of Howard Arkley. Licensed by Kalli Rolfe Contemporary Art.

Peter Garrett doesn't hold back.

The Comedy Company's Kylie Mole in a rooly excellent jumper.

Scott Robinson (Jason Donovan) and Charlene Mitchell (Kylie Minogue) taking neighbourliness seriously.

The First Fleet comes into view with advice for Bicentennial revellers.

Aboriginal protestors issue a reminder that white Australia has a black history.

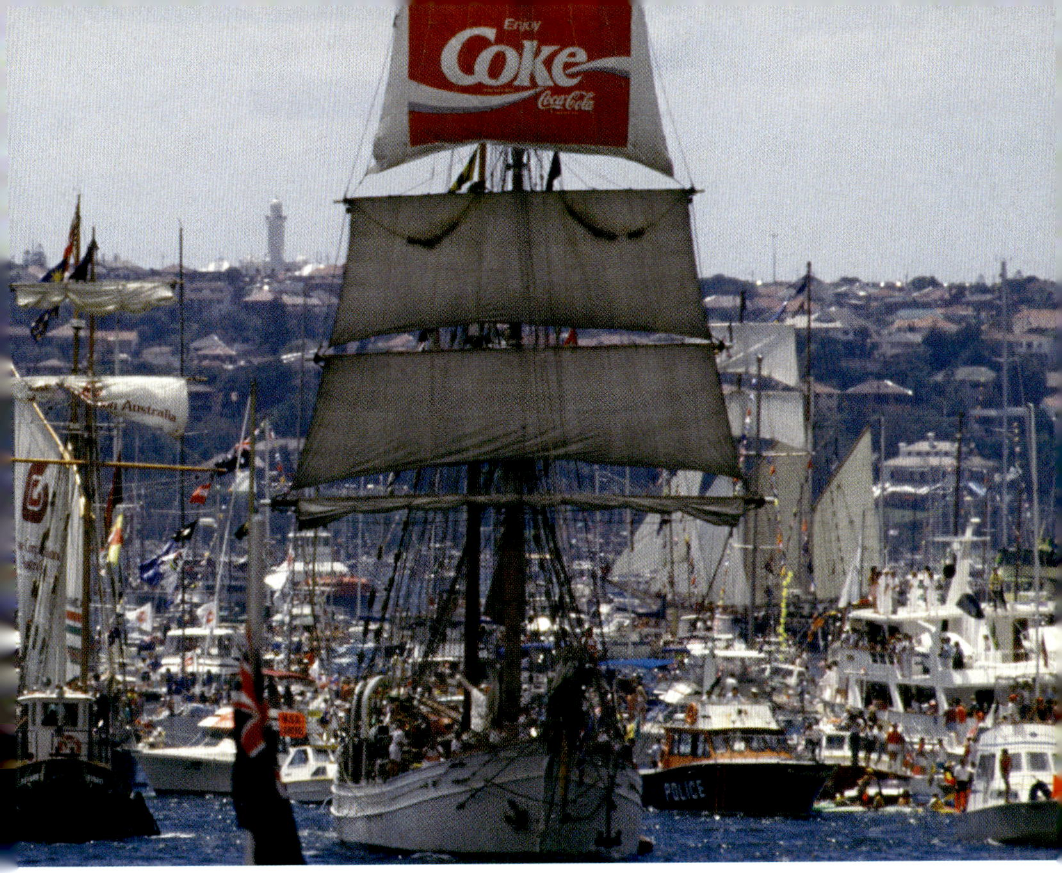
Enjoy
Coke
Coca-Cola
POLICE

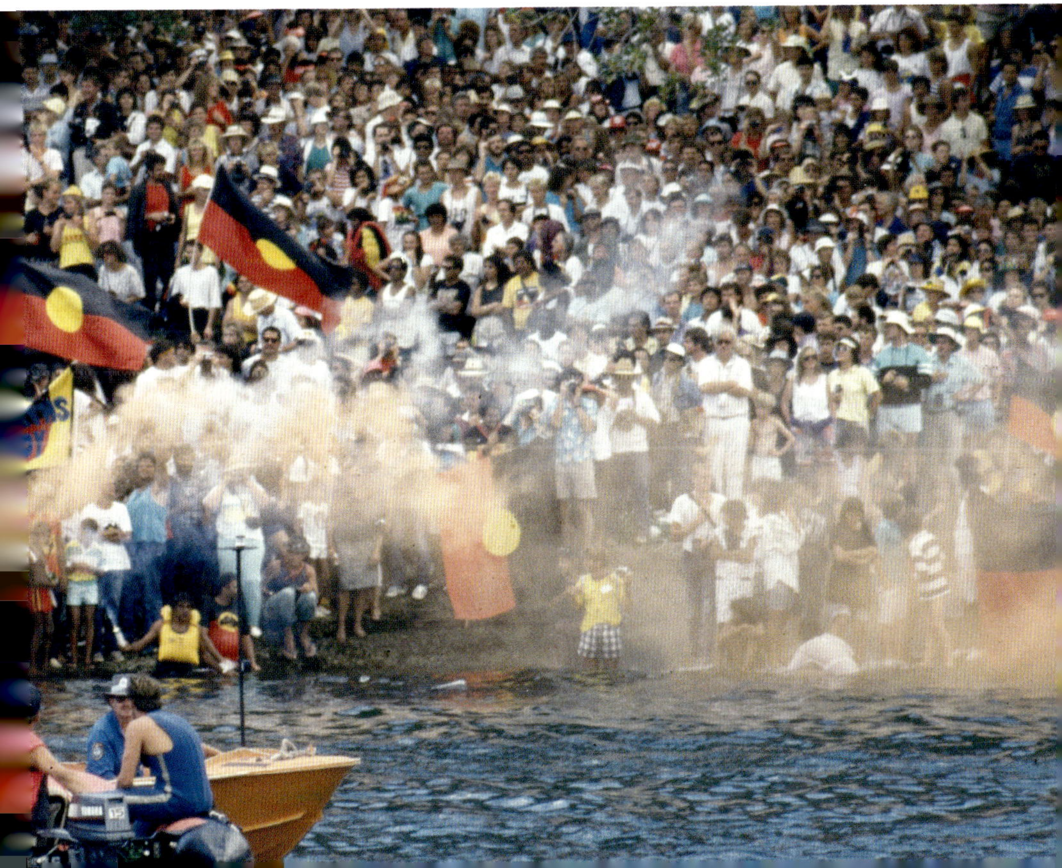

Protestors show that jailed BLF boss Norm Gallagher was gone but not forgotten.

Plans for the Multifunction Polis were only a little less fantastic than depicted here.

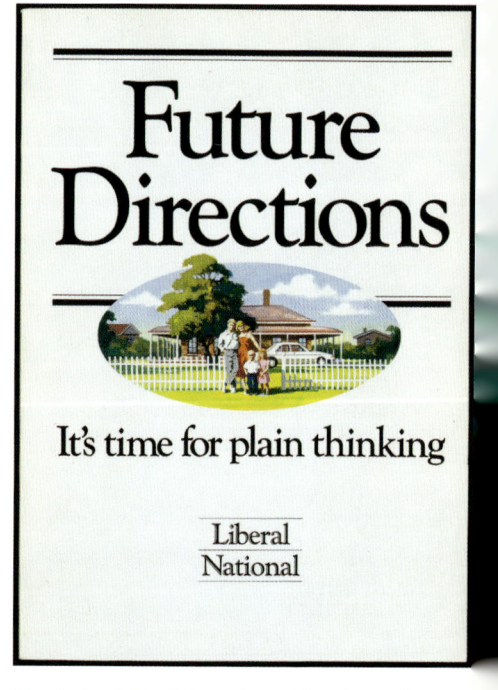

The federal Coalition tries taking Australia back to the future.

Irene Bolger and striking nurses take a walk.

Joh Bjelke-Petersen demonstrates where he intends taking Queensland – and Australia.

Bob Hawke under pressure.

8
The Identity Card

If the Government sends me an identification card I shall return it with a letter to explain that I do not need it; I already know who I am.
　　Douglas Graham (Ringarooma), *Australian*, 8 September 1987

In 1998 the novelist David Malouf celebrated Australians' discovery of a style he called 'loosely Mediterranean', which he thought epitomised by people eating at pavement tables. But where they dined was only the beginning of it. Australians now ate dainty and stylish dishes, drank wine and dressed up or stripped off for display. They had come to accept their own bodies and were thoroughly at ease in enjoying themselves. Australia, he said, had become a place 'where play seems natural, and pleasure a part of what living is for' – a contrast with what he saw as the more limited possibilities in the British and Irish Australia of his youth.[1]

The 1980s were the critical decade in the emergence of this way of living, thinking and feeling and, as Malouf recognised, the country's foodways – the intersection of food and culture – were among the most vivid illustration of a new cosmopolitan sensibility. 'Do not overload any meal with cream or butter,' the chef Stephanie Alexander advised in one of her early books, as she went about her mission of dismantling notions of taste entrenched by almost 200 years of chops, stews and roasts. Alexander emphasised cooking with fresh and seasonal ingredients, a greater number of small courses rather than the piling up of large portions, and the idea of a meal as a 'ceremony' that had 'a beginning, a middle and an end'. Basing her cooking 'on French classical methods' but in keeping with her view that cooks needed to be attuned to the society in which they lived, Alexander also became interested in Asian and Aboriginal food. Graham Little, a political psychologist and one of Alexander's loyal subjects, distinguished her culinary nationalism from 'a rough old nationalism', in that it 'respected ... the other worlds of food'. Yet it was decidedly Australian: even the waiting style in her restaurant, he thought, far from displaying the intrusiveness and deference found elsewhere, was consistent with the democratic spirit.[2]

As Malouf suggested, restaurant dining had become one easily recognisable mark of the new refinement, a turning of the back on the world of beer, pies and blue singlets. Victorians could from 1987 even buy alcohol in cafés and restaurants without ordering a meal as well; such a community clearly had the world at its feet.[3] The cosmopolitan citizen could tell her shiraz from her cabernet sauvignon and knew how to pronounce both *focaccia* and *roulade*. Salad, meanwhile, was no longer shorthand for iceberg lettuce, sliced tomatoes and grated carrot. Alfalfa, chives, snow peas and mustard cress now graced the bowl, which might also include warm duck or lobster. 'Eating Italian' meant something more exotic than spaghetti bolognese, while the appearance of Vietnamese, Japanese, Thai and high-quality Chinese restaurants meant that chicken chow mein ceased to be the Asian culinary frontier.[4]

These changes were the result of a restaurant revolution that climaxed in an increasingly sophisticated national culture of fine dining. The nouvelle cuisine was taken up in Australia but in the hands of local mimics it became synonymous with pretentious presentation, stingy portions and high prices. Yet it also 'taught a lighter, fresher style of cooking', and innovative restaurateurs took up the cause and adapted it to local conditions. Melbourne had an especially vibrant restaurant scene in the 1980s, one in which restaurateurs such as Alexander, Dennis Gowing, Mietta O'Donnell and Tony Knox figured prominently. Just outside Sydney, nestling on the Hawkesbury, Gay and Tony Bilson's Berowra Waters Inn also acquired a towering reputation. Chef-owners such as these believed they had 'an educative function', a role in guiding public taste. Their efforts helped change the way Australians experienced food.[5]

The new cosmopolitanism also influenced what Australians were doing at home. They were embracing new and not-so-new technologies such as the microwave, the electric knife and the sandwich-maker. In many households, the venerable Sunbeam Mixmaster, possibly still wearing a floral cover, was forced to surrender to the food processor as pride of the kitchen bench. Chicken, once for a special occasion, was becoming a regular dish, regarded as healthier than red meat. Fruit juice was embraced as 'healthy'. Pasta, once ignored as a suspect foreign dish, was becoming a staple and an expression of unpretentious cosmopolitanism. And the reverberations of the salad revolution were also to be felt in the home.[6]

Even so, foodways for many remained traditional. There was still a tendency to regard mothers as primarily responsible for their family's nutrition, at a time when the proportion of married women in the workforce climbed from around four in ten in 1983 to over half in 1991.[7] And many women themselves saw their performance in the kitchen, especially in the evening meal, as a test of their competence as wives and mothers, even as their role outside the home left little time for preparing meals. Eating out, once 'a very unusual treat', was becoming commonplace, although some thought Australians not very good at it – amateurish, said Stephen Knight, the British expatriate academic. For his part, Hugh Mackay suggested that as it became more common, the pleasure that people derived from dining out seemed to be diminishing: people complained of the cost, the quality, the hassle.[8]

Another ambiguous measure of the new cosmopolitanism was the change in Australians' drinking habits. The development of the wine industry had long been treated as a mark of civilisational sophistication, a habit that continued into the 1980s. Between 1980 and 1987, per capita consumption increased from 17.3 litres to 21.3 litres, while there was a spectacular growth of exports from 1986, stimulated by the low dollar: they tripled in volume between 1986 and 1988. A third of wine exports were in bulk and of low quality; oddly, for a few years Sweden became the main market for this kind of Australian wine, probably as a result of concerns about the effects of the Chernobyl nuclear disaster on European vineyards.[9] But on the eastern seaboard of the United States, the arrival of good-quality bottled wine presented a new and unfamiliar image of a country known mainly through the recent success of *Crocodile Dundee*; Walkabout Creek seemed an unlikely place to find a nice glass of chardonnay. In Australia, cheap cask wine accounted for almost two-thirds of table wine sold, and white wine was four times as popular as red, but tastes were becoming drier as chardonnay came to replace riesling as the most favoured drop. Wine cooler – a mixture of wine and fruit juice – enjoyed popularity especially among young women, for whom it was a sweet, cheap road to oblivion. Boutique or pub-brewed beers, increasingly available by the late 1980s, provided a means of combining cosmopolitan sophistication, contempt for Bond and Elliott, and the love of drink still most commonly associated with the old Australia.[10]

*

As the culture of home life changed, so too did its physical surroundings. The fate of the old Melbourne industrial suburb of Richmond was mirrored in many Australian cities. Factories that had provided the mainstay of the local economy for generations were closing down, in many cases moving their operations to cheaper land elsewhere. Small-scale manufacturing sometimes moved in to take their place. The Rosella food-processing plant with 480 employees closed in 1983, its 7.7-acre site sold off the following year. The canning operation went to rural Tatura, the food processing to outer-suburban Rowville. The Vickers Ruwolt engineering works also announced that it was moving out of Richmond in 1984; 500 workers would lose their jobs. 'Some of us have been here for over 30 years,' explained one shop steward. 'I started in 1956. It's home to us.' The Bryant and May match factory in the same suburb would also close in the 1980s, as imports made local production unprofitable.[11] Yet in the same locale, as these relics of an old way of life passed into history, a new way was vigorously promoted by government and business. The Olympic Swimming Pool was converted into the Melbourne Entertainment Centre, a new National Tennis Centre was built, and the Cain government erected lights at the Melbourne Cricket Ground and blocked the Victorian Football League from moving the grand final to the outer-suburban VFL Park.[12]

In this manner, governments embraced what the historian Seamus O'Hanlon has called 'the events strategy' as a basis for urban renewal. In Melbourne, the redevelopment of the derelict South Bank of the Yarra River was one manifestation of the new approach. In Sydney the Wran government's redevelopment of Darling Harbour was inspired by a widely admired project to redevelop the port area of the American city of Baltimore. The Darling Harbour area, which included a new National Maritime Museum, was to be serviced by a monorail, a train set above the street that would connect the old port with the city centre. And under the leadership of government minister Laurie Brereton, a razor-sharp political operator, it was all going to happen in just four years, in time for the Bicentenary. But the monorail's construction – like the project as a whole – was vigorously contested. Patrick White called it the 'Monsterail', although the concept had its defenders, such as the cultural critic John Docker, who argued that it would contribute to a playful postmodernism sorely needed by a city still recovering from postwar brutalism.[13]

The smaller cities invested even greater hope in big projects and major events, for these could transform a backwater into an international city, an overgrown country town into a modern metropolis. Adelaide installed a casino in the railway station and staged the Formula One Australian Grand Prix from 1985. The international recognition implied by the award of a glamorous major event was deeply gratifying to a city whose cosmopolitan gloss – largely the product of the 1970s premiership of Don Dunstan – only partly obscured its fear of being considered backward. Soon it would win the right to host the Multifunction Polis, the joint Japanese–Australian project for a high-tech city, a success local promoters of the project treated as a boost to Adelaide's cosmopolitan identity.[14]

To the west, optimism about the port of Fremantle managed to survive even the unwelcome victory of *Stars and Stripes* in the America's Cup summer of 1986–87. Stimulated by $83 million of government spending, as well as the relocation of hundreds of state and federal public servants to the town, Fremantle underwent something more substantial than either a clean-up or a face lift. Public and private buildings were restored or developed, the waterfront transformed into an attractive leisure space, the city's infrastructure renewed and new public housing built. While a third of residents thought the cup defence would leave the city worse off, all but a few changed their minds once the yachties and tourists had taken their leave. 'Freo is chic where once it was rough,' concluded an airline magazine.[15]

In Brisbane, local boosters were fond of calling Expo '88 a turning point in the city's fortunes, a 'coming of age', the moment when a sleepy, subtropical town became 'an international city'.[16] Expo gave further momentum to a business already well in hand: the destruction of old Brisbane by an alliance of the Bjelke-Petersen government and property developers. The rugged working-class South Bank of the Brisbane River found itself with a supporting role in the new cosmopolitan script.[17] South Brisbane, explained a local satirical magazine, 'has always been the wrong side of the river', the place where the blacks and the migrants lived and 'the prostitutes and sly grog were sold openly' under police protection. All of this had to go as the city spread 'across the river in the interest of art, leisure and technology. Beneath it all is the stink of patronage, donations to the Bjelke-Petersen Foundation and real estate tips given long ago.'[18] ''Together, We'll Show the World' was the Expo '88 slogan, but there was always an ambiguity about who the 'we' actually were; it assuredly did not include the South Brisbane renters kicked out of their homes to make way for Expo visitors. The Expo audience, in any case, was predominantly from Queensland, so it is doubtful whether 'the world' considered it had been shown anything much at all. Still, many recall Expo with great fondness. The ostensibly international character of the event did not prevent its becoming a celebration of Queensland pride, identity and optimism amid bright sunshine and vivid colours, such as those offered by Ken Done's gaudy *Australia* sculpture, the Australian pavilion's exterior.

The image of Queensland that Expo presented might have been a familiar one – a land of sunshine, beaches and fun – but its high-tech US and Japanese gadgets and displays also conveyed a sense of a city and a state joyfully embracing modernity. Especially for people who had not much travelled, getting your replica passport stamped in each of the national pavilions provided a sense of having experienced cultural diversity or, as one grateful couple put it, having been 'given one last chance to see the world'. Sidewalk dining and extended opening hours for hotels and eateries survived the event's conclusion.[19]

*

The cosmopolitan identity associated with the inner city needed a bête noire, and in Sydney, a city with well-differentiated regions of affluence and poverty, this position was occupied by 'westies – who are dags because they wear jeans on the beach and always bring an esky'.[20] The term 'bogan', emerging in the mid-1980s, lacked a specific regional flavour, but it too provided a way to talk about class differences as a matter of cultural style rather than material deprivation – in a society that still nurtured the idea that anyone prepared to 'have a go' would do nicely. Without cosmopolitanism, there could have been no bogan or westie, for these identities took their meaning from their relationship with one another. To be cosmopolitan was to hold a licence for commentary on the taste of those seen to lack cultural savoir faire. Yet popular culture added layers of complexity; it continued to celebrate lifestyles and identities that maintained some distance from the new cosmopolitanism. Two of the most spectacularly successful Australian cultural products of the era drew on older identities supposedly being swept away by the advent of urbanity.

When the new television soap opera *Neighbours* began its career on Channel Seven in 1985, *TV Week* declared it 'our own *Coronation Street*', in a reference to the long-running British soap. *Neighbours*, however, was from the outset quite different, being filmed not in a proletarian street but the middle-class Melbourne suburb of Vermont, the fictional Ramsay Street, Erinsborough. The new cosmopolitans who hung around hip precincts such as Brunswick Street in Melbourne and Oxford Street in Sydney might have thought of suburbia as daggy, but *Neighbours* was a quiet celebration of the Australian suburb at a time when it remained the setting for most people's lives.[21] Yet Ramsay Street was also a long way from most Australians' experiences of suburban life, having more in common with a village or, in the world of Australian soaps, with Wandin Valley, the town depicted in *A Country Practice*. Erinsborough was not a dormitory suburb in which the tired commuter sought refuge after a busy day in the office, but an intimate community where people lived, loved and (occasionally) laboured without seeming to need very much that the rest of the world had to offer.[22] Suburbia, as depicted in *Neighbours,* was a place of community, social drama and, above all, nice-looking young people with tanned skin and perfect teeth.

None of this made for instant success. The early history of *Neighbours* illustrates one of the most neglected features of the 1980s: the continuing salience of the local. *Neighbours* fared reasonably well in Melbourne, but poorly in Sydney. It did not rate well enough nationally to justify its relatively high cost, and the show was cancelled in mid-1985.[23] The executives responsible for this decision would in due course possibly feel like the record company executive who advised Beatles manager Brian Epstein that groups of guitarists were on the way out. Later in the year Channel Ten, the lowliest of the three commercial networks, picked up the soap. It received a makeover and was also marketed aggressively, especially in Sydney.[24]

Most significantly, it recruited a number of young actors who proved to have star quality. Of these, two especially stood out. Jason Donovan, who had been raised by his divorced father, Terence, himself a well-known television actor, was a handsome young blond with a winning smile, a pot habit and a luxuriant mullet hairstyle. He played Scott Robinson: the all-Australian suburban lad. Scott's love interest was Charlene Mitchell, played by Kylie Minogue, a small, pretty teenager with her hair a mess of curls and waves. There was little indication, as the tomboyish Charlene made the transition from a school uniform to the overalls of an apprentice mechanic, that by the end of the decade she would be one of the most famous women on the planet.

During 1986 *Neighbours* became a hit: less so in Sydney than Melbourne, but a hit nonetheless. One of the marketing techniques its promoters favoured was the personal appearance at suburban shopping malls. These were not discreet occasions for orderly autograph signing but spectacles full of screaming – and occasionally fainting – young girls. This mania would soon spread well beyond Australia's shores. The company that produced the show, Grundy's, sold *Neighbours* to the BBC, which from October 1986 used it to fill a couple of obscure daytime slots.[25] After the show quietly built up a following among housewives, university students, younger kids on school holidays and Britain's massive army of unemployed, BBC management decided to repeat each episode in the late afternoon – with spectacular results. Although *Coronation Street* remained the prince of British soapies with more than 24 million viewers per episode, by the late 1980s *Neighbours* managed an average of about 18 million, placing it just behind another BBC serial, *EastEnders*, with 20 million.[26]

While *Neighbours* would, in due course, find its way to dozens of other countries, fathoming the reasons for the show's appeal to British audiences sparked a mini-industry. *Neighbours* was 'just quaintly foreign enough to please without confusing', offering what the producer of *EastEnders* perceptively called 'an almost different type of culture – a breakaway from the stale English environment'.[27] Others surmised that 'a street full of good citizens' – all of them white – 'who have a house, job and self-reliance automatically leading to good neighbourliness', was just the thing in Thatcher's Britain.[28] Unlike its British rivals, *Neighbours* shunned social and political issues and so did good service as escapist fantasy. And due to the show's filming location of Melbourne, while the sun often shone on Ramsay Street, it did so less constantly or fiercely than some British viewers might have expected. The accents were unmistakably Australian, but they were not so foreign as to confound or offend any but the most easily confounded or offended ears – especially ears already raised, as so many young British ears had been, on the dulcet tones of Rolf Harris.[29]

Neighbours presented an image of Australia somewhat out of time. It was white, even Anglo, in an era when most Australian governments promoted the virtues of a multicultural citizenry. A British-based Aboriginal poet and filmmaker, Rikki Shields, argued in 1988 that the introduction of an Aboriginal character to the show would do much to advance the cause of his people 'because then everyone could see that we are Australian too'.[30] Yet '[i]t is quite unthinkable that the ravaged countenance of an Australian black could suddenly pop up on *Neighbours*', judged Germaine Greer in 1989, possibly indulging in a bit of stereotyping of her own. '[I]f a gang of Aborigines were to camp on one of those manicured lawns, and pass around the flagon, the good neighbourliness would evaporate long before anyone actually relieved himself in the shrubbery.' *Neighbours* certainly projected a nostalgic view of Australia, one largely unaffected by the migrations of the 1940s to 1960s, let alone those from Asia since the 1970s. 'How many wogs are there in *Neighbours*?' asked the actor Arky Michael: the answer was very few.[31]

Yet none of the criticism diminished the show's popularity. Both Minogue and Donovan – who had themselves quietly entered a relationship – launched music careers on the back of *Neighbours*, each quickly turning out a string of hits courtesy of the assembly line of British producers Stock, Aitken and Waterman. Neither Kylie's 'I Should Be So Lucky' nor Jason's 'Nothing Can Divide Us' qualified as a profound reflection on the modern condition, but that mattered not at all to the millions of children who turned them into pop stars. Meanwhile episode 523 of *Neighbours*, Scott and Charlene's oddly anachronistic teenage wedding, attracted massive audiences – an estimated 20 million in the United Kingdom, where viewers helped push the song that accompanied their nuptials, Angry Anderson's power ballad 'Suddenly', to number three on the charts. (It was beaten to number two by the duet 'Especially for You', sung by Kylie and Jason themselves.) Other members of the cast recorded songs, appeared on the British pantomime circuit and, in the case of Guy Pearce, went on to a highly successful international film career. Minogue would do even better than that. After taking up for a time with Michael Hutchence, she sprouted feathers, sequins and an endless capacity to reinvent herself for the global entertainment market, a market that, almost miraculously, an obscure, low-budget suburban soap with wobbly sets had opened up for her.

Neighbours had only one rival as 'showbiz surprise of the decade'.[32] The global success of the film *Crocodile Dundee* (1986) astonished critics, if not the supremely confident duo of Paul Hogan and John Cornell responsible for unleashing it on the world.[33] In Australia, it surpassed the American film *ET* as the largest-grossing film on record; in the United States, where Hogan had appeared in several cities as the face of Australian tourism promising 'to slip an extra shrimp on the barbie', it became the second-highest grossing film of 1986 behind *Top Gun*, as well as the most commercially successful foreign film of all time.

With a budget of $8.8 million – high for an Australian film, much of it put up by Hogan and Cornell themselves – after just a few weeks in American cinemas it had already earned $114.3 million.[34] Audiences loved the simple story of a legendary crocodile hunter from the Australian outback who meets a visiting American journalist, Sue Charlton (Linda Kozlowski), when she visits Walkabout Creek in pursuit of a story. After a few days in the Kakadu region of the Northern Territory, where Mick – among other things – saves Sue from the clutches of a hungry crocodile, the story moves to New York. Much of the humour then turns on Dundee – a noble savage at once wise and innocent – being dropped into the urban jungle, where his adventures include trying to work out the purpose of the bidet in his plush hotel. There was much more 'fish out of water' comedy of this kind – with the fish invariably triumphant – culminating in the show's most famous scene, in which Mick and Sue are threatened with a knife by a black hoodlum who wants Mick's wallet. 'That's not a knife,' proclaims a relaxed and laughing Mick, pulling out a huge concealed blade of his own. '*That's* a knife.'[35]

It was easy to see why Americans liked it: their country's problems, it seemed, might yet be solved by an antipodean Davy Crockett with a big knife. The hero from the Australian outback had a homely solution to every problem raised by an overgrown city and an over-civilised society. Thugs, pimps, petty thieves, cocaine addicts, transvestites, pretentious eastern intellectuals: Mick takes them all on, with knife, punch, grope, avuncular demonstration or tin can aimed unerringly at a bag-snatcher's head. No one is immune to his charm, while he seems to enjoy the quirks he discovers among the New York natives. Robert Hughes, the Australian expatriate art critic, concluded that '[t]he reason Americans like such a flagrant example of Australian kitsch is the same reason Australians like it: Americans feel nostalgia for the vanished frontier which they think survives in Australia, but of course it's disappeared there, too.'[36] Some criticised the film for its outdated stereotypes, as well as for its conservative – or at least complacent – politics. But what these critics missed was the way the figure of Mick Dundee, for all his supposedly primitive ways, embodied a cosmopolitan present.

Crocodile Dundee is often compared with an earlier Australian 'fish out of water' comedy, *The Adventures of Barry McKenzie* (1972), in which the humour depends so largely on Barry's antipodean gaucheries in the mother country. But Mick was a very different kind of figure from Barry: rural rather than urban; more assured in dealing with women, the bourgeois and the educated; innocent, like Barry, but combining with it the cleverness of the trickster. Above all, Mick had a touch of class; he was able to hold his own in polite company, and life was for him something more than the quest for the next Foster's. Indeed, Hogan was consciously avoiding the ocker film tradition of the 1970s, appealing instead to an older, more innocent Hollywood tradition of family entertainment, the Saturday afternoon matinee and the plain, simple hero. As he explained: 'Crocodile Dundee never loses his dignity. Even if he is naive and uneducated, he doesn't make a melon of himself all the time. He's got some grace.'[37] The historian Jim Davidson pointed out that this was not just another re-enactment of 'ancient rites of passage to the former seat of imperial power [London]'; rather, it was a film 'fully in character with the aggressive nationalism of the Age of the Winged Keel', evoking an 'increasingly assertive people ... determined to take on America'.[38]

Crocodile Dundee was the greatest, although not the only, international commercial success of the era. *The Man from Snowy River* (1982) did splendidly at home and respectably abroad, incidentally helping along sales of the retro bush fashion made by companies such as R.M. Williams and Driza-Bone. The uniforms Prue Acton designed for the Australian team at the 1984 Los Angeles Olympics included clothing emblazoned with Australian fauna, woollen wattle-coloured Driza-Bone–style stockmen's coats and the increasingly popular Akubra hats.[39] The post-apocalyptic *Mad Max* trilogy (1979, 1981, 1985), directed by George Miller, conveyed a rather less homely national image but was commercially successful, as well as unleashing the young US-born Australian actor Mel Gibson on the world. The impact of Australians on Hollywood had never been greater: Peter Weir, Bruce Beresford and Fred Schepisi all directed hit US movies during the 1980s, and they were accompanied by an array of actors and cinematographers. There was also a developing habit of referring to an Australian film 'industry', a reflection, in part, of the so-called 10BA provisions introduced in 1981. These provided tax concessions for film investment, beginning at 150 per cent of the capital spent in the first year – until the scheme was abolished in 1988. Rather like in manufacturing, subsidies were seen to have resulted in too many films, some of them poor in quality, many unable to find an audience at home or abroad. A smaller number of high-quality films would better reflect the ethos of a confident, globalising nation.[40] Hogan himself was a proponent of this view. *Crocodile Dundee* had taken advantage of 10BA to attract investors, but Hogan believed Australians made '[t]oo many little art films' that were 'never going to make money or appeal to the public'.[41] Still, art-house cinema retained a place in the 1980s, with Paul Cox bringing to Australian film an 'emotional and psychic depth' of which no one could accuse Hogan or Dundee.[42]

The age of the 'period film' had largely run its course by early in the decade – *Gallipoli*, *The Man from Snowy River* and *Phar Lap* were successful late examples – but the genre received a new lease of life from that quintessentially 1980s phenomenon, the historical mini-series. These, too, were essentially a product of 10BA and could be made to pay by television pre-sales. There were dozens of them – fifty between 1980 and mid-1986 alone – and the range of subjects covered was vast, stretching from the convict era (*Against the Wind*, *For the Term of His Natural Life*), the gold rushes (*Eureka*), bushranging (*The Last Outlaw*) and paddle-steamers (*All the Rivers Run*), through to the labour movement (*Waterfront*, *Land of Hope*), politics

(*The Dismissal, True Believers*), war (*Anzacs, The Last Bastion, Vietnam*), aviation (*A Thousand Skies*), sport (*Bodyline*), music (*Melba*) and religion (*Brides of Christ*).[43] Viewers received something like an extended tutorial in Australian history, often placing considerable weight on the perfidy of Albion or, for more recent times, of Uncle Sam, with Australia's imperial oppressor loyally supported by assorted local quislings. Generally, the mini-series rated either well or spectacularly, after being promoted as a major television event. Though viewers would have to look elsewhere for stories of the Aboriginal experience of past and present, these series helped make white Australians more conscious of their history than ever before – even when they amounted to little more than the melodramatic acting out of the sensibilities of the present in the stories, hairstyles and funny dress of the past.[44]

*

The international success of Australian film and television might have reassured many Australians at a time when one of their most prominent politicians was warning of their possible fate as citizens of a banana republic. Yet the essentially familiar, sunny and optimistic tone of *Neighbours* and *Crocodile Dundee* was seemingly belied by a strange and unexpected outbreak of national stroppiness. The angriest such explosion occurred in September 1987 and few if any members of the political class saw it coming. Some of the usual suspects were there, stirring the pot as before: Peter Garrett, the troublemaker of 1984; former Treasury secretary John Stone, now a National Party senator for Queensland; Alan Jones, Rugby Union coach, media personality and Liberal Party identity; Ben Lexcen, America's Cup hero-genius, recently a supporter of Joh for Canberra; even Norm Gallagher, the burly survivor of the class war and Pentridge Prison. The national economic summit of 1983 had failed to achieve such an impressive consensus; Bob Hawke had finally succeeded in bringing Australians together.

Right and left seemed to have found common cause in opposition to the Australia Card. The idea of a compulsory identity card emerged from the tax summit of 1985, a new weapon in the fight against tax and welfare fraud. Its passage since then had been troubled, sufficiently so to have alerted a less preoccupied government that it needed to be handled with special care. In 1986 a joint select committee came out against the proposal, and the majority included one government member, John Saunderson, who argued that a system of tax file numbers would be sufficient. Still, the government persisted, despite the Senate's defeating the Australian Card Bill on two occasions. The second of these was used as the trigger for the double dissolution election of 1987, although the Australia Card barely figured in the campaign.

This reticence would cause the government a major problem, for Hawke claimed a mandate to proceed with the bill, which he said would be considered by only the second ever joint sitting of the parliament. Opinion polling up to this point had been solidly in favour of an identity card, with at least two out of three voters supportive.[45] As Les Murray recognised in his poem 'The Australia Card', the proposal appealed to people's sense of grievance: they liked the idea of sterner measures for dealing with tax and welfare cheats. 'They guessed they could depend, Blue, on your meanness in the end, Blue / to insinuate a burglar's set of plastic / between you and your rights, Blue'.[46]

Yet during September 1987, rallies, meetings and sackloads of mail indicated a major revolt. A Perth protest on 23 September attracted between 20,000 and 40,000 people, and brought together state Liberal Party politicians and BLF men carrying the Eureka flag, mothers pushing strollers, and goosestepping youths dressed in Nazi-style uniforms, who displayed pictures of Bob Hawke wearing a Hitler moustache. The rally ended with an emotional rendition of 'Advance Australia Fair'; 'the identity card has clearly struck a raw nerve', concluded the *West Australian*.[47] It had. On 19 September, the *Australian* reported that since the beginning of the month it had received over 800 letters on the subject, with the proportion of seventeen to one against.[48] Polling by this time showed that a clear majority wanted the Australia Card to go away.[49] Proponents compared the noisy clamour to the hostility the government had faced over its fringe benefits and capital gains taxes, but it is hard to believe that anyone really believed this. Such taxes affected the few rather than the many and did not touch on questions of identity, rights and tradition.

In the Australia Card revolt, citizens protested against 'this drastic change to our way of life', about a proposal 'totalitarian in concept', about an instrument for making the state 'our master, rather than our servant'.[50] In an age when the microchip was both increasingly ubiquitous yet still little understood, they worried about the dangers to their privacy from prying officials and skilful hackers. People also drew on the past to make sense of what their government was trying to do to them. One letter-writer in the *Australian* described the Australia Card as 'the greatest danger to our freedom ... since the Japanese bombed Darwin', while Geoffrey Blainey reminded his readers that the licences to which the Eureka rebels had objected were the identity cards of their time.[51]

Most of all, people objected to being reduced to a bit of green and gold plastic and a number. The terminology of the formidable 130-page bill itself – which referred to people as 'Card-subjects' – invited the ridicule and contempt that rained down on it. But the bill itself was almost impossible to obtain by September 1987; such was the demand for copies that the government printer had run out. If it had been more widely circulated, it is unlikely to have assuaged public concern with its rich panoply of offences carrying large fines and prison sentences. Despite many suggestions to the contrary in national mythology, Australians usually respect lawful authority, but there are hints that civil disobedience would have resulted if the government had persisted. The scheme required the whole population, both adults and children, to report for photographing. Birth certificates would need to be acquired from state governments, two of which – Queensland and Tasmania – announced that they would refuse to cooperate. Media outlets previously supportive or indifferent turned against the government in its hour of need. Hawke's problem was that having used the Australia Card as a pretext for an early election, he could not easily back away; and having for years proclaimed the card to be essential in the fight against fraud – the government claimed it would save a billion dollars – he could not now drop it as unnecessary. But a way out emerged from an unlikely quarter.

Ewart Smith was a retired lawyer and senior public servant with a libertarian streak, who had over time come to see the Australia Card as a 'menace to our way of life'. Woken in his Canberra home early on 22 September by the warbling of magpies, he re-read the bill and noticed that it contained a line which required a regulation to be passed to bring the card into operation, even after approval by a joint sitting of the parliament.[52] This was an Achilles heel, since a regulation could be disallowed by either house and the government lacked a Senate majority. After Smith announced his discovery, the bill's opponents in the Senate, the Australian Democrats and the Coalition parties, made it clear that they were prepared to use their numbers to prevent the bill from operating. At this point, the government abandoned the bill to great rejoicing throughout the land, with Smith an unlikely St George to the Australia Card dragon.

*

The Australia Card affair had exposed a raw nerve of suspicion of the state, an insistence that the virtues of people and nation were cultivated and maintained despite, rather than because of, the qualities and conduct of the political class. The Bicentennial celebrations that began just a few months later were similarly dominated by a feeling that the things which made life in Australia worth living had little to do with the nation's political system or its politicians. It was the land, the beach and the sunshine – and the kind of relaxed lifestyle that these gifts made possible – which most white Australians thought to celebrate. Many had declining patience with elite appeals to their identity as citizens of a multicultural Australia.

It is perhaps for this reason that intellectuals and historians have not been kind to Australia's Bicentenary of 1988. It 'is likely to be forgotten soon enough', declared a group of critics from the University of Wollongong in 1988. 'It is one of history's one-night stands'.[53] The road to the Bicentenary was certainly a winding and treacherous one. The Fraser government established the Australian Bicentennial Authority (ABA) in 1979 under the chairmanship of John Reid – 'an impeccably mannered, immaculately tailored, permanently tanned' patrician whose company, James Hardie, had been slowly killing thousands of Australians while Reid deprecated the health risks posed by asbestos. He was a pillar of the business establishment but in 1985 both Reid and his chief executive officer, David Armstrong, lost their jobs amid allegations of ABA extravagance with taxpayers' money.[54] Jim Kirk, chairman and chief executive of Esso, took over running the ABA and proved to be a surer set of hands.

By this time, the Bicentenary was entangled in ideology, becoming the subject of a 'history war' in which contending understandings of the nation's past were upheld or condemned. The right criticised the ABA for its fashionable embrace of multiculturalism, its vision of the event as a national guilt trip, and its failure to give due regard to Australia's British heritage, democracy, constitution, Christian traditions, private enterprise, the family, the monarchy, the American alliance and much else.[55] The left, in the face of a powerful Aboriginal counter-narrative that declared Australia had been invaded rather than settled – that 'White Australia Has a Black History' – argued that the celebration was bound to fail as a performance of national unity. The official motto, meanwhile, had changed from 'Living Together' to the more celebratory 'The Australian Achievement' in 1981, and then, after Hawke's election, back to 'Living Together'. The advertiser Mojo-MDA ultimately took matters out of the hands of bureaucrats and politicians by transforming it into 'Celebration of a Nation' via a jingle.[56] Inevitably, critics of the Bicentenary – and probably a few naughty schoolchildren – turned this into 'Masturbation of a Nation'.

For its part, the ABA did its best to discourage thinking of the Bicentenary as being about a foundational moment, since it was considered that this would lead to contention and embarrassing protest.[57] Rather, the anniversary would be 'a celebration of Australia by all Australians whether their ancestors came here fifty thousand years ago, on the First Fleet or during the gold rushes or off a refugee boat from Kampuchea a fortnight ago'.[58] Under Reid, whose pet project it became, the ABA adopted as the centrepiece of its plans a scheme to bring tall ships from around the world for an Australia Day 'Parade of Sail' on Sydney Harbour, an idea borrowed from the US Bicentenary of 1976. Here was a nice, politically safe (if expensive) commemoration that would also be visually appealing. But then there emerged a rival, less politically safe private venture for a First Fleet Re-enactment, which stalked the ABA right up to 26 January 1988 and beyond.

Jonathan King's boyish enthusiasm for history drove a quest extending over a decade to stage a re-enactment of the voyage of Captain Arthur Phillip and the eleven ships of the First Fleet. The historians have treated King – a lecturer in politics, who was also a descendant of a First Fleeter and early governor – harshly; that one of his fleet bore a large Coke logo on its sail as it entered Sydney Harbour on 26 January 1988 invited ridicule, even contempt.[59] Yet this treatment in many ways seems unfair: his venture was highly ambitious and captured the imaginations of many. And more pragmatically, in the absence of ABA support, the project could not have survived without corporate sponsorship, which supplemented income from the sale of berths to adventure travellers and of rights to media organisations.

Under Reid and his CEO, David Armstrong, the ABA long resisted the idea of offering money or official endorsement to the re-enactment. But as early as 1984 the responsible minister, Barry Cohen, was leaning towards some kind of re-enactment – if a less elaborate and expensive one than that envisaged by King. As he told Armstrong, 'One cannot deny the fact that the Bicentenary is about European settlement and that a key date in the 1988 calendar will be 26 January.' Suggesting a change of posture, he wondered 'whether we aren't now beginning to adopt a too defensive position'.[60] Neville Wran also sensed that the concept was a winner, and swung the NSW government behind the project. A talkback radio appeal raised hundreds of thousands of dollars at a time when the fleet looked like it might get no further than Brazil, and eventually the ABA, too, provided financial backing in the form of an unsecured loan; despite the opinion of senior cabinet minister John Dawkins that the re-enactment was 'a tasteless and insensitive farce . . .

inspired by a clumsy mixture of commercial gain together with an exaggerated view of the importance of the original voyage in Australia's history'.[61]

One can easily dismiss King's conclusion that the occasion of the fleet's arrival in Sydney 'was the first day on which we had experienced the sensation of being a nation, when all Australians came together for the first time'.[62] Yet he had identified an undoubted weakness in official Australia's conception of the Bicentenary: the downplaying of British origins so as to evade 'convict roots' as well as the history of conflict between the newcomers and Aboriginal people.[63] His hope was to instil in his own people the kind of patriotism and pride in origins that he saw as flourishing in the United States; he was astute in recognising that the old shame about convict origins had given way to an intense pride. As recently as the mid-twentieth century many Australians had remained embarrassed by their country's penal origins, but by the 1980s such feelings had largely passed into history, along with the eugenic assumptions that had ensured their resilience. That Australians were prepared for a more intense engagement with their convict past became clear in the reception accorded Robert Hughes's *The Fatal Shore*, which appeared in bookshops in time for the Bicentenary. Hughes might be considered another Bicentennial entrepreneur; he had superbly judged the market for an epic history of the convict era.[64] Many Anglo-Celtic Australians were researching their family histories with an enthusiasm stimulated by 1988 – sometimes assisted by Bicentennial funding – and many nurtured a quiet hope that they might find a convict ancestor or two to adorn the branches of the family tree. Here was a chance to weave family stories into the national narrative: it is striking, and in tune with this sensibility, that Peter Carey's 1988 Booker Prize–winning novel *Oscar and Lucinda* is couched as a family history, a modern-day descendant's account of the curious, tragic lives of his ancestors in Victorian England and colonial New South Wales.

King and his partners were not insensitive to Aboriginal opinion, although if Indigenous critics of his venture had been privy to his 1984 letter to the prime minister, they are unlikely to have been pleased by his comment that '[w]e plan to stress the Aboriginal occupation of Australia prior to the arrival of the first fleet, the warm reception given by the aboriginals to the new arrivals'.[65] King built up a small network of Aboriginal advisers that included Burnum Burnum, who would himself stage one of the truly memorable political gestures of the Bicentenary when he travelled to England and, on 26 January 1988, claimed it on behalf of his people in Folkestone

Harbour.[66] The First Fleet's departure from Portsmouth also attracted Aboriginal protest, including that of the artist Tracey Moffatt, arrested after disrupting a ceremony in which she asked King who had given him permission to fly the Aboriginal flag.[67] There were subsequent protests as the ships arrived in Australian ports on their way to Sydney. At Eden, an Aboriginal man told the crew: 'You people have hurt us by putting this Fleet on; you are hurting our feelings because people died through this First Fleet … Our people say stop now and go back from where you came from.'[68]

Australia Day in Sydney saw these conflicts play out in the streets and on the harbour. The wealthy took to pleasure craft or gathered in homes with harbour views; the rest of the estimated 2 million spectators crammed into the spaces alongside Sydney Harbour with their picnic baskets, rugs and flags for the nation's largest ever party. Few, unless they were listening on a radio, would have heard the speeches delivered in the official ceremony in the shadow of the Opera House at Bennelong Point by Bob Hawke, Prince Charles and other dignitaries; it was the maritime spectacle – of Tall Ships and First Fleeters amid countless other vessels – that generated most excitement, rivalled in the minds of some only by the exhilarating presence of Princess Diana. Not all were exhilarated. Malcolm Turnbull, a pudgy young lawyer and banker, appalled that the Prince of Wales was the main speaker at Australia's 'celebration of a nation', decided from that moment to commit himself to the cause of a republic.[69]

Nor was the sight of Diana so exhilarating to the Aboriginal protesters perched on the shore at Lady Macquarie's Chair, where they had set up an 'embassy' and participated in what turned out to be a glorious festival of pan-Aboriginality and a celebration of survival. In the days before 26 January, as they converged on the city, sections of the media played up the possibility of violence from such protesters; afterwards, they reported the demonstrations, marches and ceremonies as free of bloodshed, as if there had been a strong indication beforehand that it would be otherwise. Such fears of disruptive protest were widespread and not confined to Sydney. At Brewarrina, where there had been a violent confrontation a few months before, local police managed to conjure out of a couple of Aboriginal men sitting on a car bonnet a plot 'to organise protests or similar disturbances'. A report from north-western New South Wales went further: Aboriginal people were thought to have acquired firearms through Michael Mansell, a radical Tasmanian activist who had recently visited Libya. The authorities in Sydney responded to these fantastic rumours of an armed Aboriginal insurrection by sending Tactical Response Group members up north. Meanwhile, in Sydney a white racist group calling itself BARK – or Bicentennial Australian Revolutionary Kommandos – in the weeks leading up to 26 January went on a violent rampage which included vandalism of an Aboriginal educational institution, Tranby College, as well as an attack on the home of the state Labor minister for Aboriginal affairs.[70]

Sydney was the centre of Bicentennial activity on 26 January; throughout much of the rest of the country, people watched the celebrations on television, sometimes as they prepared a special lunch to mark the occasion. '[W]e really do have to wonder whether this Bicentenary is a celebration of a nation or just a birthday bash for Sydney,' one Melbourne paper concluded sourly.[71] Yet larger cities held concerts and fireworks, and small towns organised breakfasts, parades and carnivals where soldiers, convicts, ladies in bonnets and even the occasional Ned Kelly rubbed shoulders. Local citizens competed against each other in egg-and-spoon and three-legged races. The radio station in Mount Isa organised several events, including a thong-throwing championship in partnership with a local shoe shop. At Alice Springs, the family fun day at one hotel included gumboot throwing, arm and green-jelly wrestling, stubby-drinking races, and beer-belly and wet t-shirt contests; the territory's Aboriginal population observed a quiet day of mourning. A 'First Fleet' managed to find its way to Lake Mulwala, a reservoir located on the Victoria–New South Wales border; another arrived at Lake Ainsworth at Lennox Head, where the re-enactment included whites acting the part of 'natives' who attacked the newcomers before very quickly becoming 'friendly' and joining the ceremony onshore. A history of violence and dispossession was in this way readily resolved, at least to the satisfaction of the revellers.[72]

This was a Bicentenary focused on the local, the family, the personal and an unpretentious, light-hearted display of patriotism. It was ritual that continued an established folk tradition that had been hardly less evident when Australia celebrated its sesquicentenary in 1938. One of Hugh Mackay's informants recalled that she 'loved our own private Bicentenary celebrations. We had a flag-raising ceremony on the clothes line, and we had a canoe in the pool that we called "Our Endeavour" with sails on it. I was very, very proud when we did the flag-raising.'[73] These were European 'land rites', ceremonies of mock formality linking family and friends to each other and the nation in ways that tried to evade the racial politics of the Bicentenary even as their activities unwittingly disclosed them.[74] Such private celebrations, often conducted amid a sea of green and gold balloons and streamers, might have almost completely escaped the attention of posterity except that the official historian of the Bicentenary, Denis O'Brien, wrote to country newspapers asking people to report on what they had done on 26 January.[75]

The letters revealed that people did things in their own way. A barbeque and dress-up day organised by the Richardsons of Healesville near Melbourne attracted an impressive array of characters, including tennis stars Evonne Goolagong and Pat Cash, bushrangers Ben Hall and Ned Kelly, Dame Edna Everage, Ginger Meggs and Daisy Bates as well an Aboriginal, a convict, assorted ockers, a bush padre, a gumnut baby, a colonial schoolgirl, 'a typical all-Australian mum' and, as a daring counterpoint, a 'lady of the night'.[76] At Samford near Brisbane, Karen and John Spiller invited some 100 friends to their place for a barbeque to mark 'this momentous occasion' with the only requirement being 'that they came in some appropriately Australian garb'. The guests included a trouserless Malcolm Fraser impersonator in a towel, recalling an embarrassing incident involving the ex–prime minister in the lobby of a Memphis hotel.[77]

There was also much more to the Bicentenary than 26 January. The June Birthday Beacons were the brainchild of another Bicentennial entrepreneur, Chilean-born Claudio Veliz, a conservative academic from Melbourne's La Trobe University. Appealing to the place of fire across so many cultures represented in Australia – and its importance to the Australian continent itself – the event invited communities throughout Australia to light beacons in a chain around the whole country as a display of national fellowship and community spirit. The Birthday Beacons attracted the praise of the New Right as a counterweight to the left-wing emphases Veliz and his allies saw as dominating the official program. The event was unfortunately hampered by wet weather: participants at one central Victorian bonfire thought that, through the mist, they could see the beacon at Mount Tarrengower, 'until someone pointed out that it was Dulcie Lloyd's back door light'.[78]

The ABA sponsored a vast number of events – about 24,000 – and provided funds for a major travelling exhibition, the completion of a Stockman's Hall of Fame at Longreach, the cataloguing of historical records and the publication of many, many books.[79] There was the glamorous $4 million Bicentennial fashion parade, sponsored by the International Wool Secretariat and the Australian Wool Corporation, and staged at the Sydney Opera House in the presence of Charles and Diana. Wool and royalty: it seemed a bit like old times. But this extravaganza was intended to signify not the old empire but a post-imperial nation's globalisation, as nine international and six local designers explored the theme of 'the ancient continent of Australia – its earth, water, air and fire', revealing what splendid things they and their models could achieve on the sheep's back.[80]

Meanwhile, Ken Done's colourful designs, while spurned by art critics, were snapped up in the form of clothing, prints and other merchandise. Done, too, was an astute Bicentennial entrepreneur, his distinctive brand chiming perfectly with the national look that many white Australians desired to project – bright, colourful, apolitical – and which, in the age of globalised consumerism, was also an image that foreign tourists enjoyed taking home with them. Sydney itself, or rather its glorious harbour, was the centrepiece of his vision.[81] Yet for those who regarded Done's art as fluff, Manning Clark, the septuagenarian historian whose six-volume *A History of Australia* had been completed in 1987, was available as the Bicentenary's public figure par excellence, an Old Testament prophet in a big hat who embodied the nation because he had written its history. Clark's media role was to call on the deep well of his cultural authority to interpret the nation for the nation, delivered with a gravitas that no mere journalist could muster. A musical based on his *History* flopped but had no appreciable impact on Clark's reputation as the wise old man with a unique insight into the state of his country's soul.

★

The Jelbart family of Jindera told O'Brien that they had enjoyed a delightful Australia Day 1988, not least because both of their daughters – although born six years apart – had birthdays on that day. They decorated the house in green and gold, hosted a party, enjoyed a singalong and kept an eye on the celebrations in Sydney which made 'us all feel included and so, so happy'. By the early hours of the morning, 'a quite heated discussion on the aboriginal question' was in progress, and '[a]fter a few drinks over the evening, we all had a point of view, and it was all so stimulating. You can imagine!'[82] Such conversations must have been common during 1988. The Bicentenary raised the profile of Aboriginality at home and abroad. Foreign coverage drew attention to the manner in which Aboriginal protest had 'dulled the shine of Australia's self-congratulatory bicentennial celebrations', turning '[w]hat should have been a primrose path' for political leaders 'into so many stations of the cross'.[83] But there were signs that the occasion encouraged among white Australians reflection and debate on the legacy of dispossession. There was greater pressure to articulate one's feelings about the claims being made by Aboriginal advocates, to recognise a difficult, uncomfortable history.[84]

Between the mid and late 1980s, the historical and contemporary Aboriginal experience arrived on the national stage in a way that has had profound implications for the nation's subsequent history.[85] The revolution had several aspects. It was embodied in the most expensive exercise in symbolism Australia had ever undertaken, the new Parliament House, officially opened by Queen Elizabeth II in May 1988. Where the old parliament had been dominated by the symbolism of empire, the new one embraced a renovated national identity. In place of Westminster green and red, there were softer tones intended to suggest the Australian bush and desert; Italian marble had a counterpoint in predominantly Australian timbers; a mosaic by Papunya Tula artist Michael Tjakamarra Nelson dominated the forecourt: the boomerang-shaped building's whole atmosphere was designed to evoke Aboriginality and landscape.[86]

Another indication of the new Aboriginal prominence was literary. Dispossession and violence figured in books that reached a global market, among them *The Fatal Shore*, and *Oscar and Lucinda*, which climaxes in the raw, brutal tale of an exploration party's massacring of blacks. The English author Bruce Chatwin's sprawling international bestseller *The Songlines* (1987) presented a spiritually charged landscape crisscrossed by Dreaming-tracks, a country where each 'man's verses were his title deeds to territory'. Chatwin paid tribute to the complexity and richness of Aboriginal culture by presenting it within a larger set of ruminations about humanity, which he saw as nomadic in its purest state. The country itself he presented not as a wilderness, but a place brought into the history of humanity by the songs and stories of an ancient, living people.[87]

Mainstream publishers were also calling on Aboriginal people. Penguin produced an anthology of Aboriginal poetry edited by Aboriginal author and activist Kevin Gilbert, *Inside Black Australia* (1988), while the University of Queensland Press launched a black Australian writers series. Aboriginal story, memoir, autobiography and family history was also making its mark. Ruby Langford's *Don't Take Your Love to Town* (1988) was a battler's tale but instead of the familiar story of a white bushman or pioneer, we are invited to empathise with the hard and too often tragic life of a Bundjalung woman at the heart of a large, turbulent family. Black historians were also beginning to produce their own histories of colonisation; a notable early example was *Koori: A Will to Win* (1985), the work of James Miller, a Wonnarua (Hunter Valley) man based at the Armidale College of Advanced Education.

For white historians, too, violence and dispossession occupied an increasingly prominent place in the nation's origin story. Penguin published a series of books by the Townsville-based academic Henry Reynolds, which included studies of frontier violence as well as his influential defence of Aboriginal property rights, *The Law of the Land* (1987). These politically charged works unsettled many prevailing national myths, or rather stood them on their head; Reynolds invested Aboriginal people with positive qualities, such as patriotism, improvisation, courage and resilience, with which white myth-makers had traditionally credited their own national heroes. His books reshaped both the historical understanding and emotional disposition of the many Australians who read them.[88]

But the most important book of them all was the work of a first-time author, an Aboriginal woman from Perth, publishing with the Fremantle Arts Centre Press. Sally Morgan's *My Place* (1987) was the story of the author's discovery of her Aboriginal heritage through the pursuit of family history. Containing some of the pleasures of a detective story, *My Place* sold hundreds of thousands of copies and became standard fare in schools and universities. No book since Darwin's *On the Origin of the Species* (1859) had exercised such a powerful influence over the attitude of white Australians towards black Australians. But the acclaim was far from universal, with the historian Bain Attwood criticising Morgan's romantic approach to Aboriginal identity, and Indigenous critics condemning her assumption that Aboriginality could simply be taken up without being lived and earned. Aboriginal critics also puzzled over the book's mass appeal to white audiences, suggesting that *My Place* acted to reassure them 'that they are no longer racist because they have read it'.[89] But *My Place* assuredly did not offer catharsis to the Drake-Brockmans, the pastoral dynasty depicted in the book; they were outraged by the claim, attributed to Morgan's grandmother Daisy, that Howden Drake-Brockman fathered Daisy, and even more by the insinuation that he later formed an incestuous relationship with her that produced Morgan's mother, Gladys.[90] *My Place*, however, was designed not for old pioneering families but for a modern, cosmopolitan and white Australia more than ever convinced that individuals could fashion meaningful identities for themselves.

Aboriginal music was also winning a place in popular culture. Bob Marley's 1979 tour provided a stimulus to young Aboriginal musicians, with two Adelaide-based groups – Us Mob, and No Fixed Address – performing and recording reggae rock in the early 1980s; 'We have Survived' by No Fixed Address came to acquire anthem status among Indigenous Australians. In 1986 Midnight Oil accompanied the mainly Aboriginal group the Warumpi Band on what was billed as the Blackfella–Whitefella tour of the Northern

Territory. It was not an unalloyed triumph in any conventional sense. Some performances by both bands fell flat, and the Oils – despite their soaring reputation – had to work hard to win over remote communities.[91] The experience might well stand as a simulacrum for the hard work of reconciliation, but Midnight Oil's number-one hit album *Diesel and Dust* (1987) reflected their desert sojourn and deepening engagement with Aboriginal politics and land rights. Songs such as 'Beds Are Burning' and 'The Dead Heart' – the latter originally written for a film about the handover of Uluru – exposed their young Australian fans to the ethical and political dilemmas of living in a country stolen from someone else. In 1988 Midnight Oil toured the United States with a Yolngu band, Yothu Yindi, which melded traditional Aboriginal music and rock to produce a distinctive sound. Their 1991 song 'Treaty', besides being an international dance-floor hit, lamented the failure of the federal government to sign a treaty with Aboriginal Australians.[92] In 1987 Hawke had suggested that a 'treaty' or 'compact' be signed during the Bicentennial year; in June 1988 he reaffirmed his commitment when Central and Northern Land Councils presented him with a set of claims that became known as the Barunga Statement, after the site of the festival where the ceremony occurred. But in the face of conservative opposition, the treaty went the same way as so many of Hawke's commitments to Aboriginal people: it was abandoned.

Indigenous dance and theatre benefited from the formation of the Bangarra Dance Theatre in Sydney in 1989 by Carole Johnson, a charismatic African American migrant. Bangarra was Wiradjuri for 'to make fire'. The same period saw contemporary Aboriginal art rise to a position of pre-eminence in Australia and abroad. Papunya Tula, the most famous of the contemporary Aboriginal art movements, emerged in the turbulent NT settlement near the border with Western Australia in the early 1970s under the encouragement of a white art teacher, Geoffrey Bardon.[93] But the art world, as distinct from the anthropologists, only really began to pay serious attention to the school's distinctive dot paintings a decade later, as critics came to see in them an innovative form of abstraction that eluded the categories and conventions of 'modernism' and 'postmodernism'. By 1984 the director of the National Gallery of Australia, James Mollison, was prepared to call the Papunya Tula acrylic paintings 'possibly the finest abstract art achievements to date in Australia'.[94] Discerning local collectors acquired works; specialist galleries, craft shops and dealers set up; Sotheby's started an Australian office with an eye on the burgeoning 'tribal art' market; major exhibitions were mounted in

Australia and overseas; Australian institutions allocated more money to their contemporary Aboriginal art budgets; overseas galleries and collectors bought up big. Especially after the stock-market crash provoked a boom in art investment, the prices paid for Aboriginal paintings skyrocketed. In 1989 one estimate put the value of the Aboriginal art industry at over $18 million.[95]

Fashion designers, too, looked to traditional Aboriginal motifs. Australian fashion, a *New York Times* journalist commented in 1986, was now synonymous with 'vivid colors, wild textures and provocative shapes'.[96] Influential Sydney designers Jenny Kee and Linda Jackson drew on images from a variety of cultures and 'tribal art', but in their quest for the unique and internationally marketable, they gave a privileged place to the local flora and fauna and to Aboriginal motifs. Sydney was instrumental in defining the new Australian 'look', not only through designers such as Kee and Jackson but also via the city's association with beachside fun, bright colours and dazzling sunshine. According to *Vogue Australia* in January 1988, Sydney had 'a kind of summer dressing all its own. Fresh. Easy. Confident. Its basis: short skirt, light jacket and a top that bares the neck to the prevailing north-easterly'.[97]

Kee and Jackson each spent time in remote Indigenous communities such as those in the Tiwi Islands and at Utopia Station, and they collaborated with Aboriginal artists, craft workers and designers, who were making a mark in their own right. Aboriginal designers and artisans on Bathurst Island provided Pope John Paul II with the vestments that he wore to say Mass in Darwin during his 1986 visit to Australia. The visual impact of the leader of the world's Catholics wearing Tiwi design was as powerful in registering the presence of a living culture as his sermon in Alice Springs that called on Aboriginal people to remain faithful to their traditions while opening their hearts to Jesus Christ. The Bundjalung artist Bronwyn Bancroft ran a Sydney store called Designer Aboriginals and was an innovative creator of women's fashion with a political message. Desert Designs, started in Western Australia by artist Jimmy Pike, opened clothing stores and signed licensing agreements that carried its creations into the global marketplace. And the Jumbana Company, established by John and Ros Moriarty, promoted an Indigenous graphic style that was ancient, contemporary and increasingly understood as 'Australian', not only 'Aboriginal'; their designs would eventually grace Qantas jets. The Australian image at home and abroad was perhaps becoming a little less Eurocentric and colonial, as it shifted to accommodate – and bring into the global market – the culture and visions of people who had once been dismissed as being among the most primitive and barbaric on the face of the earth.[98]

All of this stimulated debate about the dangers of white cultural appropriation, plagiarism and even of a new form of assimilation or 'ethnocide'.[99] Yet far from the art schools and city galleries where such matters seemed pressing, in the outback towns of New South Wales and Queensland a rather more familiar story of oppression and violence was still playing out. The so-called riots in Bourke, Goondiwindi and Brewarrina each arose from an incident that crystallised Aboriginal accusations of pervasive white racism and discriminatory policing. The Bourke 'riot' resulted from a perception of police leniency towards a white man who had backed his car over the head of an Aboriginal man.[100] In Goondiwindi, a town just inside Queensland's border with New South Wales, in January 1987 the ejection of an Aboriginal man from a Friday night disco led to retaliation on the Saturday by a large group of Aboriginal men, who damaged buildings and attacked hotel patrons.[101] In Brewarrina a few months later, a wake in a local park for a man who had died in police custody – and whom many Aboriginals suspected police had killed – led to a bitter verbal exchange with whites who had armed themselves on the balcony of a hotel, and a short but violent clash with police.[102] The national attention that the Brewarrina riot attracted finally led the Hawke government to agree to a royal commission into Aboriginal deaths in custody.

In each of these instances, violence directed national attention to the poisonous race relations of many country towns. Local whites resented media attention that sometimes implied they were a bunch of rednecks, but even superficial media inquiry turned up bitter racial hatred, contempt for blacks who lived on government 'handouts', and Aboriginal alienation and deprivation. At Goondiwindi, the riots prompted an investigation by the Human Rights and Equal Opportunity Commission that found in the nearby Aboriginal settlement of Toomelah atrocious and overcrowded housing, a lack of fresh water and massive unemployment. Residents complained of racism at Goondiwindi High School, and of a town where they were made to feel unwelcome by whites when they visited to do business.[103] One local white woman responded that her silence was not a sign of racism or contempt but simply the result 'of not knowing what to say'.[104] It would be hard to conjure a more vivid illustration of race relations in Goondiwindi, and – it seems likely – in many other corners of the nation.

★

Market researchers in the second half of the 1980s found a 'bewildered', 'pessimistic' and 'apprehensive' population 'deeply concerned about the pace of change'. The title of one 1988 study commissioned by the advertising firm Clemenger – *Present Tense* – captured the mood well.[105] Hugh Mackay also found a sense of anxiety about change: crime, the breakdown of school discipline, the lack of a work ethic, Aboriginal land rights and the formation of ethnic enclaves in cities. Many Australians, he reported, were 'visibly shaken by what they perceive as the quite unexpected impact on Australian life of Asian migrants'.[106] In mid-1988 a federal government inquiry chaired by a former ambassador to China, Stephen FitzGerald, while calling for an immigration policy better designed to meet Australia's economic needs, also warned that multiculturalism was becoming unpopular among many Australians who saw it as divisive and threatening. Clearly, some other term was needed. So what did FitzGerald and his fellow committee members suggest? 'Cosmopolitanism' seemed perfectly suited to doing the work required, and the report used it as a virtual synonym for multiculturalism. A cosmopolitan national vision implied variety, openness, diversity, tolerance and sophistication – even 'cultural patronage and creativity' – and all without the supposedly fragmentary implications of multiculturalism.[107]

When set against a background of continuing New Right propaganda against multiculturalism – Blainey, for instance, warned in 1988 that Australia was becoming a 'cluster of tribes' – the potential for a public backlash seemed considerable. John Howard, as leader of the Opposition, was working hard to provoke just such a reaction. Emboldened by the FitzGerald report, he unveiled the theme of 'One Australia' in a speech to the WA Liberal Party in late July. The Liberal leader criticised multiculturalism for having 'gone off the rails', condemned the idea of 'a federation of cultures' (a term seemingly adapted from Blainey's more incendiary phrase), and argued that Australians had apologised too much for both their history and their identity: 'Why is it that we are frightened to ask people to put loyalty to Australia above loyalty to any other part of the world?'[108]

Howard's subsequent fumbling of the immigration issue would prevent his party from exploiting the national mood. On 1 August, on radio and television, he began talking about Australia admitting fewer Asians; even worse, he raised the prospect of Asian migration being lowered in the interests of social cohesion, implying that he favoured such a course. Howard then went on to compound this folly by stubbornly digging in, often getting angry during interviews and, above all, refusing to admit that he had erred in suggesting the revival of an immigration policy based on race. Later in the month, Hawke humiliated him with a parliamentary motion that invited support for continued bipartisanship over a non-discriminatory immigration policy. In the most telling passage of his speech, Hawke clarified that he was not accusing Howard of racism but making 'the more serious charge... of cynical opportunism'. The prime minister accused Howard of policy by 'code word' – an approach that would later be dubbed 'dog-whistling' – while Howard also provided a taste of the future when he declared that he would 'never ever abandon the sovereign right of this country to decide who will be a permanent citizen'. Four Liberal MPs crossed the floor to vote with the government, and two others abstained. Howard's leadership was badly damaged.[109]

The federal Coalition's manifesto *Future Directions: It's Time for Plain Thinking* was launched a few months later on 4 December 1988. The cover image is a justly famous example of Australian political iconography – fair-haired husband and wife, boy and girl miniature versions of their parents; white picket fence; large, comfortable home with a grand colonial veranda; modest late-model car out the front. The somewhat fantastic nature of the visual imagery was underlined at the pre-launch press conference in Parramatta when a journalist suggested the house seemed to be on four acres, which would require a $500,000 mortgage in Sydney. 'It's very much a Coalition house,' replied a grinning Howard.[110] Shadow ministers evidently liked it, arguing behind the scenes after the launch that 'as the family logo is now well established as our "property", we should incorporate it in all future Party publications'.[111]

That the document of over 100 pages contained a strong strain of nostalgia all commentators could agree. The suggestion – sometimes couched as an accusation – that the Coalition was trying to take the country back to the future gained additional weight from the song released to coincide with the document. Bryce Courtenay, a creative director with the Coalition's George Patterson advertising agency, and future bestselling author, claimed he had written it in an hour. 'Pseudo-intellectuals who write for newspapers', he predicted, 'will give it a drubbing', a prediction that proved unerringly accurate.[112] The lyrics depicted a young boy on his mother's knee; she tells him, 'Son you're Australian / That's enough, for anyone to be':

> It's enough to be a good man
> Plain thinking men stay honest and stay true,
> Don't heed the fast talker or the con man,
> Australian needs plain thinking men like you.

The son grows into a man:

> I watched as things began to change around me,
> The fancy dancers got to have their say,
> They changed the vision, spurned the wisdom
> And made Australia change to suit their way.
> It's time we cleansed the muddy waters,
> And do the things we know must be done,
> So that we teach our sons and daughters,
> What it means to be a true Australian.[113]

The text of *Future Directions* portrayed Australia as a nation in decline: 'Taught to be ashamed of their past, apprehensive about their future, pessimistic about their ability to control their own lives let alone their ability to shape the character of the nation ... many came to see change as being in control of them ... hope and confidence in the future were transformed into concern and despair'. But a solution was at hand: the Coalition parties would 'restore hope and certainty to an Australian community which is anxious about the future and has lost that sense of security and direction that in the past enabled it to plan ahead with confidence'.[114] Howard was the leader of a strong party that would restore stability to society while he paradoxically promised ever more economic change – faster and more extensive deregulation, privatisation of public assets, and a quicker winding down of tariffs than even Labor was proposing.

For *Future Directions*, society comprised responsible citizens in harmonious families forming a united nation. The implication was that these identities should be emphasised over the narrowly ethnic identities of migrants and Aboriginal people, and the document opposed a treaty with Aboriginal Australians as based on 'the absurd proposition that a government can make a treaty with itself in favour of some of the citizens it is elected to serve at the expense of others'.[115] *Future Directions* was very much on the side of those who had criticised the alleged left-wing slant of the ABA, to the extent of including the Bicentennial slogan discarded by the Hawke government, 'The Australian Achievement', among its subheadings. Australians, it indicated, should feel pride in the country's European history, but no guilt for anything done by their ancestors to Aboriginal people.

★

Future Directions voiced a conservative understanding of national identity, one no longer defined explicitly by whiteness yet which celebrated Australia's British heritage, Western identity and special relationship with the United States. But changes in the global balance of economic power were wearing away the foundations of this world view. By 1988 Japan had emerged as the most dynamic economic power on earth, and Tokyo seemed to be displacing New York as the centre of the capitalist world. 'Like New York under the robber barons,' a visiting Australian academic recorded in his diary, 'Japan can afford to import anything it wants.'[116]

By this time a controversy over Japanese investment was taking place in Australia, apparently sparked by the purchase of a popular koala sanctuary in Brisbane.[117] Japanese investment in Australia had already increased by more than five times in the first half of the decade, and by 1987–88 had become Australia's largest source of foreign capital. Some 60 per cent of this investment was in property, often high-profile resorts and golf courses.[118] Japan seemed destined to become an increasingly powerful player in the global economy, a glittering empire based on high-tech gadgetry, financial clout and a will to succeed that was less perceptible among the Anglo democracies. 'Do we want to become like Japan, where kids commit suicide in high school if they aren't getting good enough marks?' asked one member of a focus group in 1988.[119]

The idea of Australian complacency in the face of Japanese economic aggression was echoed in popular culture. A children's book, *The Laziest Crocodile in Australia* (1989), has a 'Mr Yen ... famous Japanese hotel builder and real-estate tycoon', arriving in the sleepy north Queensland town of Port Paradise to build a luxury hotel. The local crocodiles who, with the exception of Lazy Les, normally put on a bit of a show for the 'Spot-a-Croc tourist boat', are attracted by the prospect of 'rots and rots of rovery fish every day' which the tycoon promises them if they will let him build his resort on their swamp. The crocodiles agree to give up their home and although there are initially protests from local residents who believe they have accepted a bum deal, the people's resistance, like the crocodiles', cannot survive the lavish hospitality that Mr Yen lays on. Only Les, the laziest crocodile, refuses to cooperate. The story is largely of the efforts of this decidedly laid-back reptile, shaken out of his lethargy by the invasion of his home, to sabotage the Japanese resort. Les has the last laugh when he destroys the hotel by gnawing through the pylons on which it rests. Mr Yen gives up, announcing he will never again build in Australia, and soon everything is back to normal: Les returns to his hammock, his one-crocodile campaign against Japanese economic imperialism an outstanding success.[120]

On the Gold Coast, where Japanese investment in real estate was increasingly substantial and conspicuous, Les the crocodile had an ally in the improbably named Bruce Whiteside, a dealer in second-hand clothing and a New Zealand citizen. The first meeting he called to protest against foreigners buying up Australian land attracted 1500 people, who listened to Whiteside, backed by an Australian flag inscribed with the slogan 'Heart of a Nation', call for a ban on the sale of land to foreigners.[121] Speakers variously characterised the Japanese as the 'yellow peril', a people who were 'ruthless, cruel and intrusive'.[122] Whiteside saw himself as the spearhead of a national organisation mobilising 'the sons and daughters of ANZAC' against foreign land ownership in defence of an 'identity' and a 'way of life'. His political leadership, however, was amateurish, his rhetoric archaic and his attitudes extreme: he advocated the compulsory resumption of all land bought by foreigners since 1900.[123] But anti-Japanese protests, which soon extended to Cairns, did elicit a response from politicians across the political spectrum, some of whom developed a sudden concern with the 'problem' posed to the national interest by Japanese economic imperialism. The Queensland government revived an idea that had been kicking around for years: a foreign land register.[124] The results of a 1988 *BRW* survey of people in the five mainland capitals help explain the politicians' nervousness, for it found that while over half wanted to encourage foreign investment, 63 per cent were worried about the prospect of more *Japanese* investment.[125]

Those with such attitudes may also have worried a government increasingly preoccupied with Australia's enmeshment with Asia. A 1989 report commissioned by the Hawke government welcomed the 'great opportunity' offered by what its author, Ross Garnaut, called 'the Northeast Asian ascendancy'. Australia, once fearful of its neighbours, could now take advantage of its proximity by throwing over 'the dead weight of a protectionist past' and forming closer relations with the dynamic north-east Asian economies.[126] In the same year, the Australian government played a key role in the formation of APEC (Asia-Pacific Economic Cooperation), a forum to advance this vision of an economically integrated and prosperous region.

This cherished vision of an Asia-focused 'open' nation had its critics on the left as well as the right. For the former, Japanese investment was 'the third wave' of capitalist imperialism in Australia, following the British and

American ones.[127] Whiteside himself gradually recognised the need to play down the more obviously racist dimension of his propaganda as he sought to build wider alliances. And there were other late 1980s manifestations of anti-Japanese sentiment. One objection to the Japanese-inspired high-tech Multifunction Polis (MFP) – slated to be built on some disused marshland in Adelaide – was that it would create a foreign 'enclave'. Right-wing racists and left-wing socialists occasionally found themselves in uncomfortably close proximity in the anti-MFP campaign, while restored Liberal leader Andrew Peacock sought to harvest the 'enclave' issue for votes in the 1990 federal election campaign.

By the late 1980s, racist taunts, graffiti, posters and violence were attracting greater publicity, although it is impossible to know if they were becoming more frequent. Far-right groups such as the Sydney-based National Action fostered hatred through bill-posting, leaflet-drops and sticker campaigns, while the Australian Nationalist Movement in Western Australia extended its campaign of hate to a series of arson attacks on Perth Chinese restaurants.[128] At the end of 1988 the Human Rights and Equal Opportunity Commission launched a National Inquiry into Racist Violence in Australia. When it reported in 1991, it found many instances of 'discrimination against, harassment of and violence towards Australians of Asian origin'. Victims reported that police rarely showed much interest in their complaints. In February 1988 a Malaysian-born Perth taxi driver, Peter Tan, died after being bashed by a seventeen-year-old, Nicholas Meredith, who explained his actions to police thus: 'I don't like Chinese, to start with, so I belted shit out of him.'[129]

But these social anxieties were only part of the story. More Australians were now travelling each year to Asia than to Europe; adventurous students grappled valiantly with Asian languages; youths went on exchange to Japan; backpackers included Asian countries among the places where they would 'discover themselves' while abroad; and Bali boomed as a destination for a short and more exotic break than Surfers Paradise could offer.[130]

*

Anti-Japanese sentiment was often mobilised around memory of the Pacific War.[131] The prisoner of war (POW), previously somewhat marginal in public memory and military commemoration, became 'a figure to rival the iconic centrality of the original Anzacs'.[132] The suffering endured by POWs at the hands of the Japanese lent itself to use as a political parable, a warning of the Japanese will to dominate and victimise innocent Australians. Edward 'Weary' Dunlop, the surgeon and POW, was an advocate of reconciliation with the former enemy rather than the stoking of old hatreds, but his emergence as a national icon during this period was one sign of a change in war commemoration: a shift from the warrior to the carer and healer, and from the legendary Gallipoli hero to the Second World War victim of Japanese brutality.[133] Meanwhile, the qualities traditionally attributed to Anzacs – 'mateship, resourcefulness, egalitarianism and courage' – were translated to POWs but with one major difference: war trauma, as conveyed through personal testimony, was becoming central to the way their experience figured in public consciousness.[134]

Anzac's resurgence in the 1980s as a foundation of national identity depended on the bitterness and division engendered by the Vietnam War giving way to greater public sympathy for those Australians who had participated in it. Redgum's 1983 number-one hit 'I Was Only Nineteen' shifted popular consciousness of the war from Cold War politics to its traumatic effect on veterans. The angry Vietnam vet was a stock type in popular culture of the period and just before Anzac Day in 1984, a veteran in Brisbane burned his service medals in the eternal flame of the city's war memorial to protest his treatment by the government. 'The Gallipoli men came home heroes,' he explained. 'The Vietnam blokes came home losers who nobody wants to know. But they didn't lose. The politicians lost Vietnam.'[135]

The Welcome Home parade, staged in Sydney in the spring of 1987 in front of over 100,000 spectators, was a landmark in the reimagining of Vietnam veterans' relationship to Australian society. It mattered not at all that the whole enterprise was founded on the false belief that no such parades had been staged during the war itself: reportage of this event made much of the weeping of veterans, and the event's 'emotional purging of anger, frustration, bitterness, confusion and rejection'.[136] It is impossible to imagine a major spectacle involving returned soldiers being staged and reported in these terms before the mid-1980s; an emotional transformation had occurred in public life. Of the Melbourne Anzac Day ceremony in 1988, the *Age* declared '[t]he spirit of Anzac revived', as 'thousands of extra Vietnam veterans took their place for the first time'.[137]

The Hawke government's engagement with these developments was uncertain. It came up with funding for the Welcome Home march and provided money for the Australian Vietnam Forces National Memorial, but this was tentative engagement rather than warm embrace. It was noticed that some veterans had declined to give Hawke the 'eyes-right' when they marched past him in Sydney, which was interpreted by the event's organiser as 'a final gesture of resentment against the Labor Party' over the war.[138]

The 1980s also saw the resurgence of the original Anzacs, beginning in 1981 with the Peter Weir film *Gallipoli* and the bestselling memoir, later a mini-series, *A Fortunate Life*, written by WA Gallipoli veteran Albert Facey. Weir's hit film portrayed the affair as a tragedy and a loss of Australian innocence, with Britain, as Australia's imperial master, cast as villain. Facey's memoir, meanwhile, presented the war as an episode in the struggle of a working-class battler. Such films and books often provoked a highly emotional response in people otherwise remote from the experience of war. The increasingly popular practice of pilgrimage could also evoke strong emotions in visitors to war graves and battle sites. A young Australian visitor to Gallipoli in the late 1980s recalled the effect of visiting Lone Pine: 'I cried, not for the soldiers, but for myself. I wanted to be a part of the Anzac legend, yet I was forced to stand and watch unattached.'[139] Increasingly, young tourists would cease to see themselves as 'unattached'. They would imagine through their nationality, and sometimes through their family history, that they were very much part-owners of the story of Anzac.

Feminist activism was also a part of Anzac Day during the 1980s, with women protesting against rape in war staging demonstrations in several Australian cities. Some demanded inclusion; others wanted Anzac Day abolished, arguing that a 'women's march or wreath-laying would lead to women being co-opted into a misogynist tradition'.[140] A Sydney protester, the sociologist Rosemary Pringle, explained their aim. 'There are rapists in that crowd who are marching proudly for this country,' she said, 'and we intend to make them feel guilt.'[141] The protests by organisations such as Women Against Rape and the Anti-Anzac Day Collective were deeply unpopular, sometimes provoking violence, invariably leading to sexist abuse, and often resulting in arrests.[142] The Victorian RSL president Bruce Ruxton did not mince words in 1983. 'If one looked at them,' he declared, 'I wonder how rape would be possible.'[143] In the following year, the NSW RSL president recognised that rape occurred in war, only to reinforce the enduring myth of national innocence: 'Australian servicemen have a pretty clean record in this regard – they were too busy fighting for the freedom of their country.'[144] The protests against rape in war petered out in the late 1980s and while they did not win popular acclaim, in one respect they belonged to an emerging Anzac mainstream: they drew attention to the traumatic impact of war.[145]

Others wanted inclusion yet met with similar resistance from the ageing keepers of the Anzac legend. Ruxton and his comrades interposed themselves when members of a Gay Ex-Services Association in Melbourne sought entry to the Shrine of Remembrance in 1982 to lay a wreath; in 1983 the Shrine ruled that non-recognised groups could lay wreaths 'discreetly' outside the context of the ceremony. A member of the Gay Ex-Services Association declared that they 'didn't want any hassle. All we wanted was to lay a wreath.' But he had found that 'the first reaction was just part of the thinking that poofters don't join up and that they don't serve their countries overseas'.[146]

And just as Ruxton did not, as he said, mind 'poofters' marching on Anzac Day with their units, so it was with Aboriginal people. There was no controversy while they remained willing to march with their old units, but the application of the newly formed Aboriginal and Islander Ex-Services Association to allow Indigenous ex–service personnel to march as a group received a predictable rebuff. So a dawn service and march – claimed as the 'first Aboriginal Anzac march' – occurred in inner-suburban Northcote. At the service, an Aboriginal pastor, Neville Lilley, standing between an Aboriginal flag and an Anzac cross, told those present 'that Aboriginal people had been privileged by God to fight for their country and for freedom'. The organisers of the march were deliberately contesting an idea that had long lurked around efforts to deny Aboriginal people's claims to land rights: that they had not defended Australia in time of war.[147]

In spite of this kind of challenge, the historian Mark McKenna has suggested that a reinvented Anzac Day offered itself in the late 1980s 'as a less complicated and less divisive alternative' to Australia Day, especially in the wake of the failure of the 1988 Bicentenary to enact national unity.[148] Certainly, Hawke seems to have recognised Anzac's potential as a source of national symbolism, even if he felt initially hampered by the legacy of the Vietnam War. More attracted in his speech-making to Curtin and the Second World War at first, the prime minister came to Gallipoli and the First World War gradually, drawn by circumstance and a highly developed political instinct. In 1984 he announced that his government would ask its Turkish counterpart to rename the beach on which the Australians had landed on 25 April 1915 Anzac Cove.[149] This change occurred in 1985, with an Ataturk Peace Park being established in Canberra as part of the Australian end of this exercise in memorial diplomacy (much to the disgust of local Kurdish nationalists, who turned up at the opening to trade insults with Turkish government supporters).[150] In 1986 Hawke gave an Anzac Day address while visiting Greece, the site of a disastrous campaign in 1941.[151] But it was the 1990 seventy-fifth anniversary pilgrimage to Gallipoli that truly gave Hawke the opportunity to put his mark on the legend.

Fifty-eight Gallipoli veterans aged between 93 and 104 accompanied Hawke and the new Opposition leader, John Hewson, and about 10,000 Australian 'pilgrims', many of them young backpackers who responded to the old-timers as if they were 'rock stars'.[152] Hawke's speech at the dawn service borrowed – to put it politely – from Lincoln's Gettysburg Address, as an agnostic prime minister declared the beach 'sacred because of the bravery and the bloodshed of the ANZACs'. In a speech delivered later at Lone Pine on that same morning, Hawke saw in the story of Anzac 'recognition of the special meaning of Australian mateship'.[153] So after a decade in which Australian identity had been vigorously contested, it had again come to rest, at least in the mind of the prime minister, on a very familiar foundation.

9
The Crash

It was so hard these days to know what you felt. Once it had been straightforward: get out of Vietnam, higher wages, a better deal for women. Then it got so complicated; it was all economics and what seemed at first abhorrent could be portrayed as only a short-term evil leading ultimately to better things and there were just so many variables, you couldn't keep track of them in your head all at once.

AMANDA LOHREY, *THE READING GROUP* (1988)

On most days in the mid-1980s, Sydney's Simpsons restaurant – co-owned by the economist and future Liberal Party leader John Hewson – was 'wall-to-wall pin stripe at lunch time', its screens allowing stockbrokers, bankers and analysts to follow what was happening back on the stock-exchange floor. But around noon on Tuesday 20 October 1987, as the strains of jazz singer Vince Jones wafted from the sound system, the restaurant was almost deserted.[1] Not far away in the Sydney Stock Exchange building in Bond Street, the morning's trading had been the most frantic of the decade, but for the first time in years, it was almost exclusively on one side: everyone wanted to sell. Wall Street had just had its Black Monday, which wiped $800 billion, or almost 23 per cent, off the value of shares, compared with 13 per cent in the famous 1929 crash. Australia's Black Tuesday crash saw a 25 per cent, or $55 billion, drop in value.[2]

'From the opening trading bell' at ten o'clock, 'it was pandemonium'.[3] 'It's just been bloody chaotic,' explained one dealer, 'just intense panic, everyone's selling, the banks weren't lending in the afternoon, and no-one's buying.'[4] At 11.30 am, to add to the excitement, a rumour did the rounds that Iran had declared war on the United States.[5] Anxious investors – large and small – squeezed into the crowded public galleries of the country's stock exchanges or, braving the Sydney rain, remained on the steps looking at the ribbon passing across the monitor reporting on the carnage inside, where dealers waved their arms about frantically trying to sell shares that no one wanted. Leading Sydney stockbroker Rene Rivkin ran his worry beads red-hot; he would later sum up the day for journalists as 'disaster, disaster, disaster'.[6] Yuppies and grey-hairs among the dealing fraternity indulged in black humour about soup kitchens, jumping out of skyscrapers, getting shot by disgruntled investors, working for McDonald's. And when John Howard interrupted the weekly meeting of the parliamentary Liberal Party in Canberra to report that a fifth of the value had already been wiped off the share market, two of his parliamentarians, John Moore and John Spender, immediately rushed out the door to call their stockbrokers.[7]

Hours after the day's trading was finished, 'most brokers remained shell-shocked'.[8] But who was responsible for the bloodbath? Sober commentary pointed to American budget deficits and trade imbalances before – in the case of the *Australian* – moving on to identify the usual suspects closer to home: union power, high wages and government spending. Some blamed greedy Americans, others Japanese investors awash with money yet too ignorant to know a good deal from a bad one.[9] Commentators drew attention to internationalised financial markets and computers which had ensured that '[t]he very feel of Wall Street or London or Tokyo flows through the cathode ray terminals which are the nerves and muscles of world markets'.[10]

As the nation's commentariat contemplated the wreckage, they tried to decipher what it all meant. The title of the *Australian Financial Review*'s editorial declared that '1987 is NOT 1929', but possibly more in hope than conviction. Newspapers which had spent much of the 1980s celebrating free enterprise and bemoaning government intervention now assured readers that 'governments are more involved in overseeing and regulating stock markets and banks nowadays'.[11] And banks, they said, had been very careful in their lending practices, demanding 'fairly stringent security against loans for share trading, providing themselves good protection against sliding prices'.[12]

Before long, it became clear enough that at least one bank had not been demanding 'fairly stringent security against loans'. Indeed, there were claims that Laurie Connell's Rothwells had lent money in some cases without even bothering to record the name of the debtor.[13] Several hundred million dollars had in recent years passed to Connell himself in the form of unsecured loans, to bankroll his dubious investments and extravagant lifestyle. Reality began closing in when it got about that the National Australia Bank had been bouncing Rothwells cheques. A run on the bank began on Wednesday

21 October, the day after the stock-market collapse. So Connell returned to Perth from Sydney where he had been busy with the ill-starred Fairfax takeover, and began making frantic phone calls.

Brian Burke was among those Connell spoke to about the bank's troubles. The danger to his government of a scandal was plain enough, for Connell was highly conspicuous among Burke's Tammany Hall–style political network. With gross and characteristic impropriety, Burke arranged for the Government Employees Superannuation Board and the State Government Insurance Commission (SGIC) to buy millions of dollars worth of Rothwells assets and bills, but it was going to take more than this to make any dent on its problems.[14]

Corporate Australia rallied to save Connell's skin – and its own. For if Rothwells went down, so might other financial institutions, as well as a number of business empires whose book value, but not indebtedness, had shrunk alarmingly in the recent share-dumping. Connell, Alan Bond and Bond's managing director, Peter Beckwith, met in Perth over the weekend and worked around the clock with various other executives, bankers and state Labor government minister David Parker to organise a rescue. Burke was only ever a phone call away. Bond took charge, and Connell agreed to commit $70 million of his own money; an empty undertaking, since his personal finances were on a par with those of the bank. In any case, he continued looting Rothwells much as he had before, taking out another $40 million within weeks. In the end, about $150 million worth of commitments were assembled to prop up Rothwells, the money coming from Kerry Packer, Robert Holmes à Court, John Elliott, Richard Pratt and Larry Adler – a glittering array of corporate stars. Burke offered a government guarantee of up to $150 million, which persuaded the National Australia Bank to get in on the act, and it lent Rothwells the same amount.[15]

Rothwells stumbled on, harried by creditors and depositors. Burke, always with an eye for danger as well as the main chance, retired in early 1988 to take up an appointment as Australia's ambassador to Ireland and the Holy See. The career of his successor, Peter Dowding, would soon be destroyed by further ill-advised efforts to prevent Rothwells from falling over. The most extraordinary of his government's expedients was its October 1988 purchase from Connell and a partner of a company called Petrochemical Industries Co. Ltd for $400 million – about 100 times the value of its assets. While this allowed some of Rothwells's creditors to get their money back courtesy of the taxpayer, it was too late for Connell and his bank – a liquidator was appointed the following month.[16]

Paul Barry has called Rothwells's demise 'the harbinger of doom, the first star to fall in the great Australian corporate collapse'.[17] Several of the Perth entrepreneurs whose stars had shone brightly during the 1980s were now more like sailors desperately bailing water out of listing ships. Holmes à Court – aged by the corporate battles of recent years, suffering from diabetes and addicted to cigars – realised quickly that the game was up. His goal now was to offload his public companies to save his private one, Heytesbury. In this he was greatly assisted by the enterprise that came to be known as WA Inc. – the mutual back-scratching of the Labor government and big business – which ensured that his landing was a great deal softer than it would otherwise have been.[18] The crash had ended his dream of a controlling share of BHP, which itself bought up half of Holmes à Court's shares while the WA government picked up another parcel worth around $50 million, in addition to several Perth properties. But there was more: the State Government Insurance Commission agreed to buy just under a fifth of Holmes à Court's Bell Group, while the cash-strapped Alan Bond, desperate to get his hands on the loot sitting inside Bell Resources, offered to pick up a share of the same size. This appeared to be a very shady arrangement, one in which the parties colluded to prevent ordinary shareholders from selling their shares at the same price as Bond and the SGIC had paid. The National Companies and Securities Commission was having none of it, and advised that Bond needed to make an offer to all holders of Bell stock, one that would only worsen his already serious cash-flow problems – effectively forcing him into a full takeover that he could ill-afford.[19]

Western Australia's entrepreneurial golden age was over. Carmen Lawrence, a psychologist and single mother who succeeded Dowding, appointed a royal commission in November of 1990 to investigate WA Inc. Holmes à Court would have been a star witness, except that he had died in September, his heart and health broken by the failure of his bid for BHP and a crash that ended his dreams of ever taking the company from the eastern establishment.[20] Laurie Connell *was* a star witness at the royal commission, but his life would also prove short: he died bankrupt in early 1996. Others were more resilient, living on like period pieces from a time of embarrassing excess. Brian Burke, only in his early forties when he resigned and with ambitions for a career in federal politics, was in Dublin, but as the royal commission uncovered its sorry tale he had to return to Perth to tell his side of the story. Burke would eventually serve two prison terms, in each case for matters that seemed trivial when viewed against the background of the vast system of cronyism over which he had presided.

Alan Bond initially looked as if he would survive Black Tuesday, just as he had the downturn of 1974, but his ability to tread water finally failed him in 1989, as auditors revealed a loss of almost $1 billion for the most recent financial year – the largest in Australian history. There was grim irony in Bond learning that the receivers had been called in just as he stepped ashore as victor of the Sydney–Hobart race in his yacht *Drumbeat*. This hollow nautical triumph provided a tidy bookend to his 1980s.

Kerry Packer took back Channel Nine the following year, his $200 million of preference shares – a legacy of the original deal with Bond – being all the 'money' he needed to regain control. In other words he had pocketed more than $800 million for his dealings with the WA businessman and received, in return, an expanded network: no wonder Packer remarked, 'You only get one Alan Bond in your life, and I've had mine'. [21] Bond was declared bankrupt in 1992 and later imprisoned for various offences, including having taken $1.2 billion out of Bell Resources to prop up the rest of his failing business. Journalists and regulators continued to look for money trails in the usual places – such as Switzerland – for Bond lived luxuriously despite apparent financial ruin. Yet he was irrepressible, making it back onto the lower rungs of the *BRW* list of the 200 richest Australians in 2008, and five years later appearing in the media alongside Bob Hawke as the hero of 1983 at a thirty-year commemoration of the America's Cup victory. For that, it seemed, Australians were prepared to forgive much.

*

The only state that could rival Western Australia in the exuberance of its economic life, or outdo it in the corruption of its most senior politicians, was Queensland. A thin veneer of parliamentary democracy only partly obscured the reality that Queensland had descended into the closest thing imaginable in Australia to a police state. Sir Terence Lewis, plucked in the mid-1970s from obscurity on the Charleville beat, was a de facto member of cabinet, consulted by the premier on all manner of issues off-limits to police commissioners elsewhere. But all of this would begin to unravel almost from the moment the National Party won re-election in late 1986. While Bjelke-Petersen was distracted by his push for Canberra, federal agencies and investigative journalists were laying a series of mines that would eventually destroy his premiership and bring to an end thirty-two years of conservative government in the state.

Brisbane journalists had been sniffing around the godly state's illegal casinos, drug rings, sex shops and brothels for some years before their reporting began to bite. But when a young *Courier-Mail* journalist, Phil Dickie, began writing articles about Brisbane's flourishing vice industry from January 1987, the timing was exquisite; a group of journalists led by Chris Masters at the ABC's *Four Corners* was also working on a program that would go to air on 11 May 1987 as 'The Moonlight State'.[22] Dickie would eventually win a Walkley Award for his slow drip of stories on the crookedness at the heart of law enforcement, but the impact of Masters's 'The Moonlight State' was immediate and explosive. The main differences were the national exposure and the powerful pictures. *Four Corners* used the film footage gathered on its reporters' excursions in Brisbane's Fortitude Valley with great skill, opening with scenes from a strip joint, and then cutting away to images of Bjelke-Petersen and Lewis at a public event. The episode ended with an image of Bjelke-Petersen at a church service, his wife playing the organ, and the congregation singing 'Onward Christian Soldiers'. In between these scenes, Masters introduced viewers to a rogue's gallery of brothel owners, casino operators, SP bookmakers, drug dealers, bagmen and crooked cops: the names of Hector Hapeta, Vittorio Conte, the Bellino brothers and Jack Herbert would for years be all over the national media. Of the brothels themselves, Masters declared in the program: 'While police and politicians can't find them, the public can't miss them.' Parlour operators, it was alleged, were paying about $100,000 a month into a syndicate, money which was passed on to police in return for protection. The message was unmistakable: Queensland's premier and police commissioner were blind, crooked or hypocrites.

Bjelke-Petersen himself was overseas when 'The Moonlight State' went to air, and the acting premier, Bill Gunn, promised a searching inquiry. When Bjelke-Petersen returned, he did his best to shut it down but without success. 'You've got the tiger by the tail and it will end up biting you,' he told Gunn – but he should have said 'biting me'.[23] The government appointed a leading barrister, Tony Fitzgerald QC, to lead a Commission of Inquiry into Possible Illegal Activities and Associated Police Misconduct. Even as the hearings began, the payments to police – a longstanding arrangement code-named 'the Joke' by those involved in it – continued for another couple of months.[24]

Lewis was the first witness, but it was his diaries more than his testimony that proved sensational, for they showed that the police commissioner was both powerful and corrupt. The government forced him to stand aside in September, but the revelations continued to tumble from witnesses, notably the corrupt police whom Fitzgerald had seen fit to offer indemnities. The star witness was 'bagman Jack Herbert', as he was invariably called: and for reporters he was almost too good to be true. Herbert was a British migrant and ex-cop who had been an intermediary between the criminal syndicates and the police, accepting payments on behalf of the former which he distributed to the latter. His own take was around $1.25 million out of a total of $3 million paid over several decades, and he and his family lived a luxurious lifestyle, one that would have been unimaginable to the working-class boy from south London he had once been.[25] He had taken a 'holiday' in Britain when things became a little too hot after the airing of 'The Moonlight State', but the authorities tracked him down and returned him to Brisbane. As the man at the centre of the Joke, Herbert was in a strong position to explain how it had worked, how much was involved and who had been in on it.[26]

The inquiry, expected to be short and sharp, heard from 339 witnesses over more than two years.[27] And even while they provided testimony about police accepting money and free sex in exchange for their blind eye, the National Party government and its police force continued to pose as the guardians of morality against the corrupting influence of trendies and southerners, launching pre-dawn raids on university campuses to seize condom vending machines.[28] Seen in light of the Fitzgerald Inquiry's revelations, there was something here more dangerous to the government than mere ridicule or accusations of hypocrisy: it looked morally bankrupt. Bjelke-Petersen's approval rating slumped to 22 per cent, and in November 1987 he made a move to save his skin that was probably also designed to shut down the inquiry. To help bring this about, he demanded the resignations of five of his ministers, ostensibly on grounds of disloyalty, although the premier was vague about the reasons for his actions. When they refused, Bjelke-Petersen asked the governor, Sir Walter Campbell, to sack them. Campbell demurred, though Bjelke-Petersen eventually persuaded him to accept three dismissals. But on 27 November the National Party voted to get rid of Bjelke-Petersen, electing Mike Ahern as leader and Gunn his deputy. Bjelke-Petersen is said to have called Buckingham Palace in a futile effort to get the Queen to save him, and even tried to do a deal with the Labor Party.[29] On 1 December he resigned, but only after his National Party colleagues issued a threat that if he continued to hold out, he would have to foot the bill for the various defamation actions he had taken out against his manifold enemies.[30]

The order over which the premier had presided for almost twenty years was crumbling around him. Lewis would eventually receive a fourteen-year jail sentence for his corruption, which included over $600,000 of bribes.[31] Don 'Shady' Lane, an ex-policeman and former Liberal who had defected to the Nationals to help give them a majority in their own right in 1983, was the Joke's man in cabinet.[32] He eventually went to jail for stealing ministerial funds. Big Russ Hinze would have almost certainly joined him, if he had not died before he could be prosecuted. The Fitzgerald Inquiry would eventually report that during four years between 1983 and 1987, over $800,000 'described as "loans forgiven" and "loans written off" was processed through the Hinze group financial accounts to the credit of individual accounts of Hinze and his wife'.[33] Bjelke-Petersen, no longer premier, was himself questioned during the inquiry about the lucrative multi-million-dollar construction contracts awarded to companies that donated money to the National Party. The most sensational exchange turned on the question of political donations, for his office was awash with cash. A curious Fitzgerald wondered what effect the arrival of $50,000 might have on office life, asking whether one of Bjelke-Petersen's secretaries would come in and say: 'We've just had somebody drop by and leave $50,000 in cash but we don't know who he is?'

> Bjelke-Petersen: Sir, honestly, you don't talk like that, really. Nobody comes in and says 'I've got $50,000' ... I have nothing to do with the funds. I do not recollect it. I do not sit at the door waiting for people to come in.
> Fitzgerald: Obviously you didn't have to.[34]

Bjelke-Petersen would go on trial for having perjured himself. He was fortunate not to go to prison: after the jury became deadlocked, it was found that the foreman was an active member of the National Party. In its symbolism, if not in its justice, this was as fitting an end to the Queensland premier's public career as could be imagined.

Beyond those who found their corruption exposed or their careers curtailed by its activities, the inquiry had its critics. The journalist Brian Toohey entitled a 1989 article 'How Fitzgerald flunked it' and noted that he 'seemed to have plenty of time to take evidence about whether some constable copped a "freebie" from some prostitute operating ... from the back of a panel van' but 'did not call evidence from the businessmen who had engaged in various financial transactions with Hinze and Joh'.[35] A local commentator similarly wondered what was to be done about all of the corruption not linked to the police: 'land deals, milk quotas, government contracts, selling knighthoods', but recognised that the inquiry 'could conceivably go for twenty years and still not get to the bottom of all the muck'.[36] Here was the rub: Fitzgerald would have been aware of the difficulties Frank Costigan had encountered as his inquiries into the Painters and Dockers Union fanned out to businessmen who devoted their days to making their affairs exceedingly complicated. Fitzgerald never set out to catch every crook, but rather to change the culture of a state.

In that he was successful: 'Fitzgerald', as it became known, was a landmark in the politics of Queensland, the history of Australian policing and the treatment of corruption. And rather like Expo '88, with which it coincided, it paved the way for a renovated state identity – one with which Queenslanders would feel less like curiosities on display for the amusement of supposedly more sophisticated southerners. Jokes about Queensland police and money in brown paper bags would live on, but after Fitzgerald and Joh, Queenslanders would, for good or ill, increasingly feel – and become – more like other Australians.

*

Christopher Skase had become an adopted son of Queensland. In 1987 he was awarded the honour of Queensland Business Executive of the Year, but the cash prize of $20,000 would barely have kept him in aftershave, and it is unclear if he found any use for the Apple ImageWriter II colour printer – Skase wrote all his ideas down on old-fashioned notepads – or, considering that he had his own jet, the first-class tickets to London. By the end of the decade, however, the money and plane tickets would have been welcome, as Qintex sank under a mountain of debt and its chief's plans for overseas expansion.[37]

Skase's ambitious acquisition of Channel Seven stations in five mainland capitals meant his audience reach exceeded the 60 per cent allowed by the government's new media laws.[38] Meanwhile, the combination of the sharemarket crash, high interest rates and a pilots' strike exposed the cash-flow problems of his resort empire. Skase began selling assets, offloading just under half of his three resorts to a Japanese buyer.[39] But he also went on an American buying spree, one that reflected his desperation to find a big hole into which to shovel the large and growing problems of the Qintex group. In 1987 he had invested in Hal Roach studios, a company that colourised old black-and-white film – a fad of the period.[40] But two years later – in a move that took financial journalists' breath away – the media reported that he had acquired the legendary film studio Metro-Goldwyn-Mayer/United Artists for $1.2 billion.[41] In reality, the deal was much more complicated, and modest, than a straight takeover, for MGM effectively remained in the hands of its existing owner. After a competing offer from Rupert Murdoch meant that Skase had to bid even more to stay in the game, he was unable to muster the funds for the deposit, the deal fell through, and his US company filed for bankruptcy.[42] Once analysts grasped that the Qintex group as a whole had a high level of exposure to the failed US operation, Skase was no longer able to repel the barbarians at the gate, which included the Australian media, the federal Labor government, 'socialist theorisers', regulators, bankers, investors and shareholders – 'tall poppies' had no hope in Australia, he later declared.[43] In October 1989 the major Qintex companies were suspended from the stock exchange. Revelations that Skase's management company had received over $40 million in fees while Qintex's debt to the banks ballooned to over $1 billion and its shares plunged in value cut away whatever remained of his credibility. The National Companies and Securities Commission was investigating the group, creditors withdrew their support and in November 1989, Qintex collapsed.[44]

Skase subsequently lived in Europe, returning from time to time for court appearances. Charged in 1991 with breaches of corporations law arising from his pocketing of management fees of over $19 million, he also faced a tax liability, an accusation that he had bribed a Gold Coast mayor, the examination of his assets by creditors and, once he was declared bankrupt, the prospect of being prevented from leaving the country.[45] But Skase persuaded a court to return his passport and took up residence on the Spanish island of Majorca, never to return.[46] By now, he unquestionably had a disease of the lungs but, ever the showman, he went to great lengths to demonstrate that his life would be imperilled by extradition to Australia, deploying for the benefit of the media a breathing apparatus and oxygen tank that made him look like a frogman.[47] He became an object of hatred and ridicule.

Skase was a scapegoat for what had gone wrong in Australia's 1980s. A nation that had made heroes of its entrepreneurs, and held up their lifestyle as both enviable and the reward for their success, now turned bitterly against them.[48] Skase was perfectly fitted for this role not only because he fled instead of taking his medicine, but also because his lavish parties and luxurious lifestyle, as well as his empire of posh resorts, jewellery retailers and media companies, epitomised the excesses of 1980s consumer capitalism. And he had always seemed effete and even un-Australian beside the likes of those two sporting men and brewers of beer, Elliott and Bond. Skase died in his Spanish exile in 2001. He was just fifty-two.

*

Adelaide never could quite match the Sunshine State in its embrace of a 1980s high life. But even before the beginning of the decade, the city was wearing its old 'City of Churches' garb with a degree of embarrassment, preferring a more glamorous image as a paradise of progressive social reform, high culture and fine dining. Yet South Australia also remained a manufacturing state, with the battling car industry as its beating heart, and the steel industry one of its limbs. During the 1980s South Australian elites tried to shake off the state's dependence on this old economy, emphasising financial services, tourism and big events. A grand casino was built to rival the striking Festival Centre which had nestled on the bank of the Torrens since 1973. The Formula One Grand Prix overtook the Adelaide Festival as the most eagerly anticipated event in the city's annual calendar. The world was coming to Adelaide – or at least a rich and famous party set, which devoted its time and money to following racing-car drivers around the world.

Adelaide was also going out to the world. The State Bank of South Australia (SBSA) quickly became central to the state's aspirations to hit the big time. It appointed as managing director a member of a Sydney establishment family, Timothy Marcus Clark, who led the bank on an extraordinary course of expansion, all conveniently backed by a state government guarantee and with no share price to worry over.[49] Between 1984 and 1989, its assets soared from just over $3 billion to five times that amount, while its profits climbed from around $19 million to over $90 million.[50] All of this looked impressive, but even a glance at the figures indicated that assets, and therefore risk, were growing rather more quickly than profits.

The danger was actually far worse than it appeared. A large part of the bank's problem – although it was touted at the time as a mighty achievement – was that its business had shifted dramatically from home loans to much riskier commercial developments in which the bank was a highly exposed venture partner. Housing loans – the bank's traditional fare – had come to be seen as lousy business because returns were steady rather than spectacular, dribbling in over many years. By contrast, commercial loans yielded quick results and the salaries of bank executives were happily linked to 'asset growth', as loans were euphemistically called.[51] By the end of the 1980s, the bank had expanded its operations to New Zealand, had branches in London and New York, and offices in Chicago, Los Angeles and Hong Kong. It was doing two-thirds of its business outside South Australia.[52] In the financial year to June 1990 the SBSA's lending expanded wildly as the book value of its 'assets' increased by about 50 per cent, from $14 billion to $21 billion, in a final spin of the roulette wheel. Profits had meanwhile declined from over $90 million to just $24 million as the recession started to bite.[53]

By the time the bank issued its annual report in 1991, it was a less glossy document than those of previous years, largely shorn of the smiling faces of happy South Australians. The bank, it announced, had a new chairman, a new managing director and a new board. It also had a government indemnity which would allow SBSA 'to retain its relatively high credit ratings' – a polite way of explaining that SA taxpayers would be footing the bill for the profligacy and incompetence of the previous management.[54] In the early 1990s, a royal commission and an auditor-general's inquiry would ensure that the SBSA received continuing media exposure. It was eventually split into a 'bad bank', into which failed or failing loans were emptied for the taxpayer to cover, and a 'good bank', which retreated into the reliable home-loan market, was sold for $730 million and yielded healthy profits to its new shareholders.[55]

How had this happened? It was in many respects a typical story of the 1980s but, as usual, with local peculiarities. Like most such scandals it had at its heart an arrogant and forceful figure in Tim Marcus Clark, whom the state auditor-general, in surveying the wreckage, called 'the bank's growth hormone'.[56] Clark, who was also chairman of the Grand Prix board, brooked no dissent from his vision of the bank's future, and he was sufficiently plausible to persuade both the SBSA board and the premier–treasurer, John Bannon, that the bank was going from strength to strength. Bannon and his advisers lacked experience of commercial banking, and even if they had known the right questions to ask, the profits that the SBSA group was sending their way each year would have dampened their curiosity.[57] The Reserve Bank worried about the SBSA's exposure, but it did not speak to Bannon and had only an advisory prudential role in relation to state banks. Clark, in any case, treated the RBA's warnings with contempt and on one occasion walked out of a meeting with RBA officials when he did not like what they were saying.[58]

The SBSA affair irreparably weakened the state Labor government. Bannon resigned in September 1992, succeeded by Lynn Arnold. As losses from the SBSA passed $3 billion and the recession bit, Labor had little chance at the December 1993 election.[59] The financial disasters of the early 1990s also sapped the ambitions that had driven the SBSA's expansion in the first place.

As one annual report from happier times had explained, the bank's 'presence in Australasia and the world's major financial centres' was providing the state with 'an important financial network ... where high technology industry and export trade' would flourish.[60] The intention was that South Australia should not be left a provincial city wallowing in decline as part of a post-industrial rust belt.

*

South Australia's trials in the late 1980s and early 1990s were essentially problems for South Australia. Victoria's had wider ramifications: it was a state of more than 4 million people, and Melbourne was the traditional centre of Australian manufacturing and finance. But by the time of John Cain's third election victory in October 1988, his government's energy had largely dissipated. Its strategy of picking winners by taking equity in businesses through the Victorian Economic Development Corporation (VEDC) meant that it inevitably shared in the losses that came in the wake of the stockmarket crash. An accountant's report criticising the VEDC's decision-making appeared soon after the election, and the VEDC's eventual losses, at around $100 million, while piddling compared with the scale of corporate collapse in the private sector, undermined public confidence in a premier who had made much of his suburban solicitor–like caution and probity.[61]

The VEDC's problems were a setback, but those of the State Bank of Victoria (SBV) were a more serious matter. Tricontinental, its merchant banking arm, already had a reputation for chasing marginal clients with loan money, but after the SBV assumed full ownership in 1985 – it previously had a 25 per cent share – the market raised the merchant banker's credit rating from BBB to A+. As had been the case with the SBSA, a state government guarantee now stood behind Tricontinental.[62] Under the 31-year-old Ian Johns, who had risen from bank teller to managing director in little more than a decade, Tricontinental saw itself as a world apart from the SBV.[63] As one of Tricontinental's senior managers later told a royal commission into its affairs, 'I still do not believe that the State Bank is a commercial institution. I believe it is very much a way of life.'[64] He did not intend this as a compliment. By way of contrast, Tricontinental directed its efforts towards 'getting its hands dirty' alongside 'a view to cultivating the entrepreneurial spirit that will provide the greatest growth to Australia'.[65] In reality, it had little choice but to chase the business of those in whom the big banks were uninterested if it were to grow rapidly. Tricontinental did, however, attract the likes of

Bond, Skase and Herscu who, as the same executive quoted above put it, were 'blue chip ... for Tricontinental'.[66]

Tricontinental markedly increased its exposure to the booming commercial property market after the stock-market crash and by early 1989, it was in serious strife. At a board meeting in April, a former managing director, Jack Ryan, likened its lending policy to 'a desperado trying to get out of trouble on the last race at Flemington'.[67] The SBV wanted to sell it, which further undermined confidence in its solvency. Then, in May, the government learned that Johns himself was about to face criminal charges arising from his share-dealing. (He would eventually serve a seven-month prison sentence.) Having sacked Johns, the SBV took over direct management of Tricontinental, only to have its losses blow out in the next few months to over $1.7 billion. To cover the $2.7 billion losses of the whole SBV group, the Victorian government sold the SBV to the Commonwealth Bank. The 1980s had claimed yet another of the nation's venerable institutions; in this case, one which had begun its career in 1842.[68]

The Tricontinental affair shook confidence in the Cain government's prudence; the Pyramid scandal destroyed it. Even a government that was travelling well would have suffered some damage from the collapse of a business such as the Geelong-based Farrow group of companies. But the Victorian government, far from travelling well, was descending into bitter factional warfare. A government plan to dispense with conductors on the city's famous trams by introducing a new ticketing system produced chaos. For three weeks in January 1990 angry unionists parked long lines of trams in the city's streets – a conspicuous sign of a government no longer able to govern.[69] In the March federal election, the Labor Party lost ten of its twenty-four House of Representatives seats in Victoria. Few doubted that state issues had contributed significantly to creating this electoral killing field.

By this time, there had already been a run on the Pyramid Building Society. Pyramid was in one sense a classic story of provincial Australia; in another, a tale of what happened in the 1980s when small fish tried to become big ones in the much larger ocean opened up to them by deregulation. Building societies had traditionally provided loans for homebuyers, and Pyramid, founded in 1959, was a typical example, with deep roots in the Geelong community.[70] New Victorian legislation in 1986 had allowed building societies greater freedom to engage in financial activities beyond their traditional fare, a freedom that the Farrow group of companies exploited to the utmost and more; its horizons increasingly extended well beyond the

Bellarine Peninsula. In a little more than two years at the end of the 1980s, the group's assets tripled from around $900 million to over $3 billion.[71]

Farrow, which included the Pyramid, Geelong and Countrywide building societies, was from the mid-1980s controlled by two men, both Geelong locals. Bill Farrow inherited the business from his father; when the group ran into difficulties in the late 1980s, he had 80 per cent control, the other 20 per cent belonging to David Clarke, a former Geelong football star who now spent most winter weekends on the ski slopes. Farrow himself seemed to be most people's idea of a good Geelong bloke, and he stuffed the group's board with other good Geelong blokes, most of them from Geelong College like him and Clarke, none of them with experience of high finance – also like him and Clarke.[72] Clarke, however, secretly borrowed money from the Farrow group through proxies, on notably favourable terms, to finance his own multi-million-dollar commercial property deals. At the same time, both men received millions in management fees, while they attracted a gush of deposits from customers by paying a rate of interest well above their rivals.[73] Yet they were still able to lend money at discount rates, using the application fee as a major source of profit, a business model which provided an incentive to offer new loans while flattening the income from old ones.[74]

These activities were poor business practice although not illegal. But to get around the legislative requirement that half their loans be for owner-occupied homes, Farrow and Clarke classified commercial developments as 'residential' and thereby exposed the business to the vagaries of the commercial property market.[75] Two-thirds of the group's money was tied to such assets and even before prices headed south, state regulators in Melbourne and the Reserve Bank in Sydney were aware that all was not rosy.[76] But neither acted decisively and in February 1990 a run on the Pyramid Building Society began. Depositors took out $134 million in just a fortnight; the Victorian government responded with a soothing statement assuring the public that their funds were 'secure', and that the '[r]umours circulating about the society are without foundation'.[77]

This turned out to be far from the case. As a report into the disaster later remarked, Pyramid's problems were not of liquidity but of solvency, and another run on Pyramid occurred in May and June.[78] Efforts by Pyramid and the government to secure bank support failed as the depth of the group's problems became clearer, and the government called in an accountant to assess just how soiled the shop really was. He promptly recommended the suspension of trading. Cain then foolishly denied that his government would guarantee the funds of depositors, despite the assurance provided earlier in the year. The result was a predictable storm of outrage, much of it emanating from battling Geelong where depositors – many of them small ones – had well over $500 million locked up in the Farrow group. They attracted little sympathy from Cain: it would be hard to imagine a man more unsuited by temperament or experience to dealing with the Pyramid crisis. He understandably had no time for Farrow and Clarke, whom he claimed were not running a building society but a finance company, yet he showed little more feeling for depositors and investors who, so far as he was concerned, had been happy to take the high interest rates and then cry poor when the company went belly up. At a time when the Farrow group's problems were still widely understood to have arisen from a lack of short-term liquidity, or possibly even 'malicious gossip', Cain appeared insensitive as well as hypocritical in light of the bailout being performed on the SBV.[79]

Angry and frightened depositors protested outside Parliament House in Melbourne, and in the rain and wind at Kardinia Park in Geelong where they joined hands to say the Lord's Prayer for the Farrow group. Some gave way to despair; there was a report in the local press that one man with his savings tied up in Pyramid had killed himself by leaping off the Barwon Heads bridge.[80] As Cain and his cabinet continued to equivocate, there was a caucus revolt in which Geelong MPs were predictably prominent in demanding that the $1.3 billion of more than 200,000 depositors in the Farrow group be paid out. Cain gave way, possibly influenced by the class action with which angry depositors threatened his government in addition to the political pressure being applied from all sides.[81]

The Farrow collapse had demonstrated the inadequacy of building-society supervision and regulation at the state level. More than that, it hinted at a wider problem with the deregulated financial sector in Australia. Reserve Bank supervision did not extend to state-owned banks, nor to building societies; yet a building society that closed its doors while it held more than $1 billion in deposits would induce a wider panic. And so it proved, especially after it also emerged in July 1990 that three friendly societies which between them controlled $350 million were also in difficulty. A run on the Bank of Melbourne followed; it had only recently converted from a building society to a bank and was apparently well-managed, with a level of liquidity above requirements. In any case, since it fell within the responsibility of the Reserve Bank, the RBA issued a statement on 16 July guaranteeing depositors' money, but not before the bank had received a barrage of calls from worried depositors and false rumours circulated that there were 150 people queued up outside its Hawthorn branch demanding their money. A commentator likened the crisis to 'a cancer eating into the fabric of the state financial system'.[82] If so, it was a cancer that contributed to killing off Cain's premiership.[83] He resigned in August 1990 in favour of his deputy, Joan Kirner; she would lead the government to a crushing defeat at the hands of Liberal leader Jeff Kennett in October 1992.

John Elliott, the Melbourne businessman who had devoted part of his busy public life in the 1980s to ridding the country of 'socialist' governments of this type, was by this time in no position to gloat. For Elliott's fortunes, like those of the city over which his presence had once towered, plummeted during the late 1980s as he desperately sought to raise his status from a highly paid executive to a super-wealthy, free-wheeling, all-powerful entrepreneur. He and some of his IXL cronies created a company called Harlin Holdings as the vehicle for a management buyout of Elders-IXL – an ethical minefield since it involved him taking possession of a company that he was being paid by shareholders to run in their interests. In 1988, backed by BHP money, Harlin acquired about 18 per cent of the group. In the following year Elliott, worried that the emergence of another large investor would dilute his influence, agreed to take up another 17 per cent of the company at $3 per share from friendly shareholders. At this point, Elliott's problems began to get out of control, for the regulatory authorities insisted that he make the same offer to all shareholders. Elliott expected that few would wish to sell at what he regarded as a low price, but he was inundated with offers and ended up with 56 per cent of the company and a $3 billion debt: far more than could be serviced by the dividends he would receive from his investment.[84] In 1990 he stood down as chairman of Foster's Brewing Group, as the company was now called, after it reported a $1.3 billion loss; he was booed at its annual general meeting. BHP finally pulled the plug on its financing of Elliott's activities in mid-1992, calling in a $1 billion debt.[85] Pursued by the National Crime Authority (NCA) for years in connection with one of his deals in the 1986 play for control of BHP, a decade later Elliott was acquitted of charges of theft and conspiracy involving $66.5 million after a court found the NCA's pursuit of Elliott unlawful.[86]

Elliott seemed to enter the 1990s with plenty of money – if less than he once had hoped for – and became a major grower of rice and miller of flour, and retained the presidency of his beloved Carlton Football Club, which named a new stand after him. He was a survivor of the 1980s, albeit much diminished in stature from the business star who would enter politics to save the country from socialism and mediocrity. Yet in the more straitened early 1990s, Elliott's style of business, politics and masculinity already seemed to belong to a bygone era. The magic was gone: more of his businesses collapsed in the early 2000s, and breaches of the rules governing player payments brought his downfall at Carlton, too. His name was erased from the grandstand that had honoured him.

*

As it approached the end of the decade and its fourth election, the Hawke government struggled with the usual trials of political longevity – declining public enthusiasm, managing leadership succession – as well as a few peculiar to its time and place. The stock-market collapse had not produced a depression, or even signs of a downturn in the real economy. Instead, low share prices and interest rates encouraged a plunge into property as a safe place to park money. Demand remained robust, much to the surprise of many experts who had feared the worst after the crash and fully expected that the budget and trade deficits being run in the world's largest economy, the United States, must eventually flow through to hurt smaller fry. While the buoyancy was welcome, one effect of a surge in demand would be to increase the flow of imports, which would blow out the current account deficit – the difference between what Australia earned and what it bought from the rest of the world – and Keating in particular had come to see this as the key indicator of the country's economic performance.

The Australian government, now endowed through its own regime of self-denial with fewer instruments than its predecessors, turned again to interest rates as its solution to an overheated economy. In the latter half of 1988, a powerful investment boom provoked an increasingly aggressive approach to raising interest rates by Keating, his economic adviser, Don Russell, and senior Treasury officials such as Chris Higgins and David Morgan. Hoping that the economy would make a 'soft landing' when demand eased, they pushed up cash rates from 10 per cent in March 1988 to almost 18 per cent in November 1989. The Treasury secretary, Bernie Fraser, was more cautious about heading off at the pass something that the government had been wanting for years – business investment – while in cabinet, political hardheads like Graham Richardson argued that rising home-loan interest rates, unless checked, would kill the government.[87]

It was the hawks who won this battle, and their victory sent the economy into a downward spiral which Keating later famously described as 'a recession that Australia had to have'.[88] Despite five cuts in interest rates during 1990, there would be no 'soft landing', especially for the million Australians who found themselves without a job. These were the victims of what the journalist Paul Kelly sees as a recession which 'was largely a result of the difficulties in the transition from a closed to an open economy'. It is unlikely that any took comfort from their contribution as sacrificial lambs in the quest for the greater good that he believes was ultimately served, the movement towards a 'new order' of deregulated labour markets, zero protection, low inflation and hands-off government.[89] It is true that as a result of global factors, Australia was unlikely to have avoided the global recession of the early 1990s. However, George Megalogenis has pointed out that although Australia went into recession around the same time as the United States, it took longer to get out of it and experienced far higher unemployment.[90] Yet it has become the habit of many commentators – Megalogenis among them – to credit this recession with setting up a quarter-century of economic prosperity. The recession cleaned up inefficiencies, mopped up 1980s excesses and allowed governments finally to break the problem of inflation. But this is the view from the summit rather than the suburbs, where the recession would exact a pitiable toll.

In the short term, towering interest rates shredded jobs and destroyed businesses whose failure, in turn, placed growing pressure on the banks. Westpac, which had begun the decade as the country's largest, found itself with billions of dollars in bad or doubtful debts, and its global expansion of the 1980s ended in disaster.[91] Among the banks, it was the biggest loser, with bad-debt write-offs and provisioning of well over $6 billion between 1989 and 1993.[92] Business empires once hailed as works of genius fell apart under the pressure of the times, taking vast sums of shareholder equity, bank loans and jobs along with them. Skase was not the only failed entrepreneur to leave the country a step or two ahead of creditors and police. One overextended and – by 1990 – bankrupt businessman, Abe Goldberg, a Holocaust survivor who had gained control of the Linter group in the mid-1980s, fled the country when his business went bust, escaping to his native Poland, and leaving behind hundreds of millions of dollars in debt and ten arrest warrants. Westpac was conspicuous among his creditors, but it had been similarly generous to George Herscu, whose real-estate group Hooker Corporation also collapsed at this time. Herscu would serve prison time for paying bribes to Russ Hinze.[93]

The recession brought down small businesses too, and the experience of Lucas Morris Homes, a Melbourne company owned by Ken Morris, was not unusual. Having begun as a small outfit building houses during the 1960s, Morris expanded with the help of the banks in the heady 1980s, building retirement homes on the south coast of New South Wales and even mansions at Sanctuary Cove in Queensland. By early 1992 he was one of about eighty builders who had crashed since 1990. Morris had to put off his permanent staff of thirty, to say nothing of the hundreds of subcontractors and tradesmen that his company's projects had kept in work.[94]

Reporting on evidence of 'the recession mentality' among his focus groups in May 1991, Hugh Mackay recorded an 'emphasis ... on maintenance, survival, postponement'.[95] While economic growth resumed after 1991, unemployment continued to climb, reaching just under 11 per cent in 1993, a figure massively higher than the OECD average of 8 per cent.[96] In December 1992, unemployment in Australia was 11.2 per cent, the worst rate since the Second World War.[97] Meanwhile, the number of long-term unemployed trebled between 1989 and 1993, growing from 108,200 to 337,700.[98] The 1980s 'boom' had never been kind to workers such as these, but recession devastated them. The transformation of the economy had included a shift away from manufacturing towards services, from male to female employment, from full-time breadwinning to part-time and casual labour, from bush and town to city and suburb. Opportunities opened up in the new industries, but usually for far fewer workers than had been employed in the old economy. The differences between old and new were visible in the northern Victorian town of Wangaratta, where the biggest employer, Bruck Textiles, had reduced its workforce from 1150 to 620 by the early 1990s. The business had invested millions in a new plant, but still felt vulnerable to tariff reductions and cheaper imports. Yet at the other end of the town, IBM had a computer factory which employed 175 people all year round and more during busy times, and it was generating over $100 million per year in exports. These companies were doing the kinds of things that government ministers, financial writers and dry economists said they should – investing in technology, developing exports – yet the future looked brighter for the relatively small number of workers at IBM than the larger number at Bruck.[99] (Ironically, Bruck remained in business in Wangaratta in 2015, having been transformed into a manufacturer and distributor of 'value-added, high performance and protective fabrics'; IBM sold off its operation in the town in 1997.[100])

Structural adjustment – the displacement of workers from factories in the interests of greater efficiency – included schemes to retrain them, yet opportunities for those with limited education and low skills were sparse everywhere, and especially so outside the big cities. The biggest employer in the small Victorian town of Rochester, Jockey Australia, a manufacturer of t-shirts and skivvies, closed its doors in 1991, putting fifty women out of work. The company offered them jobs at its factory in another town thirty kilometres away, but only a dozen went. No doubt many had domestic responsibilities that prevented them working so far from home, a daily journey which in any case would have eaten into their low wages, while the prospect of a redundancy payout would have been attractive in hard times. And perhaps these women saw the writing on the wall, since the company had already closed its factories elsewhere. It was reported that many of the townspeople had taken to selling Amway products.[101]

Some businesses cited tariff cuts as one of their problems. The government wound back protection in parts of the economy on an industry-by-industry basis in its first five years, but by the second half of the decade it was preoccupied with promoting global free trade against a background of 'trade war' between the United States, Europe and Japan. Australia formed the Cairns Group of agricultural producers in 1986 to push for free trade, and Australian negotiators would be in a stronger position to argue their case in the interests of exporters if tariffs were being reduced at home. But this international agenda could not have led to lower tariffs without the growing intellectual force of arguments for liberalisation, which were backed by the formidable cabinet firepower of Hawke, Keating, Button, Kerin and Walsh.[102] For this government of economic modernisers, tariffs were the key example of the decades of feather-bedding and rent-seeking that had produced gross inefficiencies, a hopelessly uncompetitive manufacturing economy, and excessive retail prices for ordinary consumers. During a cabinet meeting in August 1986, Kerin passed a note to Button that neatly summarised the attitudes of the modernisers to this legacy:

> The cost to this country of Menzies's adherence to British Imperial Preference, McEwen's high secondary industry tariffs, Country Party endorsement of cargo cultism on minerals plus 30 years of Cabinets dominated by cockies since 1949 will take another 30 years to overcome.[103]

'YES, I AGREE', Button replied.[104] After the 1988 cabinet decision to reduce most tariffs to 10 or 15 per cent by 1992 – only motor vehicles, and textiles, clothing and footwear, already subject to industry plans, were excluded – Hawke passed a note to Button complimenting him on his role in 'one of our most significant decisions' as a government.[105]

In March 1991, in the middle of the recession, the government cut general tariff rates further – to 5 per cent by 1996. Car tariffs would go down from 35 per cent to a modest 15 per cent by 2000, and those on textiles, clothing and footwear to between 15 and 35 per cent (effective levels of protection in the late 1980s were 78 per cent for textiles, and 183 per cent for shoes and clothing).[106] In reply to objections in cabinet to the proposed reductions from a left-wing minister, Gerry Hand, Keating compared the textile manufacturers to Iraqi despot Saddam Hussein (who had recently invaded Kuwait), driving 'away in Mercedes from these little plants ... using those old ducks as shields, these poor old buggers sewing buttons for eight hours a day with their eyes hanging out ... if you support the workers, why not give them a cheap shirt; why not give them cheap shoes – not three times the world price'.[107] As he had done in selling the entry of foreign banks to his party in the mid-1980s, Keating represented a more open, internationally competitive economy as a blow against a greedy local establishment for the benefit of ordinary folk, a claim requiring considerable chutzpah in the midst of the worst unemployment since the 1930s. Paul Kelly has celebrated the 1991 decision as having 'demolished the edifice of Protection' after its century-long reign, but it did not at the time meet with popular acclaim.[108] Public opinion continued to lean towards tariffs and there were attacks on economic rationalism – including on free trade – from both the right and the left for its dogmatic insistence that the state should stay out of the market, and its reliance on 'abstract and rarefied theory' that seemed impervious to lived reality.[109]

Such critics pointed to the example of countries such as Japan and Singapore, where the state had played an instrumental role in economic development. Australian interest in the Multifunction Polis (MFP), which kicked around government from 1987 onwards, reflected a wider interest in applying aspects of the Japanese economic model to Australia, at a time when Japan was still regarded by many as a great success story. Beginning as an idea of the Japanese Ministry of International Trade and Industry for a cooperative venture with Australia to create a 'City of the Future', it was seen to have advantages for both countries. For the Japanese, it was about exporting economic ideas, management practices and technologies at a time when that country was awash with cash, and looking to lift its international influence. For Australian modernisers, the emphasis on high-tech industry, education, research and development, and commercialisation was attractive at a time when they were desperate to move the country away from its reliance on commodity exports and to restructure industry.[110]

The MFP gave rise to a bewildering amount of paper in the next few years, as state governments prepared bid documents, and consultants, bureaucrats, business leaders and politicians tried to make the original Japanese concept meaningful in an Australian context. But the rhetoric surrounding the project was often ridiculous, as were not a few of the ideas that clung to it, like a plan to build a runway for a spaceship, and a suggestion that the city would make itself truly international by deploying automatic translation technology. MFP documents are replete with references to 'high-touch', 'soft infrastructure', 'leading edge', 'smart holidays' and – a Japanese favourite that came out of the original basic concept – '5th sphere living'. So who was to have the honour of hosting the MFP? The federal government announced in June 1990 that Queensland was the successful bidder, and the MFP would go to the Gold Coast. But when that state's recently elected Labor premier, Wayne Goss, learned that he would need to spend over $300 million buying up private land to make it a reality, he declined to involve his state, while Button joked that some of the land's owners were star witnesses at the Fitzgerald Inquiry. In the blink of an eye, the MFP was awarded to Adelaide, which planned to build the city at Gillman, a degraded and contaminated former tidal marsh about ten kilometres from the city.[111]

By this stage, the MFP was attracting lively criticism, some of it concerned with Japanese economic imperialism; some with the elitist notion that bureaucrats planned to create a utopian city of 200,000 people, all of them wealthy professionals; and some simply that these professionals would be foreigners. Others just thought the scheme daft. One SA woman remarked at an Adelaide meeting of the MFP in mid-1991 just before it descended into chaos, 'People like me are sick and tired of being told what Utopia we have coming. What do you have to do to get rid of them?'[112] The MFP project limped on into the 1990s in Adelaide, giving rise to some modest environmental projects and housing developments, but no utopian city of the future. South Australians had to content themselves with their lives in the 4th sphere.

The Japanese model appealed to some critics of economic rationalism because it showed that the state could play a critical role in economic success, but its attractiveness to the left was limited by the control Japanese business exerted over labour conditions. Australian unions, in fact, played virtually no role in the MFP, which Bill Kelty believed to be a 'mickey mouse' project.[113] For some trade union leaders, it was another faraway country – known to most Australians mainly as a powerhouse in pop music and tennis – that provided the most attractive exemplar. Sweden's statist version of social democracy posed an alternative to the economic rationalist turn of Australian Labor in the mid-1980s. Long ruled by the leftist Social Democratic Party, the country also had a trade union movement intimately involved in policymaking. Its economic performance included 'low inflation, reasonable growth ... low unemployment', high export performance and a degree of 'social cohesion' unfamiliar to the more economically free-wheeling English-speaking democracies such as Britain and the United States. Laurie Carmichael, a former communist firebrand and research officer at the Amalgamated Metal Workers' Union, was the most forceful advocate of 'the Swedish model'.[114] His work gave rise to the report *Australia Reconstructed* (1987), the result of a union fact-finding mission, which set out an alternative vision to the Labor economic rationalists' embrace of financial markets and hands-off government; one that emphasised strategic state intervention, full employment, industrial democracy, social policy, and education and training.[115] *Australia Reconstructed* was a landmark for the union movement, not least because it redirected attention from tariff protection and state ownership to markets, productivity, skills and competitiveness – a shift entirely in tune with the government's own, and one that blunted opposition to tariff cuts.

The new emphasis on connecting education to productivity was no better illustrated than in higher education, which experienced unprecedented upheaval in the late 1980s. The architect of the revolution was John Dawkins, who had come from Finance and then Trade, and the very name of the portfolio he received after the 1987 election – Employment, Education and Training – spoke eloquently of the direction in which he would take policy. While trade minister, Dawkins had persuaded the government to introduce full fees for international students, a field that had previously been considered a de facto arm of the aid budget. Once he took over the higher education portfolio, the new minister quickly built up an informal group of allies and advisers among senior academics and university leaders, which came to be derided as 'the purple circle'. They gained a reputation – one almost certainly exaggerated – as a secretive cabal given to boozy meals with the minister, during which they exercised a malign influence on higher education policy.[116]

The official beginning of the Dawkins revolution arrived with the Green Paper of December 1987, which was designed to provide the illusion that the minister was consulting the universities about their future; the White Paper of July 1988 set out a new government policy largely in line with the earlier document. Coming in the aftermath of the stock-market collapse, both documents reflected a sense of urgency about the economic future. Australia, said the Green Paper, could no longer rely on its traditional export base but would need to adapt its economy to 'advanced manufacturing and new service industries'.[117] A well-educated workforce with transferable skills would be needed to help the country adjust to this increasingly competitive world. Universities had to be much better attuned to the changing needs of the labour market; they would need to take in a much larger number of students and educate them more effectively to become productive economic units.

The White Paper promised commitment to diversity, yet the impulse towards homogeneity was evident in common funding arrangements, tighter government control, minimum size and the shift towards more managerial structures – what it called a 'unified national system'. The vice-chancellor's role was redefined as that of a chief executive officer. Research would be geared more closely to 'the needs of the society and economy which support it', and links with industry were to be promoted. In short, higher education policy would serve the government's economic goals, and universities would become more like businesses.[118]

The policy additionally demanded 'fewer, larger institutions'. This promoted a spate of amalgamations, which many of the academics involved regarded as shotgun marriages.[119] Dawkins appears to have recognised from the outset that the vice-chancellors would find it impossible to maintain a united front against his reforms, and he skilfully played institutions off against one another. Vice-chancellors who stood to gain from the changes, by enlarging the size of their empires, were willing to come on board.[120] But for students, the most significant aspect of the new system as it evolved was the reintroduction of tertiary fees. Here, Dawkins followed a middle way between a market solution and free tuition. An economist from the Australian National University, Bruce Chapman, came up with a plan that would allow students to defer payment until they were earning a minimum salary after graduation, when they would be able to repay their fees through the taxation system. Many students opposed the Higher Education Contribution Scheme (HECS), but their objections had no effect on a government that had already dealt harshly with cows far more sacred than free tertiary education. Dawkins scorned what he called the 'undisguised and unabashed self-interest' of student agitation, in contrast with his own generation, who had protested over the 'great issues' of the day: Vietnam, apartheid, black rights.[121] HECS also attracted the criticism of more gung-ho free-market warriors than Dawkins, who indicated that an opportunity for creating a higher-quality system fully responsive to consumer demand had been lost.

One of these critics was Don Watts, a WA scientist who became the inaugural vice-chancellor of Bond University on the Gold Coast, the nation's first private university. As an initiative of the ubiquitous Alan Bond – a joint venture with a Japanese partner, EIE Development – the new university suffered from Bond's declining solvency and reputation in the late 1980s. Its marketing, moreover, did the fledgling institution no favours by making absurd comparisons with Harvard, Yale and Princeton. Yet although still covered with incomplete buildings, busy construction workers and a great deal of mud, the university took in its first group of students in May 1989.[122]

A private university on this scale – it cost about $300 million – was a bold experiment that could probably only have been conceived by the likes of Bond in the 1980s. Watts, who was one of Dawkins's purple circle, was a trenchant critic of publicly funded university education and an energetic advocate of the alternative his own university offered. He argued that if no price was attached to tertiary education, it would not be properly valued: 'it is a foolish notion to make education free because it doesn't offer any incentives to the student or express the power of education'.[123] And he argued – accurately enough – that institutions excessively dependent on federal funding would not be independent.[124] Universities should do more to produce 'innovative, entrepreneurial professional graduates' of the kind that Australia needed in a highly competitive world.[125] Public universities, he considered, had been unable to do so – and in this respect at least, Watts's views were surely not a very long way from those of Dawkins himself.

This stress on education, research and productivity represented a new vision of Australia's economic future: as 'the clever country' – to use a phrase that the government embraced for a time – populated by innovative researchers, entrepreneurial businesses and skilled employees making sophisticated products that the rest of the world wanted to buy. Manufacturers would no longer shelter behind tariff walls producing poor-quality, overpriced goods for their long-suffering compatriots. Nor would lazy management run off to the government at the first sign of trouble, looking for help to see them through to the next crisis. Rather, a restructured, diversified, capital-intensive and high-tech industrial economy would be sufficiently competitive to insulate the country from the kind of external shock it had received in 1986.[126] This was a noble vision and as the country's manufacturing export performance improved in the second half of the 1980s with the help of a low Australian dollar, it also looked like an increasingly realistic national aspiration.

Signs were not wanting that Australian manufacturers might indeed be able to follow where successful exporting countries such Japan and Sweden had led. As the country emerged from the early 1980s recession, productivity in the steel industry increased markedly and by the middle of the decade, not only were exports improving but Australian manufacturers' share of the local market was up around 89 per cent. Steel's revival, moreover, occurred while the combined workforce at Port Kembla, Newcastle and Whyalla declined from 24,500 in 1983 to 18,500 by 1989. At Port Kembla alone, new plant and job reorganisation over just twelve months in 1988–89 reduced the size of its workforce by over a fifth at the same time as production increased by 18 per cent. The car industry, too, was doing better by this time than in the early 1980s: quality, efficiency and exports were up, and tariffs and prices were down.[127]

Also down, however, was the size of the manufacturing workforce: restructuring meant job losses, and these bit especially hard where a community was largely dependent on a single industry. The Holden plant in South Australia's Elizabeth, near Adelaide, had employed six or seven thousand people in the 1960s but just 4500 twenty years later. The town's rate of adult male unemployment in 1986 was almost 17 per cent and the historian Mark Peel concluded rather grimly in 1995, 'many of Elizabeth's people are the wrong kind of people for a restructured Australia'. This community had paid a heavy price for its enforced role in trying to save Australian manufacturing: 'Men sitting on pavements, waiting for buses. Teenagers lolling around aimlessly, nothing to do. Men pushing the babies, in prams, to the shops'. All of this was reminiscent of 'the aimlessness and hopelessness' that a local school principal had witnessed during the 1930s Depression in England.[128] At Port Kembla, which had been devastated by job losses in the first half of the 1980s, unemployment in 1986 was a startling 17.6 per cent, while the proportion of workers in the Wollongong district employed in manufacturing dropped from almost 30 per cent in 1981 to less than 18 per cent a decade later.[129]

By the mid-1980s it had well and truly dawned on the residents of such places that when Hawke and his ministers talked about 'saving the steel industry', they had in mind restoring profitability, not the thousands of jobs that had been already lost.[130] Unemployment in many of Australia's industrial towns was no longer cyclical: jobs, many of them skilled, disappeared forever and with them, the communities they had sustained. The legacy of restructuring, with its personal hardships, social costs and the end of a way of life, was a harsh one.[131] But in view of what restructuring was intended to achieve, the longer-term national gain has also been disappointing. The steel industry today is a shadow of its former self, with the great Newcastle works – which once employed 12,000 – closing its doors in 1999. The car industry's future is even more bleak: all production is due to cease by 2017. Confounding the dreams of 1980s economic modernisers, Australia's prosperity today rests not on sophisticated manufacturing exports, but on demand for its minerals in China and India.[132] The country has become a quarry after all.

*

The Hawke–Keating relationship had always been central to the story of the Labor government – and, indeed, to the story of Australia's 1980s. Since his youth, Keating had often looked to older, more experienced men as mentors and teachers, and Hawke played something like this role for a time. But once Keating gained in confidence and Hawke revealed his feet of clay in the lead-up to the 1984 election and the 1985 debate over tax reform, Keating came to believe that he was the one at the wheel; Hawke had relegated himself to passenger while continuing to accept the credit for steering the ship.

There were also temperamental differences between the two men that were always likely to create tension. Hawke was the boozy larrikin who abandoned his old ways to become prime minister. The self-discipline he had imposed became part of his sustaining myth, that of the bloke who was both ordinary enough to like the kinds of things that the average bloke liked, yet extraordinary in giving up the least wholesome of them to become national leader (or so he claimed – he moderated rather than discontinued his philandering when he became prime minister and resumed an affair with his biographer, Blanche d'Alpuget, late in 1988).[133] This delicate balance was central to Hawke's self-myth of his love affair with the Australian people. A true lover will sacrifice himself for his love; Hawke came to see his self-discipline as central to his own leadership, just as discipline on the part of others was needed to ensure that his government did not degenerate into a Whitlamite shambles.

All of this was a long way from Keating's world. While, unlike Hawke, he was a product of the working class, he made little effort to pretend that he was an ordinary man. He knew that the antiques, the classical music and the expensive suits set him apart from popular taste, and he refrained from the charade of pretending to enjoy the spectacle of a group of men kicking a piece of leather around a paddock or a bunch of nags running in circles. Where Hawke found parliament a chore and was never terribly good at it, Keating was a consummate performer in the house – one who made an art of the creative insult – and in this role, he was often critical in maintaining the morale of caucus during difficult times.[134] Nor did Keating feel the need to play up his commitment and self-discipline, which, he rightly felt, could be taken for granted; he worked hard and had never shown much interest in the dissolute pleasures that had been such a feature of Hawke's pre-prime-ministerial life.

Keating's rivalry with Hawke became increasingly intense, as Hawke showed few signs of wishing to hand over the reins to the man whom everyone regarded as his natural successor. The treasurer talked behind the scenes of leaving politics – his 'Paris option'. When he delivered a budget surplus in August 1988 – calling it 'the one that brings home the bacon' – Hawke responded the following day by telling a journalist that if Keating were to leave politics, there were 'people of very considerable talent in the Ministry and the position would be filled'. Keating was furious, and although Hawke at first refused to budge over the succession, he realised that all the media talk about leadership was damaging the government. So on the evening of 25 November 1988 Hawke and Keating met in the presence of two witnesses – Bill Kelty, who was close to Keating, and businessman and Hawke confidant Peter Abeles – at the prime minister's Sydney residence in Kirribilli. Hawke agreed to vacate the prime ministership in favour of Keating after the 1990 election, but then made himself ridiculous by complaining that Keating was late for cabinet meetings and would need to mend his ways.[135]

With the leadership conflict put aside for a time, Labor could look to the election due in 1990 with hope, if not confidence. But unfortunately for the government, 1989 proved a difficult year and, as two political scientists commented afterwards, the 'current theories of electoral behaviour' suggested that Labor should have lost the election that followed.[136] As well as rapidly climbing interest rates, from August the government had to contend with one of the bitterest industrial disputes of the era, when almost the entire workforce of domestic airline pilots – around 1600 of them – went on strike.

The pilots were worried about loss of status and pay rates. They were subject to the Prices and Incomes Accord, but viewed themselves as rather more than highly skilled transport workers – more like the executives who were making squillions in the nation's boardrooms. They also had a history of militancy, of conducting short, sharp strikes to attain their objectives. Under Australia's two-airline system – the duopoly of government-owned Trans Australia Airlines (TAA, called Australian Airlines by 1989) and the privately owned Ansett – a higher wages bill could simply have been passed on to consumers. But in 1987 the government had given notice that it would terminate the two-airline agreement in 1990, which would give rise to a more competitive industry. The Pilots' Federation, under the leadership of Brian McCarthy, claimed a pay increase of almost 30 per cent, which placed it well outside Accord guidelines.[137]

Hawke worried that if pilots were to gain large salary increases, it would lead to a wage breakout and the destruction of the Accord and his government. But the dispute also appealed to his hankering after conflict and crisis; 'consensus' had never represented the whole Hawke, who had an infamously belligerent side. And then there was the presence of his close friend and mentor Peter Abeles at the head of Ansett. During the dispute one protesting pilot in Perth held up a placard that read: 'Vote 1 Abeles, Cut Out the Middleman'.[138]

The prime minister's attacks on the pilots were somewhat intemperate. He responded to a ban on flights outside the hours of 9 am to 5 pm by declaring 'war' on the pilots, later calling them 'glorified bus drivers'.[139] Then, like Ben Chifley during the miners' strike of 1949, Hawke mobilised the military to break the strike, allowing RAAF planes to be used to carry domestic passengers. With the government's help, the airline companies lined up foreign planes and pilots, and the government spent $50–100 million ensuring that the strike did not spread to other unions. The companies also took out writs against individual pilots – which it later abandoned – and successfully sued the Pilots' Federation and six of its leaders for $6.5 million in damages. Hawke backed this use of the common law against the pilots despite its blatant contravention of party policy, in a tactic that recalled the emblematic New Right disputes of the mid-1980s such as Mudginberri and Dollar Sweets (see chapter 6).[140]

In what was possibly a tactical error, although one guided by a fear of losing their superannuation and being sued for damages, the pilots resigned en masse but continued to form picket lines, harass 'scabs' and complain of a conspiracy by the government, the ACTU and the airline companies. In view of the forces ranged against them, they stood little chance. As highly paid workers who were seen to have tickets on themselves, they failed to attract public sympathy, and Hawke succeeded in presenting them as greedy and unscrupulous. But what of the rights to strike and to enjoy freedom of association? There was an apparent confusion in Hawke's mind between government policy and the law of the land. The Accord was government policy, but in the absence of any constitutional authority to regulate wages, backroom deals with Bill Kelty did not actually have the status of federal law.[141] In demanding the right to negotiate directly with their employers, moreover, the pilots wanted no more than what every union in the country would have within a few years, as both centralised wage determination and the Accord passed into history. But that would be too late for the humiliated pilots, most of whom had no choice but to leave the industry or seek employment overseas.

Labor Party research found that one result of the strike was that electors now had an image of Hawke as 'an angry, snarling, alienating, confrontationist'.[142] Yet while the conflict inflicted considerable damage on the tourist industry, and angry pilots maintained the rage against Labor during the March 1990 election campaign, it seems not to have shifted many votes one way or another. Rather, Labor was able to approach the election with several advantages. First, even by its own remarkable standards in the 1980s, the Coalition proved impressively dysfunctional in the lead-up to the vote. As the result of a successful party-room coup in May 1989, Howard lost the leadership to Peacock. Two of the plotters – Wilson Tuckey and John Moore – then appeared on an ABC television program to provide the inside story, boasting of their success. It was an inauspicious start to Peacock's second term as leader, and did not get much better from there. Peacock later had to remove Tuckey from his frontbench as the price of persuading Howard to rejoin it. Meanwhile in Victoria, a series of bitterly contested preselection battles had resulted in the defeat of party 'wets' such as Ian McPhee and a distinct move to the right, suggesting little interest in contesting the middle ground that Labor had so successfully occupied since March 1983. This was not a happy family, but it was one increasingly prone to airing its dirty linen in public. Finally, a couple of months before the election, shadow health minister Peter Shack, one of the coup plotters, called a press conference at which he admitted that in his area of responsibility the Coalition did 'not have a particularly good track record'. His own party's health policy, he added, would cost somewhere between zero and $2.6 billion. Labor could hardly believe its luck.[143]

A second issue working for Labor in 1990 was the pure chance of the electoral cycle in the states. Labor lost ten federal seats in Victoria and a seat each in Western Australia and South Australia – states in which there were longstanding and increasingly unpopular state Labor governments – yet it picked up two seats in each of New South Wales and Queensland. In the former, a coalition government led by Nick Greiner, the son of Hungarian migrants and a Harvard MBA who thought that governments should be run in the manner of corporations, had been making itself unpopular with big spending cuts since its election in 1988.[144] Meanwhile, in Queensland the Labor Party led by former lawyer Wayne Goss won a resounding victory at the election of December 1989, ending more than three decades of conservative rule. At the time of the March 1990 federal election, Goss was still enjoying a honeymoon after displacing the discredited National Party government. Indeed, Labor's federal fortunes there had been improving since the mid-1980s; it picked up a combined total of six Queensland federal seats in the 1987 and 1990 elections. In other words, federal Labor was lucky that the losses incurred as a result of its manifold problems in Victoria were partly offset by gains in Queensland.

But the issue that worked most influentially in favour of federal Labor at this time was 'the greening of Australian politics'. The saving of the Franklin in 1983 was only the first of many conservation struggles. It lent both confidence and momentum to the environmental movement, even if the Hawke government, preoccupied with economic problems in its early years, seemed less enthusiastic about building on this success. It was unwilling, for instance, to prevent the construction of a road through North Queensland's Daintree Rainforest, despite the heroic efforts of conservationists in trying to stop the bulldozers in their tracks. These protests in 1983 and 1984, however, placed protection of the wet tropics on the national agenda.[145]

The replacement of Barry Cohen with Graham Richardson as environment minister in 1987 proved a turning point in the political history of conservation. Richardson was a famously adept political operator – if one with a shady reputation – and he had come to believe that the environment held the key to the Labor Party's survival in office. Impressed by the passions that had been aroused over the battle for the Queensland forests, in April 1986 Richardson took up an invitation from Bob Brown to visit Tasmania. After flying by helicopter over some stunning forests, they stopped next to a lake for 'a lunch of soggy sandwiches', walked around the area and talked about its future. Brown wanted the area protected and by the time Richardson returned to Hobart, he 'was a convert ... I wanted to become a warrior for his cause. That was a bad day for the logging industry ... but a very good one for me, the environmental movement and the Labor Party.'[146] Richardson elevated the standing of the issue in the media and government, placing it at the heart of Labor's strategy for holding on to office in 1990.[147]

There was a general quickening of interest around environmental issues from the mid-1980s. The defeat of the campaign against uranium mining and the easing of the Cold War saw a transfer of both activists and attention from nuclear issues to broader environmental ones. Global problems such as the hole in the ozone layer and the greenhouse effect – or what we now call global warming – raised the prospect of a catastrophic future, rather as the danger of nuclear war had long done. Another ingredient was the nationalist upsurge of the mid-1980s, in which the country was packaged up for the tourism industry and the Bicentenary. Natural wonders figured prominently in such efforts, while the *Crocodile Dundee* films, which were credited with having increased international interest in Australia, were filmed in Kakadu in the Northern Territory, an area subject to a long-running debate over plans to mine it for uranium. In this way, Hogan and Cornell might ultimately have done as much for environmentalism in Australia as Brown and Richardson. The Bicentenary, meanwhile, featured references to the land, geography and the environment as sources of Australian identity and belonging.[148]

These matters were of national import but especially transformative in Tasmania, where conflicts between development and conservation had been at the heart of politics for years, including such issues as woodchipping and logging, the listing of World Heritage areas, and a proposal to build a pulp mill at Wesley Vale in the north of the state. Beginning with a meeting in the local primary school, Christine Milne, a teacher and mother who had been arrested during the Franklin protests, mobilised community concern about the threatened destruction of 'a way of life' through chemical pollution.[149] Supporters of the campaign included farmers who were able to see the threat to their own livelihoods from such projects. As one commented just before the 1989 state election, 'A few years ago I would happily have run over Bob Brown with my bulldozer. Now if I saw him up a tree I'd take his lunch up to him.'[150] New initiatives such as Landcare, which began in Victoria in 1986, also involved farmers concerned about the impact of land degradation on their productivity.[151] A national Landcare scheme came from joint lobbying of the federal government by Phillip Toyne of the Australian Conservation Foundation (ACF) and Rick Farley of the National Farmers' Federation (NFF) – an alliance of environmentalists and farmers that in itself highlighted the growing prominence of conservation issues. Their joint proposal, which included plans for the formation of 1600 Landcare groups across Australia, attracted a Hawke promise of $320 million in 1989.[152]

If there had been any doubts about the new electoral potency of the environment, they were surely laid to rest at the Tasmanian state election of 13 May 1989. Green Independents were able to take advantage of the proportional electoral system to win five seats in a house of thirty-five, representing the votes of 17 per cent of Tasmanians, and sufficient to give them the balance of power between the Liberals and the ALP. Milne, one of the successful candidates, told her supporters in the final days of the campaign: 'The rest of the world is watching.'[153] But Robin Gray, the Liberal premier, refused to give in without a fight and tried to remain in office. While negotiations between the Labor Party and the Greens continued, a Tasmanian media proprietor and chairman of the logging company Gunns, Edmund Rouse, attempted to bribe Labor MP Jim Cox to switch sides. Cox informed police of the $110,000 offer, and Rouse was arrested, tried and sent to prison.[154] Labor and the Greens signed a pact, and Gray was defeated by their combined numbers on the floor of the house. Labor formed a government with Greens support, a new experiment in Australian politics and possibly the first such alliance in the world, although it proved a fraught relationship that lapsed in 1990 over the issue of woodchipping and a feeling on the part of the Greens that they were being ignored.[155]

Environmental issues remained divisive, and especially so as the country slid into a recession. The economics ministers in the Hawke government, such as Dawkins, Kerin, Button and Walsh, resisted Richardson's efforts to elevate such issues; Keating, although the leading economics minister, was more equivocal, partly because he wanted the party's leadership and could less afford to alienate potential supporters. Peter Walsh did not feel similarly hampered, and even less so after his resignation from the ministry following the 1990 election. As he remarked in a note passed to Button: 'In reply to the question what are we going to do about the recession, you should have said we are going to have a chain of marine national parks around our coast – as the P.M. announced yesterday.'[156] Walsh was even contemptuous of the joint ACF–NFF Landcare initiative, which he regarded as a customary rent-seeking effort on the part of two practised mendicants.[157] He held Hawke in particular scorn for one of his 1991 decisions as prime minister – the prevention of mining at Coronation Hill in Kakadu National Park – even though the basis for this decision was not environmental but the objections of Aboriginal people who claimed that the site had spiritual significance. Walsh, characteristically, thought they had been well 'coached' by the ACF and the Northern Land Council.[158]

*

Labor won the 1990 election with 39.4 per cent of the primary vote, considerably lower than its share of almost 43 per cent in its landslide defeat at the 1975 election and down from almost 46 per cent in 1987, 47.5 per cent in 1984 and around 49.5 per cent in 1983. It was carried to an eight-seat majority by the second-preference votes it received from Australian Democrats and Greens candidates. Few doubted that the environment had played a significant role, not so much because voters had it at the top of their list of election issues – a post-election survey found it ranked fifth – but because Labor's advantage over the Coalition on this issue was so massive. The ALP was seen as having policies that more closely aligned with a much larger group of voters than the Coalition did.[159] All the same, the peculiar nature of Labor's 1990 victory contributed to a sense of crisis about the party's identity and future. The collapse of European communism in 1989 – a year now widely recognised along with 1918 and 1945 as one of the 'watershed years' in twentieth-century world history – removed one of the things that had helped define world ideology for over seventy years.[160] The apparent triumph of capitalism over its only serious rival in the twentieth century – the command economies of the communist states – suggested that future political debate in Western countries would be conducted on the basis of an acceptance of market solutions to economic questions. For a party that had traditionally favoured state ownership of parts of the economy and would have liked to see more of it, the triumph of the market raised tricky ideological questions. Admittedly, for much of the Labor right and the centre, there was no real dilemma; they were already committed to the market and did their best to ignore research which found that a majority of voters favoured continuing public ownership in a mixed economy.[161] Keating had already used the Commonwealth Bank's purchase of the troubled State Bank of Victoria to carry out a partial privatisation of the people's bank, traditionally regarded as one of the party's gifts to the nation. A special party conference in September 1990 also agreed to subject the publicly owned Telecom to competition, and to allow the government to sell Australian Airlines and a minority stake in Qantas, the international carrier. Those supporting the change drew a long bow to suggest that the failure of communist command economies proved the wisdom of off-loading government assets in Australia. Hawke joked that Australia might end up in a troika with Cuba and Albania; NSW Labor leader Bob Carr, while conceding that privatisation was indeed a departure from Labor tradition that bewildered the party rank and file, thought it was necessary to recognise 'that a great deal of old Laborism has failed, just as old-fashioned Australian capitalism had failed'. He pointed out that the West German power utilities had just absorbed the East German power system – and without an agonised debate over it.[162]

Still, some on the Labor Left found opportunities for advancing traditional 'social justice' goals. Brian Howe, who would rise to become deputy prime minister in the early 1990s, epitomised this approach. A Methodist clergyman who had been active in struggles to improve the quality of life of working-class people in Melbourne during the 1970s, Howe was social security minister through the second half of the 1980s. With a portfolio that accounted for about a quarter of the federal budget, he came to recognise that there was scope for effecting savings in one area to introduce new initiatives in another, a strategy he was well placed to pursue after he joined the Expenditure Review Committee in 1987. The families package Hawke announced in his 1987 election policy speech, with its plans for an assault on child poverty, was one product of Howe's approach. It was just the kind of initiative that helped convince some wavering ALP loyalists, often disgusted with both economic rationalism and the prime minister's mateyness with the super-rich, that their government still had a Labor soul.[163]

There was a bloodlessness, nonetheless, about the appeal to 'efficiency' and 'competitiveness' that lay behind the right's push for privatisation, and even to some extent in the language of 'social justice' that underpinned Howe's efforts to reduce poverty. The professionalisation of politics, the embrace of markets and the impulse to be rid of unnecessary ideological baggage risked abandoning one of the central defining features of the Labor Party since its emergence in the 1890s: its 'moral critique of capitalism'.[164] A draft review of the ALP that appeared at the end of 1990 reported that '[p]arty members express difficulty in defining what the Party stands for and what its purpose is and there is disillusionment with aspects of Government policies ... and there is consequently disengagement from the Party process'.[165] Such soul-searching would intensify as the Labor Party approached its centenary during the recession and the leadership crisis of 1991.

Under its young defence minister Kim Beazley in the mid-1980s, Australia revised its military doctrine to emphasise the defence of the continent and its northern approaches, a formal confirmation of the movement away from the policy of 'forward defence' that had underpinned involvement in the Vietnam War. In 1990, however, the government faced an international crisis that had nothing at all to do with continental defence; it concerned the prospect of the 'New World Order' that optimists imagined might emerge with the end of the Cold War. In response to Iraq's invasion of Kuwait in August 1990, the Hawke government agreed to send three vessels – two frigates and a supply ship – to help enforce sanctions against Saddam Hussein's regime. A tense meeting of senior ministers in late November – Hawke, Keating, Button, Gareth Evans (in charge of foreign affairs since Hayden's appointment as governor-general in 1988) and Robert Ray, the defence minister – agreed that if war broke out because of Iraq's intransigence, Australia should make a small contribution of ships to the conflict, and that it would be best to avoid any appearance of responding to a US request for help. Clearly, there were concerns about the attitude that might be taken by sections of the party to the first Australian commitment to a war since Vietnam, particularly if the nation was seen to be following the US.[166]

When the fighting broke out in January 1991, Hawke gained the chance to become a war leader, to match his developing self-image as a significant international statesman, one who took pride in having taken on Margaret Thatcher over the question of Commonwealth sanctions against South Africa, as well as in successfully lobbying her, the French and the Americans to prevent the mining of Antarctica. The Gulf War, while supported by a majority of Australians, attracted protests on various grounds: loathing of war, that sanctions had been given insufficient opportunity, that lives should not be risked over oil, that Australia should not be subservient to the US, and that interference in Arab affairs was unwarranted. Nonetheless, despite a good deal of anguish on the part of some Labor parliamentarians – especially in the Left and the Centre Left – there was limited parliamentary opposition: feverish negotiation with the factions ensured that Australia's commitment would be a limited one. In the end, a small group of Labor members and senators signalled their opposition to the war, but Hawke defended the commitment as being in line with Labor's traditional support for the United Nations, and later revelled in his country's part in the victory over Iraq, minor though it was.[167]

These happenings only postponed the looming confrontation with his treasurer, since Hawke was showing no sign of standing aside in accordance with the Kirribilli Agreement, and he gained in confidence from the Gulf War. On 7 December 1990 Keating gave an off-the-record speech to a group of journalists at the National Press Club that reignited the leadership contest. The previous day, the 47-year-old Treasury secretary Chris Higgins had died suddenly of a massive heart attack. Keating, who had formed a close bond with him, was in a dark mood, but also an expansive one. He spoke at length – and eventually came to the subject of leadership: 'if you look at some of the great countries ... like the United States – we've never had one leader like they've had. The United States has had three great leaders, Washington, Lincoln and Roosevelt ... We've never had one such person.' He dubbed John Curtin 'a trier' – and then went on to compare his own performances to those of the great tenor Placido Domingo.[168]

Inevitably, the speech was reported in the media, and Hawke was furious, not just at what he saw as the treacherous censure of his own leadership but at the insult to his hero, Curtin. It proved a critical moment in the unravelling of the Hawke government. In late January, Hawke told Keating that he would not be stepping aside, using the Placido Domingo speech as part of his justification. Hawke had convinced himself that only he could lead Labor to a fifth election victory. On 30 May 1991, in preparation for Keating's leadership challenge to Hawke, Graham Richardson revealed to the journalist Laurie Oakes the existence of the Kirribilli Agreement; it was on the news that evening, the biggest political story in years. In the vote on 3 June, Hawke defeated Keating sixty-six to forty-four, a comfortable margin but certainly not wide enough to be the end of Hawke's difficulties. Keating, who had known he lacked the numbers, moved to the backbench, being replaced as treasurer by the capable and genial primary industries minister, John Kerin.

On 21 November 1991 the Coalition released its *Fightback!* package. After the 1990 election, the Liberals had turned to a relative political novice, John Hewson, to lead the party. A free-market economist and university professor before his election in 1987, Hewson – with his Ferrari, share in a restaurant, lucrative consultancies and efficiently organised tax affairs – was the epitome of 'eighties man'. His elevation to the Liberal leadership broke the impasse created by years of bitter rivalry between Howard and Peacock, but it would in time raise problems of its own.[169]

Fightback! was a massively detailed 'dry' economic policy document that included a proposal for a 15 per cent goods and services tax. In the days that followed its release, Hawke and Kerin showed no sign of being able to counter the manifesto's impact; so much so that after the new treasurer blundered in being unable to recall the meaning of an economic acronym during a press conference, Hawke sacked him on 6 December. A few days later, six of Hawke's closest supporters in cabinet tried in vain to persuade him to resign. By this time, it seemed likely that Keating had the numbers for a successful challenge, but Hawke remained resolute. 'I know that we can win the next election,' he told Button on 17 December. 'I understand the Australian people better than anyone. Because of my own deep understanding of them I know I can win the next election. Everywhere I go the feeling is good.'[170] Considering the polls showing Labor headed for a massive defeat, the deep recession and the sombre national mood, Button must have wondered whether they were talking about the same country.

In a ballot held two days later on a fine summer's evening in Canberra, Keating defeated Hawke by five votes. As the meeting broke up, each side in the contest lined up to wish a weeping Hawke well. A group of supporters then escorted Labor's longest-serving prime minister – the man who more than any other had defined Australia's 1980s – from the caucus room back to his office.[171]

Afterword
What Did It All Mean?

In January 1990 the fashion magazine *Vogue* invited its readers to use the quiet time over the summer 'to rethink what we want in this decade. We need less, rather than more ... pare down, slow down' was its message for the 1990s and beyond.[1] There was implied censure of the decade that had just passed in such advice, as there was in the claim of a *Sydney Morning Herald* journalist in 1992 that '[s]hame for the binge of the 1980s has set in'.[2] This was how the 1980s looked to many who had just lived through it: as an era to be repudiated on account of its excess.

The image of the 1980s as the age of greed and extravagance remains, but it is no longer dominant in our public discourse. It has been overtaken by another 1980s: the story of how we came to be rich and successful. This 1980s, of course, had to wait for the recession we 'had to have', the east Asian financial crisis, the dot-com boom and the global financial crisis. There is an inevitable tone of smugness in it, but also a forgetfulness: this 1980s could only emerge once the anger, shock and disappointment that so many people felt about the lived 1980s – and especially the crash with which it ended – had dissipated.

The 1980s as the origin of our present happy state have been told as a story of Australian exceptionalism: our good fortune marks us off from the rest of the world.[3] Yet the 1980s retreat of the state in the face of market power was one of the least distinctive features of Australia's experience: histories of other Western countries during the era disclose similar stories. This is especially true of Anglophone democracies such as the United States, Britain, Canada and New Zealand, but there are also parallels with the decline of French statism during François Mitterrand's Socialist Party presidency. Globalisation is conceived as both the sum total of these national stories and something more: the power of liberated financial markets combined with computer technology, economic liberalism and mass consumption to create something new and powerful.

What is distinctive and interesting about the Australian 1980s is less what was shared with other liberal capitalist nations than how the new pressures and impulses were handled in local ways. It has been a feature of Australia's economic history since 1788 that its institutions and policies have proven remarkably adaptive to changing challenges and opportunities, and in this sense, the 1980s – far from being special or exceptional – conform to a longer-term pattern.[4] This is a point that has rarely been acknowledged by what might fairly called the 1980s cheer squad, a group still led by Paul Kelly. Nor can their now ingrained habit of reading the 1980s predominantly in light of what happened next capture the meaning of the period as it was experienced by those living through it. The early 1990s 'memory' of the 1980s as an age of greed and excess embodied a powerful sense that things had gone very wrong, that something valuable in the Australian tradition of the 'fair go' had been too easily set aside in the new celebration of productivity, efficiency and competitiveness. But what was distinctive about the Hawke government's approach was that it sought to combine a shift towards the market with a commitment to social spending to reduce poverty, a basic level of government support for all, and a continuing role for unions in the workplace. This effort sets Australia apart from both Britain and the United States in the 1980s.

What of the identity question? Australia in the 1980s was a settler society, demographically dominated by people of British and European origins, and its emergence as a fully independent nation was a relatively recent event. The decade, in this chronology, can be seen as a further working-out of the dilemma posed by the end of the British Empire in the 1960s. What kind of country should we be? Some still looked to the bush as a source of Australian values, and the popularity of Cliff Young, R.M. Williams clothing and *Crocodile Dundee* surely attested that this dream was far from over. Others held up multiculturalism, cosmopolitanism or even suburbanism as the essence of being Australian. Another move was to look to ancient Aboriginal culture to provide a historical depth missing from the more recent European experience, an idea that rhymed with the habit of regarding the land itself as a common source of identity and belonging.

The rapid, unexpected changes in the international order during the late 1980s and early 1990s contributed to the bewildering nature of these debates. The end of the Cold War reduced the fear of a major conflict between the superpowers, but the hopes invested in the 'New World Order' soon proved illusory – in the face of crises in the Middle East, Rwanda and even in the heart of Europe itself, in the former Yugoslavia. Any prospect that greater market freedom in China might be accompanied by expanded political liberty was dashed by the communist government's brutal suppression of protest in Tiananmen Square in June 1989. But the end of apartheid in South Africa was a landmark in the achievement of global racial equality, to which Australia's own abandonment of the White Australia Policy in the 1970s had also contributed something.

Australia's 1980s exposed plenty of unfinished business in the area of race relations – in the continuing controversies over Asian migration, as well as the debate over Aboriginal land rights. The 1991 report of the Royal Commission into Aboriginal Deaths in Custody revealed the continuing impact of colonisation, but by now Australia was on the cusp of a revolution in Aboriginal affairs. At the end of the 1980s few Australians had heard of Eddie Mabo, the Torres Strait Islander who spent most of the decade in protracted litigation to have his people's ownership of their land legally recognised. The High Court's Mabo decision of 1992, by overturning the legal fiction of terra nullius, would lend the land rights debates of the 1980s a distinctly old-fashioned feel.

Australia's 1980s continue to cast their shadow over our lives. The decade stalks debate about the poor quality of our present politics and politicians, the inadequacy of our national leadership and the perils of dependence on commodity exports for which world demand fluctuates much as it did thirty years ago. The songs of the 1980s fill our journeys, its fashions live in our nightmares, its popular heroes regularly figure in the media – even if only to signal their passing.

News of the death of one of the most famous of them, Alan Bond, is all over the weekend papers as I write these words. Most commentators are struggling to strike a balance in discussing such a man, the hero of the America's Cup and the villain who stole more than $1 billion from Bell shareholders. But as this book has shown, there is no single story of the 1980s that can be neatly packaged for the myth-makers of our own times – not, in any case, without producing a caricature of them. Bond was hero and crook, just as the decade elevated greed to the status of public benefaction at the same time as it cultivated our sense of responsibility for the common good through the rise of environmentalism, the continuing concern with poverty and the quest for an inclusive sense of national belonging.

A recent book concerned mainly with the United States calls the 1980s 'a critical and transitional decade'.[5] It is an apt description for Australia, too: its

1980s brought to a climax the debates over personal intimacy, national identity and the economic future which had been bubbling for a generation. But it did not resolve them. We are still a long way from sorting out how men and women, gays and straights, can live as equals. We are yet to work out how we can be open, global and cosmopolitan without surrendering national sovereignty or cultural integrity, or what it means for a predominantly European country aligned with the United States to have an Asian future, or how a settler people can ever be reconciled with those whom it has violently dispossessed. Nor did the 1980s usher in a free-market utopia: we are still grappling with how to insulate our economy from the shock of falling export prices, still wondering about whether manufacturing has a future, still puzzling over how the claims of efficiency, competition and productivity can be reconciled with those of economic security, justice and a decent quality of life. In the 1980s, the government worried over the duopoly exercised by two airlines; thirty years later, we are stuck with a similar duopoly, exercising a similar kind of control, but this time, over our shopping trolleys. Seen in this way, the 1980s were neither 'the end of certainty' nor the beginning of 'the Australian moment'; more a magic mirror in which the legacies of the past and the crises of the present were seen with greater clarity than before, and the possibilities of the future made faintly visible: a child's picture drawn with a finger on glass.

Acknowledgments and Author's Note

To write of one's own times – and perhaps even more of the period of one's youth – presents both opportunities and difficulties. As I completed this book, I came more and more to wonder how much of my sense of the period's coherence came out of my own life story. My father had long predicted that Bob Hawke would eventually become Australia's prime minister but he did not live to see the day, for he died of cancer in November 1982. Early the following year, as a thirteen-year-old, I began Year 9 at my Catholic school's main campus in outer-suburban Bundoora, a spacious contrast to the junior school I had attended nearer to home in the northern suburbs of Melbourne. This combination of major and minor upheaval does provide a sense of 1983 as a threshold between one phase of life and another – perhaps childhood and youth, but such categories are too precise to capture the complexities of life.

After completing my Higher School Certificate in 1986, I went on to study arts at Melbourne University. I was the first generation of my immediate family to attend university; becoming a schoolteacher – which was then my aim – was the highest ambition I had ever been encouraged to conceive. After my undergraduate education, I left to do postgraduate work in Canberra, beginning early in 1991 as the country dipped into its worst economic downturn since the Depression. I was lucky to be on a scholarship, and therefore out of the workforce, for three more years.

My remembered 1980s, then, were a Melbourne working-class experience, and they coincided with my teenage years, my later high school education, and my university days. And they largely centred on family, school, church and sport – a traditional combination, and one that would have been familiar to similarly placed male youths at pretty much any time in the previous half-century or more. We lived in an inner-suburban home that was all arches, brown stain and wood panelling; an unmistakable relic of a 1970s renovation. I have very little consciousness of being much affected – not directly, at any rate – by the new technologies of the era. My younger sister and I played games like Space Invaders and Pac-man on our second-hand Atari, but computer technology had minimal impact on my education. At school, I always hand-wrote assignments and at university, I either still hand-wrote or, less often, typed my essays up on a borrowed electric machine. I didn't have a passport or a credit card, and I did all my banking with a passbook. The fax machine might have been revolutionising business, but I can't recall ever having seen, let alone used, one. The car phone and the brick-like mobile were making their appearance, but for me – and I suspect most of those I knew – they belonged to Hollywood rather than daily life. My first car, bought in 1987 for about $2000, was an orange 1971 Toyota Corona.

Such is not the stuff of celebrity autobiography but it has probably increased my sensitivity to the continuities of life for many during a decade that the subtitle of this book proclaims 'transformed Australia'. Still, there were some modest gestures to the times. We bought our first video recorder around 1988 – and our second in 1989, after the first was nicked by a burglar. I was still buying cassettes and vinyl records at the end of the decade, and my favourite group was the Beatles. Uncanny X-Men and Pseudo Echo each played at 'socials' held at my school – I attended the latter, in 1986, but recall little other than it was loud, I didn't much like them, and I threw up outside the school hall as an adverse reaction either to 'Funky Town' or my dinner. I don't think the era's fashions had much impact on me, although I had an early teenage partiality to clothing with a nationalist theme, a mid-teenage attraction to turquoise, peach and lemon, and a later preference for pastel-coloured jumpers. At the end of the decade I took to wearing to university a pink Lacoste shirt under a blue denim jacket.

Many of the major public events of the era passed over me fairly lightly, as one might expect of a teenager. In February 1983 I happened to be on a school camp not far from one of the Ash Wednesday bushfires, a coincidence that – I later learned – provoked a great deal of understandable concern among parents back in Melbourne watching the horror unfold on their televisions. I was interested in politics, if in a fairly superficial way, and I recall all of the federal elections of the era. I must have had my first vote at the 1987 election. But I lived at home throughout university and did not get involved in either student or neighbourhood politics beyond writing a couple of letters to the local paper. I have no recollection of 26 January 1988 at

ACKNOWLEDGMENTS AND AUTHOR'S NOTE

all: I was with a group of old schoolfriends holidaying on Great Keppel Island in Queensland, where the main interest was in girls and drinking. Like the rest of the country, I was proud of the America's Cup win in 1983 and, again rather like pretty much everyone else, indifferent to the defeat of 1987. Any Carlton loss in the Victorian Football League hurt like hell until about 1987 – and, for some inexplicable reason, much less after that.

Some of the debts I incurred in writing this book go back to the 1980s. I am especially conscious of what I owe to my teachers, who introduced me to many of the themes I have explored here. In particular, I want to thank John Nicholls of Parade College, an immensely talented teacher of legal studies and politics. Later, I also learned a great deal about Australia's 1980s from six fine teachers of politics, history and literature at the University of Melbourne: the late Albert Paolini, the late Graham Little, Verity Burgmann, Bruce Watson, Stuart Macintyre and Chris Wallace-Crabbe. There are the debts to my family, and especially my mother, who raised me during the 1980s, and who died just as I was beginning my research.

I owe an enormous debt of gratitude to Megan Kelly, a child of the 1990s, who provided superb research assistance for this book but also engaged patiently with my ideas about it. Despite the increasingly outrageous nature of my requests for research materials in Canberra's collections, her kindness, generosity and good humour were unfailing. Blake Singley provided both research and advice on dealing with foodways – again, my thanks. The Menzies Centre for Australian Studies at King's College London provided a Bicentennial Fellowship which facilitated travel to London in October 2014, while the Australian National University (ANU) kindly granted me study leave in the second half of 2014 to write the book. I am grateful to both universities for their support.

I presented papers at several seminars and workshops which were excellent opportunities for trying out my ideas. I am especially grateful to Robert Crawford and Jackie Dickenson, who invited me to a workshop at the University of Technology Sydney on the history of the office. My thanks, also, to Gideon Haigh for his conversation on that occasion and encouragement of what I thought I was trying to do. Later, I presented papers to the Melbourne Feminist History Group, the Menzies Centre for Australian Studies at King's College London, the History Research Seminar at Flinders University, the 2015 conference of the Australian Society for the Study of Labour History in Melbourne, and in my own department, the School of History at the ANU. David Headon and John Uhr ran a most stimulating conference at the ANU in December 2014 on Eureka which sent me down a path that was helpful at a critical time in the writing of the book, while John Uhr and Ryan Walter provided a welcome opportunity to discuss *Future Directions* at a conference on political rhetoric, also at the ANU.

I am very grateful to Robert Manne, who generously read much of the manuscript at short notice, and commented very helpfully on its strengths and weaknesses. I subjected chapter 7 to the forensic, but always encouraging, scrutiny of my colleagues in the ANU History Reading Group: my thanks for Carolyn Strange for her role in bringing us all together, and to Gemma Betros, Nick Brown, Mary Kilcline Cody, Tania Colwell, Alex Cook, Ben Mercer and Patty O'Brien for their comments. The School's PhD students have been unfailingly indulgent in enduring my enthusiasm for this period of Australian history, and they do much to provide a stimulating environment for writing and researching Australian history. My thanks, also, to Selwyn Cornish for his conversation and generosity in reading and commenting on chapter 2, and to David Chessell, for bringing his vast economic expertise and knowledge of the era to bear on the same material. Naturally, I am responsible for any misapprehensions and errors that remain.

At an early stage in thinking about a book on Australia's 1980s, I benefited from the inspiration and ideas of my colleague at King's College London, Richard Vinen, author of the exemplary *Thatcher's Britain*. I am also grateful, as ever, for conversations, information, support and advice from friends and colleagues such as Linda Addison, Andrew Bonnell, Judith Brett, Peter Browne, Brian Costar, Doug Craig, Jim Davidson, David Day, Nick Dyrenfurth, Hannah Forsyth, Murray Goot, Adam Graycar, Bridget Griffen-Foley, Ian Hancock, Ian Henderson, David Horner, David Lee, Mark McKenna, Humphrey McQueen, Lyndon Megarrity, Doug Munro, Paul Strangio, Marija Taflaga, Pat Troy, Christine Wallace, Stuart Ward and Hugh White. I also thank the national offices of both the Labor Party and the Liberal Party for access to their collections in the National Library. My debts to various institutions will be clear from the endnotes and the picture credits, but I would like especially to thank the Canberra and Sydney offices of the National Archives of Australia, Bruce Ibsen of the University of Queensland Archives, and Virginia MacDonald of the Reserve Bank Archives for her generosity in making available to me material on the float. My thanks also to John Casamento, Tony De Bolfo and Liz Ross in connection with the illustrations.

At Black Inc., my thanks once again to Chris Feik, for his encouragement, expert eye and invariably sound advice, to Kirstie Innes-Will for the professionalism, patience, enthusiasm and skill she brought to the task of transforming manuscript into book, and to Siân Scott-Clash for help with permissions, images and production issues. And I am yet again indebted to Nikola Lusk for her wonderful editorial work.

Finally, many thanks to Nicole McLennan, who endured the customary ordeals when I have my head in a big project, and was characteristically generous about it all – her advice on chapter 7 was especially valuable; and to our daughter Amy, whose enquiries about my progress were a spur to get it all finished. I expect that she will one day be able to compare these 'eighties' to the next lot. When she does, I hope she might faintly recall that I dedicated this book to her, with my love.

Endnotes

ABBREVIATIONS

AFR	Australian Financial Review
ALP	Australian Labor Party
BRW	Business Review Weekly
CPD	Commonwealth Parliamentary Debates
CT	Canberra Times
GCB	Gold Coast Bulletin
H of R	House of Representatives
NAA	National Archives of Australia
NLA	National Library of Australia
NYT	New York Times
RBA	Reserve Bank of Australia
SBSA	State Bank of South Australia
SLV	State Library of Victoria
SMH	Sydney Morning Herald

INTRODUCTION: STORIES OF THE 1980S

1   *GCB*, 12 January 1988, p. 22.
2   ibid., 13 May 1988, p. 4.
3   ibid., 8 January 1988, p. 5.
4   ibid., 28 December 1985, pp. 52–3.
5   ibid., 3 September 1991, pp. 1–2.
6   Paul Kelly, *The End of Certainty: The Story of the 1980s*, Allen & Unwin, St Leonards, 1992, pp. 1–16.
7   George Megalogenis, *The Australian Moment: How We Were Made for These Times*, Viking/Penguin, Camberwell, 2012.
8   Gareth Evans, *Inside the Hawke–Keating Government: A Cabinet Diary*, Melbourne University Press, Carlton, 2014, p. vii.
9   'Friends Push Picture of Magic Mike after Baird's Rapid Rise to Premier', *Age*, 19 April 2014, www.theage.com.au/it-pro/friends-push-picture-of-magic-mike-after-bairds-rapid-rise-to-premier-20140419-zqwmr.html, accessed 13 May 2015.
10 *Folklife: Our Living Heritage: Report of the Committee of Inquiry into Folklife in Australia*, Australian Government Publishing Service, Canberra, 1987, p. 1.
11 Graeme Turner, *Making It National: Nationalism and Popular Culture*, Allen & Unwin, St Leonards, 1994, pp. 3–4.

12 Tim Duncan and John Fogarty, *Australia and Argentina: On Parallel Paths*, Melbourne University Press, Carlton, 1984, p. 164.

Chapter 1: A Good Run

1   *Daily Telegraph*, 17 February 1983, p. 3; *SMH*, 17 February 1983, p. 1.
2   John Button, 'Some Political Notes', 16 January 1983, John Button Papers, Series III Notebooks, Box 8, Folder 9, Files N-P 1983 & 1999, SLV.
3   John Button, 'Memorandum of Discussion – January 6, 1983', ibid. There are also accounts of this conversation in Paul Kelly, *The Hawke Ascendancy: A Definitive Account of Its Origins and Climax, 1975-1983*, Angus & Robertson, Sydney, 1984, pp. 344-7 and John Button, *As It Happened*, Text Publishing, Melbourne, 1998, pp. 191-2.
4   Kelly, *Hawke Ascendancy*, pp. 2-4.
5   ibid., p. 393.
6   John Stubbs, *Hayden*, Mandarin Australia, Port Melbourne, 1990, p. 253.
7   [Robert Hawke], *Policy Speech: Federal Election Campaign Launch*, Sydney Opera House Opera Theatre, 16 February 1983, p. 2.
8   Graham Richardson, *Whatever It Takes*, Bantam Books, Sydney and Auckland, 1994, pp. 46-7.
9   Hawke, *Policy Speech*, pp. 5, 16, 36.
10 J. Oliver, N.R. Britton and M.K. James, *The Ash Wednesday Bushfires in Victoria 16 February 1983*, Disaster Investigation Report No. 7, Centre for Disaster Studies, James Cook University of North Queensland, Townsville, 1984, pp. 6, 32; Stephen J. Pyne, *Burning Bush: A Fire History of Australia*, University of Washington Press, Seattle and London, 1998.
11 *Drought, Dust and Deluge: A Century of Climate Extremes in Australia*, Bureau of Meteorology, Australian Government, Canberra, 2004, p. 55.
12 Oliver, Britton and James, *Ash Wednesday*, pp. 8-9, 19, 21, 75.
13 *Advertiser* (Adelaide), 19 February 1983, p. 1.
14 Robert Murray and Kate White, *State of Fire: A History of Volunteer Firefighting and the Country Fire Authority in Victoria*, Hargreen Publishing Company, North Melbourne, 1995, p. 226.
15 Oliver, Britton and James, *Ash Wednesday*, p. 22.
16 This account of the Cockatoo bushfire depends on Edward Mundie, *Cockatoo Ash Wednesday 1983 The People's Story*, Hyland House, Melbourne, 1983; Icia Molloy (ed.), *Baked Apples on a Tree: Ash Wednesday Reflections*, Cockatoo Neighbourhood House, Cockatoo, 2011; Oliver, Britton and James, *Ash Wednesday*; *SMH*, 18 February 1983, p. 3; *Herald* (Melbourne), 17 February 1983, p. 3.
17 Mundie, *Cockatoo*, p. 38.
18 ibid., p. 48.
19 *Australian*, 18 February 1983, p. 1.
20 ibid., p. 3.
21 *SMH*, 17 February 1983, p. 3.
22 *Advertiser*, 19 February 1983, p. 3.
23 *Age*, 17 February 1983, p. 3; *Sun* (Melbourne), 18 February 1983, p. 1.
24 Murray and White, *State of Fire*, pp. 237, 230-1.
25 *Advertiser*, 19 February 1983, p. 3.
26 *Sun*, 18 February 1983, p. 3; Murray and White, *State of Fire*, p. 234.
27 *Herald*, 17 February 1983, p. 3; *Age*, 18 February 1983, p. 3.

ENDNOTES

28 Pyne, *Burning Bush*, p. 412.
29 *Sun*, 18 February 1983, pp. 3, 11.
30 ibid., 19 February 1983, p. 7; 18 February 1983, p. 7.
31 Molloy (ed.), *Baked Apples*, pp. 117, 129; Pyne, *Burning Bush*, p. 415.
32 Pyne, *Burning Bush*, pp. 413–19.
33 *Australian*, 21 February 1983, pp. 1–2.
34 Troy Bramston (ed.), *The Wran Era*, The Federation Press, Annandale and Leichhardt, 2006.
35 Quentin Beresford, *The Godfather: The Life of Brian Burke*, Allen & Unwin, Crows Nest, 2008, p. 43.
36 ibid., p. 46.
37 Trevor Sykes, *The Bold Riders: Behind Australia's Corporate Collapses*, Allen & Unwin, St Leonards, 1994, pp. 65–8; Beresford, *Godfather*, pp. 45, 99; Evan Whitton, *The Hillbilly Dictator: Australia's Police State*, ABC, Crows Nest, 1989, pp. 70–1, 73; Noel Bushnell, 'In the Court of King Joh', *Australian Business*, 11 November 1987, p. 58.
38 Bill Hayden, *Hayden: An Autobiography*, Angus & Robertson, Pymble, 1996, p. 305.
39 David Marr, *The Ivanov Trail*, Nelson, Melbourne, 1984, pp. 38, 65, 177–8, 180, 201–2; Peter Sekuless, *The Lobbyists: Using Them in Canberra*, George Allen & Unwin, Sydney, 1984, pp. xi, 8–9.
40 David Combe, 'The CIA's Role in Labor's Downfall', *Bulletin*, 12 January 1982, pp. 29–31; Marr, *Ivanov*, pp. 68–9; Combe narrates his career in the Royal Commission on Australia's Security and Intelligence Agencies, Transcript (hereafter *Combe Ivanov RCT*), 24 August 1983, pp. 3795ff.
41 Marr, *Ivanov*, pp. 43–6.
42 ibid., pp. 40–2, 53–7, 61.
43 ibid., pp. 66–7.
44 Harvey Barnett, *Tale of the Scorpion*, Susan Haynes/Allen & Unwin, North Sydney, 1988, pp. 130, 140, 144; *Combe Ivanov RCT*, 6 August 1983, p. 2836; Bob Hawke, *The Hawke Memoirs*, Mandarin, Port Melbourne, 1996 [1994], pp. 197–8.
45 'Edited Transcript of Conversation between Mr. Ivanov and Mr. Combe on 4 March 1983', pp. 22, 26, 33, in *Combe Ivanov RCT*.
46 Tim Duncan, 'Fraser Departs in a Shambles of Flash Bulbs', *Bulletin*, 15 March 1983, p. 23.
47 *AFR*, 7 March 1983, p. 3.
48 John Edwards, *Keating: The Inside Story*, Penguin Books, Ringwood, 1996, pp. 171–7; *Australian*, 7 March 1983, p. 1; *AFR*, 7 March 1983, pp. 1, 48; *AFR*, 8 March 1983, pp. 1, 52; *AFR*, 9 March 1983, pp. 1, 8, 44.
49 Edwards, *Keating*, p. 196.
50 *AFR*, 9 March, pp. 1, 8, 10; Maximilian Walsh, 'How John Stone Retained the Treasury', *Bulletin*, 29 March 1983, pp. 20–24; Edwards, *Keating*, pp. 172–3, 177–8; Hawke, *Memoirs*, pp. 147–8, 153–4.
51 Hawke, *Policy Speech*, pp. 5–6.
52 'Address by the Prime Minister, the Hon R.J. Hawke, A.C., M.P. to the National Economic Summit Conference House of Representatives Canberra 11 April 1983', pp. 9–10.
53 Colleen Ryan, 'Summit Business', *National Times*, 15–21 April 1983, p. 37; *Age*, 16 April 1983, pp. 10, 11.
54 *Age*, 12 April 1983, p. 5; 13 April 1983, p. 13; John Hurst, 'Crean and Kelty Steal the Show', *National Times*, 15–21 April 1983, pp. 16–17.

55 C.R. Rye, 'Meeting with Mr Kelty', Minute Paper, 17 March 1983, p. 1, NAA: E1983/88 PT2.
56 *National Economic Summit Conference 11-14 April 1983: Documents and Proceedings, Volume 2, Record of Proceedings*, Australian Government Publishing Service, Canberra, 1983, pp. 30-6.
57 ibid., pp. 56, 86.
58 *Age*, 13 April 1983, p. 3.
59 Sue Johnson, 'The Well-Mannered Summit', *National Times*, 15-21 April 1983, p. 4.
60 *Summit Proceedings*, vol. 2, p. 194.
61 *Age*, 16 April 1983, p. 10.
62 Geoff Kitney, 'The Big Issue No Amount of Consensus Could Solve', *National Times*, 15-21 April 1983, p. 5.
63 *Age*, 13 April 1983, p. 27.
64 Johnson, 'The Well-Mannered Summit'. See also *Age*, 16 April 1983, p. 11; Anne Gorman, 'The Sound of Marking Time', *Australian Society*, 1 May 1983, pp. 22-3; *Age*, 12 April 1983, p. 6.
65 Johnson, 'The Well-Mannered Summit'.
66 Frank Stilwell, 'The Economic Summit and Beyond', *Arena*, no. 63, 1983, pp. 16-25; Max Teichmann, 'Is There Rain after the Hawke Lightning?', *Australian Society*, 1 April 1983, p. 28. See also Geoffrey Barker in the *Age*, 16 April 1983, p. 11.
67 Peter Beilharz, 'The View from the Summit', *Arena*, no. 64, 1983, p. 17.
68 Kitney, 'Big Issue', pp. 4-5; *Age*, 13 April 1983, p. 4.
69 Edna Carew, *Keating: A Biography*, Allen & Unwin, Sydney, 1988, p. 84; Edwards, *Keating*, pp. 177-8.
70 P.J. Sheehan, 'Notes on Draft Outline: Economic Prospects to 1985/86 – Draft of 11 March 1983', 15 March 1983 and N.F. Hyden, 'Note for File: National Economic Summit – Preparations', 17 March 1983, p. 5, NAA: E1983/88 PT 1; C.R. Rye, 'Note for File: Economic Summit', 29 March 1983, NAA: E1983/88 PT 2.
71 John Cain, *John Cain's Years: Power, Parties and Politics*, Melbourne University Press, Carlton, 1995, p. 159.
72 Hawke, *Memoirs*, pp. 152-3.
73 *Age*, 16 April 1983, p. 18; Liz Ross, *Dare to Struggle Dare to Win! Builders Labourers Fight Deregistration 1981-94*, The Vulgar Press, Carlton North, 2004, p. 71.
74 *Report of Commissioner Appointed to Inquire into Activities of the Australian Building Construction Employees and Builders Labourers Federation* (hereafter *Winneke RC*), vol. 2, F.D. Atkinson, Government Printer, Melbourne, 1982, p. 379.
75 *Winneke RC*, vol. 2, p. 327 and vol. 1, p. 18.
76 ibid., vol. 1, *passim*; the story of the Grollo truck is at p. 106.
77 Humphrey McQueen, *We Built This Country: Builders' Labourers and Their Unions*, Ginninderra Press, Port Adelaide, 2011, pp. 328-9; Ruth Ostrow, *The New Boy Network: Taking Over Corporate Australia*, William Heinemann Australia, Richmond (Vic.), 1987, pp. 31, 44; Ross, *Dare to Struggle*, ch. 4.
78 M.W. Butlin to N.F. Hyden, 'Return to Centralised Wage Fixation – Some Further Issues', 19 April 1983, p. 2, NAA: E1983/88 PT 2.
79 Bob Carr, 'Post-Summit Challenge Must Be Crushed', *Bulletin*, 26 April 1983, pp. 24-5.
80 David Combe, 'Inside the Star Chamber', *Matilda*, March 1985, pp. 27-8.

81 Humphrey McQueen, 'The Pain of Coming Home to Deficit Government', *Australian Society*, 1 December 1983, p. 27.
82 Hawke, *Memoirs*, pp. 89–92.
83 *Combe Ivanov RCT*, 3 August 1983, pp. 2499–502.
84 ibid., pp. 2507–9.
85 ibid., 5 August 1983, pp. 2698–9.
86 ibid., 12 August 1983, p. 3221.
87 *Sunday Telegraph*, 8 May 1983, p. 39.
88 *SMH*, 10 May 1983, p. 1.
89 Federal Caucus, Minutes, 10 May 1983, Bob Hawke Prime Ministerial Library, University of South Australia; *CPD*, H of R, vol. 131, 11 May 1983, pp. 389, 452, 493–4 and the *Australian*, 11 May 1983, p. 1.
90 *CPD*, H of R, vol. 131, 10 May 1983, pp. 344, 348–9, 350.
91 *Daily Mirror*, 10 May 1983, p. 1.
92 *Combe Ivanov RCT*, 18 August 1983, p. 3631.
93 *CPD*, H of R, vol. 131, pp. 450–1.
94 *Combe Ivanov RCT*, 30 August 1983, p. 4094.
95 Meena Blesing, *'Was Your Dad a Russian Spy?': The Personal Story of the Combe/ Ivanov Affair by David Combe's Wife,* Sun Books, South Melbourne, 1986, pp. 5, 193.
96 Australian Labor Party 36th Biennial National Conference, Transcript, 12 July 1984, p. 570.
97 Hawke, *Memoirs*, p. 191.
98 Rob Watts, 'No Hope for Combe', *Arena*, no. 66, 1984, pp. 66–77.
99 Barnett, *Scorpion*, pp. 54, 130.
100 *Royal Commission on Australia's Security and Intelligence Agencies: Report on Term of Reference (c), December 1983*, Australian Government Publishing Service, Canberra, 1983, pp. 100, 104–5.
101 Royal Commission on Australia's Security and Intelligence Agencies, *Report on the Sheraton Hotel Incident*, February 1984, AGPS, Canberra, 1984; P.N. Grabowsky, *Wayward Governance: Illegality and Its Control in the Public Sector*, Australian Institute of Criminology, Canberra, 1989, ch. 8.
102 Neville Nicholls, 'Climate Outlooks: From Revolutionary Science to Orthodoxy', in Tim Sherratt, Tom Griffiths and Libby Robin (eds), *A Change in the Weather: Climate and Culture in Australia*, National Museum of Australia Press, Canberra, 2005, pp. 18–29; J.L. McBride and N. Nicholls, 'Seasonal Relationships between Australian Rainfall and the Southern Oscillation', *Monthly Weather Review*, vol. 111, 1983, pp. 1998–2004.
103 *Wheat Australia*, vol. 16, no. 3, April 1983.
104 *Kaniva Times & Nhill Free Press*, 29 March 1983, p. 3.
105 *Chronicle* (Toowoomba), 21 March 1983, p. 1; 22 March 1983, p. 5; 6 April 1983, pp. 1–2.
106 *Daily Liberal* (Dubbo), 23 March 1983, p. 45; *Cobar Age*, 6 April 1983, p. 3.
107 *Daily Liberal*, 5 April, 1983, p. 3; 6 April 1983, p. 2.
108 *Land*, 7 April 1983, p. 3.
109 *Daily Liberal*, 15 March 1983, p. 3; 18 March 1983, p. 1.
110 *SMH*, 11 September 1983, p. 18; *Daily Liberal*, 24 March 1983, p. 5; *Weekly Times*, 4 May 1983, p. 3; *Land*, 24 March 1983, p. 3; 28 April 1983, p. 3.
111 *Daily Liberal*, 5 April 1983, p. 3.
112 *Land*, 24 March 1983, p. 6.
113 ibid., 7 April 1983, p. 6.

114 *Australian*, 4 May 1983, p. 26.
115 Cliff Young, *Cliffy's Book*, High Country Publishing, Dargo, 1995, pp. 18, 21, 23–4; *Age*, 5 April 1983, p. 11.
116 *People*, 23 May 1983, pp. 22–3.
117 Julietta Jameson, *Cliffy: The Cliff Young Story*, Text Publishing, Melbourne, 2013, pp. 90, 94.
118 The following account of the race, unless otherwise stated, depends on: Jameson, *Cliffy*; Young, *Cliffy's Book*; *Australian*, 2 May 1983, p. 1; 3 May 1983, p. 1; *Sun* (Melbourne), 29 April 1983, p. 71; 30 April 1983, p. 55; 2 May 1983, pp. 1, 2; 3 May 1983, pp. 1, 2; 4 May 1983, pp. 1, 2; *Geelong Advertiser*, 2 May 1983, p. 1; 3 May 1983, p. 1; *Colac Herald*, 2 May 1983, p. 6; 4 May 1983, p. 24.
119 Young, *Cliffy's Book*, p. 49.
120 *Australian*, 3 May 1983, p. 6.
121 *Colac Herald*, 4 May 1983, p. 1.
122 ibid.
123 ibid., 29 April 1983, p. 1; 9 May 1983, p. 6; 4 May 1983, p. 1; 6 May 1983, p. 1; 9 May 1983, p. 1; 11 May 1983, p. 17.
124 Young, *Cliffy's Book*, p. 57.
125 Al Simmons, *The Ballad of Cliff Young*, Judy Simmons Publications, Cheltenham, 1983; Drew Kettle, 'Cliff Young's "Great Race": Sydney to Melbourne 1983', in *Cliff Young: Champion Endurance Runner*, Lions International, Colac, n.d. [1983].
126 *Sun*, 4 May 1983, p. 73; Young, *Cliffy's Book*, p. 55; Jameson, *Cliffy*, pp. 155, 168.
127 *Colac Herald*, 9 May 1983, p. 6.
128 *SMH*, 11 September 1983, p. 19.
129 *Wheat Australia*, vol. 17, no. 4, April 1984; Australian Wheat Board, *Crop Report for 1983–83 Australian Wheat*.
130 *Weekly Times*, 2 February 1984, p. 9; *Land*, 12 January 1984, pp. 3, 6.

Chapter 2: Keeping Afloat

1 David Armstrong and Michael Meagher, 'The End of a Magnificent Obsession', *Bulletin*, 11 October 1983, p. 99; Bruce Stannard, *The Triumph of Australia II: The America's Cup Challenge of 1983*, Lansdowne, Sydney, 1983, pp. 11–39, 125.
2 Paul Barry, *The Rise and Fall of Alan Bond*, Bantam Books, Sydney, 1990, pp. 26, 31–4.
3 ibid., pp. 35–58.
4 ibid., pp. 61–4; John Bertrand, as told to Patrick Robinson, *Born to Win: A Lifelong Struggle to Capture the America's Cup*, Bantam Books, Sydney, 1985, pp. 433–4.
5 Alan Bond with Rob Mundle, *Bond*, HarperCollins, Sydney, 2003, pp. 64–5, 105–7.
6 *Australian*, 28 September 1983, p. 36.
7 Stannard, *Triumph*, pp. 59–61.
8 Rick Feneley, 'The "Lie" That Captured the America's Cup', *SMH*, 14 October 2009, www.smh.com.au/news/sport/the-lie-that-captured-the-americas-cup/2009/10/13/1255195786058.html, accessed 18 August 2014.
9 *Australian*, 28 September 1983, p. 36.
10 Stannard, *Triumph*, pp. 63–125; Bertrand, *Born*, pp. 32, 34–5, 288–89, 335–63.
11 Donald Horne, 'Cup Fever', *National Times*, 30 September–6 October 1983, pp. 3–4; *SMH*, 28 September 1983, p. 4.
12 *Courier-Mail*, 28 September 1983, p. 4.

ENDNOTES

13 *Australian*, 26 September 1983, p. 8.
14 ibid., 28 September 1983, p. 12.
15 ibid., 29 September 1983, p. 8.
16 *AFR*, 28 September 1983, p. 12.
17 *Age*, 28 September 1983, p. 13.
18 Warren Jones to Kevin Bray, telex, 2 February 1983; Bray to Prime Minister [Malcolm Fraser], Briefing Notes, 2 and 9 February 1983; Richard Pratt, Aide Memoire, 4 February 1983, NAA: A1209/1983/455 PART 1.
19 *AFR*, 28 September 1983, p. 6.
20 Graeme Davison, 'The Imaginary Grandstand', *Meanjin*, vol. 61, no. 3, 2002, pp. 4–18.
21 *West Australian*, 28 September 1983, p. 8.
22 *Australian*, 28 September 1983, p. 12.
23 Paul James, 'Australia in the Corporate Image: A New Nationalism', *Arena*, no. 63, 1983, pp. 65–106.
24 *Australian*, 28 September 1983, p. 2; *AFR*, 28 September 1983, p. 12. See also *Age*, 28 September 1983, p. 24.
25 *Australian*, 28 September 1983, p. 31.
26 *AFR*, 28 September 1983, p. 19.
27 *Australian*, 20 September 1983, p. 1.
28 *AFR*, 28 September 1983, p. 12.
29 ibid., p. 3.
30 *SMH*, 28 September 1983, p. 4.
31 *Australian*, 28 September 1983, p. 2.
32 *AFR*, 28 September 1983, p. 3.
33 Alan Ramsey, 'Hawke Leads the Public Razzamatazz', *National Times*, 30 September–6 October 1983, p. 7.
34 *Bulletin*, 31 January 1984, p. 23.
35 *AFR*, 28 September 1983, p. 3.
36 Turner, *Making It National*, p. 26.
37 Cabinet Minute, Perth, 27 September 1983, decision no. 2197, 'Without Submission – The America's Cup 1983 – Successful Australia II Challenge', NAA: A13979/2197; Cabinet Minute, Canberra, 5 October 1983, decision no. 2216, 'Submission No. 454 – Tourism Promotional Initiatives to Capitalise on America's Cup Victory', NAA: A13977/454.
38 *SMH*, 28 September 1983, p. 8.
39 Carew, *Keating*, p. 93.
40 Armstrong and Meagher, 'The End of a Magnificent Obsession', p. 96.
41 Stephen Bell, *Australia's Money Mandarins: The Reserve Bank and the Politics of Money*, Cambridge University Press, Cambridge, 2004, pp. 21–5; Kelly, *End of Certainty*, pp. 78–9.
42 Carew, *Keating*, pp. 96–7.
43 Kelly, *End of Certainty*, p. 70.
44 Peter Walsh, *Confessions of a Failed Finance Minister*, Random House Australia, Milsons Point, 1995, p. 103.
45 Carew, *Keating*, p. 89.
46 Gregory McCarthy and David Taylor, 'The Politics of the Float: Paul Keating and the Deregulation of the Australian Exchange Rate', *Australian Journal of Politics and History*, vol. 41, no. 2, August 1995, p. 226.
47 Hawke, *Memoirs*, p. 235.

48 Reserve Bank of Australia, 'Foreign Exchange Arrangements', Press Release, Sydney, 28 October 1983, NAA: A9488, O1983/106, PART 7.
49 Edwards, *Keating*, p. 231.
50 C.R. Rye, 'The Float: Treasury Involvement', Note for File, 13 December 1983, Reserve Bank of Australia Archives, Martin Place, Sydney.
51 Greg Hywood, 'The Night Keating Gave Australia Its Brave New World', *AFR*, 18 December 1989, p. 7.
52 Hywood, 'The Night Keating Gave Australia Its Brave New World'.
53 Carew, *Keating*, p. 101.
54 Rye, 'The Float: Treasury Involvement'; John Stone, 'Floating the Dollar: Facts and Fiction', *Quadrant*, January–February 2012, p. 18.
55 *Weekend Australian*, 10–11 December 1983, p. 14; *AFR*, 12 December 1983, p. 1.
56 Hywood, 'The Night Keating Gave Australia Its Brave New World'.
57 Kelly, *End of Certainty*, p. 76.
58 Craig Beaumont and Li Cui, 'Conquering Fear of Floating – Australia's Successful Adaptation to a Flexible Exchange Rate', IMF Discussion Paper, Asia and Pacific Department, July 2007, www.imf.org/external/pubs/ft/pdp/2007/pdp02.pdf, accessed 18 September 2014.
59 Carew, *Keating*, p. 91.
60 McCarthy and Taylor, 'Politics of the Float', p. 230.
61 Hawke, *Memoirs*, pp. 237–8.
62 ibid., pp. 239–42.
63 Paul Keating, 'Paul Keating's Account of the Decision to Float', in Edwards, *Keating*, pp. 544–5.
64 *Sunday Telegraph*, 1 January 2012, www.dailytelegraph.com.au/news/opinion/paul-keating-recalls-his-first-approach-to-bob-hawke-about-floating-the-australian-dollar-in-1983/story-e6frezz0-1226233871491, accessed 16 September 2014.
65 'Discussions with Treasurer', 9 September 1983, RBA Archives.
66 Keating to Johnston, 23 November 1983, NAA: A9488, O1983/106, PART 7.
67 Johnston to Keating, 23 November 1983, RBA Archives.
68 M.J. Phillips, 'Discussions with Treasurer', Note for File, 30 November 1983, RBA Archives.
69 See Stone, 'Floating the Dollar: Facts and Fiction' and 'Floating the Dollar: More Facts and More Fiction, *Quadrant*, March 2012, pp. 51–7.
70 Stone, 'Floating the Dollar: Facts and Fiction', p. 13.
71 [Robert Whitelaw and David Borthwick], Overseas Finance Branch, Overseas Economic Relations Division, 'Possible Evolutionary Changes to Exchange Rate Management', 19 September 1983, NAA: A9488, O1983/106, PART 6.
72 Stone to Keating, Memorandum, 16 October 1983, NAA: A9488, O1983/106, PART 6.
73 Selwyn Cornish, 'A Float to Remember', *AFR*, 21 November 2014, Review, p. 7.
74 Stephen Mills, *The Hawke Years: The Story from the Inside*, Viking, Ringwood, 1993, p. 101.
75 A.G. Griffiths to P.J. Keating, 8 November 1983, NAA: A9488, O1983/106, PART 1.
76 Ann Nevile, 'Financial Deregulation in Australia in the 1980s', *Economic and Labour Relations Review*, vol. 8, no. 2, December 1997, pp. 273–92.
77 Carew, *Keating*, p. 91.
78 Australian Labor Party 36th Biennial National Conference, *Transcript*, 9 July 1984, pp. 182, 184.
79 Cain, *John Cain's Years*, p. 160.

ENDNOTES

80 *Victoria: The Next Step*, The Economic Strategy for Victoria: A Statement by the Treasurer, 9 April 1984, p. 12.
81 Australian Labor Party 36th Biennial National Conference, *Transcript*, 9 July 1984, p. 160.
82 Sykes, *Bold Riders*, pp. 472–8; Chris Kenny, *State of Denial*, Wakefield Press, Kent Town, 1993, pp. 67–9.
83 Carew, *Keating*, p. 105.
84 Linda Cowan (Secretary, North Sydney Branch) to Bob McMullan, 23 July 1984, (no. 82), ALP National Secretariat Papers, NLA MS 4985, 84/2/22 (Box 451).
85 Deborah Light, 'Button, Minister in a No-Win Portfolio', *BRW*, 10–16 November 1984, p. 64; Button, *As It Happened*, pp. 274–87.
86 Button, *As It Happened*, pp. 282, 305–6; Stuart Simson, 'Amber Light Flashing for Car Industry', *BRW*, 7–14 January 1984, pp. 24–5 and 'Button Moves with Ford', *BRW*, 2–8 June 1984, pp. 11–14.
87 Button to Hawke, 11 February 1984, Button Papers, MS 13728, Box 1, Folder 7, SLV.
88 'Notes of Meeting with Nixon Apple', typescript, 17 June 1994, typescript, ibid., Box 9, Folder 5; Button, *As It Happened*, pp. 253–4; Australian Labor Party 36th Biennial National Conference, *Transcript*, 13 July 1984, p. 794.
89 Andrew Scott, *Fading Loyalties: The Australian Labor Party and the Working Class*, Pluto Press, Leichhardt, 1991.
90 Sol Encel, 'Labor's New Class Takes Command', *Australian Society*, 1 May 1984, pp. 6–9.
91 Susan Ryan, *Catching the Waves: Life In and Out of Politics*, HarperCollins, Sydney 1999, pp. 214–15.
92 John Dawkins [Minister for Finance] to Bob Hawke, 25 September [1984], M3826/1, Series RH14, Box 1, F9 (Personal Correspondence Dillon Family), Bob Hawke Papers, Bob Hawke Prime Ministerial Library, University of South Australia.
93 Anne-Marie Boxall and James A. Gillespie, *Making Medicare: The Politics of Universal Health Care in Australia*, NewSouth Publishing, Sydney, 2013, chs 7–8.
94 *CPD*, H of R, vol. 135, 1 March 1984, p. 370.
95 *CPD*, Senate, vol. 100, 8 November 1983, p. 2298.
96 Mrs Betty Hocking MHA, ACT Coordinator, Women Who Want to Be Women, 27 May 1983, ALP National Secretariat Papers, NLA MS 4985, 84/2/29, Box 452.
97 *Women Who Want to Be Women, Newsletter*, no. 22, September 1983, p. 9.
98 *CPD*, Senate, 21 October 1983, vol. 100, p. 1929.
99 ibid., 8 November 1983, p. 2295.
100 *CPD*, H of R, 1 March 1984, vol. 135, p. 401.
101 Peter Beilharz and Rob Watts, 'Tories in Labor Drag?', *Australian Society*, 1 May 1984, pp. 32–3.

Chapter 3: 'Vanishing Aussie?'

1 *Warrnambool Standard*, 19 March 1984, in Renata Singer, assisted by Michael Liffman (ed.), *The Immigration Debate in the Press 1984*, Updated Edition, The Clearing House on Migration Issues, Richmond (Vic.), 1984, p. 3. See also Geoffrey Blainey, 'Multi-Cultural Australia: Now and Then' ['Summary of Blainey address as provided by Rotary, to participants at Warrnambool Conference, March 18, 1984'], ibid., p. 1.
2 Tran My-Van, 'Vietnamese Refugees in Australia', in James Jupp (ed.), *The Australian People: An Encyclopedia of the Nation, Its People and Their Origins*, Cambridge University Press, Cambridge, 2001, p. 722.

3   *Richmond Times*, 14 February 1984, p. 8; 28 August 1984, p. 6.
4   Morag Loh, *Dinky-Di: The Contributions of Chinese Immigrants and Australians of Chinese Descent to Australia's Defence Forces and War Efforts 1899–1988*, Australian Government Publishing Service, for the Office of Multicultural Affairs, Canberra, 1989.
5   Andrew Jakubowicz, 'State and Ethnicity: Multi-Culturalism as Ideology', in James Jupp (ed.), *Ethnic Politics in Australia*, George Allen & Unwin, Sydney, 1984, pp. 14–28; Tim Rowse, 'The Trouble with Hegemony: Popular Culture and Multiculturalism', *Politics*, vol. 20, no. 2, November 1985, pp. 70–6; Stephen Castles, Bill Cope, Mary Kalantzis and Michael Morrissey, *Mistaken Identity: Multiculturalism and the Demise of Nationalism in Australia*, Pluto Press, Sydney, 1988.
6   Lachlan Chipman, 'The Menace of Multiculturalism', *Quadrant*, vol. 14, no. 10, October 1980, p. 5.
7   Frank Knopfelmacher, 'The Case against Multi-Culturalism', in Robert Manne (ed.), *The New Conservatism in Australia*, Oxford University Press, Melbourne, 1982, p. 63.
8   John Hirst, 'More or Less Diverse', in Hirst, *Looking For Australia: Historical Essays*, Black Inc., Melbourne, 2010, p. 211.
9   *Richmond Times*, 19 December 1983, p. 3; 21 February 1984, p. 1.
10 *Liverpool-Fairfield Champion*, 23 May 1984, p. 2; 6 June 1984, p. 19.
11 Tim Duncan, 'Our Isolated Vietnamese', *Bulletin*, 15 March 1983, p. 31.
12 *Newcastle Herald*, 21 January 1983, p. 1; 22 January 1983, p. 1; 10 February 1983, p. 1; *SMH*, 18 February 1983, p. 11.
13 Duncan, 'Our Isolated Vietnamese'.
14 *Liverpool-Fairfield Champion*, 16 May 1984, p. 1.
15 ibid., 7 December 1983, p. 4; 21 December 1983, pp. 1, 6; 18 January 1984, p. 9; 8 February 1984, p. 1.
16 Anne Blair, *Ruxton: A Biography*, Allen & Unwin, Crows Nest, 2004.
17 ibid., pp. 95, 97–9.
18 *Australian*, 5 March 1984, in Singer (ed.), *Immigration Debate*, p. 2.
19 Morag Fraser, 'The Media Game', in Deborah Gare, Geoffrey Bolton, Stuart Macintyre and Tom Stannage (eds), *The Fuss That Never Ended: The Life and Work of Geoffrey Blainey*, Melbourne University Press, Carlton, 2003, p. 149.
20 Andrew Markus, 'The Politics of Race', in Gare et al. (eds), *Fuss That Never Ended*, p. 113.
21 *Age*, 20 March 1984, in Singer (ed.), *Immigration Debate*, p. 4.
22 Geoffrey Blainey, *Our Side of the Country: The Story of Victoria*, Methuen Haynes, North Ryde, 1984, pp. 49–52 and *All for Australia*, Methuen Haynes, North Ryde, 1984, pp. 21–2.
23 *Age*, 19 March 1984, in Singer (ed.), *Immigration Debate*, p. 4; *Age*, 22 March 1984, p. 12; Blainey, *All for Australia*, p. 28.
24 *Age*, 19 and 20 March 1984, in Singer (ed.), *Immigration Debate*, pp. 4, 6.
25 Robert Birrell, 'Changing patterns', *Australian Society*, 1 October 1983, p. 18.
26 *Herald*, 3 April 1984, in Singer (ed.), *Immigration Debate*, p. 18.
27 Peter Shergold, 'Immigration Today: Fact and Fiction', in Frances Milne and Peter Shergold (eds), *The Great Immigration Debate*, Federation of Ethnic Communities' Councils of Australia, Sydney, Second Edition, 1984, p. 30 and Adrian Chan, 'The Mythology of Race', in Milne and Shergold (eds), *Great Immigration Debate*, p. 115.
28 *CT*, 17 May 1984, p. 2.

29 *Age*, 19 May 1984, pp. 1, 12.
30 Andrew Markus and M.C. Ricklefs (eds), *Surrender Australia? Essays in the Study and Uses of History: Geoffrey Blainey and Asian Immigration*, George Allen & Unwin, Sydney, 1985.
31 *Australian* and *Age*, 21 March 1984 and *AFR*, 7 May 1984 in Singer (ed.), *Immigration Debate*, pp. 8, 10, 24; Markus and Ricklefs (eds), *Surrender Australia?*.
32 Keith Simkin and John Nicholson, 'Concepts of Racism in Popular Discourse: The 1984 Immigration Controversy in Letters to the Editor', in Andrew Markus and Radha Rasmussen (eds), *Prejudice in the Public Arena: Racism*, Centre for Migrant and Intercultural Studies, Monash University, Clayton, 1987, pp. 45–55. For a list of such letters, see Markus and Ricklefs (eds), *Surrender Australia?*, pp. 133–42.
33 *Age*, 21 March 1984, p. 12.
34 *Sun*, 26 June 1984, p. 9.
35 *Age*, 27 March 1984, p. 12.
36 *Herald*, 27 April 1984, p. 6; *CPD*, H of R, vol. 138, 23 August 1984, p. 269.
37 *CPD*, H of R, vol. 137, 8 May 1984, p. 2008.
38 *CT*, 7 May 1984, in Singer (ed.), *Immigration Debate*, p. 25.
39 *CPD*, H of R, vol. 137, 8 May 1984, p. 2013.
40 *CPD*, H of R, vol. 138, 23 August 1984, p. 277.
41 James Curran and Stuart Ward, *The Unknown Nation: Australia after Empire*, Melbourne University Press, Carlton, 2010.
42 Blainey, *All for Australia*, p. 114.
43 *CPD*, H of R, vol. 137, 8 May 1984, pp. 2016–17.
44 *Age*, 10 May 1984, in Singer (ed.), *Immigration Debate*, p. 36.
45 *Age*, 12 May 1984, p. 10, in ibid., p. 43.
46 Ghassan Hage, *White Nation: Fantasies of White Supremacy in a Multicultural Society*, Pluto Press, Annandale, 1998.
47 *Australian*, 21 March 1984, in Singer (ed.), *Immigration Debate*, p. 10.
48 Kelly, *End of Certainty*, pp. 132–4.
49 *Age*, 12 July 1984, in Singer (ed.), *Immigration Debate*, p. 65.
50 *Age*, 19 October 1984, in ibid., p. 83.
51 *Age*, 10, 12 May 1984; *AFR*, 14 May 1984, in ibid., pp. 36, 43, 44.
52 *CPD*, H of R, vol. 137, 8 May 1984, p. 2026.
53 Blainey, *All for Australia*, pp. 31, 101–2, 138–41.
54 ibid., pp. 131–3.
55 *Herald*, 19 May 1984, pp. 1, 2; Murray Goot, 'Public Opinion and the Public Opinion Polls', in Markus and Ricklefs (eds), *Surrender Australia?*, pp. 56–7.
56 Bruce Stannard and Susan Molloy, 'Asians in Australia: More Harmony Than Hatred', *Bulletin*, 9 October 1984, p. 81.
57 ibid., p. 82.
58 *Liverpool-Fairfield Champion*, 27 June 1984, p. 5.
59 *Sydney Morning Herald*, 27 August 2014, www.smh.com.au/federal-politics/political-news/paul-keating-gives-blistering-critique-of-bob-hawke-20140827-1093n7.html, accessed 31 August 2014.
60 Pal Ahluwalia and Greg McCarthy, 'The Politics of Intimacy: A Conversation with Bob Hawke', in Gerry Bloustein, Barbara Comber and Alison Mackinnon (eds), *The Hawke Legacy*, Wakefield Press, Kent Town, 2009, pp. 21–2.
61 *Land Rights News*, September 1985, p. 4.
62 Ronald T. Libby, *Hawke's Law: The Politics of Mining and Aboriginal Land Rights in Australia*, University of Western Australia Press, Nedlands, 1989, p. 16.

63 Beresford, *Godfather*, pp. 75–84.
64 Murray Goot and Tim Rowse, *Divided Nation? Indigenous Affairs and the Imagined Public*, Melbourne University Press, Carlton, 2007, p. 70.
65 Libby, *Hawke's Law*, pp. 56–60.
66 Hugh Morgan, 'Religious Traditions, Mining and Land Rights', in Ken Baker (ed.), *The Land Rights Debate: Selected Documents*, Institute of Public Affairs, Melbourne, 1985, pp. 22–6; Libby, *Hawke's Law*, p. 60.
67 Gerard Henderson, *Australian Answers*, Random House Australia, Sydney, 1990, p. 243.
68 Both Clyde Holding, the minister for Aboriginal affairs, and Barry Cohen, the minister for home affairs and the environment, were present.
69 Libby, *Hawke's Law*, pp. 76–7.
70 Andrew Markus, *Race: John Howard and the Remaking of Australia*, Allen & Unwin, Crows Nest, 2001, p. 118.
71 Tim Duncan, 'The State of the Debate', in Baker (ed.), *Land Rights Debate*, p. 3.
72 *Kaniva Times & Nhill Free Press*, 6 September 1983, p. 1; 20 September 1983, p. 1; 4 October 1983, p. 3.
73 Goot and Rowse, *Divided Nation?*, pp. 85–96.
74 Libby, *Hawke's Law*, pp. 80–1.
75 Cabinet Minute 24 September 1984, Cabinet Submission 1039 – National Aboriginal Land Rights – Decision 4391, NAA: A13977/1039.
76 Libby, *Hawke's Law*, pp. 107–9.
77 Quentin Beresford, *Rob Riley: An Aboriginal Leader's Quest for Justice*, Aboriginal Studies Press, Canberra, 2006, p. 191.
78 Evans, *Inside the Hawke–Keating Government*, p. 34.
79 ibid., pp. 35, 39, 57, 167.
80 Beresford, *Rob Riley*, p. 190.
81 Western Australia, *Hansard*, Legislative Assembly, 26 March 1985, p. 1342; 27 March 1985, pp. 1420–1, 1443.
82 ibid., 26 March 1985, p. 1337; 27 March 1984, pp. 1424, 1429. See also David Barnett, 'New Land Rights Plan Creates Australian Apartheid', *Bulletin*, 12 March 1985, pp. 26–30. This claim also featured on the magazine's cover, so the message would have been received by many who never read the *Bulletin*. The article was mentioned approvingly in the WA debate by an opponent of the land rights bill. See also Howard Jacobson, *In the Land of Oz*, Hamish Hamilton, London, 1987, p. 68.
83 Western Australia, *Hansard*, Legislative Assembly, 26 March 1985, p. 1336; 27 March 1985, pp. 1958–9.
84 ibid., 26 March 1985, p. 1355.
85 ibid., p. 1362.
86 ibid., 27 March 1985, pp. 1422, 1958, 1969.
87 ibid., 26 March 1985, pp. 1346, 1349.
88 Mungo MacCallum, 'Backtracking on Blacks', *Matilda*, May 1985, p. 27.
89 *CT*, 14 May 1985, p. 1; 16 May 1985, p. 1; 17 May 1985, p. 3; *Land Rights News*, no. 34, August 1985, pp. 4–5, 7; Beresford, *Rob Riley*, pp. 189–90.
90 Libby, *Hawke's Law*, pp. 7, 113–14.
91 *Land Rights News*, no. 34, August 1985, p. 10.
92 ibid., p. 12.
93 ibid., p. 4.
94 Ruby Langford, *Don't Take Your Love to Town*, Penguin Books, Ringwood, 1988, p. 234.

95 Ann McGrath, quoted in Roslynn D. Haynes, *Seeking the Centre: The Australian Desert in Literature, Art and Film*, Cambridge University Press, Cambridge, 1998, p. 265.
96 Denis O'Brien, *The Bicentennial Affair: The Inside Story of Australia's 'Birthday Bash'*, ABC, Crows Nest, 1991, pp. 123–5; Phil Jarratt, 'True Blue Goes to Uluru', *Bulletin*, 16 December 1986, p. 33.
97 Michael Chamberlain, *Heart of Stone: Justice for Azaria*, New Holland, London, 2012, p. 30.
98 Ken Crispin, *The Crown versus Chamberlain: 1980–1987*, Albatross Books, Sutherland, 1987; Dianne Johnson, 'From Fairy to Witch: Imagery and Myth in the Azaria Case', in Deborah Staines, Michelle Arrow and Katherine Biber (eds), *The Chamberlain Case: Nation, Law, Memory*, Australian Scholarly Publishing, North Melbourne, 2009, pp. 7–20.
99 Graham Seal, 'Dread, Delusion and Globalisation: From Azaria to Schapelle', in Staines, Arrow and Biber (eds), *Chamberlain Case*, p. 83.
100 Johnson, 'From Fairy to Witch', pp. 14–15.
101 Haynes, *Seeking the Centre*, p. xi.
102 Crispin, *Crown versus Chamberlain*, p. 16.
103 *Australian*, 23 October 1985, p. 10.
104 Robert Langton, *Uluru: An Aboriginal History of Ayers Rock*, Aboriginal Studies Press, Canberra, 1989, pp. 80, 88, 93–4, 105, 108–9, 117–18.
105 *Northern Territory News*, 2 October 1985, p. 1; 10 October 1985, p. 6.
106 *Australian*, 8 October 1985, p. 9.
107 ibid., 28 October 1985, p. 1.
108 *Herald*, 21 May 1984, p. 4.
109 Western Australia, *Hansard*, Legislative Assembly, 26 March 1985, p. 1385.
110 Megalogenis, *Australian Moment*, p. 120.

Chapter 4: Power and Passion

1 The foregoing discussion depends on: James Norman, *Bob Brown: Gentle Revolutionary*, Allen & Unwin, Crows Nest, 2004, *passim*; Peter Thompson, *Bob Brown of the Franklin River*, George Allen & Unwin, North Sydney, 1984, esp. pp. 166–74; Lenore Nicklin, 'With the Greenie Guerrillas on the Franklin Front', *Bulletin*, 1 February 1983, pp. 36–42; Ian Terry, 'A Matter of Values: Stories from the Franklin River Blockade, 1982–83', *Papers and Proceedings: Tasmanian Historical Research Association*, vol. 60, no. 1, April 2013, p. 55; Stefan Petrow, 'Saving Tasmania?: The Anti-Transportation and Franklin River Campaigns', *Tasmanian Historical Studies*, vol. 14, 2009, esp. pp. 111, 115, 121.
2 Keith Scott, *Gareth Evans*, Allen & Unwin, St Leonards, pp. 120–3.
3 Martin Clark, interview with Michael Black, transcript, p. 7, http://blogs.unimelb.edu.au/opinionsonhigh/files/2013/07/Remembering-Tasmanian-Dams-Interview-Transcripts2.pdf, accessed 17 January 2015.
4 Quoted in Norman, *Bob Brown*, p. 105.
5 Paul Dibb, *The Nuclear War Scare of 1983: How Serious Was It?*, Special Report, Australian Strategic Policy Institute, Canberra, October 1983, p. 2.
6 Jim Falk, *Taking Australia Off the Map – Facing the Threat of Nuclear War*, William Heinemann Australia, Melbourne, 1983, p. 54.
7 Dibb, *Nuclear War Scare*.
8 Desmond Ball, *A Suitable Piece of Real Estate: American Installations in Australia*, Hale & Iremonger, Sydney, 1980, esp. ch. 16.

9   'A Preliminary Appraisal of the Effects on Australia of a Nuclear War', Office of National Assessments, December 1980, NAA: A10756, LC5130.
10 Desmond Ball and R.H. Mathams, 'The Nuclear Threat to Australia', in Michael Denborough (ed.), *Australia and Nuclear War*, Croom Helm Australia, Fyshwick (ACT), 1983, pp. 38–54.
11 ibid.
12 J.A. Ward, 'Can We Survive a Nuclear Attack Upon Australia?', in Denborough (ed.), *Australia and Nuclear War*, p. 101.
13 Falk, *Taking Australia*, p. 14.
14 Christopher Forsyth, *Can Australia Survive World War III?* Rigby, Adelaide, 1984.
15 *Australian*, 28 March 1983, p. 1; *Age*, 28 March 1983, p. 1; 16 April 1984, p. 5; 1 April 1985, p. 1; *SMH*, 28 March 1983, p. 3; *Courier-Mail*, 28 March 1983, p. 3; 16 April 1984, p. 3; *Advertiser* (Adelaide), 1 April 1985, p. 1.
16 *Australian*, 28 March 1983, p. 1; 16 April 1984, pp. 1–2; *Age*, 28 March 1983, p. 1; *Advertiser*, 28 March 1983, p. 3; *SMH*, 16 April 1984, pp. 1–2.
17 Hayden, *Hayden*, p. 383.
18 ibid., pp. 339–41.
19 Ashley Lavelle, '"Conflicts of Loyalty": The Australian Labor Party and Uranium Policy, 1976–82', *Labour History*, no. 102, May 2012, p. 184; Cabinet Minute, 31 October 1983, decision no. 2353, Attachment B, NAA: A13977, 385.
20 Cabinet Minute, 31 October 1983, decision no. 2353, NAA: A13977, 385; *CT*, 4 November 1983, p. 1.
21 ALP, Federal Caucus, Special Meeting, Minutes, 7 November 1983, Bob Hawke Prime Ministerial Library.
22 *CT*, 11 July 1984, p. 1; Greg Adamson, *Stop Uranium Mining: Australia's Decade of Protest 1975–85*, Resistance Books, Chippendale, 1999, p. 37.
23 ALP National Conference, Transcript, 10 July 1984, pp. 333, 283, 292–3, 264, 340, 339–40.
24 ibid., p. 294–5.
25 *CT*, 11 July 1984, p. 1.
26 ALP National Conference, Transcript, 11 July 1984, pp. 418, 422, 460; *CT*, 12 July 1984, pp. 1, 9.
27 *CT*, 18 June 1984, p. 3.
28 Gillian Fisher, *Half-Life: The NDP: Peace, Protest and Party Politics*, State Library of New South Wales Press, Sydney, 1995, pp. 10–15.
29 Ian McFarlane, *The Encyclopedia of Australian Rock and Pop*, Allen & Unwin, St Leonards, 1999, pp. 410–11; John O'Donnell, Toby Creswell and Craig Mathieson, *The 100 Best Australian Albums*, Hardie Grant Books, Prahran, 2010, pp. 84–7.
30 Toby Creswell and Martin Fabinyi, *The Real Thing: 1957 – Now: Adventures in Australian Rock & Roll*, Random House, Milsons Point, 1999, p. 137.
31 Fisher, *Half-Life*, p. 14.
32 *Royal Commission on the Activities of the Federated Ship Painters and Dockers Union, Final Report*, vol. 1, pp. 4–5.
33 ibid., vol. 3, pp. 15, 27.
34 Paul Barry, *The Rise and Rise of Kerry Packer Uncut*, Bantam, North Sydney, 2007, pp. 264–5; Brian Toohey, 'Costigan: More Extracts and a Special Sitting', *National Times*, 21–27 September 1984, p. 17.
35 Evans, *Inside the Hawke–Keating Government*, pp. 4–5.

36 Geoff Kitney, 'Costigan set to drop another bombshell into Canberra', *National Times*, 7–13 September 1984, pp. 6–7.
37 'Some Cases from Costigan's Files', *National Times*, 14–20 September 1984, pp. 4–6.
38 Barry, *Rise and Rise of Kerry Packer Uncut*, p. 270.
39 Evans, *Inside the Hawke–Keating Government*, p. 5.
40 Barry, *Rise and Rise of Kerry Packer Uncut*, p. 313.
41 Rodney Tiffen, *Scandals: Media, Politics & Corruption in Contemporary Australia*, University of New South Wales Press, Sydney, 1999, pp. 131, 187.
42 Jonathan Holmes, 'Recollections of a Cutting-Room Technician', in Sally Neighbour (ed.), *The Stories That Changed Australia: 50 Years of Four Corners*, ABC Books/HarperCollins, Sydney, 2012, pp. 87–8.
43 *Daily Mirror*, 2 May 1983, pp. 1–2; *SMH*, 11 May 1983, p. 1.
44 Evan Whitton, *Can of Worms II*, The Fairfax Library, Broadway (NSW), 1987, pp. 293–5; *SMH*, 2 January 2012, www.smh.com.au/nsw/time-runs-out-for-disgraced-prisons-minister-20120101-1ph9s.html, accessed 3 January 2015.
45 Chris Masters, 'The Big Dig', in Neighbour (ed.), *Stories*, pp. 111–12.
46 Gillian Appleton, *Diamond Cuts: An Affectionate Memoir of Jim McClelland*, Macmillan, Sydney, 2000, p. 217.
47 *Age*, 2 February 1984, p. 1.
48 Garry Sturgess, 'Murphy and the Media' and A.R. Blackshield, 'The "Murphy Affair"', in Jocelynne A. Scutt (ed.), *Lionel Murphy: A Radical Judge*, McCulloch Publishing in association with the Macmillan Company of Australia, Melbourne, 1987, pp. 211–229 and 230–40.
49 Jenny Hocking, *Lionel Murphy: A Political Biography*, Cambridge University Press, Cambridge, 1997, p. 290.
50 Wendy Bacon, 'Behind the Murphy Affair', *National Times*, 31 August–6 September 1984, p. 6.
51 Nick Dyrenfurth, *Mateship: A Very Australian History*, Scribe, Melbourne and London, 2015.
52 *CPD*, H of R, 13 September 1984, p. 1255.
53 Blackshield, 'The "Murphy Affair"', pp. 246–9.
54 Evans, *Inside the Hawke–Keating Government*, pp. 317–18; Hocking, *Lionel Murphy*, p. 303.
55 Evans, *Inside the Hawke–Keating Government*, p. 323.
56 ibid., p. 363.
57 Blackshield, 'The "Murphy Affair"', p. 256.
58 Appleton, *Diamond Cuts*, pp. 221–5.
59 ibid., p. 227; *SMH*, 28 October 1986, p. 2.
60 *CPD*, H of R, 13 September 1984, p. 1252.
61 Geoff Kitney, 'Where Hawke Is Vulnerable', *National Times*, 21–27 September 1984, pp. 7–9 and 'Hawke Bear-Trapped Following Wran Train', *National Times*, 7–13 September 1984, pp. 3–4.
62 *SMH*, 21 September 1984, p. 4.
63 Brian Toohey, 'How Judge Foord Upheld Sue Hawke's Appeal', *National Times*, 31 August 1984–6 September 1984, p. 8.
64 *SMH*, 21 September 1984, p. 4.
65 ibid., 22 September 1984, p. 1.
66 Tom Skotnicki, 'Victims of Success', *BRW*, 26 July 1985, pp. 36–47; *SMH*, 17 March 1985, p. 5; 10 June 1986, p. 17.

67	Paul Sendziuk, *Learning to Trust: Australian Responses to AIDS*, University of New South Wales Press, Sydney, 2003, ch. 7.
68	James Button, *Speechless: A Year in My Father's Business*, Melbourne University Press, Carlton, 2012, pp. 191–2, 198.
69	Creswell and Fabinyi, *Real Thing*, p. 146.
70	*New Musical Express*, 13 August 1988, p. 3.
71	Andrew McMillen, *Talking Smack: Honest Conversations About Drugs*, University of Queensland Press, St Lucia, 2014, pp. 11–16.
72	Paul Kelly, *How to Make Gravy*, Hamish Hamilton, Melbourne, 2011, p. 79–80.
73	Toni Makkai and Ian McAllister, *Patterns of Drug Use in Australian Society: An Analysis of National Trend Data 1985–91*, Australian Government Publishing Service, Canberra, 1993, pp. 33–8.
74	Nikki McWatters, *One Way or Another: The Story of a Girl Who Loved Rock Stars*, Black Inc., Collingwood, 2012, pp. 188–9.
75	Wayne Hall, 'The Demand for Methadone Maintenance Treatment in Australia', Technical Report no. 28, National Drug and Alcohol Research Centre, University of New South Wales, 1995, p. 8, http://ndarc.med.unsw.edu.au/resource/demand-methadone-maintenance-treatment-australia, accessed 4 January 2015.
76	Makkai and McAllister, *Patterns of Drug Use*, pp. ix, 3–4, 45–8.
77	*Illicit Drugs in Australia: Situation Report 1988*, p. 28.
78	Maggie Brady, *Heavy Metal: The Social Meaning of Petrol Sniffing in Australia*, Aboriginal Studies Press, Canberra, 1992, pp. 11–16, 27–34, 150–1.
79	Louis Nowra, *Kings Cross*, NewSouth, Sydney, 2013, pp. 390–9.
80	Ian Tyrell, *Deadly Enemies: Tobacco and Its Opponents in Australia*, University of New South Wales Press, Sydney, 1999, pp. 193–6.
81	*Year Book Australia 1990*, pp. 266–7.
82	Tyrell, *Deadly Enemies*, p. 201.
83	Administrative and Clerical Officers Association, *Clearing the Air: Smoking in the Workplace: A Manual for ACOA Delegates*, ACOA, Sydney, 1985, p. 3.
84	Tyrell, *Deadly Enemies*, p. 205; *CT*, 3 September 1986, p. 1; 28 February 1987, p. 11; 3 March 1987, p. 3.
85	*CT*, 2 March 1988, p. 1.
86	Makkai and McAllister, *Patterns of Drug Use*, pp. 16–24.
87	*SMH*, 21 September 1984, p. 4.
88	*Age*, 21 September 1984, p. 1.
89	*SMH*, 21 September 1984, p. 1; *Age*, 21 September 1984, p. 1.
90	*Australian*, 21 September 1984, p. 1.
91	*Age*, 23 September 1983, p. 13; 21 September 1984, p. 1.
92	Staley to Hawke, 3 October 1984, Series RH 14/Box 1, F9, Bob Hawke Papers, Bob Hawke Prime Ministerial Library.
93	Dawkins to Hawke, 25 September [1984]; Leslie to Bob and Hazel Hawke, 26 September 1984, ibid.
94	*Weekend Australian*, 22–23 November 1984, p. 4.
95	Graham Little, 'Hawke in Trouble', *Meanjin*, vol. 44, no. 3, September 1985, p. 291.
96	Fox to Hawke, 25 September 1984, Series RH 14/Box 1, F9, Bob Hawke Papers, Bob Hawke Prime Ministerial Library.
97	Christian Ryan, *Golden Boy: Kim Hughes and the Bad Old Days of Australian Cricket*, Allen & Unwin, Crows Nest, 2009, chs 13–14.
98	ibid.

99   ibid., p. 244; *Australian*, 27 November 1984, p. 1.
100 Ryan, *Golden Boy*, pp. 246, 254; *CT*, 2 December 1984, p. 2; *Daily Express*, 27 November 1984, pp. 8–9; *Guardian*, 28 November 1984, p. 1; *Australian*, 27 November 1984, p. 1.
101 *Guardian*, 27 November 1984, p. 21.
102 Brooks to Hawke, 3 September 1984 (no. 133), NLA MS 4985, 84/2/22, Box 451.
103 'Campaign Director's Report 1984 Federal Election: Draft for Consideration by National Campaign Executive', 1984, Bob Hawke Papers, RH18/2/F46, Box 2, Bob Hawke Prime Ministerial Library.
104 Bill Kerr, 'The Politics of the NDP Split', *Arena*, no. 72, 1985, pp. 51–6; Fisher, *Half-Life*, pp. 56–81.
105 Robert W. Baring (Sec., Ocean Grove Branch) to Bob McMullan, n.d. [Dec. 1984] (no. 3.), NLA MS 4985, 84/2/22, Box 451.
106 Gerald Hensley, *Friendly Fire: Nuclear Politics & the Collapse of ANZUS, 1984–1987*, Auckland University Press, Auckland, 2013, pp. 86–115, 134, 137.
107 ibid., pp. 29–30, 43, 66, 123, 186–7.
108 ibid., pp. 156, 193.
109 Peter Garrett, *Political Blues*, Hodder and Stoughton, Sydney and Auckland, 1987, p. 62.
110 Hensley, *Friendly Fire*, p. 46.
111 Marian Wilkinson, 'Hawke Takes Lange to Task on ANZUS', *National Times*, 25–31 January 1985, p. 5.
112 *CT*, 29 January 1985, p. 1; 30 January 1985, p. 3; 31 January 1985, p. 1.
113 'Record of Conversation', Hayden and Lange, 26 September 1984, UN New York, NAA: A1838/336, 370/1/20, Part 21.
114 Peter Batchelor, Telex, 15 March 1985, NLA MS 4985, 1984/2/51, Box 522.
115 *Australian*, 1 April 1985, p. 3; *Age*, 1 April 1985, p. 1.
116 Falk, *Taking Australia*, pp. 47, 52–4, 57, 109, 169, 218, 234–5.
117 Geoff Kitney, 'The Treaty Trembles: Hawke's Humiliation Signals the End of an Era', *National Times*, 8–14 February 1985, pp. 1, 3.
118 Geoff Kitney, 'Why Bob Hawke Will Have To Say No', *National Times*, 1–7 February 1985, pp. 3, 7.
119 *Australian*, 6 February 1985, 2.
120 NLA MS 4985, 1984/2/51, Box 522.
121 *The Report of the Royal Commission into British Nuclear Tests in Australia*, 1985, vol. 1, p. 11.
122 Turner, *Making It National*, pp. 57–61.
123 Paul Charman, 'Judge's Dread', *Time Out*, 21–27 March 1985, p. 9; Mungo MacCallum, 'Diamond Jim ... A Larger-Than-Life Legend', *Matilda*, November 1985, p. 37.
124 *Report of the Royal Commission into British Nuclear Tests*, vol. 1, pp. 308–9.
125 'Maralinga (Rainy Land)', in Paul Kelly, *Don't Start Me Talking: Lyrics 1984–2012*, Allen & Unwin, Sydney, p. 36.
126 Dieter Michel, 'Villains, Victims and Heroes: Contested Memory and the British Nuclear Tests in Australia', *Journal of Australian Studies*, vol. 27, no. 80, 2004, pp. 221–8.

Chapter 5: The Deal-Makers

1   Hugh Stretton, 'The Cult of Selfishness', in *Political Essays*, Georgian House, Melbourne, p. 189.

2   *BRW*, 12–18 November 1983, p. 24.
3   Ostrow, *The New Boy Network*.
4   *BRW*, 12–18 November 1983, 18–24 August 1984.
5   Deborah Light, Michael Meagher and Alan Deans, 'Road to Riches: The Holmes à Court Story Part 4', *BRW* 26 September 1986, p. 53.
6   *BRW*, 16 August 1985.
7   Robert Gottliebsen, 'The Takeover Revolution', *Australian Way*, January 1987, pp. 6–15.
8   *BRW*, 15 August 1986, p. 151.
9   ibid., p. 78.
10 *CT*, 6 September 1985, p. 3; *Time Magazine*, 16 September 1985, p. 74, *The Times*, 6 May 1985, p. 4; *NYT*, 16 May 1985, p. A31.
11 Evans, *Inside the Hawke–Keating Government*, p. 379.
12 Brian Toohey, 'Fairfax and the New Establishment', *Eye*, October 1987, pp. 12–14.
13 Paul Chadwick, *Media Mates: Carving Up Australia's Media*, Macmillan, South Melbourne and Crows Nest, 1989, ch. 1.
14 John McManamy, *Crash! Corporate Australia Fights for Its Life*, Pan Books, Sydney and London, 1988, pp. 82–4.
15 Chadwick, *Media Mates*, chs. 1–2; Evans, *Inside the Hawke–Keating Government*, pp. 234–5, 237–41; Alan Ramsey, 'Media Blowup Begins', *Time Australia*, 8 December 1986, pp. 36–41.
16 Lawrence Van der Plaat, *Too Good to Be True: Inside the Corrupt World of Christopher Skase*, Macmillan, Sydney, 1996, p. 65.
17 Tom Prior, *Christopher Skase: Beyond the Mirage*, Information Australia, Melbourne, 1994, pp. 93–5; Sykes, *Bold Riders*, p. 305.
18 *BRW*, 15 August 1986, p. 135; 2 September 1988, p. 141; *SMH*, 14 November 1987, pp. 81, 84; Catherine Ann Hoyte, 'An Australian Mirage', PhD Thesis, Griffith University, 2003, p. 359.
19 *Sunday Age*, 19 November 1989, Agenda, p. 2.
20 Van der Plaat, *Too Good to be True*, p. 40–1.
21 Prior, *Christopher Skase*, p. 87.
22 *Weekend Herald*, 28–29 December 1985, p. 11.
23 *Herald*, 26 December 1986, p. 2. For Skase's parties, see also Prior, *Christopher Skase*, pp. 83–91.
24 *BRW*, 14 August 1987, p. 44.
25 *SMH*, 29 August 1985, pp. 15, 17; 7 April 1986, p. 26; 9 April 1986, p. 39; 1 May 1986, p. 19; 5 May 1986, p. 29; 1 June 1986, p. 24; 17 June 1986, p. 25; 24 June 1986, p. 27; 4 July 1986, p. 17; 22 August 1986, p. 21; 16 October 1986, p. 27; Barry, *Rise and Fall of Alan Bond*, pp. 168–79.
26 Sykes, *Bold Riders*, pp. 208–9.
27 *BRW*, 14 August 1987, p. 42.
28 ibid., p. 6.
29 Hoyte, 'Mirage', p. 61.
30 *BRW*, 14 August 1987, p. 6.
31 Don Stammer, 'Picking the End of the Boom', *BRW*, 14 August 1987, pp. 24–25.
32 James Belich, *Replenishing the Earth: The Settler Revolution and the Rise of the Anglo-World, 1783–1939*, Oxford University Press, Oxford and New York, 2009.
33 *BRW*, 14 August 1987, p. 42.

ENDNOTES

34 Michael Cannon, *The Land Boomers*, Melbourne University Press, Melbourne, 1966.
35 *Eye*, August 1987, p. 12.
36 David Meredith and Barrie Dyster, *Australia in the Global Economy: Continuity and Change*, Cambridge University Press, Cambridge, 1999, pp. 244, 249.
37 Sykes, *Bold Riders*, p. 445.
38 McManamy, *Crash!*, p. 5.
39 *SMH*, 5 January 1987, p. 9.
40 *SMH*, 19 October 1985, p. 12.
41 *Weekend Australian*, 19–20 February 1983, p. 18; Peter Denton, *Elliott: A Biography of John D. Elliott*, Little Hills Press, London and Sydney, 1987, chs 1–4.
42 Denton, *Elliott*, chs 5–8; Peter Thompson and Robert Macklin, *The Big Fella: The Rise and Rise of BHP Billiton*, William Heinemann, North Sydney, 2009, p. 128.
43 'How King John Saved the Throne', *BRW*, 17 December 1983–6 January 1984, pp. 11, 15.
44 *AFR*, 12 December 1983, p. 48.
45 *SMH*, 30 July 1987, p. 15.
46 *CT*, 31 October 1987, p. 3.
47 David Marr, 'Thunder on the Right', *National Times*, 22–28 June 1984, p. 16.
48 *Australian*, 17 April 1973, p. 9.
49 *SMH*, 12 November 1984, p. 7.
50 *Age*, 16 October 1986, p. 24; 27 February 1987, p. 5; 10 September 1988, Saturday Extra, pp. 1–2; *Weekend Australian*, 18–19 April 1987, pp. 9, 11; *AFR*, 7 May 1987, p. 3; 24 July 1987, p. 5; *SMH*, 9 May 1987, pp. 41, 44; 20 July 1987, p. 3; *Courier-Mail*, 28 July 1987, p. 9.
51 *BRW*, 14 August 1987, p. 42; Thompson and Macklin, *Big Fella*, p. 127.
52 David Uren, 'Takeovers on the High Seas: The Corporate Raiders', *Australian Left Review*, no. 96, Winter, 1986, p. 7.
53 Gideon Haigh, *The Battle for BHP*, Information Australia with Allen & Unwin Australia, Melbourne, 1987, pp. 33, 36.
54 Evans, *Inside the Hawke–Keating Government*, pp. 296–7.
55 Haigh, *Battle for BHP*, pp. 17–20.
56 Hugh Mackay, *The Mackay Report: Big Business*, July 1985, pp. 17–18, 38.
57 Haigh, *Battle for BHP*, p. 1.
58 Thompson and Macklin, *Big Fella*, pp. 139–40; Evans, *Inside the Hawke–Keating Government*, pp. 277, 282–3.
59 Brian Toohey, 'The Death of Labor', *Eye*, July 1987, p. 10.
60 Denton, *Elliott*, ch. 16; Thompson and Macklin, *Big Fella*, pp. 128–38.
61 Haigh, *Battle for BHP*, p. 75; Thompson and Macklin, *Big Fella*, pp. 141–6; Denton, *Elliott*, ch. 16.
62 Haigh, *Battle for BHP*, p. 86; *SMH*, 5 January 1987, p. 9.
63 Patricia Edgar, *Janet Holmes Court*, HarperCollins, Sydney, 1999, p. 193.
64 Barry, *Rise and Fall of Alan Bond*, p. 164–5.
65 Geoff Kitney, 'Brewers shape up for battle of the beers', *Times on Sunday*, 7 September 1986, p. 18.
66 Barry, *Rise and Fall of Alan Bond*, pp. 166–7.
67 Edna Carew, *Westpac: The Bank that Broke the Bank*, Doubleday, Sydney, 1997.
68 Maureen Murrill and Laura Tingle, 'High Performance Knocks Out Old Rules', *BRW*, 30 May 1986, p. 46.
69 Sykes, *Bold Riders*, ch. 8; Carew, *Westpac*, pp. 196–204.

70 V.J. Carroll, *The Man Who Couldn't Wait*, William Heinemann, Port Melbourne, 1990, pp. 124–5, 11.
71 ibid., p. 284.
72 Sykes, *Bold Riders*, ch. 13.
73 ibid., pp. 450, 444; Robert Murray and Kate White, *A Bank for the People: A History of the State Bank of Victoria*, Hargreen Publishing Company, North Melbourne, 1992; Hugo Armstrong and Dick Gross, *Tricontinental : The Rise and Fall of a Merchant Bank*, Melbourne University Press, Carlton, 1995, pp. 88–9.
74 Martin Thomas, *The Fraud: Behind the Mystery of John Friedrich, Australia's Greatest Conman*, Pagemasters, Richmond (Vic.), 1991.
75 *Courier-Mail*, 30 March 1989, p. 9.
76 Sykes, *Bold Riders*, p. 260.
77 *Age*, 28 March 1989, pp. 1, 4; Thomas, *Fraud*, pp. 16, 34–5, 48, 68, 73, 76–8, 139, 156; John Friedrich with Richard Flanagan, *Codename Iago: The Story of John Friedrich by John Friedrich*, William Heinemann Australia, Port Melbourne, 1991, pp. 114, 158; Sykes, *Bold Riders*, pp. 249–50.
78 Friedrich, *Codename Iago*, pp. 150, 153, 246–56; Murray and White, *Bank for the People*, p. 453; Thomas, *Fraud*, p. 57.
79 *Courier-Mail*, 1 May 1983, pp. 1, 3; *Weekend Australian*, 7–8 January 1989, p. 3.
80 *BRW*, 15 August 1986, p. 50.
81 Hoyte, 'Mirage', p. 49.
82 Uren, 'Takeovers', p. 9.
83 *Australian*, 4 December 1983, p. 19.
84 *Age*, 29 September 1991, Money, p. 1; *AFR*, 8 February 1990, pp. 1–2; *Australian*, 4 December 1983, p. 19.
85 *CT*, 13 November 1989, p. 14.
86 ibid.; *Weekend Australian*, 14–15 September 1991, p. 1; 18–19 December 1993, pp. 18–19; *Age*, 29 September 1991, Money, p. 1; *Australian*, 8 February 1990, p. 2; *AFR*, 8 February 1990, pp. 1–2; *Australian*, 30 April 1989, p. 10; Sykes, *Bold Riders*, pp. 564–5.
87 *Australian*, 30 April 1989, p. 10; *CT*, 13 November 1989, p. 14.
88 *Australian*, 14–15 September 1991, p. 1.
89 *Weekend Australian*, 18–19 December 1993, pp. 18–19; *Age*, 14 January 1992, p. 23; Sykes, *Bold Riders*, p. 565.
90 Mackay, *Big Business*, pp. 38, 26, 30.
91 Anne Coombs, *Adland: A True Story of Corporate Drama*, William Heinemann Australia, Port Melbourne, 1990, pp. 264–6.
92 *SMH*, 24 October 1987, p. 67.
93 ibid.; Keith Dunstan et al., 'Big Spenders: The Changing Tastes of Our Rich', *BRW*, 19 December 1986, pp. 44–51; Sally Loane, 'Mega Homes', *National Times*, 21–27 February 1986, pp. 14–15.
94 Dunstan et al., 'Big Spenders', p. 47; Loane, 'Mega Homes', p. 15.
95 Bruce Stannard, 'At Sea with Australia's Boating Barons', *Bulletin*, 31 January 1984, pp. 33–8.
96 *SMH*, 24 October 1987, p. 67.
97 Ostrow, *New Boy Network*, pp. 30–1.
98 *SMH*, 24 October 1987, p. 67.
99 Paul Barry, *Going for Broke*, Bantam Books, Sydney, 2000, pp. 25–31 and *The Rise and Rise of Kerry Packer Uncut*, pp. 529–31.
100 Dunstan et al., 'Big Spenders', pp. 47, 51; *SMH*, 31 October 1987, p. 73.

ENDNOTES 333

101 Ian Heads and David Middleton, *A Centenary of Rugby League 1908–2008: The Definitive Story of the Game in Australia*, Pan Macmillan, Sydney, 2008, pp. 439–500.
102 Dave Nadel, 'Colour, Corporations and Commissioners, 1976–1985', in Rob Hess and Bob Stewart (eds), *More Than A Game: An Unauthorised History of Australian Rules Football*, Melbourne University Press, Carlton South, 1998, pp. 200–24.
103 Ian Andrews, 'From a Club to a Corporate Game: The Changing Face of Australian Football 1960–1999', *International Journal of the History of Sport*, vol. 17, nos 2–3, p. 238.
104 John Elliott, *Big Jack: My Sporting Life*, Schwartz & Melbourne Books, Melbourne, 2003, pp. 42–9.
105 Kerrie Gordon and Alan Dalton, *Too Tough to Die: Footscray's Fightback 1989*, Flett, Henderson & Arnold [Printers], Abbotsford, 1990, p. 138; Dave Nadel, 'The League Goes National, 1986–1997', in Hess and Stewart (eds), *More Than A Game*, p. 233–4.
106 *National Times*, 24–30 May 1985, pp. 3–4.
107 *SMH*, 10 January 1985, p. 3.
108 *Age*, 10 January 1985, p. 20.
109 *SMH*, 10 January 1985, p. 3; *Sunday Telegraph*, 27 July 1986, p. 8.
110 *CT*, 6 July 1986, p. 7.
111 *Woman's Day*, 26 July 1988, p. 16.
112 *Age*, 1 August 1985, p. 1.
113 Kevin Taylor, *The Sydney Swans: The Complete History 1874–1986*, Allen & Unwin Australia, North Sydney, 1987, p. 141.
114 Glennys Bell, 'Edelsten Hopes It's Only Au Revoir', *Bulletin*, 15 July 1986, pp. 28–9.
115 *CT*, 12 September 1985, p. 1.
116 *SMH*, 14 September 1985, p. 36; Kate Beauchamp, 'Australian Sport Gets a Godfather', *Matilda*, no. 7, September 1985, pp. 27–9.
117 *SMH*, 27 August 1986, pp. 1, 6.
118 *Courier-Mail*, 28 September 1987, p. 1.
119 Geoffrey Edelsten, *Enigma*, New Holland, Sydney, 2012.
120 *Herald*, 26 September 1986, p. 1.
121 *Weekend Herald*, 27–28 September 1986, p. 2; personal observation by author.
122 *Sun*, 29 September 1986, p. 68; *Herald*, 29 September 1986, p. 24 and Grand Final Supplement, p. 2; Lionel Frost, *The Old Dark Navy Blues: A History of the Carlton Football Club*, Allen & Unwin, St Leonards, 1998, p. 173.
123 *Sun*, 29 September 1986, pp. 55; *Herald*, 29 September 1986, Grand Final Supplement, p. 2.
124 Cabinet Minute, 15 May 1984, Decision no. 3242, 'Without Submission – Purchase of Australia II and America's Cup Defence', NAA: A13979, 3242; Cabinet Minute 3 June 1985, Decision no. 6117, 'America's Cup – Customs Duty and Sales Tax Aspects' and 'Income Tax Deductibility for Public Donations to America's Cup Defence Campaign Funds', NAA: A14039, 2794.
125 *West Australian*, 21 January 1987, p. 3.
126 ibid., 21 January 1987, p. 1.
127 ibid., 29 January 1987, p. 15; 30 January 1987, p. 18; 2 February 1987, p. 3; 3 February 1987, pp. 1, 4; John Selwood and Elaine McEwon, 'Hedonists, Ladies and Larrikins: Crime, Prostitution and the 1987 America's Cup', *Visions in Leisure and Business*, vol. 14, no. 3, 1995, pp. 28–51.

128   *West Australian*, 5 February 1987, pp. 2–3.
129   ibid., 31 January 1987, p. 1.

Chapter 6: Taking Credit

1   George Turner, *The Sea and Summer*, Grafton Books, London 1989 [1987], p. 426.
2   *Richmond Times*, 1 May 1984, p. 1; 8 May 1984, p. 1; 22 May 1984, p. 3; 5 June 1984, p. 1; 19 June 1984, p. 1.
3   Peter Ewer, Winton Higgins and Annette Stevens, *Unions and the Future of Australian Manufacturing*, Allen & Unwin, Sydney, 1987, p. 21; *Year Book Australia 1990*, p. 551; Meredith and Dyster, *Australia in the Global Economy*, p. 255.
4   *Year Book Australia 1988*, p. 305; Meredith and Dyster, *Australia in the Global Economy*, pp. 244, 285.
5   Linda X and Kim X, interviewed by Loretta Ribaudo, 17 September 1985, transcript, p. 38, National Library of Australia Unemployment Project, OH 2518/8, J.S. Battye Library of West Australian History, Oral History Unit.
6   Six anonymous interviewees, Balga, CYSS, interviewed by Loretta Ribaudo and Melissa Watson, 18 September 1985, pp. 25–6, OH 2518/9, in ibid.
7   Kylie X and Joanna X, interviewed by Melissa Watson and Loretta Ribaudo, 18 September 1985, OH 2518/10, pp. 10–11, in ibid.
8   Linda X and Kim X, interview, pp. 29–32, in ibid.
9   Julie X, interviewed by Melissa Watson, 17 March 1986, OH 2518/53, p. 46, in ibid.
10 Anonymous Male, interviewed by Stuart Reid, 24/29 January 1986, OH2518/39, p. 52, in ibid.
11 Hugh Mackay, *The Mackay Report: Money*, March 1984, p. 10.
12 Peter Saunders, *Welfare and Equality: National and International Perspectives on the Australian Welfare State*, Cambridge University Press, Cambridge, 1994, pp. 282–4.
13 ibid., pp. 17–23; Christabel Young, *Young People Leaving Home in Australia: The Trend Towards Independence*, Australian Family Formation Project Monograph no. 9, Department of Demography, Research School of Social Sciences, Australian National University, Canberra, 1987, pp. 121–4, 140–42; *CT*, 23 July 1984, p. 2; Kelly, *End of Certainty*, p. 142.
14 Kelly, *End of Certainty*, p. 196.
15 *AFR*, 15 May 1986, pp. 1, 4, 8–9, 14.
16 Kelly, *End of Certainty*, pp. 212–13.
17 ibid., p. 220.
18 Walsh, *Confessions*, pp. 149–51; *AFR*, 29 July 1986, p. 1.
19 Walsh, *Confessions*, pp. 150–1.
20 *AFR*, 29 July 1986, pp. 1, 4, 7; *Australian*, 29 July 1986, pp. 1, 4, 14; Kelly, *End of Certainty*, p. 220.
21 *AFR*, 29 July 1986, p. 3.
22 *Australian*, 15 May 1986, pp. 10, 14.
23 Mackay, *The Mackay Report: Money*, p. 31.
24 Margaret Griffiths, 'The Sustainability of Consumer Credit Growth in Late Twentieth Century Australia', *Journal of Consumer Studies and Home Economics*, vol. 24, no. 1, March 2000, p. 23.

25 Mackay, *The Mackay Report: Money*, pp. 18, 25, 37.
26 Griffiths, 'Sustainability', pp. 23–33.
27 Evan Jones, 'The Foreign Currency Loan Experience in 1980s Australia with Particular Reference to the Commonwealth Bank of Australia: Bank Documents, Bank Culture, and Foreign Currency Loan Litigation', Working Papers, School of Economics and Political Science, University of Sydney, Sydney, 2005, http://sydney.edu.au/arts/political_economy/downloads/JonesFCLsLegalCultureWP1205.pdf, accessed 14 December 2014.
28 Michael Meagher and Laura Tingle, 'Swiss Loans Trap', *BRW*, 12 September 1986, pp. 18–27; Tom Skotnicki, 'Lawyers Target Swiss Loan Business', *BRW*, 10 October 1986, pp. 59–64.
29 Whitton, *Hillbilly Dictator*, pp. 78–9; Phil Dickie, *The Road to Fitzgerald and Beyond*, University of Queensland Press, St Lucia, 1989, pp. 274–5.
30 Meagher and Tingle, 'Swiss Loans Trap'; Skotnicki, 'Lawyers Target Swiss Loan Business'; Carew, *Westpac*, pp. 263–4; 'The Swiss Loans Affair: Farmers From All Over Australia Are Now in Serious Financial Trouble', *Countrywide*, 24 March 1989, transcript, http://parlinfo.aph.gov.au/parlInfo/search/display/display.w3p;query=Id:%22media/tvprog/VR200%22, accessed 10 January 2013.
31 The Honourable Justice Andrew Rogers, 'Developments in Foreign Currency Loan Litigation', *Journal of Banking and Finance Law and Practice*, September 1990, p. 202.
32 Meagher and Tingle, 'Swiss Loans Trap', p. 18.
33 *Weekend Australian*, 21–22 September 1985, p. 5.
34 Nicholas Brown and Susan Boden, *A Way Through: The Life of Rick Farley*, NewSouth, Sydney, 2012, pp. 103, 121.
35 Geoffrey Lawrence, *Capitalism and the Countryside: The Rural Crisis in Australia*, Pluto Press, Sydney and London, 1987, pp. 3–4, 14, 23, 25, 33–4, 43–4, 49, 58–66 and 'Progress and Poverty: The Farmer's Plight', *Arena*, no. 72, 1985, p. 120; *Herald*, 16 April 1986, p. 8.
36 Lawrence, *Capitalism and the Countryside*, pp. 23, 25.
37 ibid., pp. 12–13, 139–45, 153; *Age*, 25 June 1985, p. 1; Brown and Boden, *Way Through*, pp. 117–18.
38 *CT*, 2 July 1985, p. 11; *Australian*, 2 July 1985, pp. 1–2, 15 May 1986, p. 9; *Herald*, 16 April 1986, p. 8; *Age*, 18 April 1986, p. 3; *Sun*, 18 April, 1986, p. 1; Brown and Boden, *Way Through*, pp. 117–18; Lawrence, *Capitalism and the Countryside*, pp. 12–13.
39 *AFR*, 15 May 1986, p. 5.
40 J. Whitelaw to R.J. Hawke, 7 March 1983, NAA: A9488, O1983/106 Part 2.
41 Jim Kitay and Rod Powe, 'Exploitation at $1000 per Week? The Mudginberri Dispute', *Journal of Industrial Relations*, vol. 29, no. 3, September 1987, pp. 365–71; Bernie Brian, 'The Mudginberri Abattoir Dispute of 1985', *Labour History*, no. 76, May 1999, pp. 109–114.
42 Kitay and Powe, 'Exploitation', pp. 368–9; *Weekend Australian*, 10–11 August 1985, p. 11.
43 Kitay and Powe, 'Exploitation', pp. 366–8; Brian, 'Mudginberri', pp. 112–14.
44 Kitay and Powe, 'Exploitation', pp. 365–400; Brian, 'Mudginberri', pp. 109–19.
45 *AFR*, 30 July 1986, p. 5.
46 *Australian*, 1 January 1986, pp. 1, 7.
47 Jay Pendarvis, interviewed by Ray Aitchison, 14 June 1986, Transcript, p. 17, NLA: ORAL TRC 2086.

48 Adrian Lynch, 'Big Union Shaft from the Bush', *Rydges*, September 1986, pp. 156–7.
49 Pamela Williams, 'Westpac's Big Role in NT Union Battle', *BRW*, 2 May 1986, pp. 18–22.
50 Brian, 'Mudginberri', p. 121.
51 *CT*, 12 September 1988, p. 5.
52 See, for instance, *Age*, 28 August 1986, pp. 1, 4.
53 *Year Book Australia 1988*, pp. 331–2.
54 David H. Plowman, 'Economic Forces and the New Right: Employer Matters in 1986', *Journal of Industrial Relations*, vol. 29, no. 1, March 1987, pp. 84–91; *Age*, 3 April 1986, p. 13.
55 Gerard Henderson, 'The Industrial Relations Club', in John Hyde and John Nurick (eds), *Wages Wasteland: A Radical Examination of the Australian Wage Fixing System*, Hale & Iremonger in association with the Australian Institute for Public Policy, Sydney, pp. 42, 44. Originally in *Quadrant*, vol. 27, no. 9, September 1983, pp. 21–9.
56 The economic historian Edward Shann, in whose honour the lecture was held, had been a forthright critic of Australia's statist economic policies between the wars.
57 John Stone, '1929 and All That', *Quadrant*, vol. 28, no. 10, October 1984, p. 19.
58 Gerard Henderson, 'The Fridge-Dwellers-Dreamtime in Industrial Relations', in *'Arbitration in Contempt': The Proceedings of the Inaugural Seminar of the H.R. Nicholls Society held in Melbourne 28 February–2 March, 1986*, H.R. Nicholls Society, Melbourne, 1986, pp. 281–2.
59 Ray Evans, 'Justice Higgins: architect and builder of an Australian folly', in Hyde and Nurick (eds), *Wages Wasteland*, p. 31.
60 Quoted in John Stone, 'Introduction', in *'Arbitration in Contempt'*, p. 11.
61 John Rickard, *H.B. Higgins: The Rebel as Judge*, George Allen & Unwin, Sydney, 1984, pp. 186–8.
62 John Stone, Ray Evans, Barrie Purvis and Peter Costello, 'The H R Nicholls Society', 16 January 1986, in *'Arbitration in Contempt'*, pp. 317, 314.
63 *Sun*, 22 April 1985, p. 1; *Age*, 22 April 1985, p. 7.
64 *Coburg Courier*, 24 April 1985, p. 1; *Melbourne Times*, 24 April 1985, p. 2; *Sun*, 22 April 1985, pp. 1–3, 8; 23 April 1985, p. 2; *Age*, 22 April 1985, pp. 1, 7, 13; Evans, *Inside the Hawke–Keating Government*, pp. 102–4.
65 Peter Costello with Peter Coleman, *The Costello Memoirs: The Age of Prosperity*, Melbourne University Press, Carlton, 2008, p. 33.
66 *Age*, 13 December 1985, p. 6; 21 February 1986, p. 16.
67 Costello with Coleman, *Costello Memoirs*, pp. 33–7; Shaun Carey, *Peter Costello: The New Liberal*, A Sue Hines Book/Allen & Unwin, Crows Nest, 2001, pp. 112–16.
68 Douglas Blackmur, 'Industrial Conflict in the Public Sector: The Origins and Nature of the 1985 Queensland Electricity Dispute', *Australian Journal of Public Administration*, vol. 48, no. 2, June 1989, p. 166.
69 Tom Bramble, *Trade Unionism in Australia: A History from Flood to Ebb Tide*, Cambridge University Press, Cambridge, 2008, pp. 140–1; Margaret Gardner and Rob McQueen, 'Law and Order: The Queensland Power Dispute', in Roman Tomasic and Ric Lucas (eds), *Power, Regulation and Resistance: Studies in the Sociology of Law*, Canberra Series in Administrative Studies, no. 8, School of Administrative Studies, Canberra College of Advanced Education, Canberra, 1986, pp. 57–69; Paul McCarthy, 'Power Without Glory: The Queensland Electricity Dispute', *Journal of Industrial Relations*, vol. 27, no. 3, 1985, pp. 364–82; *Courier-Mail*, 21 August 1985, p. 1; 22 August 1985, p. 1.

70 Mark Sherry, *Sellout: The Story of the SEQEB Strike*, Rank and File Press, Brisbane, 1993.
71 Wayne Gilbert, 'The Queensland Power Dispute', in *'Arbitration in Contempt'*, p. 29.
72 *Northwest Telegraph*, 13 August 1986, p. 2.
73 Howard Smith and Herb Thompson, 'Industrial Relations and the Law: A Case Study of Robe River', *Australian Quarterly*, vol. 59, nos 3 and 4, Spring and Summer 1987, p. 298 and 'The Conflict at Robe River', *Arena*, no. 79, 1987, pp. 88–9.
74 Larry Graham, 'The 1987 Robe River Dispute', *Papers in Labour History*, no. 2, October 1988, pp. 71–2.
75 Adrian Hudson, interviewed by Stuart Reid, 21 September 1986, Pannawonica, Robe River Dispute, OH 2305, no. 25, State Library of Western Australia (SLWA).
76 Trevor and Sue Grey, interviewed by Stuart Reid, 24 September 1986, Pannawonica, Robe River Dispute, OH 2305, no. 36, SLWA.
77 Welfare Committee, interviewed by Stuart Reid, 19 September 1986, Wickham, Robe River Dispute, OH 2305, no. 15, SLWA.
78 David Baxter, Robina Bonner and Keith and Margaret Williamson, interviewed by Stuart Reid, 22 September 1986, Pannawonica, Robe River Dispute, OH 2305, No. 30, SLWA.
79 *West Australian*, 4 September 1986, p. 1.
80 ibid., 6 September 1986, p. 2.
81 M. Kaempf, *Politics and Industrial Relations: The Robe River Dispute*, Discussion Paper 15, Department of Industrial Relations, University of Western Australia, Nedlands, 1989, pp. 11, 17.
82 Charles Copeman, 'Light on the Hill: Industrial Relations Reform in Australia: The Robe River Affair', Proceedings of the H.R. Nicholls Society, Mooloolaba, June 1987, http://archive.hrnicholls.com.au/archives/vol3/vol3-8.php, accessed 15 December 2014; Patrick Gethin, *The Power Switch at Robe River*, Australian Institute for Public Policy, Perth, 1990.
83 This discussion, and that in the following paragraph, is informed by Braham Dabscheck, *Australian Industrial Relations in the 1980s*, Oxford University Press, Melbourne 1999, pp. 107, 146; Shaun Carey, *Australia in Accord: Politics and Industrial Relations Under the Hawke Government*, Sun Books, South Melbourne, 1988, pp. 96–102; Kelly, *End of Certainty*, p. 262.
84 Kelly, *End of Certainty*, pp. 206–7.
85 McQueen, *We Built This Country*, p. 324.
86 Ross, *Dare to Struggle Dare to Win!* pp. 110–16; *Victoria: The Next Step*, pp. 3, 17–19, 28–31; McQueen, *We Built This Country*, pp. 328–9.
87 *Age*, 18 April 1986, p. 5; 19 April 1986, p. 3; *Herald*, 16 April 1986, p. 3; *Sun*, 17 April 1986, p. 4; Ross, *Dare to Struggle Dare to Win!* pp. 149–54, 225–30.
88 *Australian*, 29 July 1986, pp. 1, 4, 5.
89 Joe Hajdu, *Samurai in the Surf: The Arrival of the Japanese on the Gold Coast in the 1980s*, Pandanus Books, Research School of Pacific and Asian Studies, The Australian National University, Canberra, 2005, pp. 4, 57.
90 *GCB*, 26 November 1985, p. 1; 17 December 1985, p. 7; 24 December 1985, p. 2; 15 February 1986, p. 2; 14 August 1986, p. 1; Dickie, *The Road to Fitzgerald*, pp. 249–50.
91 David Monaghan, 'The vision of "Blood and Guts" Mike Gore', *SMH*, Good Weekend, 11 October 1986, p. 26.
92 *GCB*, 28 December 1985, pp. 52–3.

93 *Age*, 5 December 1987, p. 5.
94 *SMH*, 15 November 1987, p. 22.
95 Kelly, *End of Certainty*, p. 296.
96 Chris Fisher, *Coal and the State*, Methuen Australia, North Ryde, 1987; Brian Galligan, *Utah and Queensland Coal: A Study in the Micro Political Economy of Modern Capitalism and the State*, University of Queensland Press, St Lucia, 1989, esp. pp. 219–23; David Lee, 'Between Booms – Mining in the 1980s and 1990s', unpublished manuscript.
97 *Courier-Mail*, 17 July 1986, pp. 1–2; 18 July 1986, p. 2; 21 July 1986, p. 1; Evans, *Inside the Hawke–Keating Government*, p. 353.
98 Kelly, *End of Certainty*, p. 297.
99 *Sun-Herald*, 19 October 1986, in 'Joh Crusade' folder, Liberal Party Federal Secretariat Papers, NLA MS 5000, Box 1363.
100 *National Times on Sunday*, 9 November 1986, in ibid.
101 John Howard, *Lazarus Rising: A Personal and Political Autobiography*, HarperCollins, Pymble, 2010, pp. 155–6; Rob Borbidge, interviewed by Roger Scott and Maree Stanley, *Queensland Speaks*, www.queenslandspeaks.com.au/rob-borbidge, accessed 29 June 2015.
102 Sally Loane, 'Ponytailed pollster who inspired Joh', *Times on Sunday*, undated, in 'Joh Crusade' folder.
103 Frank Robson, 'Mike Gore', *Australian Penthouse*, April 1988, p. 53.
104 ibid.; Loane, 'Ponytailed pollster who inspired Joh'; David Fagan, Obituary for Mike Gore, *Australian*, undated clipping, [c. December 1994], Mike Gore Biographical File, National Library of Australia; Kelly, *End of Certainty*, p. 293.
105 Robson, 'Mike Gore'.
106 Kelly, *End of Certainty*, pp. 336–40; Brown and Boden, *Way Through*, pp. 140–2.
107 David Russell, Interview, Queensland Speaks, 16 December 2011, www.queenslandspeaks.com.au/david-russell, accessed 17 June 2015; Paul Davey, *Joh for PM: The Inside Story of an Extraordinary Political Drama*, NewSouth Publishing, Sydney, 2015, p. 38. For Bjelke-Petersen's attitude to the Fraser government, see Davey, *Joh For PM*, pp. 7-11, 73.
108 'The Joh Conundrum', Note for File, 21 December 1986, in 'Joh Crusade' folder.
109 'Review of Joh and "Silly Season"', 8 January 1987, in ibid.
110 *Times on Sunday*, 1 February 1987; *Border Morning Mail* (Albury-Wodonga), 2 February 1987, pp. 1, 2, 11; *Daily Advertiser* (Wagga Wagga), 2 February 1987, in ibid.
111 *Australian*, 10 February 1987 and Tony Eggleton, 'Tactics and the Queensland National Party', 3 March 1987, in ibid.
112 'Summary of Media Coverage 9 February–1 March 1987', in ibid.; Howard, *Lazarus Rising*, p. 161.
113 Paul Davey, *Ninety Not Out: The Nationals 1920–2010*, University of New South Wales Press, Sydney, 2010, p. 220.
114 Davey, *Joh for PM*, p. 78.
115 John Howard, 'The Coalition', Press Release, 28 April 1987, in 'Joh Crusade' folder.
116 Howard, *Lazarus Rising*, p. 167.
117 Davey, *Ninety Not Out*, p. 236.
118 Toohey, 'Death of Labor', p. 8.
119 'Draft Report for Campaign Committee: Government's Electoral Standing – Strategy for 1988 Election', pp. 3–4, October 1986, Bob Hawke Papers, RH 18/2/F52 (Box 2), Bob Hawke Ministerial Library, University of South Australia.

120 Andrew Leigh, *Battlers and Billionaires: The Story of Inequality in Australia*, Redback, 2013, ch. 3; Saunders, *Welfare and Inequality*, p. 144; Ann Harding and John Landt, 'Policy and Poverty: Trends in Disposable Incomes: March 1983–September 1991', *Australian Quarterly*, vol. 64, no. 1, Autumn 1992, pp. 19–48; David O'Reilly, 'Retreat Australia Fair', *Bulletin*, 25 April 1989, pp. 52–9.
121 Saunders, *Welfare and Inequality*, pp. 269–71; Harding and John Landt, 'Policy and Poverty', pp. 26–7.
122 Frank Castles, 'Australia's Inequality Paradox', *Australian Society*, November 1989, pp. 44–5.
123 *BRW*, 14 August 1987, p. 6.
124 *SMH*, 12 June 1987, p. 8.
125 ibid., 14 July 1987, p. 3.
126 Toohey, 'Death of Labor', p. 8.
127 Hawke, *Hawke Memoirs*, pp. 403–4.
128 ibid., p. 400.
129 Gerald Stone, *Singo, The John Singleton Story: Mates, Wives, Triumphs, Disasters*, HarperCollins, Sydney, 2003, pp. 217–20.
130 Ian McAllister and Alvaro Ascui, 'Voting Patterns', in Ian McAllister and John Warhurst (eds), *Australia Votes: The 1987 Federal Election*, Longman Cheshire, Melbourne 1988, p. 226; David Day, *Paul Keating: The Biography*, Fourth Estate, Sydney, 2015, p. 297.
131 David O'Reilly, 'That Old Hawke Magic', *Bulletin*, 4 April 1989, pp. 37–8.

Chapter 7: New Dangers, New Pleasures

1 A.N. Malden, 'Once More, with Feeling', *Time Australia*, 15 December 1986, pp. 60–1.
2 Julie Clark, 'Is Sex Dead? (Or At Least In Trouble?)', *Cleo*, April 1983, pp. 34, 36.
3 *Dolly*, November 1985, p. 58.
4 Adele Horin, 'Sex in Life', *National Times*, 5–11 April 1981, p. 36; Sung-Mook Hong, 'Permissiveness, More or Less: Sexual Attitudes in the General Public, *Australian Journal of Sex, Marriage & Family*, vol. 5, no. 2, May 1984, pp. 89–96.
5 *Dolly*, May 1986, p. 59.
6 ibid., August 1983, pp. 50–8.
7 John McCallum, 'Belief versus Church: Beyond the Secularisation Debate', in Jonathan Kelley and Clive Bean (eds), *Australian Attitudes: Social and Political Analyses from the National Social Science Survey*, Allen & Unwin, North Sydney, pp. 176–86; Jonathan Kelley and M.D.R. Evans, 'Should Abortion Be Illegal? Australians' Opinions and Their Sources in Ideology and Social Structure', in Kelley and Bean (eds), *Australian Attitudes*, pp. 3–25; *Dolly*, August 1983, p. 58.
8 Rebecca M. Albury, *The Politics of Reproduction: Beyond the Slogans*, Allen & Unwin, St Leonards, 1999, pp. 66, 122.
9 McWatters, *One Way or Another*, p. 63.
10 Horin, 'Sex in Life', p. 40.
11 'Love and the Unmarried Woman', *Woman's Day*, 27 December 1984, p. 43.
12 *Dolly*, May 1986, p. 58.
13 Siew-Ean Khoo, *Living Together*, Australian Institute of Family Studies Working Paper No. 10, Collins Dove, Blackburn (Vic.), August 1986, pp. 1, 5.
14 Peter McDonald, 'Household and Family Trends in Australia', Australian Bureau of Statistics, 1301.0 – *Year Book Australia*, 1994, www.abs.gov.au/

ENDNOTES

Ausstats/ABS@.nsf/94713ad445ff1425ca25682000192af2/72dc873d21f1e2ecca-2569de00221c82!OpenDocument, accessed 16 May 2015.
15. Kelly Bourne, 'Here's to You, Mrs Robinson!' *TV Week*, 27 June 1987, p. 7.
16. Susan Linacre, 'Lifetime Marriage and Divorce Trends', Australian Bureau of Statistics, Canberra, 2007, pp. 1–2, www.ausstats.abs.gov.au/ausstats/subscriber.nsf/0/0B6F42BBA4622404CA25732F001C93F1/$File/41020_Lifetime%20marriage%20and%20divorce%20trends_2007.pdf, accessed 16 May 2015.
17. Kelly Bourne, 'Marry Me!' *TV Week*, 13 June 1987, p. 5.
18. Australian Bureau of Statistics, 3306.0.55.001 – Marriages, Australia, 2007, www.abs.gov.au/ausstats/abs@.nsf/mf/3306.0.55.001, accessed 20 June 2015; McCallum, 'Belief versus Church', p. 178.
19. Bettina Arndt, 'Are Women Giving Sex a Bad Name?' *Cleo*, March 1983, pp. 44, 46.
20. Jan Stockley, 'No Fear or Favour in Dame Leonie's Controversial Words', *Women Australia*, no. 10, August–September 1985, p. 8.
21. *Dolly*, July 1989, p. 22.
22. Janeen Baxter, 'The Sexual Division of Labour in Australian Families', *Australian Journal of Sex, Marriage & Family*, vol. 9, no. 2, May 1988, pp. 87–93.
23. Richard Neville, 'From Playpower to Playpen', *Matilda*, March 1985, p. 14.
24. Peter McDonald, 'Conflicting Messages: Marriage in the 1980s', *Australian Journal of Sex, Marriage & Family*, vol. 8, no. 2, May 1987, p. 74.
25. Deirdre James and Graeme Russell, 'Reproduction and the New Man', *Australian Journal of Sex, Marriage & Family*, vol. 8, no. 3, August 1987, p. 125.
26. Kathy Lette, *Hit and Ms*, Penguin Books, Ringwood, 1984, p. 18.
27. Alice Garner, *The Student Chronicles*, The Miegunyah Press, Carlton, 2006, pp. 63–4.
28. *CT*, 30 January 1986, p. 1; 20 October 1986, p. 2.
29. ibid., 15 April 1984, p. 2. Navratilova was a star tennis player of the era and a lesbian.
30. ibid., 12 April 1984, p. 18.
31. ibid., 12 February 1989, p. 26.
32. Bev Roberts, 'Ockers and Malespeak', *Australian Society*, 1 August 1984, p. 14.
33. *Age*, 21 May 1983, p. 1.
34. ibid., 13 June 1983, p. 3.
35. ibid., 25 May 1983, pp. 1, 28; 28 June 1983, p. 4; 29 June 1983, p. 24.
36. Sally Gray, 'Super Bodies: Heroic Fashion from the 1980s in Melbourne', *Art Monthly Australia*, no. 206, December 2007–February 2008, pp. 25–7.
37. Joanne Entwistle, 'Fashioning the Career Woman: Power Dressing as a Strategy of Consumption', in Maggie Andrews and Mary M. Talbot (eds), *All the World and her Husband: Women in Twentieth-Century Consumer Culture*, Cassell, London and New York, 2000, pp. 224–38.
38. Ann Pilmer, 'Dressing for Success', *Women Australia*, no. 8, April–May 1985, pp. 20–2.
39. Megalogenis, *Australian Moment*, p. 267.
40. Ilsa Colson, *More Than Just the Money: 100 Years of the Victorian Nurses Union*, Prowling Tiger Press, Northcote, 2001, pp. 58–71.
41. *Herald*, 6 November 1986, p. 6.
42. *Sun*, 4 November 1986, p. 1; 6 November 1986, p. 1; 7 November 1986, p. 1.
43. Carol Fox, *Enough Is Enough: The 1986 Victorian Nurses' Strike*, School of Health Services Management, University of New South Wales, Kensington, 1991, pp. 99–175.
44. *Sun*, 6 November 1986, p. 2.

45 *CT,* 26 May 1985, pp. 40, 41, 42, 44; Adele Horin, 'Talented Women', *National Times,* 22-28 June 1984, p. 3; Grabowsky, *Wayward Governance,* ch. 11.
46 'Love and the Unmarried Women', p. 44.
47 G.N. Soutar, L.K. Savery and N.F. Dufty, 'Sexual Harassment in the Banking Industry: Some Australian Evidence', *Human Resource Management Australia,* vol. 25, no. 3, November 1987, pp. 82-7.
48 'Love and the Unmarried Woman', p. 44.
49 *Courier-Mail,* 11 January 1983, p. 5.
50 Fia Cumming, 'Sexual Harassment', *Women Australia,* August-September 1984, p. 45.
51 Marian Sawer, 'Human Rights: Women Need Not Apply', *Australian Society,* September 1988, p. 9.
52 *GCB,* 10 June 1988, pp. 1-2; 15 June 1988, p. 6.
53 *Daily Telegraph,* 5 February 1983, p. 20.
54 Dennis Altman, 'The Ockerism of Gay Sydney', *Meanjin,* vol. 42, no. 2, June 1983, p. 216.
55 *Daily Telegraph,* 5 February 1983, p. 5; 7 February 1983, p. 12; Clive Faro with Garry Wotherspoon, *Street Seen: A History of Oxford Street,* Melbourne University Press, Carlton South, 2000, pp. 248-9.
56 *Daily Telegraph,* 5 February 1983, p. 20.
57 Sendziuk, *Learning,* pp. 13, 18, 39, 57.
58 Quoted in ibid., p. 57; Fred Nile, 'The Facts on AIDS - "The Gay Plague"', Supplement to *Australian Christian Solidarity,* [p. 2]; Hiram Caton, 'The AIDS Apocalypse', *Quadrant,* vol. 29, no. 11, November 1985, p. 28.
59 Department of Community Services and Health, *Report of the Third National Conference on AIDS, 4-6 August 1988, Hobart, Tasmania,* Australian Government Publishing Service, Canberra, 1988, p. 739.
60 *GCB,* 7 January 1988, p. 3; 8 January 1988, p. 7.
61 Adele Horin, 'Gay Life after AIDS', *National Times,* 8-14 November 1985, pp. 9-10.
62 Gary W. Dowsett, 'Sexual Conduct, Sexual Culture, Sexual Community: Gay Men's Bodies and AIDS', in Jill Julius Matthews (ed.), *Sex in Public: Australian Sexual Cultures,* Allen & Unwin, St Leonards, 1997, p. 81.
63 G.W. Dowsett, 'The Place of Research in AIDS Education: A Critical Review of Survey Research among Gay and Bisexual Men', in *Report of the Third National Conference on AIDS,* pp. 159-66.
64 Sendziuk, *Learning.*
65 Department of Community Services and Health, *Report of the Third National Conference on AIDS,* p. 686.
66 Sendziuk, *Learning,* ch. 6.
67 *Present Tense: The Plight of Australians Today,* A Clemenger Report in conjunction with Arbes Strategic Research, February 1988, pp. 5-6.
68 Makkai and McAllister, *Patterns of Drug Use,* p. 4.
69 Sendziuk, *Learning,* p. 151.
70 Kaz Cooke, *The Modern Girl's Guide to Safe Sex,* McPhee Gribble/Penguin Books, Fitzroy, 1988, p. 6.
71 Julian Assange, *Julian Assange: The Unauthorised Autobiography,* Canongate, Edinburgh, 2011, p. 55.
72 ibid., p. 56.
73 ibid., pp. 62-3.
74 *Australian Personal Computer,* December 1988, p. 472.

75   ibid., January 1985, p. 12.
76   ibid., April, 1983, pp. 18, 20.
77   ibid., January 1984, p. 15.
78   ibid., January 1985, p. 13.
79   ibid., December 1988, p. 483; August, 1983, p. 63; May 1984, p. 167.
80   ibid., April, 1983, p. 53.
81   ibid., May 1984, p. 161; February 1984, p. 21.
82   Jonathan King with David Iggulden, *The Battle for the Bicentenary*, Hutchinson Australia, 1989, p. 129.
83   *Australian Personal Computer*, February 1984, p. 4.
84   ibid., May 1983, p. 76; December 1988, p. 493.
85   Australian Bureau of Statistics, 'Special Feature – Leisure at Home', 4102.0 – Australian Social Trends, 1995, www.abs.gov.au/AUSSTATS/abs@.nsf/2f762f95845417aeca25706c00834efa/a1b5d7636e6719f7ca2570ec00753522!OpenDocument, accessed 17 May 2015.
86   Barry Jones, *Sleepers, Wake! Technology and the Future of Work*, Oxford University Press, Melbourne, 1982, pp. 114, 256.
87   Denise Beale, *How the Computer Went to School: Australian Government Policies for Computers in Schools, 1983–2013*, Monash University Publishing, Clayton, 2014, ch. 3.
88   *Office News*, March 1985, p. 26.
89   ibid., July 1985, p. 25.
90   *Office News & Automation*, September 1986, p. 14.
91   ibid., January 1989, p. 16.
92   *Office News*, February 1986, p. 9.
93   ibid., p. 10.
94   K.N. Baidya and M.G. Stevenson, *A Study of Repetitive Strain Injuries Reported to the Department of Industrial Relations, New South Wales*, 1985/IE/1, p. 1.
95   Australian Public Service Association, *Repetition Strain Injury Sufferers' Handbook*, September 1984, pp. 2, 5, 14.
96   *Office News*, December 1985, p. 20; August 1986, p. 16; March 1987, p. 28; *Office News & Automation*, December 1987–January 1988, p. 12.
97   King, *Battle for the Bicentenary*, p. 179.
98   John Laws, Interview with John Howard, Monitair, Radio 2UE, transcript, 9.30 am, 1 August 1988, Liberal Party, NLA 5000, Box 1318.
99   *Office News & Automation*, August 1986, pp. 13–14.
100 *Office News*, September 1986, p. 22.
101 *Office News & Automation*, November 1988, p. 12.
102 ibid., January 1989, p. 6.
103 Michael Dickinson, 'Why the Australian House Can Never Be the Same Again', *Bulletin*, 4 April 1989, pp. 86–9.
104 *Media Information Australia*, no. 47, February 1988, p. 127 and no. 48, May 1988, p. 128.
105 ibid., no. 48, May 1988, p. 128; Robert Crawford, *But Wait There's More . . . A History of Australian Advertising, 1900–2000*, Melbourne University Press, Carlton, 2008, pp. 197–8.
106 Michelle Arrow, *Friday on Our Minds: Popular Culture in Australia Since 1945*, University of New South Wales Press, Sydney, 2009, pp. 160–3.
107 *Books – Who Reads Them? A Study of Borrowing and Buying in Australia*, Hans Hoegh Guldberg Economic Strategies Pty Ltd, Sydney, May 1990, esp. ch. 2.

ENDNOTES

108 Irene Stevens, *A Short History of the Literature Board 1986–2000*, Australia Council for the Arts, Sydney, 2004, p. 29.
109 *AFR*, 5 December 1988, p. 13.
110 Tim Rowse, *Arguing the Arts: The Funding of the Arts in Australia*, Penguin Books, Ringwood, 1985, p. 73.
111 Delys Bird, 'New narrations: contemporary fiction', in Elizabeth Webby (ed.), *The Cambridge Companion to Australian Literature*, Cambridge University Press, Cambridge, 2000, pp. 183–208.
112 May-Brit Akerholt, 'New Stages: Contemporary Theatre', in ibid., pp. 221–3.
113 David McCooey, 'Contemporary Poetry: Across Party Lines', in ibid., pp. 158–82.
114 Arrow, *Friday On Our Minds*, pp. 163–7.
115 For Quantock, see Peter Ellingsen, 'How a Tall Silly Person Copes with Fame', *Matilda*, July 1985, pp. 46–7.
116 Garrie Hutchinson, 'The a-mazing Tim and Debbie . . . (right, right)', *National Times*, 25 November–1 December 1983, pp. 12–14.
117 Patrick Cook et al., *The Gillies Report*, McPhee Gribble/ Penguin, Fitzroy, 1985.
118 Tim Ferguson, *Carry A Big Stick: A Funny Fearless Life of Friendship, Laughter and MS*, Hachette Australia, Sydney, 2013.
119 Arrow, *Friday On Our Minds*, pp. 165–6; Tony Mitchell, 'Wogs Still Out of Work: Australian Television Comedy as Colonial Discourse', *Australasian Drama Studies*, no. 20, 1992, pp. 119–33.
120 Dickinson, 'Why the Australian House Can Never Be the Same Again'; Stephen Knight, *The Selling of the Australian Mind: From First Fleet to Third Mercedes*, William Heinemann Australia, Port Melbourne, 1990, pp. 45, 51; *SMH*, 14 January 1988, p. 6.
121 Dickinson, 'Why the Australian House Can Never Be the Same Again', pp. 86–9; Day, *Paul Keating*, pp. 243–4.
122 Dickinson, 'Why the Australian House Can Never Be the Same Again', pp. 89, 86.
123 John Wilkinson, *Affordable Housing in NSW: Past to Present*, Briefing Paper No. 14/05, NSW Parliamentary Library Research Service, Sydney, November 2005, pp. 21–2, 33. For rents in Sydney, see Ronald Henderson and David Hough, 'Sydney's Poor Get Squeezed', *Australian Society*, November 1984, pp. 6–8.
124 Australian Bureau of Statistics, 'Home Owners and Renters', 1301.0 – *Year Book Australia*, 2012, www.abs.gov.au/ausstats/abs@.nsf/Lookup/by%20 Subject/1301.0~2012~Main%20Features~Home%20Owners%20and%20 Renters~129, accessed 16 May 2015.
125 Richard White et al., *On Holidays: A History of Getting Away in Australia*, Pluto Press, North Melbourne, 2005, ch. 6.
126 ibid.
127 Derogatory term for Aboriginal Australians.
128 Clayton X, interviewed by Stuart Reid, 27 August 1985, National Library of Australia Unemployment Project, OH 2518/2, J.S. Battye Library of West Australian History, Oral History Unit, pp. 32, 47.
129 Anonymous male, interviewed by Stuart Reid, 24/29 January 1986, OH 2518/39, ibid., p. 68.
130 Kate Ceberano, *I'm Talking*, Hachette Australia, Sydney, 2014, pp. 43, 87–8.
131 Tristan Migliore, interviewed by Stuart Reid, 14 August 1985, OH 2518/1, National Library of Australia Unemployment Project, J.S. Battye Library.

132 Duro Cubrilo, Martin Harvey and Karl Stamer, *Kings Way: The Beginnings of Australian Graffiti: Melbourne 1983–93*, The Miegunyah Press, Carlton, 2010; *Age*, 24 August 1989, p. 11; *Sun* (Melbourne), 13 April, 1985, pp. 23, 30.
133 Arrow, *Friday on our Minds*, p. 143.
134 Anthony Griffis, *Air Guitar: The True Life and Daggy Times of a Lounge-Room Rock Star*, Penguin Books, Camberwell, 2003, p. 123.
135 INXS and Anthony Bozza, *INXS: Story to Story: The Official Autobiography*, Atria Books, New York, 2006, pp. 1–72.
136 INXS and Bozza, *INXS*, pp. 54, 263.
137 Susan Wyndham, 'Mister Hutchence, I Presume', *Australian Magazine*, 14–15 October 1989, p. 49.
138 INXS and Bozza, *INXS*, p. 81.
139 Stuart Maconie, 'INXS: "You British Are Too Cool for Your Own Good"', *New Musical Express*, 25 June 1988, pp. 14–15.
140 McFarlane, *The Encyclopedia of Australian Rock and Pop*, p. 322.
141 Jeff Apter, *Up from Down Under: How Australian Music Changed the World*, The Five Mile Press, Scoresby, 2013, pp.147–56, 169–81.
142 Stuart Maconie, 'Growing Up Gracefully', *New Musical Express*, 6 August 1988, p. 13.
143 Don Watson, 'Trials of the Singer', *New Musical Express*, 24 January 1987, pp. 12–14.
144 Robert Eaglestone, 'From Mutiny to Calling upon the Author: Cave's Religion', in Karen Welberry and Tanya Dalziell (eds), *Cultural Seeds: Essays on the Work of Nick Cave*, Ashgate, Farnham (UK) and Burlington (VT), 2009, pp. 139–51; Ian Johnston, *Bad Seed: The Biography of Nick Cave*, Little, Brown and Company, London, 1995, pp. 206, 239–44.
145 Johnston, *Bad Seed*, p. 248; Edwina Preston, *Howard Arkley: Not Just a Suburban Boy*, Duffy & Snellgrove, Sydney, 2002, p. 103.
146 Glennys Bell, 'Katie Pye: An Artist in Clothing', *Bulletin*, 18 October 1983, pp. 44–5.
147 Adrian Martin, 'Before and After *Art & Text*', in Rex Butler (ed.), *What is Appropriation? An Anthology of Writings on Australian Art in the 1980s and 1990s*, IMA Publishing, Brisbane, 2nd edn, 2004, pp. 114–15.
148 Jenny Watson, 'Urgent Images', *Art & Text*, no. 14, Winter 1984, p. 69.
149 Denise Morgan, with an introduction by Sasha Grishin, *Roar Re-Viewed*, Macmillan, Melbourne, 2011, pp. 7–11, 69–110.
150 [Paul Taylor], 'Symposia 1983–84: Introduction', *Art & Text*, no. 14, Winter 1984, p. 66.
151 Preston, *Howard Arkley*, pp. 150–3; John Gregory, *Carnival in Suburbia: The Art of Howard Arkley*, Cambridge University Press, Cambridge, 2006, pp. 14–21.

Chapter 8: The Identity Card

1 David Malouf, 'A Spirit of Play', in Robert Manne and Chris Feik (eds), *The Words That Made Australia: How a Nation Came to Know Itself*, Black Inc., Collingwood, 2012, pp. 213–14.
2 Stephanie Alexander, *Stephanie's Menus for Food Lovers*, Methuen Haynes, North Ryde, 1985, pp. ix–x, xiii, xvi; *Stephanie's 21 Years of Fabulous Food: December 1976–December 1997*, Stephanie's, Melbourne, 1998.
3 Seamus O'Hanlon with Tony Dingle, *Melbourne Remade: The Inner City Since the 70s*, Arcade, Melbourne, 2010, p. 125.

4   Hugh Mackay, *The Mackay Report: Food*, March 1987, p. 39; Barbara Santich, 'Featuring a Constantly Changing Menu', *Gourmet*, April–May 1982, pp. 95–8.
5   Santich, 'Featuring a Constantly Changing Menu', pp. 97–8; Rita Erlich, *Melbourne by Menu: The Story of Melbourne's Restaurant Revolution*, Slattery Media Group/State Library of Victoria, Richmond (Vic.), 2012.
6   Mackay, *The Mackay Report: Food*, pp. 13–15, 22–5; Santich, '"Featuring a Constantly Changing Menu"', p. 95.
7   Harding and Landt, 'Policy and Poverty', p. 21.
8   Knight, *Selling of the Australian Mind*, p. 129; Mackay, *The Mackay Report: Food*, pp. 35–6.
9   James Halliday, *A History of the Australian Wine Industry 1949–1994*, The Australian Wine and Brandy Corporation in association with Winetitles, Adelaide, 1994, p. 105.
10 John Beeston, *A Concise History of Australian Wine*, 3rd Edition, Allen & Unwin, Crows Nest, 2001, pp. 260–4; *NYT*, 30 November 1986, p. A9; 8 February 1989, p. C1.
11 *Richmond Times*, 17 April 1984, pp. 1, 8; 12 June 1984, p. 1; 10 July 1984, p. 1; 31 July 1984, p. 1; 14 August 1984, p. 2.
12 O'Hanlon, *Melbourne Remade*, ch. 4.
13 Patrick White, *Patrick White Speaks*, Primavera Press, Sydney, 1989, p. 175; John Docker, *Postmodernism and Popular Culture: A Cultural History*, Cambridge University Press, Cambridge, 1994, pp. 96–7.
14 *Adelaide: The Nominated Site for the Multi Function Polis (MFP)*, Department of Premier and Cabinet, Adelaide, 1990, ch. 7, p. 2.
15 Peter Newman, 'Fremantle and the America's Cup: Avoiding the Autocratic Trap', *Architecture Australia*, March 1988, pp. 72–7; Lyndall Crisp, 'Freo's Rebirth', *Australian Way*, April 1987, pp. 42–4.
16 Rachel Sanderson, 'Queensland Shows the World: Regionalism and Modernity at Brisbane's World Expo '88', *Journal of Australian Studies*, no. 79, 2003, pp. 65–75.
17 Jennifer Craik, 'Expo 88: Fashions of Sight and Politics of Site', in Tony Bennett, Pat Buckridge, David Carter and Colin Mercer (eds), *Celebrating the Nation: A Critical Study of Australia's Bicentenary*, Allen & Unwin, St Leonards, 1992, p. 156.
18 *Cane Toad Times*, issue 3, Spring 1985, pp. 6–7.
19 Donna Lee Brien, 'Celebration or Manufacturing Nostalgia? Constructing Histories of World Expo '88', p. 76 and Donna Lee Brien, 'Brisbane Will Never Be the Same: Tasting Change at World Expo '88', *Queensland Review*, vol. 15, no. 2, pp. 119–20; Tony Bennett, 'The Shaping of Things to Come', in Bennett, Buckridge, Carter and Mercer (eds), *Celebrating the Nation*, pp. 123–41.
20 Lindsay Miller and Richard Fuhr, 'The Real Sydney', *Australian Society*, 1 April 1983, p. 4.
21 Ian Craven, 'Distant Neighbours: Notes on Some Australian Soap Operas', *Australian Studies*, no. 3, 1989, p. 31.
22 James Oram, *Neighbours: Behind the Scenes*, Angus & Robertson, North Ryde, 1988, p. 52.
23 *Sun-Herald*, 21 July 1985. The newspaper articles on *Neighbours* are mainly taken from the National Film and Sound Archive.
24 Jason Donovan, *Between the Lines: My Story Uncut*, HarperCollins, London, 2007, pp. 56–60, 72–5.
25 *Mail on Sunday*, 31 January 1988, p. 3.
26 Craven, 'Distant Neighbours', pp. 2–3, notes 6–7.
27 *Daily Telegraph*, 2 February 1988, p. 12; 29 February 1988.

28 Ruth Brown, 'Caring What the Neighbours Say', *Weekend Guardian*, 18–19 February 1989, p. 20.
29 Craven, 'Distant Neighbours', pp. 18–20, 24–25.
30 *Daily Telegraph*, 3 October 1988.
31 *Radio Times*, 11–17 March 1989, p. 5; *Herald*, 31 October 1988.
32 *Telegraph* (Nashua, NH), 11 February 1987, p. 65.
33 David Stratton, *The Avocado Plantation: Boom and Bust in the Australian Film Industry*, Pan Macmillan, Sydney, 1990, p. 337.
34 James O'Toole, 'Crocodile Dundee Outguns Even 007', *BRW*, 6 November 1986, pp. 29, 33; *NYT*, 31 December 1986, p. C18.
35 Tom O'Regan, '"Fair Dinkum Fillums": The *Crocodile Dundee* Phenomenon', in Susan Dermody and Elizabeth Jacka (eds), *The Imaginary Industry: Australian Film in the Late '80s*, Australian Film, Television and Radio School, North Ryde, 1988, p. 166; Ruth Abbey and Jo Crawford, 'Crocodile Dundee or Davy Crockett? What *Crocodile Dundee* Doesn't Say about Australia', *Meanjin*, vol. 46, no. 2, June 1987, pp. 145–52.
36 *Telegraph* (Nashua, NH), 11 February 1987, p. 65.
37 *NYT*, 21 September 1986, p. A19.
38 Jim Davidson, 'Locating "Crocodile Dundee"', *Meanjin*, vol. 46, no. 1, March 1987, pp. 124, 128.
39 Liz Williamson, 'Interlaced: Textiles for Fashion', in Bonnie English and Lillana Pomazan (eds), *Australian Fashion Unstitched: The Last 60 Years*, Cambridge University Press, Cambridge, 2010, p. 107.
40 Graeme Turner, 'Crocodile Dundee, 10BA, and the Future of the Australian Feature Film Industry', *Australian Studies*, no. 2, pp. 93–103.
41 *NYT*, 21 October 1986, p. C13.
42 Tom O'Regan, 'The Enchantment with Cinema: Film in the 1980s', in Albert Moran and Tom O'Regan (eds), *The Australian Screen*, Penguin Books, Ringwood, 1989, p. 131.
43 Stuart Cunningham, 'Kennedy-Miller: "House Style" in Australian Television', in Dermody and Jacka (eds), *The Imaginary Industry*, pp. 178–99; and 'Style, Form and History in Australian Mini-Series', in John Frow and Meaghan Morris (eds), *Australian Cultural Studies: A Reader*, Allen & Unwin, St Leonards, 1993, pp. 117–32.
44 I borrow the 'funny dress' reference from Greg Dening, *Mr Bligh's Bad Language: Passion, Power and Theatre on the Bounty*, Cambridge University Press, Cambridge, 1994, p. 4.
45 See clippings from *AFR*, 12 February 1986 and *Bulletin* [undated], Hurford Papers, CH 12/17/F3(M1970/1, Item 168), Bob Hawke Prime Ministerial Library.
46 Les Murray, 'The Australia Card', www.poetrylibrary.edu.au/poets/murray-les/the-australia-card-0572049, accessed 8 March 2015.
47 *West Australian*, 24 September 1987, pp. 1–2, 10.
48 *Weekend Australian*, 19–20 September 1987, p. 20.
49 *Australian*, 22 September 1987, p. 1.
50 *Courier-Mail*, 14 September 1987, p. 8; 21 September 1987, p. 8; 16 September 1987, p. 8.
51 *Australian*, 10 September 1987, p. 10; *Weekend Australian*, 5–6 September 1987, p. 26.
52 Ewart Smith, *The Australia Card: The Story of Its Defeat*, Sun Books/Macmillan, South Melbourne, 1989, p. 99.

53 Stephen Castles, Bill Cope, Mary Kalantzis and Michael Morrisey, 'The Bicentenary and the Failure of Australian Nationalism', *Race & Class*, vol. 29, no. 3, 1988, p. 55.
54 Gideon Haigh, *Asbestos House: The Secret History of James Hardie Industries*, Scribe, Melbourne, 2006, pp. 120-1, 131-2, 159.
55 Ken Baker, 'The Bicentenary: Celebration or Apology?', *IPA Review*, vol. 38, no. 4, Summer 1985, pp. 175-82; Geoffrey Blainey, 'Mr Hawke's Other Bicentennial Scandal', *IPA Review*, vol. 39, no. 3, Summer 1985/6, pp. 15-17.
56 O'Brien, *Bicentennial Affair*, pp. 48-9, 52-3, 122-3.
57 Lyn Spillman, *Nation and Commemoration: Creating National Identities in the United States and Australia*, Cambridge University Press, Cambridge, 1997, p. 113.
58 David Armstrong, interview transcript, 30 May 1984, NAA: A463/42, 1985/491 PART 4.
59 Stuart Macintyre and Anna Clark, *The History Wars*, Melbourne University Press, Carlton, 2003, ch. 6; Wendy McCarthy, *Don't Fence Me In*, Random House Australia, Sydney, 2000, p. 217.
60 Cohen to Armstrong, [5 June 1984], NAA: A463/42, 1985/491, PART 4. See also *CPD*, H of R, 31 May 1984, p. 2611 and Sergio Sergi to Georgie Carnegie, 9 May 1984, NAA: A463/42, 1985/491 PART 5.
61 Dawkins to Kirk, [3 October 1987], NAA: A1209/75, 1985/769, PART 4.
62 King, *Battle for the Bicentenary*, p. 309.
63 ibid., pp. 36, 93-4.
64 Robert Hughes, *The Fatal Shore: A History of the Transportation of Convicts to Australia*, 1787-1868, Collins Harvill, London, 1987.
65 King to Hawke, 6 January 1984, NAA: A 463/42, 1985/491 PART 4.
66 King, *Battle for the Bicentenary*, pp. 49-50, 57, 75.
67 *SMH*, 14 May 1987, p. 5.
68 *SMH*, 15 January 1988, p. 12, clipping in First Fleet Re-enactment Company Records, 1978-1990, Mitchell Library, Sydney, MLMSS 7796, Box 1.
69 Malcolm Turnbull, *Fighting for the Republic: The Ultimate Insider's Account*, Hardie Grant Books, South Yarra, 1999, p. 2.
70 Barry Morris, *Protest, Land Rights and Riots: Postcolonial Struggles in Australia in the 1980s*, Aboriginal Studies Press, Canberra, 2013, pp. 98-99; *SMH*, 12 January 1988, p. 3.
71 *Herald* (Melbourne), 26 January 1988, p. 1.
72 'The Book of the Year – Regional Newspapers & Readers Involvement', NAA: C2705/PA50-3442 PART 2; *SMH*, 27 January 1988, p. 14.
73 Hugh Mackay, *The Mackay Report: Being Australian*, March 1988, p. 7.
74 Tom Griffiths, *Hunters and Collectors: The Antiquarian Imagination in Australia*, Cambridge University Press, Cambridge, 1996, ch. 7.
75 L. Partridge to O'Brien, 3 July 1988, NAA: C2705/PA50-3442 PART 2.
76 Karen Richardson to O'Brien, 30 May 1988, ibid.
77 Karen Spiller to O'Brien, 17 October 1988, ibid.
78 Shaun Patrick Kenaelly, *Australia's Birthday Beacons: The Story of June 18th-19th, 1988*, Seminar on the Sociology of Culture, La Trobe University, Bundoora, n.d., p. 31.
79 O'Brien, *Bicentennial Affair*.
80 Diana Bagnall, 'Night of a Thousand Baas', *Vogue Australia*, February 1988, p. 11.
81 Susie Khamis, '"I'd rather take Methadone than Ken Done": Branding Sydney in the 1980s', *Scan*, vol. 2, issue 1, 2005.

82   Judy Jelbart to O'Brien, 10 May 1988, NAA: C2705, PA50-3442 PART 1.
83   *The Times*, 27 January 1988, p. 20; 26 January 1988, p. 9.
84   Disler to O'Brien, [Rec. 12 May 1988], ibid.
85   Maria Nugent, '"The queen gave us the land": Aboriginal people, Queen Victoria and historical remembrance', *History Australia*, vol. 9, no. 2, 2012, p. 188.
86   James Warden, *A Bunyip Democracy: The Parliament and Australian Political Identity*, Political Studies Fellow Monograph no. 2, Australian Government Publishing Service, Canberra, 1994, pp. 77–83.
87   Bruce Chatwin, *The Songlines*, Jonathan Cape, London, 1987, pp. 57, 117.
88   See Bain Attwood and Tom Griffiths (eds), *Frontier, Race, Nation: Henry Reynolds and Australian History*, Australian Scholarly Publishing, Melbourne 2009, esp. the essays by Attwood and Griffiths, and Dipesh Chakrabarty.
89   Bain Attwood, 'Portrait of an Aboriginal as an Artist: Sally Morgan and the Construction of Aboriginality', *Australian Historical Studies*, vol. 25, no. 99, October 1992, pp. 302–318; Jackie Huggins, 'Always Was Always Will Be', *Australian Historical Studies*, vol. 25, no. 100, April 1993, p. 460. See also Marcia Langton, *Well, I heard It on the Radio and I saw It on the Television. . .': An Essay for the Australian Film Commission on the Politics and Aesthetics of Filmmaking By and About Aboriginal People and Things*, Australian Film Commission, North Sydney, 1993, p. 31.
90   Sally Morgan, *My Place*, Fremantle Arts Centre Press, Fremantle, 1987, pp. 333, 340; Judith Drake-Brockman, *Wongi Wongi to Speak*, Hesperian Press, Carlisle, 2001, p. 138.
91   Marcus Breen, 'Desert Dreams, Media, and Interventions in Reality: Australian Aboriginal Music', in ReeBee Garofalo (ed.), *Rockin' the Boat: Mass Music and Mass Movements*, South End Press, Cambridge (MA), 1992, pp. 160–1; Andrew McMillan, *Strict Rules*, Sceptre, Rydalmere, 1992.
92   Matthew Ricketson, 'Signs of a Treaty', *Time*, 28 October 1991, pp. 68–9.
93   Vivien Johnson, *Once Upon a Time in Papunya*, NewSouth, Sydney, 2010, pp. 3–7, 115–16.
94   Ian McLean, 'Aboriginal Art and the Artworld' and 'How Aborigines Invested the Idea of Contemporary Art', in McLean (ed.), *How Aborigines Invented the Idea of Contemporary Art*, IMA Institute of Modern Art/Power Publications, Brisbane and Sydney, 2011, pp. 35 and 334–5.
95   Adrian Newstead, with Ruth Hessy, *The Dealer Is the Devil: An Insider's History of the Aboriginal Art Trade*, Brandl and Schlesinger, Blackheath, 2014, p. 297.
96   *NYT*, 9 February 1986.
97   *Vogue Australia*, January 1988, p. 99.
98   *The Pope in Australia: Collected Homilies and Talks*, St Paul Publications, Homebush (NSW), 1986, pp. 165–72 and illustration 19; Margaret Maynard, *Out of Line: Australian Women and Style*, University of New South Wales Press, Sydney, 2001, pp. 64–7, 132–3, 168–81 and 'Grassroots Style: Re-evaluating Australian Fashion and Aboriginal Art in the 1970s and 1980s', *Journal of Design History*, vol. 13, no. 2, 2000, pp. 137–50; Williamson, 'Interlaced', pp. 118–19.
99   Anne-Marie Willis and Tony Fry, 'Symptoms of Ethnocide – 1988–89, 2007', in McLean (ed.), *How Aborigines*, pp. 286–90.
100   Morris, *Protest*, p. 108.
101   *Goondiwindi Argus*, 14 January 1987, p. 1.
102   Morris, *Protest*, p. 30.
103   *Goondiwindi Argus*, 29 July 1987, p. 6.

104 ibid., 5 August 1987, p. 3.
105 *Present Tense*, pp. 23, 4.
106 Mackay, *The Mackay Report: Being Australian*, p. 8.
107 *Immigration: A Commitment to Australia, The Report of the Committee to Advise on Australia's Immigration Policies*, Australian Government Publishing Service, Canberra, 1988, pp. 8–10; Ghassan Hage, 'Anglo-Celtics Today: Cosmo-Multiculturalism and the Phase of the Fading Phallus', *Communal/Plural*, No. 4, 1994, p. 63.
108 *CT*, 31 July 1988, p. 1.
109 *CPD*, H of R, August 1988, pp. 403, 408.
110 *Advertiser* (Adelaide), 5 December 1988, in Liberal Party of Australia, Federal Secretariat Papers, NLA 5000, Box 1318.
111 [Tony Eggleton] to Andrew Robb, Duncan Fairweather and Alastair Kinloch, 16 December 1988, in ibid.
112 *SMH*, 6 December 1988, p. 5.
113 *CT*, 5 December 1988, p. 1.
114 Liberal Party of Australia, *Future Directions: It's Time for Plain Thinking*, Liberal, National, Barton, 1988, pp. 7, 3.
115 ibid., p. 96. See also Judith Brett, 'Future Directions', *Current Affairs Bulletin*, vol. 66, no. 1, June 1989, pp. 15–16.
116 Humphrey McQueen, *Tokyo World: An Australian Diary*, William Heinemann Australia, Port Melbourne, 1991, pp. 47, 49.
117 Andrew Stewart and Robert MacDonald, 'Japanese Takeaway', *BRW*, 31 March 1988, p. 46.
118 Shigeto Tsuru, *Japan's Capitalism: Creative Defeat and Beyond*, Cambridge University Press, Cambridge, 1994, p. 201. See also Hajdu, *Samarai in the Surf*.
119 Mackay, *The Mackay Report: Being Australian*, p. 22.
120 Michael Salmon, *The Laziest Crocodile in Australia*, Peter Antill-Rose & Associates, Castle Hill, 1989.
121 *GCB*, 25 May 1988, p. 3.
122 ibid., 26 May 1988, p. 1–2, 6.
123 ibid., 4 June 1988, p. 69; 27 May 1988, p. 7.
124 ibid., 31 May 1988, p. 12.
125 Stewart and MacDonald, 'Japanese Takeaway', p. 51.
126 Ross Garnaut, *Australia and the Northeast Asian Ascendancy: Report to the Prime Minister and the Minister for Foreign Affairs and Trade*, Australian Government Publishing Service, Canberra, 1989, p. 1.
127 Abe David and Ted Wheelwright, *The Third Wave: Australia and Asian Capitalism*, Left Book Club Co-operative, Sutherland (NSW), 1989.
128 For the extreme right in Australia in the late 1980s, see Lyndall Crisp, 'Harvest of Hate', *Bulletin*, 4 April 1989, pp. 42–9.
129 Human Rights and Equal Opportunity Commission, *Report of the National Inquiry into Racist Violence in Australia*, Australian Government Publishing Service, Canberra, 1991, pp. 175, 140, 157–8.
130 Agnieszka Sobocinska, 'Innocence Lost and Paradise Regained: Tourism to Bali and Australian Perceptions of Asia', *History Australia*, vol. 8, no. 2, August 2011, pp. 199–222.
131 *Age*, 26 April 1989, p. 5.
132 Christina Twomey, 'Prisoners of War of the Japanese: War and Memory in Australia', *Memory Studies*, vol. 6, no. 3, pp. 321–30 and 'Trauma and the Reinvigoration of Anzac', *History Australia*, vol. 10, no. 3, December 2013, pp. 85–108.

133 Joan Beaumont, 'Hellfire Pass Memorial Museum, Thai–Burma Railway', in Martin Gegner and Bart Ziino (eds), *The Heritage of War*, Routledge, London and New York, 2012, p. 24.
134 Twomey, 'Prisoners of War', pp. 322, 326.
135 *Age*, 25 April 1984, p. 4; *Australian*, 25 April 1984, p. 2.
136 *Daily Telegraph*, 5 October 1987, p. 1; *Sun–Herald*, 4 October 1987, pp. 2–4.
137 *Age*, 26 April 1988, p. 4.
138 *SMH*, 5 October 1987, p. 4.
139 *Australian*, 25 April 1989, p. 10.
140 *Age*, 25 April 1984, p. 4.
141 *Australian*, 26 April 1983, p. 1.
142 *CT*, 26 April 1981, p. 1.
143 *Age*, 26 April 1983, p. 1.
144 ibid., 25 April 1984, p. 4.
145 ibid., 25 April 1987, p. 12; Twomey, 'Trauma', p. 105.
146 Bruce Scates, *A Place to Remember: A History of the Shrine of Remembrance*, Cambridge University Press, Cambridge, 2009, pp. 244–5, 289, n. 162; *Age*, 26 April 1984, p. 4.
147 *Age*, 26 April 1985, p. 5; 26 April 1986, p. 1; K.S. Inglis, assisted by Jan Brazier, *Sacred Places: War Memorials in the Australian Landscape*, The Miegunyah Press, Carlton South, 1999, pp. 446–7.
148 Mark McKenna, 'Anzac Day: How Did It Become Australia's National Day?', in Marilyn Lake and Henry Reynolds with Mark McKenna and Joy Damousi, *What's Wrong With Anzac? The Militarisation of Australian History*, NewSouth Publishing, Sydney, 2010, p. 116.
149 *Age*, 25 April 1984, p. 1.
150 *Australian*, 25 April 1985, p. 3.
151 *Age*, 26 April 1986, p. 5.
152 Carolyn Holbrook, *Anzac: The Unauthorised Biography*, NewSouth Publishing, Sydney, 2014, pp. 175–7; Michael McKernan, 'Australian Tourists at Gallipoli', unpublished paper, presented at Çanakkale/Gallipoli Wars 2015 International Conference, Çanakkale, 2015.
153 'Speech by the Prime Minister Dawn Service, Gallipoli 25 April 1990', http://pmtranscripts.dpmc.gov.au/transcripts/00008013.pdf, and 'Speech for the Prime Minister Lone Pine Ceremony Gallipoli – 25 April 1990', http://pmtranscripts.dpmc.gov.au/browse.php?did=8010, both accessed 30 November 2014.

Chapter 9: The Crash

1 *Australian*, 21 October 1987, p. 9.
2 ibid., p. 12; *AFR*, 21 October 1987, pp. 1, 8.
3 *AFR*, 21 October 1987, p. 16.
4 *Australian*, 21 October 1987, p. 12.
5 *AFR*, 21 October 1987, p. 3.
6 ibid., p. 8.
7 ibid., p. 11.
8 ibid., p. 16.
9 *Australian*, 21 October 1987, p. 8.
10 *AFR*, 20 October 1987, p. 12.
11 ibid., p. 12.

ENDNOTES

12 ibid., p. 11.
13 Beresford, *Godfather*, p. 132.
14 ibid., pp. 121–30; Sykes, *Bold Riders*, pp. 98–9, 106–8.
15 Beresford, *Godfather*, pp. 128–34; Sykes, *Bold Riders*, pp. 109–17; Barry, *Rise and Fall of Alan Bond*, ch. 18.
16 Beresford, *Godfather*, pp. 122–3.
17 Barry, *Rise and Fall of Alan Bond*, p. 216.
18 Patricia Edgar, *Janet Holmes à Court*, HarperCollins, Sydney, 1999, pp. 199–201.
19 Sykes, *Bold Riders*, pp. 225–6; ibid., pp. 206–11.
20 Edgar, *Janet Holmes à Court*, p. 198.
21 Barry, *Rise and Fall of Alan Bond*, pp. 275–6; Barry, *Rise and Rise of Kerry Packer*, p. 420; Sykes, *Bold Rider*, p. 209.
22 Chris Masters, 'Moonlight Reflections', *Griffith Review: Hidden Queensland*, no. 21, http://griffithreview.com/articles/moonlight-reflections/, accessed 8 December 2014.
23 Ross Fitzgerald, Lyndon Megarrity and David Symons, *Made in Queensland: A New History*, University of Queensland Press, St Lucia, 2009, p. 183.
24 Dickie, *Road to Fitzgerald*, p. 197.
25 Jack Herbert with Tom Gilling, *The Bagman: Final Confessions of Jack Herbert*, ABC Books, Sydney, 2004, p. 130.
26 ibid., pp. 160, 182–239.
27 Fitzgerald, Megarrity and Symons, *Made in Queensland*, p. 184.
28 Dickie, *Road to Fitzgerald*, pp. 209–10.
29 Wear, *Johannes Bjelke-Petersen*, p. 122; Whitton, *Hillbilly Dictator*, pp. 137–8.
30 Dickie, *Road to Fitzgerald*, p. 226.
31 Whitton, *Hillbilly Dictator*, p. 134.
32 Herbert with Gilling, *Bagman*, p. 109.
33 Dickie, *Road to Fitzgerald*, p. 271.
34 *Courier-Mail*, 6 December 1988, p. 1.
35 Brian Toohey, 'How Fitzgerald flunked it', *Eye*, August–September 1989, p. 7. See also Brian Toohey, 'Fitzgerald – How the Process Came Unstuck', in Scott Prasser, Rae Wear and John Nethercote (eds), *Corruption and Reform: The Fitzgerald Vision*, University of Queensland Press, St Lucia, 1990, pp. 81–8.
36 Clifford Clawback, 'The Fitzgerald Inquiry: Unturned Sods and Other Muck', *Cane Toad Times*, issue 9, Summer 1988, p. 5.
37 *Courier-Mail*, 16 October 1987, p. 9.
38 *Age*, 14 July 1989, p. 6.
39 *SMH*, 4 March 1989, p. 39.
40 *Courier-Mail*, 16 October 1987, p. 9.
41 *Australian*, 3 April 1989, pp. 1–2.
42 *Courier-Mail*, 6 June 1989, p. 5; *SMH*, 15 September 1989, p. 29; *Australian*, 12 October 1989, pp. 1, 14; Sykes, *Bold Riders*, pp. 309–15.
43 Prior, *Christopher Skase*, p. 9.
44 *SMH*, 7 November 1989, p. 1; *CT*, 21 November 1989, p. 20; *Weekend Australian*, 9–10 December 1989, p. 1; *Australian*, 29 March 1990, pp. 1–2; *AFR*, 29 June 1990, pp. 1, 16.
45 *Age*, 28 May 1991, p. 1; 29 May 1991, p. 1; *AFR*, 28 May 1991, pp. 1–2; 31 May 1991, pp. 29, 31.
46 *AFR*, 17 June 1991, p. 3.
47 Prior, *Christopher Skase*, pp. 218–43.
48 *Australian*, 28 May 1991, p. 19.

49 Greg McCarthy, *Things Fall Apart: A History of the State Bank of South Australia*, Australian Scholarly Publishing, Melbourne, 2002, pp. x–xiv, chs 5–9.
50 State Bank of South Australia (SBSA), *Annual Report*, 1989, p. 4.
51 McCarthy, *Things Fall Apart*, pp. 131, 149–50, 178.
52 SBSA, *Annual Report*, 1989, pp. 18–19; SBSA, *Annual Report*, 1990, p. 26; McCarthy, *Things Fall Apart*, p. 150.
53 SBSA, *Annual Report*, 1990, p. 20.
54 SBSA, *Annual Report*, 1991, pp. 15, 27.
55 McCarthy, *Things Fall Apart*, p. xiv.
56 Quoted in McCarthy, *Things Fall Apart*, p. 171.
57 ibid., pp. 133–7, 156–7.
58 ibid., pp. 187–90, 205–10.
59 ibid., p. 158.
60 SBSA, *Annual Report*, 1990, p. 11.
61 Kenneth Davidson, 'The Victorian Economy and the Policy of the Cain/Kirner Government', in Mark Considine and Brian Costar (eds), *Trials in Power: Cain, Kirner and Victoria 1982–1992*, Melbourne University Press, Carlton, 1992, p. 39–40.
62 Hugo Armstrong, 'The Tricontinental Affair', in ibid., pp. 46, 44.
63 Armstrong and Gross, *Tricontinental*, ch. 3.
64 Bruce Albert Ziebell, *Evidence*, Transcript of Proceedings before the Royal Commission into the Tricontinental Group of Companies, vol. 30, 7 March 1991, p. 3069.
65 Quoted in Armstrong and Gross, *Tricontinental*, p. 83.
66 Ziebell, *Evidence*, p. 3168–9.
67 ibid., p. 3115.
68 Armstrong and Gross, *Tricontinental*, p. xi; Paul Keating, in ALP, Special National Conference, Transcript, 24 September 1990, p. 75.
69 Cain, *John Cain's Years*, p. 215.
70 *Geelong Advertiser*, 30 June 1990, p. 4.
71 *Sunday Age*, 8 July 1990, p. 6.
72 ibid.; D.J. Habersberger, *Farrow Group Inquiry Final Report*, L.V. North, Government Printer, Melbourne, 1994, p. 1653–4.
73 Habersberger, *Farrow Group Inquiry Final Report*, pp. 1657, 1682, 1659, 1667–8.
74 *Geelong Advertiser*, 2 July 1990, p. 1.
75 Habersberger, *Farrow Group Inquiry Final Report*, pp. 1654, 1669–70.
76 ibid., pp. 1599, 1625–8, 1662; Sykes, *Bold Riders*, p. 388.
77 Sykes, *Bold Riders*, pp. 379, 374.
78 Habersberger, *Farrow Group Inquiry Final Report*, p. 1622.
79 ibid., pp. 1623, 1619.
80 *Geelong Advertiser*, 2 July 1990, p. 2.
81 ibid., 4 July 1990, p. 1; *Sunday Age*, 8 July 1990, p. 7.
82 *Age*, 17 July 1990, pp. 1, 10, 31.
83 Cain, *John Cain's Years*, p. 259.
84 *SMH*, 22 February 1990, pp. 29, 32–3; *Age*, 5 May 1990, p. 4; *Weekend Australian*, 19–20 May 1990, p. 1; *AFR*, 4 May 1990, pp. 1, 3.
85 *SMH*, 3 June 1992, p. 4.
86 *Australian*, 23 August 1996, p. 25.
87 Edwards, *Keating*, pp. 329, 340, 347, 353, 376.
88 Kelly, *End of Certainty*, p. 617.
89 ibid., p. 665.

90 Megalogenis, *Australian Moment*, p. 209.
91 L. Sharon Davidson and Stephen Salsbury, *Australia's First Bank: Fifty Years from the Wales to Westpac*, University of New South Wales Press, Sydney, 2005, p. 330.
92 Sykes, *Bold Riders*, p. 573.
93 ibid., ch. 10 and p. 283.
94 *Age*, 31 January 1992, p. 9.
95 Hugh Mackay, *The Mackay Report, Keynote, The Recession Mentality*, May 1991, p. 22.
96 Meredith and Dyster, *Australia in the Global Economy*, p. 285.
97 Megalogenis, *Australian Moment*, p. 210.
98 'The Long Term Unemployed, 1301.0 – Year Book Australia, 1995, www.abs.gov.au/ausstats/abs@.nsf/featurearticlesbytitle/8C560715E24051D7CA 2570FF001A1799, accessed 4 June 2015.
99 *Sunday Age*, 18 July 1992, p. 11.
100 www.brucktextiles.com.au/about-bruck/history-4; *Age*, 19 November 1997, www.computerlease.com.au/computer-lease-articles/1997/11/19/ibm-quits-plant-at-wangaratta/, both accessed 4 June 2015.
101 *Age*, 11 September 1991, p. 11.
102 Andrew Leigh, 'Trade Liberalisation and the Australian Labor Party', *Australian Journal of Politics and History*, vol. 48, no. 4, December 2002, pp. 495–502.
103 Kerin to Button, 4 August 1986, Button Papers, MS 13728, Series IV, Sub-series 1, Box 9, Folder 5, File E, SLV.
104 Button to Kerin, ibid.
105 Hawke to Button, 5 May 1988, Button Papers, MS 13728, Series IV, Sub-series 1, Box 9, Folder 5, File E, SLV.
106 Bob Hawke, Paul Keating and John Button, *Building a Competitive Australia*, 12 March 1991, Australian Government Publishing Service, Canberra, 1991; Ann Capling and Brian Galligan, *Beyond the Protective State: The Political Economy of Australia's Manufacturing Industry Policy*, Cambridge University Press, Cambridge, 1992, p. 246.
107 Edwards, *Keating*, p. 414
108 Kelly, *End of Certainty*, p. 665.
109 Murray Goot, 'Contradictory Consciousness: Polled Opinion on Protection, 1944–1992', unpublished paper, December 1992; John Carroll and Robert Manne, 'Preface', in Carroll and Manne (eds), *Shutdown: The Failure of Economic Rationalism and How to Rescue Australia*, Text Publishing, Melbourne, 1992, p. 2. See also Michael Pusey, *Economic Rationalism in Canberra: A Nation-Building State Changes its Mind*, Cambridge University Press, Cambridge, 1991.
110 Carol Baines, 'Multifunction Polis: Lost City of Opportunity', PhD Thesis, University of Adelaide, 1999.
111 *Multifunction Polis: A Concept to Create the Future*, n.d. [1989]; Gavan McCormack, 'Coping with Japan: The MFP Proposal and the Australian Response', in McCormack (ed.), *Bonsai Australia Banzai: Multifunctionpolis and the Making of a Special Relationship with Japan*, Pluto Press Australia, Leichhardt, 1991, pp. 34–67, esp. pp. 51–2 and 'A Multifunctionpolis Scheme for the Twenty-first Century' (Basic Concept) appendix in the same volume, pp. 182–218.
112 Ade Peace, 'Development, Democracy and the Australian MFP', *Chain Reaction*, no. 65, [c. 1992], p. 23.
113 Quoted in Baines, 'Multifunction Polis', p. 260.

114 Andrew Scott, *Northern Lights: The Positive Policy Example of Sweden, Finland, Denmark and Norway*, Monash University Publishing, Clayton, 2014, pp. 36–59; *Australia Reconstructed: ACTU/TDC Mission to Western Europe: A Report by the Mission Members to the ACTU and the TDC*, Australian Government Publishing Service, Canberra, 1987, p. xii.

115 ibid., *passim*.

116 Hannah Forsyth, *A History of the Modern Australian University*, NewSouth, Sydney, 2014, pp. 114–15; Stuart Macintyre, with Gwilym Croucher, Glyn Davis and Simon Marginson, 'Making the Unified National System', in Gwilym Croucher, Simon Marginson, Andrew Norton and Julie Wells (eds), *The Dawkins Revolution: 25 Years On*, Melbourne University Press, Carlton, 2013, pp. 12–13, 20–1.

117 *Higher Education: A Policy Discussion Paper*, December 1987, Australian Government Publishing Service, Canberra, 1987, p. 2.

118 *Higher Education: A Policy Statement*, July 1988, Commonwealth of Australia, 1988, pp. 30, 90.

119 ibid., p. 41.

120 Paul Brock, *A Passion for Life*, ABC Books, Sydney, 2004, pp. 185–6.

121 *Age*, 13 May 1988, p. 1, in Macintyre et al., 'Making', p. 39.

122 For Bond, see Kay Saunders and Antoinette Cass, *Bond University: The First 25 Years*, Bond University Press, Robina, 2014; Brian Orr, *Bond University: The Beginning 1985–1991: A Personal View*, Branxton Press, Canberra, 1991.

123 *GCB*, 7 June 1988, p. 2.

124 Donald W. Watts, 'The Meaning of Bond', *Quadrant*, no. 254, vol. 33, April 1989, pp. 49–50.

125 Donald W. Watts, 'The Private Potential of Australian Higher Education', in David R. Jones and John Anwyl (eds), *Privatizing Higher Education: A New Australian Issue*, Centre for the Study of Higher Education, Melbourne, 1987, p. 32.

126 Judith Brett, *Fair Share: Country and City in Australia*, Quarterly Essay, Issue 42, 2011, pp. 48–9.

127 Capling and Galligan, *Beyond the Protective State*, pp. 185, 188–9, 220.

128 Mark Peel, *Good Times, Hard Times: The Past and the Future in Elizabeth*, Melbourne University Press, Carlton, 1995, pp. 162, 170, 197, 203.

129 Julianne Schultz, *Steel City Blues*, Penguin Books, Ringwood, 1985, pp. 1–2, 118–20, 236–46; Erik Eklund, *Steel Town: The Making and Breaking of Port Kembla*, Melbourne University Press, Carlton, 2002, p. 177.

130 Schultz, *Steel City Blues*, p. 254.

131 Peel, *Good Times, Hard Times*, chs 6–7.

132 Brett, *Fair Share*, p. 49; Paul Cleary, *Too Much Luck: The Mining Boom and Australia's Future*, Black Inc., Collingwood, 2011.

133 D'Alpuget, *Hawke*, p. 232; Blanche d'Alpuget, *On Longing*, Melbourne University Press, Carlton, 2008, p. 59.

134 Michael Gordon, *Paul Keating: A Question of Leadership*, University of Queensland Press, St Lucia, 1993, pp. 65–6.

135 Day, *Keating*, pp. 305–11; Gordon, *Paul Keating*, pp. 85–7.

136 Ian McAllister and Clive Bean, 'Explaining Labor's Victory', in Clive Bean, Ian McAllister and John Warhurst (eds), *The Greening of Australian Politics: The 1990 Federal Election*, Longman Cheshire, Melbourne, 1990, p. 155.

137 Mary Sheehan and Sonia Jennings, *A Federation of Pilots: The Story of an Australian Air Pilots' Union*, Melbourne University Publishing, Carlton, 2010, pp. 146–65.

138 Mills, *Hawke Years*, p. 112.

139 Sheehan and Jennings, *Federation of Pilots*, p. 190.
140 ibid., pp. 165–80; Graham F. Smith, 'From Consensus to Coercion: the Australian Air Pilots Dispute', *Journal of Industrial Relations*, no. 3, vol. 32, September 1990, pp. 238–53.
141 Smith, 'From Consensus to Coercion', p. 246.
142 Mills, *Hawke Years*, p. 117.
143 Kelly, *End of Certainty*, chs. 25 and 27 and p. 555.
144 Ian Hancock, *Nick Greiner: A Political Biography*, Connor Court Publishing, Ballan, 2013, ch. 10.
145 Drew Hutton and Libby Connors, *A History of the Australian Environment Movement*, Cambridge University Press, Cambridge, 1999, pp. 171–5.
146 Kelly, *End of Certainty*, p. 527; Richardson, *Whatever It Takes*, p. 214.
147 Kelly, *End of Certainty*, p. 526.
148 Spillman, *Nation and Commemoration*, pp. 125–6.
149 Christine Milne, 'Pulp Mills or People Power?', in Cassandra Pybus and Richard Flanagan (eds), *The Rest of the World is Watching*, Pan Macmillan, Chippendale, 1990, p. 57.
150 Amanda Lohrey, 'The Greens: A New Narrative', in Pybus and Flanagan (eds), *Rest of the World*, p. 99.
151 Rob Youl (ed.), *Landcare in Victoria: How Landcare Helped People Government and Business Work Together in Victoria*, Rob Youl, South Melbourne, 2006.
152 Brown and Boden, *Way Through*, pp. 172–4.
153 Quoted in Cassandra Pybus, 'Introduction', in Pybus and Flanagan (eds), *Rest of the World*, p. 11.
154 Stephen Tanner, 'The Rise and Fall of Edmund Rouse', *Australian Studies in Journalism*, no. 4, 1995, pp. 72–89.
155 Hutton and Connors, *History of the Australian Environment Movement*, p. 230.
156 Walsh to Button, 29 November 1990, Button Papers, MS 13728, Series IV, Sub-series 1, Box 9, Folder 5, File E, SLV.
157 Brown and Boden, *Way Through*, p. 174.
158 Walsh, *Confessions*, pp. 209–10, 241–2.
159 McAllister and Bean, 'Explaining', pp. 170–1.
160 Kimberly R. Moffitt and Duncan A. Campbell, 'The 1980s as a Decade', in Moffitt and Campbell (eds), *The 1980s: A Critical and Transitional Decade*, Lexington Books, Lanham, 2011, p. 2.
161 John Braithwaite, 'Economic Policy: What the Electorate Thinks', in Kelley and Bean (eds), *Australian Attitudes*, pp. 26–7; Hugh Mackay, *The Mackay Report*, Keynote 2, *Privatisation*, November 1990.
162 ALP, Special National Conference, 'Transcript, 24 September 1990, pp. 36, 82.
163 Brian Howe, 'Restraint with Equity: Social Protection in Australia in the 1980s', in Susan Ryan and Troy Bramston (eds), *The Hawke Government: A Critical Retrospective*, Pluto Press Australia, North Melbourne, 2003, pp. 241–54.
164 Neal Blewett, 'Cutting the Mustard: Lectures and Chutzpah in Lieu of Keating's Memoirs', *Australian Book Review*, no. 338, February 2012, p. 11.
165 Robert Hogg, 'Review and Recommendations on the Reform of the Party's Organisation, Draft Report', Second Edition, 13 December 1990, Hawke Papers, Series RH 18, Box 17, F. 206, Bob Hawke Prime Ministerial Library.
166 David Horner, *Australia and the 'New World Order': From Peacekeeping to Peace Enforcement: 1988–1991*, Cambridge University Press, Cambridge, 2011, pp. 310–11, 325–6; Hugh White to Hawke, Briefing Paper, 29 November 1990, Button Papers, MS 13728, Series IV, Sub-series 1, Box 9, Folder 3, File C, SLV.

167 Milton Cockburn, 'The Politics of Australian Involvement', in Murray Goot and Rodney Tiffen (eds), *Australia's Gulf War*, Melbourne University Press, Carlton, 1992, pp. 42–53; Horner, *Australia and the 'New World Order'*, pp. 323–8, 415–18, 443–5; Hawke, *Memoirs*, pp. 525–6.
168 Gordon, *Paul Keating*, pp. 5, 10–11.
169 Christine Wallace, *Hewson: A Portrait*, Pan Macmillan, Sydney, 1993, pp. 139–35, 164–6.
170 Notes of Discussion with R.J. Hawke re. Leadership, 17 December 1991, Button Papers, MS 13728, Series IV, Sub-series 1, Box 9, Folder 3, File D, SLV.
171 Gordon, *Paul Keating*, p. 183.

What Did It All Mean?

1   *Vogue*, January 1990, p. 69.
2   *SMH*, 27 September 1992, p. 14.
3   Megalogenis, *Australian Moment*.
4   Ian W. McLean, *Why Australia Prospered: The Shifting Sources of Economic Growth*, Princeton University Press, Princeton, 2013.
5   Moffitt and Campbell (eds), *1980s*.

Credits

Photographs and illustrations:
'People from the McMahons Creek and Reefton areas sit out the bushfires in a Board of Works tunnel at the Upper Yarra dam', *Age*, 18 March 1983 (Fairfax Syndication); 'David Combe – This Court Finds You Guilty of the Charges Against You', *Canberra Times*, 12 May 1983 (Geoff Pryor/Pryor Collection of Cartoons and Drawings, nla.pic-an23136639, National Library of Australia); 'Sport and recreation – America's cup – Visit of "*Australia II*" team to Canberra' [Bob Hawke and Alan Bond, 1983] (National Archives of Australia: A8746, KN16/11/83/46); 'Personalities – Paul Keating – At a press conference, head and shoulders', 1984 (National Archives of Australia: A6180, 13/1/84/4); Geoffrey Blainey, 1985 (University of Newcastle); 'Young members of the Vietnamese community in Sydney's Cabramatta', *Sydney Morning Herald*, 17 November 1982 (Fairfax Syndication); Bob Brown and protestors, No Dam protest, Franklin River, Tasmania, *Age* (Photo by John Krutop/Fairfax Syndication); Cliff Young, 1983 (Photo by Andrew De La Rue/Newspix); Stephen Kernahan and John Elliott, *Age*, 10 September 1988 (Photo by Andrew De La Rue/Fairfax Syndication); Portrait of Russell Goward, 1987 (Photo by Gary Ede/National Library of Australia, PIC Box S8 #P1579/R); 'A Loser/A Winner', *Sydney Morning Herald*, 21 September 1984 (Cartoon by Jenny Coopes/National Library of Australia); 'Christopher Skase at Mirage Resort, Pt. Douglas' (Photo by Rennie Ellis, ©Rennie Ellis Photographic Archive/State Library of Victoria, Image H2011.2/2875); Michael Hutchence and Michele Bennett, Valentines Day, Sydney 1985 (Fremantle Media Ltd/Rex); Paul Hogan with John Cornell after the premiere of *Crocodile Dundee II*, Sydney, 19 May 1988 (Photo by Gregg Porteous/Newspix); Midnight Oil and Peter Garrett (Photo by Bob King/Redferns/Getty Images); Mary-Anne Fahey as Kylie Mole, Melbourne, 1989 (Photo by Impressions/Getty Images); Jason Donovan and Kylie Minogue as Scott

Robinson and Charlene Mitchell, *Neighbours*, 1987 (Fremantle Media Ltd/ Rex); 'Festivals and celebrations – Australia's bicentenary – Australia Day activities – Sydney, 1988' [First Fleet Re-enactment/Enjoy Coke] (National Archives of Australia: A6135, K8/2/88/52); 'Aboriginal Protest: Australia Day '88, Sydney Harbour' (Photo by Rennie Ellis, ©Rennie Ellis Photographic Archive/State Library of Victoria, Image H2012.140/461); Builders Labourers Federation, Free Norm Gallagher Demonstration (Photo by John Casamento); 'Multifunction Polis: A Japanese Hi-Tech City for Melbourne?', 1989 (Reason in Revolt: Source Documents of Australian Radicalism, http://www.reasoninrevolt.net.au/bib/PR0001617.htm); *Future Directions: It's Time for Plain Thinking* (Liberal Party of Australia and National Party of Australia/National Library of Australia); Irene Bolger and nurses, 1986: Australian Nursing and Midwifery Federation (Vic. Branch); Sir Joh Bjelke-Petersen, Brisbane (Fairfax Syndication); Bob Hawke, Melbourne, August 1991 (Photo by John Casamento).

Lyrics:

'The Power And The Passion', written and composed by Hirst/Moginie/Garrett, published by Sony/ATV Music Publishing Australia; 'Maralinga', written and composed by Paul Kelly, published by Sony/ATV Music Publishing Australia.

Index

Abeles, Sir Peter 17, 121, 124, 291, 292
Aboriginal and Islander Ex-Services Association 261
Aboriginal art 250–1
Aboriginal authors 248–9
Aboriginal dance and theatre 250
Aboriginal deaths in custody 252
Aboriginal fashion design 251
Aboriginal identity and culture 234
    in books 248–9
Aboriginal music 249–50
Aboriginal people
    and Anzac Day march 261
    legacy of dispossession 247
    and nuclear testing 116–18
    opinion on Bicentenary celebrations 243–5
    protests at Bicentenary 243–5, 247
    views on mining industry 77
abortion 192–3
Accord Mark II 176
acquired immune deficiency syndrome (AIDS) 202–5, 225
Acropolis Now (sitcom) 215
Acton, Prue 237
Adelaide, SA
    casino 273
    Formula One Australian Grand Prix 230–1, 273
    Multifunction Polis (MFP) 231, 258, 284–6, 285
Adelaide Hills, SA 6–7
Adelaide Steamship Company (Adsteam) 139, 164
Adler, Larry 122, 265
Adsteam, *see* Adelaide Steamship Company (Adsteam)
'Advance Australia Fair' 197
Adventures of Barry McKenzie, The 236
Age, The, tapes 100–4
Ahern, Mike 269
Air Supply (pop duo) 221
airline pilot strike 291–3
airlines 291–2
Alexander, Stephanie 227
Allen, Bill 97–8
Alter, Maurice 20

America's Cup yacht race (1983) 33, 34, 35–40, 58, 152–3, 267
amphetamines 107
Amphlett, Chrissy 223
Anderson, Warren 124
Ansett, Bob 147
Ansett Airlines 121, 292
anti-dam campaigns 85–8
anti-Japanese sentiment 256–8
anti-nuclear movement 114–15
anti-smoking campaigns 107–8
ANZ Bank 138
Anzac Cove 261
Anzac Day ceremonies 259, 260–2, 261
Anzac qualities 259
ANZUS crisis 114
apartment living 216
Appleton, Gillian 100, 103–4
Archer, Brian 56
Arkley, Howard 224, 225–6
Armstrong, David 241
Arndt, Bettina 194–5
Arnold, Lynn 274
art, Australian 224–5
art-house cinema 237
Ash Wednesday bushfires 1, 4–8, 5–7
Asia, travel to 258
Asian immigration 59, 60, 62–3, 63–71, 64–5, 65–6, 69–71, 82–3, 253, 305
'Asianisation policy' 64–5, 69–70
Asia-Pacific Economic Cooperation (APEC) 257
Askin, Sir Robert 97
Assange, Julian 206
asset sales 129
Ataturk Peace Park, Canberra 261
Attwood, Bain 249
Australasian Meat Industry Employees Union (AMIEU) 166
Australia, You're Standing in It (comedy TV series) 213
Australia Card 238–40
'Australia Card, The' (Les Murray poem) 239
Australia Day 244, 247, 261
Australia II (yacht)
    doubtful economic benefits 39–40
    winged keel design 34–5

INDEX

Australia Reconstructed (alternative national vision) 286
Australian Airlines 297
Australian authors 212–13
Australian Bicentennial Authority (ABA) 241
Australian book publishing 212
Australian Conservation Foundation (ACF) 296
Australian dollar crisis 159–60
Australian drama 212–13
Australian Football League (AFL) 149, 151–2
Australian Labor Party (ALP)
    advertising campaign 188
    and the BLF 177
    'Bringing Australia Together' campaign 4
    campaign launch 1984 112
    close to Packer 123
    conservative union membership 170–1
    corruption and mateship 102
    donations to 10
    electoral support falls 112–13
    environment policies 297
    land rights policy 72, 75, 77
    policy disputes 51–2
    relations with ASIO 20–1
    relationship with business 9–10
    uranium mining policy 93
Australian masculinity 109–10
Australian Mutual Provident (AMP) 142
Australian nationalism 36, 38, 39–40; *see also* Bicentenary celebrations
Australian Nationalist Movement 258
Australian Personal Computer (magazine) 206
Australian poetry 213
Australian Rules football 148–9
Australian Secret Intelligence Service (ASIS) 25–6
Australian Security Intelligence Organisation (ASIO) 13, 20–2, 25
Australian Workers' Union 163
Australiana 146
Australia–USSR Friendship Society 12
avant-garde fashion 224
award conditions (Robe River) 173
Ayers Rock, *see* Uluru

Baird, Mike xii
Baldwin, Peter 99
Ball, Desmond 89
Bancroft, Bronwyn 251
Bangarra Dance Theatre 250
Bank of Melbourne 278–9
banks 137–40, 162, 273–5, 297
Bannon, John 9, 93, 274
Bannon government 51
Bardon, Geoffrey 250
Barnes, Jimmy 223
Barnett, Harvey 13, 20–2, 25
Batchelor, Peter 115
Beazley, Kim 54–5, 75, 299

Beckwith, Peter 265
beer brewing industry 136–7
Beers, Garry 219
Bell Group 266
Bell Resources 121, 266
Bertrand, John 35
Bicentenary celebrations 78, 241–7, 295
Bicentennial First Fleet Re-enactment (1987–88) 207
Big Brother Movement 66
Big Gig, The (TV sketch comedy) 214
bill of rights 56
Birthday Beacons (Bicentenary celebration) 246
Bjelke-Petersen, Flo 179
Bjelke-Petersen, Joh 10
    and ETU strike 172
    on land rights 72
    launch of Rothwells 11
    link with Skase 127
    national political campaign 182–5
    perjury 270
    political donations 270
    rapport with NZ 115
    resignation 269
    Swiss franc borrowing 162
Bjelke-Petersen government 181, 267, 269
'black hand' advertisement 73–4
Black Monday stock market crash 263
Black Tuesday stock market crash 263–4, 267
Blackshield, Professor Tony 103
Blainey, Geoffrey 59, 63–5, 239, 253
    All for Australia 69
Blesing, Meena 24
Blewett, Neal 54–5, 203
Blunt, Charles 141
'bogan' (cultural identity) 231
Bolger, Irene 199–200
Bond, Alan 33–4, 37, 127–8, 136–7, 144, 146, 152–3, 162, 267, 305
Bond, Susanne 147
Bond University 288
Booker Prize winners 212
books 211–12
boom of 1987 129–30
Bottom, Bob 101
'bottom of the harbour' schemes 96
Bourke, NSW 27, 252
Bowen, Lionel 97
Braithwaite, Daryl 223
breakdancing 218
Bretton Woods exchange rates system 40–1
Brewarrina, Qld 252
Brierley, Ron 125, 132, 144
Briese, Clarrie 101, 102, 103, 105
Brisbane, Qld
    brothels 268
    Expo '88 231–2
    South Bank 231
    vice industry 268
British based society 67–8

INDEX

British migration 66
Broken Hill Proprietary Company Limited (BHP) 52, 121, 130, 133–6
Brooks, Lola 112
Brown, Dr Bob 85, 86, 87–8
Brown, John 39
Bruck Textiles, Wangaratta 282
BRW Rich List 120–2, 129
Bryant and May match factory, Richmond 230
Bryce, Mal 81
Buchanan, USS 114
budget deficit 15–16
BUGA-UP activist group 107
Builders' Labourers' Federation (BLF) 19–20, 176–7
building industry
    corruption within 20
    jobs and development through 177
building societies 276, 278
Burke, Brian 9, 10, 72, 74–5, 265, 266
Burke government 51, 75
Burns, Creighton 101
bush fashion 237
bushfires 4–8
business
    and economic recovery 17–18
    relationship with trade unions 18–19
Butlin, Matthew 20
Button, John 2–3, 14, 52–4, 53, 106, 283–4
Button car plan 53
Buttrose, Ita 204

Cabramatta, Sydney 107
Cain, John (jnr) 9, 19, 50–1, 199, 200, 275, 277–8, 279
Cain, John (snr) 9
Cain government 50–1
Cairns, Jim 92
Cairns Group of agricultural producers 283
Campbell, Sir Walter 269
Campbell report into financial system 50
Canberra Raiders Rugby League team 148
Capper, Warwick 150
car industry 52–3, 284, 289, 290
Carew, Edna 45
Carey, Peter (*Oscar and Lucinda*) 212
Carlton and United Breweries (CUB) 131–2, 136–7
Carlton Football Club 147, 151–2, 279–80
Carmichael, Laurie 54, 286
Carnegie, Roderick 131
Carr, Bob 20
Castlemaine Tooheys 127–8, 136–7
Caton, Hiram 203
Cave, Nick 106, 222–3, 224
Ceberano, Kate 218
Central Intelligence Agency (CIA) 12
Chamber of Minerals and Energy of Western Australia 73–4

Chamberlain, Azaria 79
Chamberlain, Lindy 79–80
Chamberlain, Michael 79
Chang, Dr Victor 69
Channel Nine 128, 267
Channel Seven 271
Chappell, Ian 110–11
Charles, Prince of Wales 244
Chez Oz (Sydney restaurant) 147
China 305
Chipman, Lachlan 60
Choirboys (rock band) 223
church attendance 194
cigarette smoking 107–8
cinemas 211, 235–8
Clark, Helen 115
Clark, Manning 91
    A History of Australia 247
Clark, Timothy Marcus 273, 274
Clarke, David 277
Clarko, Jim 76
Cleveland Cliffs 173, 174
'clever country' 288–9
clothing 197–8, 237
clothing industry and tariffs 284
coal mining 180
Coalition (Liberal and National parties)
    'broken' by Bjelke-Petersen 184
    Fightback! package 300–1
    Future Directions: It's Time for Plain Thinking (manifesto) 254–6
    health policy 293–4
    leadership and 1990 election campaign 293
    see also Liberal Party; National Party
Cobar, NSW 27
cocaine 107
Cockatoo, Vic. 5–7
Cohen, Barry 55, 242
Cohen, Sir Edward 132
Cold War 26, 304
Cole, Tony 48
Coles Myer 122
Comalco 38
Combe, David 11–14
    Ivanov affair 20–5
comedy and satire 213–15
Comedy Company, The (TV series) 214
Commercial Bureau 12, 14
commercial nationalism 38
Commission of Inquiry into Possible Illegal Activities and Associated Police Misconduct (Fitzgerald Inquiry) 268, 270
communism in Europe 297
compact discs 210–11
computers 205–8
condoms 204
conmen 141–2
Connell, Laurie 10–11, 51, 138, 139, 144, 146, 264–6
Connor, Dennis 35, 153

INDEX

Connor, Rex 92, 160
Conrad International Hotel, Gold Coast 179
consumer credit 161
contraceptives 193
convict origins 243
Cook, Ron 151
Cooke, Kaz 205
Copeman, Charles 173–5
Cornell, John 235
Coronation Hill uranium mining 297
Coronation Street (British TV soap opera) 234
corruption 104–8, 268–71
cosmopolitanism 231, 253
Costello, Peter 170
Costigan, Francis Xavier, QC 95, 106
Costigan Royal Commission into organised crime 95–6, 104–8, 271
Country Practice, A (TV soap opera) 233
Courtenay, Bryce, *Future Directions* song 254–5
Cox, Jim 296
Crean, Simon 17, 175
credit cards 161
Crocodile Dundee films 235–6, 295
cross-media laws 124–5
Crowded House (rock band) 221
Crowley, Rosemary 57
crying, *see* masculinity and emotion
culinary nationalism 227–9
cultural identity 212
currency crisis 159–60
currency exchange 40–4
currency float 43–4
currency speculation 42–3

Darling Harbour, Sydney 230
Davidson, Jim 236
Dawkins, John 55, 75, 110, 242–3, 286–8
de facto relationships 193–4
Deane, William 103
defence policy 299
Denborough, Dr Michael 93–4
Desert Designs (clothing design) 251
Designer Aboriginals 251
desktop computers, *see* computers
devaluation of currency 15
Diana, Princess of Wales 244
Dickie, Phil 268
dingoes 80
Dodson, Pat 77–8
Dolan, Cliff 16–17
dole 157
Dollar Sweets case 170–1
Dombrovskis, Peter 87
domestic responsibilities of women, men 195
Done, Ken 247
Donovan, Jason 233, 234–5
Don't Take Your Love to Town (Ruby Langford) 248
Doug Anthony Allstars (musical comedy team) 214

Dowding, Peter 265
Drake-Brockman, Howden 249
'dries' of Liberal Party 177–8
drinking habits 229
drought (1982–83) 26–8
drug addiction 105–8
drug overdose deaths 106
Dunlop, Edward 'Weary' 259
Dunstan, Don 231
dystopian vision of society 155–6

East Timor, self-determination 93
economic competition and migration 61–2, 82
economic crisis (1985–86) 158
ecstasy (drug) 107
Edelsten, Geoffrey 149–51
Edelsten, Leanne 150
education, *see* higher education
Einfeld, Marcus 201
El Niño 26
Elder Smith Goldsbrough Mort 131
Elders IXL 132, 135–6, 164; *see also* Foster's Brewing Group
election campaigns
  1983 8
  1984 112
  1987 184–5, 187–9
  1990 293
  see also federal elections
electoral cycle of states 294
Electrical Trades Union 172
electricity supply industry 171–2
electronic typewriters 208
Elizabeth, SA 289
Ellercamp, Paul 110
Elliott, John 130–3, 132–3, 135–6, 144, 147, 265, 279–80
Emoh Ruo (satirical film) 216
employment
  impact of recession on 282
  of women 198
  see also unemployment
Encel, Sol 54
Enright, Nick
  Come in Spinner 213
  Daylight Saving 212–13
environmental movement 294–5, 296–7
'equal rights' 81–2
Evans, Gareth 55, 56, 75, 86, 96, 101, 133, 181, xi
Evans, Ray 170
Everingham government 80
exchange rate management 41–4, 49; *see also* float of Australian dollar
Expenditure Review Committee (ERC) 42

Fairfax, James 138
Fairfax, Lady Mary 138
Fairfax, Sir Warwick 138–9, 144

INDEX

Fairfax family 120–1
Fairfax press 98–9, 123–4
Falk, Jim (*Taking Australia off the Map*) 90
families package 298
family history research 243
Family Law Act 1975 100
Farley, Rick 182, 296
farmers 163–4, 164–5
Farnham, John 223
Farquhar, Murray 98
Farriss, Andrew 219
Farriss, Jon 219
Farriss, Tim 219
Farrow, Bill 277
Farrow group of companies 276
Fast Forward (TV sketch comedy) 214
Fatal Shore, The (Robert Hughes) 243
fax machines 209–10
federal budget 1983 42
federal elections
  1983 14
  1987 184–5, 189
  1990 297
Federated Confectioners' Union (FCU) 170
Federated Ship Painters and Dockers Union 95
feminism 197
'femocrat' 197
film directors 237
film industry 235–8
financial deregulation 51–2, 278
financial pressure 157–8
financial regulation 40–54
fine dining 228
First Fleet re-enactment 242
Fitzgerald, Tony 268, 271
Fitzgerald Inquiry, *see* Commission of Inquiry into Possible Illegal Activities and Associated Police Misconduct (Fitzgerald Inquiry)
Fitzroy Football Club 148
Flannery, Christopher Dale 151
Flannery, Paul 102–3
float of Australian dollar 43–4, 45–50, 58, 159
folk culture xii
folklife inquiry xii
food and culture 227–9
Foord, Judge John 105
football clubs 147–52
Footscray Football Club 148–9
footwear industry and tariffs 284
foreign banks 50
foreign capital controls 50
foreign investment restrictions 160
foreign land register 257
foreign-exchange market deregulation 161–2
Forsyth, Christopher (*Can Australia Survive World War III?*) 90
Fortunate Life, A (Albert Facey) 260
Foster, David 213
Foster, Peter 141–2

Foster's Brewing Group 279; *see also* Elders IXL
Foster's Lager 151
Fox, Lindsay 110, 147
Franklin River 85
Fraser, Bernie 280
Fraser, Malcolm 8, 14, 40
Frederico, Hubert 197
Fremantle, WA 231
Friedrich, John 140–2
Frizziero, Carlo 170, 171

Gallagher, Norm 18, 19–20, 122, 176–7
Gallipoli (Peter Weir film) 260
Gallipoli, 75th annual pilgrimage 261
Garnaut, Ross 52, 257
Garner, Alice 196
Garner, Helen 91
Garrett, Peter 94–5, 113
Gay Ex-Services Association 261
gays 201–5
Georges, George 150–1
Gibbs, Chief Justice Harry 87, 103
Gibson, Jack 106
Gibson, Mel 237
Gillard, Julia xi–xii
Gillies, Max 213–14
global free trade 283
global recession 281
global warming 295
globalisation 303
Goanna affair 96–7
Go-Betweens (post-punk band) 221–2
Gold Coast, Qld 179, 285
Goldberg, Abe 281
goodwill (business worth) 127–8
Goondiwindi, Qld 252
Gordon-below-Franklin dam blockade 85–6, 87–8
Gore, Mike 179–80, 181, ix–x
Goss, Wayne 294
Gottliebsen, Robert 129, 186
Goward, Russell 142–4
graffiti art 218
Grattan, Michelle 68, 109
Gray, Robin 85, 296
Gray government 86
Green Independent parliamentarians 296
Gregg, Allan 182
Greiner, Nick 294
Griffiths, Alan 49
Grim Reaper 'safe sex' advertisement 204
Grollo, Bruno 20
Grollo brothers 122
Gulf War (1991) 299
Gunn, Bill 268, 269

hackers 206
Haines, Janine 57

INDEX

Hal Roach studios 271
Hall, Steele 102
Hand, Gerry 92, 284
Harlin Holdings 279
harvest bounty 30
Hawke, Bob 1–2, 290
    1983 budget 15
    1983 federal election 14
    1985 tax summit 178
    on Aboriginal land rights 71–8, 74
    airline pilots' strike 292–3
    ALP leadership 4
    America's Cup victory 38–9
    antagonism to Fairfax media 123–4
    on Anzac Day 261–2
    Anzac Day at Gallipoli 261
    Australia Card 238–40
    background in economics 46
    on Bjelke-Petersen and Coalition split 184
    booed 152
    called a 'little crook' 104–5
    'children in poverty' speech 187
    Combe–Ivanov affair 21–5
    crying 109, 110
    defeated by Keating for leadership 301
    on drug addiction 105
    float of AU$ 43–4, 45–50
    Gulf War 299
    Kirribilli Agreement 291, 300
    leadership succession 291, 300
    MX missile affair 116
    national economic summit 16–20
    and New Zealand's anti-nuclear stance 114–15
    popularity 39
    pro-American 91–3
    relationship with Bond 187
    relationship with Keating 45, 48, 178, 290
    relationships with Packer and Murdoch 123, 187
    strength 110
    on treaty with Aboriginal people 250
Hawke, Hazel 105
Hawke, Rosslyn 105
Hawke, Steven 93
Hawke, Susan 93, 105
Hawke government 4, xi
    background of parliamentarians 54–5
    economic management 185
    electoral standing 57–8
    endorsed by Packer and Bond 187
    factions 55–6
    failure to deliver land rights 77–8
    families package 298
    and Holmes à Court bid for BHP 134
    limited reform agenda 56
    market forces and social spending 304
    and New Right movement 168
    university alumni 54–5
    on Vietnam War recognition 259–60

Hawthorn Football Club 151–2
Hayden, Bill 2–3, 3–4, 66, 67, 91, 115
health insurance 56
Henderson, Gerard 73, 169
    'The Industrial Relations Club' 168
Herbert, Jack 268–9
heroin 106–7
Herscu, George 20, 122, 137–8, 146, 281
Hewson, John 300
Heytesbury Securities 133, 266
Higgins, Chris 280, 300
Higgins, Henry Bournes 169–70
higher education 286–8
Higher Education Contribution Scheme (HECS) 287–8
high-rise living 216
Hill, Jane 200
Hinze, Russ 182, 270
Hirst, John 61
Hirst, Rob 94
historical mini-series TV shows 237–8
Hodgman, Michael 63, 68
Hogan, Paul 235
Holden car plant, Elizabeth 289
Holding, Clyde 72, 81
holiday resorts 217
holidays 216–17
Hollings, Les 167
Holmes à Court, Janet 133
Holmes à Court, Robert 121–2, 125, 130, 133, 135–6, 144, 145, 265, 266
homosexuality 201–5, 203, 204–5
Hooker Corporation 281
Horin, Adele 192, 193
Horne, Donald 36
horse racing 146
house design 215–16
house prices 216
Housing Commission flats, North Richmond 156
Howard, John 169
    on Asian immigration debate 67, 253–4
    on Bjelke-Petersen 181, 184
    a 'dry' 177–8
    on fax communication 210
    on Hawke's tears 109
    industrial disputes 178–9
    leadership 255
    'One Australia' policy 253
    Peacock leadership challenge 293
    rivalry with Peacock 178
    on stock market crash 264
    on Uluru land rights 81
Howe, Brian 298
Howell, Mary 30
H.R. Nicholls Society 170, 176
Hughes, Kim 110–12
Hughes, Robert 236
human immunodeficiency virus (HIV) 204
Humphreys, Kevin 98
Humphries, Barry 112

INDEX

Hunters and Collectors (new-wave pop band) 223-4
Hurford, Chris 55
Hutchence, Michael 106, 219, 220
Hydro-Electric Commission (HEC) 86
Hywood, Greg 45, 160

'I Was Only Nineteen' (Redgum song) 259
IBM computer factory, Wangaratta 282
Icehouse (new-wave pop band) 223
identity card 238-40
immigration policy 253
'balance' in intake 68
'British race patriotism' 67
Coalition policy 66-9
multiculturalism 60
pro-Asian, anti-British 64, 66-7
pro-British, European 62-3
income inequality 185-7
Indo-Chinese migration 61
industrial conflict 168-76
industrial context 19-20
industrial relations 168-76
industry protection 19, 52-4, 283-4
Ingham brothers 121
Inside Black Australia (Kevin Gilbert) 248
intelligence agencies 25-6
interest rates 280, 281
international order, changes in 304-5
investigative reporting 98-9
investment boom 280
INXS (rock band) 106, 219-21, 220-1
Kick 221
Listen Like Thieves 221
Iraq war 299
Irises (Van Gogh) 146
iron ore, spot prices 173
Ivanov, Valery 12-14, 13, 22-3

Jackson, Linda 251
Jackson, Rex 'Buckets' 98
James, Andrew 94
Japan 256, 258-9, 284
Japanese property investment in Australia 256-7
Jockey Australia, Rochester 283
John Paul II, Pope 251
Johns, Ian 139-40, 275
Johnson, Carole 250
Johnston, Bob 43-4, 47, 159
joint defence facilities 89
Jones, Alan 111
Jones, Barry 19, 53, 55
Sleepers, Wake! 207
Jones, Kevin 98
Jones, Peter 76
judicial corruption 100-4
Jumbana Company (Indigenous graphic design) 251

Jupiters Casino, Gold Coast 179, 180

Keating, Paul 14, 291
1985 tax summit 178
on Aboriginal land rights 71-8
antagonism to Fairfax media 123-4
at *Australia II* victory 40
'banana republic' remark 158-60
defeats Hawke for leadership 301
education and early career 46
family background 50
float of AU$ 43-4, 45-50
housing affordability 215-16
increasing interest rates 280
interests 55
Kirribilli Agreement 291, 300
leadership succession 291, 300
Placido Domingo speech 300
protégé of Rex Connor 160
'recession that Australia had to have' 281
relationship with Hawke 45, 48, 178, 290
relationships with Packer and Murdoch 123
and takeover bids 134
on tariffs 284
two-station media agreement 124-5
Kee, Jenny 251
Kelly, Paul (journalist) xi, 23, 45
Kelly, Paul (singer/songwriter) 106, 118, 224
Kelty, Bill 16-17, 291
Keneally, Thomas (*Schindler's Ark*) 212
Kenneally, Mary 213
Kent, Lewis 67
Kerin, John 55, 165, 283-4, 300, 301
Keynesian economists 19
KGB 25
Kilbey, Steve 106
King, Jonathan 207, 242-4
Kings Cross, Sydney 107
Kirk, Jim 241
Kirner, Joan 279
kitchen technology 228
Kitney, Geoff 17-18
Knopfelmacher, Frank 60
Koori: A Will to Win (James Miller) 248
Kramer, Dame Leonie 195

land rights 305
Landcare 295-6
Lane, Don 101, 269-70
Lange, David 114-15
Langford, Ruby 78
Langmore, John 19
language 196-7
Law of the Land, The (Henry Reynolds) 249
Lawrence, Carmen 266
Laws, John 158, 210
Laziest Crocodile in Australia, The (Michael Salmon) 256-7

INDEX

League of Rights 66, 74
Leslie, Ian 110
Lewis, Sir Terence 11, 267, 268, 269
Lexcen, Ben 34–5
Liberal Party 132, 177–8, 183, 188, 254–6; *see also* Coalition (Liberal and National parties)
Liberty (yacht) 35–6
lifestyle 227
Lillee, Dennis 110–11
Lilley, Neville 261
liquidity crisis 14–15
Literature Board of the Australia Council 212
Little, Graham 110, 227
loan financing 137
localised bargaining 173
Lone Pine 260
Loton, Brian 134, 135
Lowy, Frank 122
Lucas Morris Homes 282
Lustig, Ted 122
Lynch, Reg 128
Lyons, Sir Edward 11

Mabo, Eddie 305
Mabo decision 305
MacCallum, Mungo 77
Macedon, Vic. 6
Mackay, Donald 97
Mackay, Hugh 134, 144–5, 253, 282
MacKellar, Michael 67
Mad Max films 237
Malouf, David 227, 228
Man from Snowy River, The 237
Mandela, Nelson xi
Manning, Peter 98
manufacturing employment 156, 289–90
marijuana 106
market forces 134–5, 297
Markus, Andrew 63
marriage 194
Marsh, Rod 110–11
Martin inquiry 42, 50
masculinity and emotion 109–10, 110–12
Masters, Chris 98, 268
Masters, Roy 98
mateship 101–2
Matheson, Laurie 12
McCarthy, Brian 292
McClelland, Justice James (Jim) 103–4, 117–18
McGilvray, Alan 111
McHugh, Jeanette 57
McKenna, Mark 261
McLachlan, Ian 163, 165, 182, 184
McLennan, Grant 106
McLennan, Sir Ian 131
McPhee, Ian 178
McWatters, Nikki 106
Meagher, Douglas, QC 96
meat industry 165–8

Meat Industry Award 166
media ownership 124–5
Medibank 56
Medicare 56
Mediterranean (Perth restaurant) 147
Megalogenis, George 281, xi
Melbourne, Vic. 228, 229–30, 276
Melbourne Cricket Club (MCC) 197
Melbourne Cricket Ground 230
men 195–6
Men at Work (rock band)
    Business as Usual 221
Merriman, Bob 111
Metro-Goldwyn-Mayer/United Artists 271–2
microfilm 208
Midnight Oil (rock band) 94–5, 221, 249–50
migrants, post-war 120
Milne, Christine 295, 296
mining industry opposition to land rights 72–4
Minogue, Kylie 233, 234–5
modems 206
mods 218
Moginie, James 94
Mollison, James 250
Mombassa, Reg 224
Monahan Dayman Adams (MDA) 38
'Moonlight State, The' (ABC *Four Corners* program) 268
Moore, John 293
Morgan, David 280
Morgan, Hugh 72–3
Moriarty, John 251
Moriarty, Ros 251
Morris, Ken 282
Mother and Son (sitcom) 215
Moura coal mine disaster 180–1
Mudginberri abattoir 165–8
multiculturalism 59, 60, 69, 253
Multifunction Polis (MFP) 231, 258, 284–6
Munro, Paul 108
Murdoch, Rupert 120–1, 122–3, 124–5, 144
Murdoch family 122
Murphy, Chris 220
Murphy, Lionel 100–4, 124
Murray, Les 213
    'The Australia Card' 239
music
    Aboriginal 249–50
    compact discs 210–11
    see also popular music
mutually assured destruction (MAD) 88–9
MX missile affair 116
My Place (Sally Morgan) 249
Myer, Sidney Baillieu 131
Myer family 122

National Action (far-right group) 258
National and International Security subcommittee (NISC) 22

s# INDEX

National Campaign against Drug Abuse 107-8
National Crime Authority 96
national economic summit 16-20
National Farmers' Federation (NFF) 163-5, 296
national identity 36, 68, 234, 248, 256, 259, 261, 304
National Inquiry into Racist Violence in Australia 258
national literature 212
National Party 181, 183-5, 270; *see also* Coalition (Liberal and National parties)
National Safety Council (NSCV) 140-2
national security, Combe-Ivanov affair 21-5
National Tennis Centre, Melbourne 230
Neighbours (TV soap) 194, 232-5
Neville, Richard 195
'New American Man, The' 119-20
New Right movement 73, 168, 169, 175, 253
New South Wales, rainfall after drought 27
New South Wales Rugby League 98
'New World Order' 299, 304-5
New York Yacht Club 38
New Zealand, anti-nuclear policy 114-15
News Corporation 122
Newtown Rugby League Football Club 148
Nicholls, Henry 170; *see also* H.R. Nicholls Society
Nile, Fred 203
1980s
    critical and transitional decade 305-6
    definitions of the period xii-xiii
    end of xiii
    familiar elements x-xi
    greed and extravagance 303-4
    market forces and social spending 304
No Fixed Address (Aboriginal reggae rock band) 249
non-sexist language 196-7
North Melbourne Football Club 147
North West Cape defence installation 89
north-east Asian economies 257
NSW Equal Opportunity Commission 200
NSW Water Board 200
nuclear attack scenarios 89-90
Nuclear Disarmament Party (NDP) 93-5, 113
nuclear ships 114
nuclear testing 116-18
nuclear weapons 88
Nurrungar defence installation 89
nurses' strike 198-9
nursing 198-9

Oakes, Laurie 23, 300
Oakley, Ross 149
O'Brien, Denis 246
office work 208-9
old-age pension 158
Olympic Swimming Pool, Melbourne 230
opposition to 71-8
organised crime 95-9, 104-8

Oscar and Lucinda (Peter Carey) 243
Ostrow, Ruth (*The New Boy Network*) 120
Otway Ranges, Vic. 28
Oxford University alumni 54-5

Packer, Sir Frank 97, 123
Packer, Gretel 147
Packer, Kerry 96-7, 120-1, 123, 124-5, 128, 142, 144, 145, 147, 187, 265, 267
Painters and Dockers (rock band) 95
Palm Sunday peace marches 91
Papunya Tula (Aboriginal art movement) 250-1
Parker, David 75, 265
Parliament House, Canberra 248
Parry, Kevin 152
passive smoking 108
peace movement 88-91
peace rallies 90-1
Peacock, Andrew 68, 77, 104-5, 109, 178, 183, 258, 293
Pearce, Guy 235
Peko-Wallsend 173-5
Pendarvis, Jay 165-8
Pengilly, Kirk 219
'period' films 237-8
Perkins, Charles 77
personal debt 161
personal recollections xiii
Petrochemical Industries Co. Ltd. 265
petrol sniffing 107
Philby, Kim 25
Pike, Jimmy 251
Pilots' Federation 292
Pine Gap defence installation 89
Piriam, Ray 54
pop art 225-6
popism (art movement) 225
popular culture 217
popular music 106, 219-24, 223, 224, 234-5
Port Kembla, NSW 289
post-punk bands 221-2
power-dressing 197-8
Pratt, Richard 37, 265
premarital sex 192
Prices and Incomes Accord 176, 292-3
Pringle, Rosemary 260
prisoners of war (POW) 258-9
privatisation of government assets 297-8
problems facing country 204
property investment 280
protest music 94-5
Psalti, Alexander 66
Pseudo Echo (rock band) 223
pub rock culture 223
punk fashion 224
punk music 221
Purvis, Barrie 170
Pyramid Building Society scandal 276

INDEX

Qantas Airways 298
Quantock, Rod 213
Qintex group 126-7, 271, 272
Quadrant magazine 168
Queensland
    1986 election 181
    leisure economy 179
    police state 267
    political corruption 268-71
    rainfall after drought 26-7

racial conflict 252, 258
racial equality 305
racism in Australia 64, 252, 258
racist policing 62
rainfall after 1982-83 drought 26-8, 30
rape in war 260
Ray, Brian 181
reading 211-12
Reagan, President Ronald 37-8, 88
recession and results 281, 296-7
recession mentality 282
regulation of financial system 40-54
Reid, John 241, 242
religious beliefs 192-3
renovation of houses 215-16
repetitive strain injury (RSI) 208-9
restaurant dining 228, 229
restrictive work practices 165-8, 173
Rhodes scholars 54-5
Richardson, Graham 92, 280, 294-5, 300
Richmond, Vic. 59-60, 229-30
right-wing politics 168-76
Riley, Rob 75, 77
Rivkin, Rene 264
ROAR (Melbourne artists) 224-5
Robe River iron ore mine, industrial disputes
    172-6
Rothwells Merchant Bank 10-11, 51, 146, 264-6
Rouse, Edmund 296
Roxby Downs uranium mine 91-2
Royal Australian Nursing Federation (RANF) 198
Royal Commission into Aboriginal Deaths in
    Custody 252, 305
Royal Commission into British Nuclear Tests
    116-18
Rugby League 147-8
rural revolt 163-8
rural unemployment raates 164
Russell, Don 280
Ruxton, Bruce 62-3, 260-1
Ryan, Jack 276
Ryan, Morgan 101, 103
Ryan, Susan 18, 55, 56-7
Rye, Dick 14

safe sex 203
Saffron, Abe 142

Sanctuary Cove, Qld. 179-80, 217, ix-x
Sanctuary Cove Resort Act 1985 180
satire and comedy 213-15
Save Victoria Committee 74
Sea and Summer, The (George Turner) 155
Seaman, Paul QC 75
Seaman report into land rights 75
security services 25-6
selfishness, cult of 119-20
Sellers, Basil 150
Seventh Day Adventist Church 79
Sex Discrimination Act 1984 56-7
sex education 193
sexism 56-7
sexual harassment 200-1
sexual inequality 195
sexual revolution 192, 225
sexuality 191-6, 203-4, 205
Shack, Peter 293-4
shearers' 'wide combs' dispute 163
Sheehan, Peter 19
Sheraton Hotel training exercise 25
Sheraton Mirage resorts 126, 217
Shields, Rikki 234
Shipton, Roger 77
Shultz, George 116
Simpsons restaurant, Sydney 263
Sinclair, Ian 23, 184, 203
Singapore 284
Singleton, John 180, 188
situation comedy 215
Skase, Christopher 11, 125-7, 140, 142, 144, 271-3
Skase, Pixie 127
sketch comedy 213-14
skinheads 217
Smith, Ewart 240
Smorgon family 121
social justice policies 298
Songlines, The (Bruce Chatwin) 248
South Africa 305
South East Queensland Electricity Board 171-2
Spalvins, John 133, 139
Sparkes, Sir Robert 183
St John, Ted 94, 95
St Kilda, Melbourne 107
St Kilda Football Club 147
Staley, Tony 110
'Star Wars' research program 88
State Bank of South Australia 51, 273-5
State Bank of Victoria (SBV) 275-6
state election cycle 294
State of Origin football series 148
Stauder, Fred 171
steel industry 52, 289, 290
steel plan 52
Stephen, Sir Ninian 81, 103
stock market crash, 1987 263-4
Stone, John 14, 15-16, 40, 45, 48, 168-9, 170
Strategic Defense Initiative 88
Street, Sir Laurence 98

INDEX

street gangs 217
Stretton, Hugh 119-20
strikes 172
   airline pilots 291-3
   Dollar Sweets 171
   nurses 198-9
   South East Queensland Electricity Board 172
structural adjustment 283
Stutchbury, Michael 159
subsidies to film industry 237
suburban life 232-3
'Suddenly' (song by Angry Anderson) 235
sunrise industries 53
Surfers Paradise, Qld x
Swan Brewery 137
Sweden 53, 286
Swiss franc borrowing 161-2
Sydney, NSW 230, 231
Sydney Morning Herald, The 101
Sydney Swans football club 149

tariff protection 52-4, 283-4
Tasmania
   1989 state election 296
   development/conservation conflicts 295
   Labor-Greens alliance 296
Tasmanian Wilderness Society (TWS) 85
tax law 10BA 37
tax minimisation 129-30
tax on debentures 160
tax summit, 1985 178
tax system changes 178
Taylor, Paul 225
technology in the home 210-11, 225
Telecom privatisation 297
television 124-5
telex machine 210
Temby, Ian 101, 102
10BA provisions (tax incentives for film production) 237
textile industry and tariffs 284
'The Big League' (ABC TV segment) 98
theme parks 217
Thiess, Sir Leslie 162
Thoroughbred racing 146
Tilley's Devine Café Gallery (Lyneham) 196
Toohey, Brian 135
   'How Fitzgerald flunked it' 270
   'The Death of Labor' 187
Toomelah Aboriginal settlement 252
Toyne, Phillip 296
Trade Practices Act 1974 167
trade unions 18-19, 167, 172
trade weighted index 41
Trans Australia Airlines (TAA) 292
Treasury 19, 48
'Treaty' (Yothu Yindi song) 250
Tricontinental (merchant bank) 139-40, 275-6
Trimbole, Robert 142

Tubby, Reg 76
Tuckey, Wilson 109, 203, 293
Turnbull, Malcolm 139
Tuxworth, Ian 80, 81
two-airline system 292
typists 208-9

Uluru 78-9, 80-1
Uncanny X-Men (rock band) 223
unemployment 156-7, 282, 289-90
unemployment benefit 157
United Kingdom, nuclear testing in Australia 116-18
United States
   Australian alliance with 93
   defence bases in Australia 89
   nuclear capability 88
universities, *see* higher education
universities, public *vs.* private 288
Unsworth, Barrie 106
uranium mining 91-2, 92-3, 295
urban renewal 229-30
Uren, David 133
Uren, Tom 23, 90
Us Mob (Aboriginal reggae rock band) 249
USSR nuclear capability 88
Utah Development Company 180

Valentine, Jo 113
Veliz, Claudio 246
Vickers Ruwolt engineering works, Richmond 230
Victoria 149
   Ash Wednesday bushfires 4-8
   Victorian Economic Development Corporation (VEDC) 51, 275
   Victorian Football League (VFL) 148-9; *see also* Australian Football League (AFL)
video cassette recorder (VCR) 211
videos and film 224
Vietnam veterans 259
Vietnam War 259-60
Vietnamese migration 59, 61-2, 70-1
virginity 192
voting system, 'above the line' 113

WA bill 75-7
WA Inc. 266
WA Industrial Relations Commission (WAIRC) 174
wage fixation 17
wage indexation 176
Walker, Frank 92
Walsh, Peter 42, 55, 75, 92, 159, 296-7
Wangaratta, Vic. 282
Ward, Russel 94
Warumpi Band (Aboriginal rock group) 249-50

Watergate scandal 98
Watts, Don 288
wealth in Australia 120, 145–7, 186–7
Weinberger, Casper 116
West, Stewart 54, 66, 81, 92, 134
Western Australia 9, 72, 77
Western Australian Development Corporation 51
Western Suburbs Rugby League team 148
Westfield Sydney-to-Melbourne Ultramarathon 28–9
'westies' (Sydney cultural identity) 231
Westmex 142–4
Westpac Bank 38, 137, 281
'wets' of Liberal Party 177–8
White, David 199, 200
White, Patrick 90–1, 94
White Australia Policy 68, 83, 305
Whiteside, Bruce 257–8
Whitlam government 11–12
Whybin, Scott 145
Williamson, David 91
    Emerald City 212
    Sons of Cain 212
Willis, Ralph 54
Windsor, Tony 163
wine industry 229
Winneke, John 19
Wogs Out of Work (comedy stage show) 215
Wollongong, NSW 289

women
    clothing and public power 197–8
    discrimination against 197
    domestic responsibilities 195
    employment of 198
    membership of clubs 197
    in professions 197
    role as wives and mothers 229
    RSI sufferers 208–9
    sexual inequality 195
    status of 18, 56–7
Women Who Want to Be Women 56–7
Wood, Wendy 188
workplace harassment 200–1
workplace smoking 108
World Heritage Convention 87
World Series Cricket (WSC) 110
Wran, Neville 9, 92, 97–8, 104, 242
Wright, Keith 91
'writing' scene 218

yachting 33
yachts 146
Yothu Yindi (Aboriginal rock group) 250
Young, Cliff 28–30
Young, Mick 22, 54
youth culture 217–19